Practical
Guide to
Environmental
Management

Practical Guide to Environmental Management

Frank B. Friedman

Environmental Law Institute
Washington, D.C.

August 1993

ᴧnowledgments

rests on the experiments and experiences of
ᴣrience, and effort required to develop, test, and
ᴐnmental program for a major corporation cannot
ᴧvidual. The ideas set forth in this book come from
ᴧs and colleagues who have applied their knowledge to
specific situations.

ᴧnals in the environmental area generally do not hold ideas for
ᴧcment of policies and programs close to their vests. This is a group
ᴧilling to share ideas and solutions. It includes environmental managers, governmental employees, citizen advocates, lawyers, consultants, and other specialists.

The true test of any idea or program comes when you are given the opportunity to put it into practice. Dr. Armand Hammer, former Chairman of the Board and Chief Executive Officer of Occidental Petroleum Corporation; Dr. Ray R. Irani, the present Occidental Chairman of the Board and Chief Executive Officer; and the management of Occidental gave me and my staff at Oxy the opportunity to test many of these programs and the backing to allow them to work. Dr. C. Erwin Piper, Rosemary Tomich, and George O. Nolley, outside directors and members of the Environmental, Health, and Safety Committee of Occidental's Board of Directors; Gerald M. Stern, Member-Board of Directors, Executive Vice President and Senior General Counsel and Secretary; and Dr. Dale R. Laurance, Executive Vice President-Senior Operating Officer were never shy about prodding us when they felt that we could move faster to resolve issues or implement programs. They were never satisfied with less than excellence.

I am particularly indebted to the late Dr. Piper, the Chairman of Occidental's Environmental, Health, and Safety Committee, who gave us the benefit of over 50 years of administrative experience and common sense. He was truly a master teacher. We will miss him. In addition, as a result of his membership in the Executive Committee of the Board and chairmanship of the Audit Committee, we were always assured that there was a commitment from the top. George Nolley, who succeeded Dr. Piper as Chairman of both committees, continues that commitment.

When I came to Oxy in 1981, I was fortunate to have Jerry Wilkenfeld on my staff and David Giannotti as my counsel. Jerry served as Occidental's Director-Health, Environment and Safety and, although since retired, continues active assistance as a consultant. Jerry's "institutional memory" and creative ability in initiating and implementing many programs played a major role in the success of our department. David, now a partner at Howry and Simon in Los Angeles, is coauthor with me of *Environmental Auditing* in the ELI Treatise on Environmental Law, from which some of the material in this book on environmental auditing and review of acquisitions originally appeared, although in a somewhat different form.

I want to thank Occidental's entire corporate health, environment, and safety professional and administrative staff (George Buxton, Catherine DeLacey, Bea Haley, Mary Kay Kelly, Ernie Rosenberg, Coni Manders, Merle Oliver, Harold Schambach, Cindy Schwarz, and Grover Vos), who continue to impress me with their dedication and creativity. They are truly the ideal group of professionals.

But no corporate staff can be successful without highly competent divisional personnel. We were truly able to work together as a team of professionals. Their willingness to be innovative, to strive for excellence, and to share concerns has provided the true test for programs. I therefore add my thanks to the senior administrators in Oxy's divisions (Bill Driscoll, Herman Fritschen, Tom Jennings, Joe Lamonica, Ernie Lindsay, Tom Timoney, and Al Meek).

Finally, I want to thank Lynn Stewart, Monica Howe Derbes, Adam Babich, and the ELI publishing staff for their many helpful comments and assistance.
—F. B. F.

Contents

Foreword

Helping corporate environmental policies become realities at the level of the individual plant manager or employee is a concern all Americans share with corporate management. Many corporate managers have made the implementation of good environmental policies one of their major objectives. Yet, surprisingly, comprehensive information on how to achieve that goal has been hard to find.

Frank Friedman's *Practical Guide to Environmental Management* fills that void in the literature. The book is a logical extension of the Environmental Law Institute's (ELI's) work in corporate environmental management. ELI's programs for corporate environmental managers have been building strength for over a decade. Struck by the dearth of materials on how to establish and operate corporate environmental management programs, we turned to Frank Friedman to create this handbook, the first and finest of its kind.

Frank Friedman is part of the small group that was present at the creation of environmental law in the late 1960s. After graduating from Columbia Law School, he joined the Lands Division of the Justice Department, handling an active natural resources litigation docket. He moved to Atlantic Richfield Corporation in 1970 when major companies began responding to the cleanup challenges presented by the new federal pollution control laws. Over the next 10 years, he became a recognized leader in the emerging fields of environmental law and management. The former Vice President for Health, Environment and Safety of Occidental Petroleum Corporation, Frank Friedman built and oversaw a large and sophisticated environmental management program covering facilities in the United States and overseas. He is now a partner, based in Los Angeles and Washington, D.C., with the Los Angeles law firm of McClintock, Weston, Benshoof, Rochefort, Rubalcava & MacCuish.

Chapter 3 tells the story of how Occidental Petroleum Corporation

1

developed its environmental management program and selected Frank to head the program in 1981. Frank has been a rare figure in a field polarized by ideology: a person who seeks to draw together environmentalists, government regulators, and industry project managers in a cooperative effort to find solutions. From 1980 through 1988, Frank was an active member of the Environmental Law Institute's Board of Directors, and he rejoined the Board in June 1990.

The Environmental Law Institute is a national nonpartisan center working for better environmental policy and management. ELI helps make "the system" work. It operates one of the nation's largest and most successful training programs in environmental law and management. ELI's courses, seminars, and training sessions are where professionals turn for solutions to some of the most complex problems of the day. ELI is also a leading publisher of the basic materials and reference texts used by environmental lawyers and managers in their daily work and their long-range planning. In addition, as a "think tank," ELI has prepared over 500 reports on the key issues of environmental management. Its research work is widely used and has become embodied in the rules and practices that help protect our air, water, and land.

Corporate environmental management is where the rubber meets the road. All the statutes, all the government regulations are aimed toward making it happen on the ground. As Frank states in his introduction:

> Good environmental management techniques benefit everyone. They help protect the environment. They make managers' jobs easier. They even save companies money, although some of these savings may not appear in the short term. Most important, environmental management, like employee relations management, is not optional. A company that does not make the effort to manage its environmental affairs well will manage them badly. If you are responsible for environmental management at your company, it is in everyone's interest for you to do as good a job as possible.

The book opens with a historical review of environmental laws and management programs. The author points out that environmental legislation is social legislation, and is liberally interpreted. The courts have routinely upheld the federal government's power to enforce stringent environmental regulations. The complex and voluminous body of environmental law rests on an extraordinarily stable political consensus favoring ambitious environmental goals: nondegraded air, rivers and lakes clean enough for fishing and swimming, and natural resources managed with respect for the needs of posterity.

Chapter 3 outlines the basics of a corporate environmental management program. A good program identifies basic objectives such as

- regular, timely, and uniform reporting from the operating line through senior management to the board of directors;
- prompt identification and resolution of environmental issues;
- establishment of preventive programs and procedures; and
- identification of developing issues or trends.

The key elements of the program are

- a computerized, centralized information system (whether in a centralized or a decentralized management system);
- a facility assessment program;
- an internal planning program and timetable;
- a capital expenditure review system;
- a willingness to address problems once they are discovered; and
- a legislative and regulatory action program.

Chapter 3 also emphasizes the importance of good communications in avoiding turf wars and in coordinating programs among divisions. Good environmental professionals can rise to the communications challenge. There is an old saying that in real estate, the three big words are location, location, and location. In environmental management, the three big words are people, people, and people. Frank's suggestions on hiring from other sectors, including government and public interest groups, underline the common goals that bond environmental professionals.

Chapter 4 gets down to the nitty-gritty of implementation. The emphasis on the importance of two-way communication continues, because in this field what you don't know will most likely end up hurting you. Frank describes in detail his recommended system of "management by exception," which ensures that responsible officials learn of and act on significant deviations from the corporate norm of compliance.

Chapter 5 focuses on the special role that environmental auditing plays in ensuring compliance and avoiding civil and criminal liability. The audit is the regular checkup that serves as preventive medicine. Chapter 6 covers a closely related topic, review of acquisitions. This has become a critical management area. The strict liability provisions of the hazardous waste laws can make innocent purchasers liable for the costs of cleaning up waste left by past owners. These provisions have made the environmental audit a prerequisite to every closing and every major bank loan, and have caused more hazardous waste cleanup than a decade of command and control regulation. Chapter 7 covers another management area that is becoming ever more important: the establishment and implementation of waste minimization programs. Like environmental auditing, waste minimization can help stop problems before they start.

Chapters 8 and 9 discuss how to deal with colleagues whose professional and political perspectives may differ. Lawyers, engineers, facility managers, and hydrologists working for the same company can find themselves talking past one another, if they are on speaking terms at all. Whether or not they are in the same field, environmental professionals can also have philosophical differences. The field is sharply divided among well-organized groups with competing visions. The players do not realize that their common interests outweigh their differences. They frequently do not understand what worries, motivates, or frustrates people in opposing camps. A successful environmental manager, corporate or otherwise, will understand these differences and motivations, and will facilitate solutions. One fertile field for this management approach is the environmental impact statement process, which is discussed in Chapter 10. If properly managed, this process can be productive for the corporation as well as protective of the environment.

Frank's conclusions are optimistic. An important theme running through his book and career is the enjoyment of working in environmental management. This is a field for problem solvers. Environmental professionals like their work and believe it is important. Their constructive attitudes and energy give cause for optimism about the long-term prospects for meeting our country's ambitious environmental agenda.

As a national environmental research and publishing organization dedicated to the development of more effective and more efficient environmental protection and pollution control programs, the Environmental Law Institute takes pride in the publication of this book. I think it will prove to be an invaluable shelf-mate to ELI's other reference works. This book stands also as a testament to ELI's commitment to better environmental management.

—J. William Futrell, President
Environmental Law Institute

Chapter 1:
Introduction

This book was written to help managers deal with the complex problems of environmental protection. Although the environmental protection field is only about 25 years old, it has already become quite complicated. I have been privileged to work in this field almost from its beginning, first as a lawyer and then as a manager-lawyer. My work has taught me many lessons, sometimes at considerable cost. In the hope that these lessons can benefit other managers, I have included in this book a wide variety of practical hints based on the experiences of myself and others in finding creative solutions to complex environmental problems. The book also tries to sort out industry concerns as to what types of regulations make sense, examine environmental programs that improve productivity and assure environmental compliance, look at the interaction of business with the community and government, and perhaps dispel some of the myths surrounding industry and its attitudes and motivations toward the environment.

Much of the book is based on my experiences at Occidental Petroleum Corporation. Oxy's environmental program is a good one, and it is the one I know best. The book emphasizes program aspects that are generally applicable, rather than those unique to Oxy. I have used my Oxy experiences to make the book more specific, concrete, and—hopefully—helpful. Therefore, my frequent references to Oxy's program should not be taken as puffery, but as illustrations of how one company uses the principles of environmental management. These principles apply to many different industries with varied cultures.

Gus Speth, the immediate past President of the World Resources Institute, noted: "Important as pressure from environmentalists and governmental direction are to stimulating change, in the end only the corporate community can efficiently provide the necessary organization, technology, and financial resources needed to design and implement change on the scale required. Companies that are trying to be leaders on a new path to a sustainable future merit our encouragement and support, just as the inevitable backsliders deserve a vigorous shove onto the trail."[1] I would add that to encourage businesses to lead the way to a sustainable future, the government must regulate intelligently. Too many regulations deliver little significant environmental protection while imposing enormous costs. Even the most responsible businesses have legitimate concerns when a company or company official can be convicted criminally for violations of environmental laws without proof of criminal intent and when record-keeping offenses can make an executive eligible for as many years in prison as a Medallin drug dealer, without many of the legal protections available to the drug dealer.

The impact of industry on the environment today needs to be placed in perspective. There is little question that U.S. industry in the past has been guilty of serious environmental depredations, some of them quite dramatic. But most of us, whether in industry, citizen organizations, or government, are wiser today than we were in the past. We have had our consciousness raised. Many of us now working for business in the environmental area came out of the environmental movement or government. Many executives today grew up with an environmental ethic or have adopted the values such an ethic implies. Economic concerns and shareholder and customer demands require that business give environmental issues a high priority. Along with expanding and tightening environmental controls, the impact of civil and criminal liabilities has made environmental irresponsibility too costly for any competent businessperson to consider.

Responsible businesses recognize that regulation is a cost of doing business. As long as regulations address real environmental problems, are understandable, avoid micro-managing a business or generating unnecessary reports, and if the "punishment fits the crime," regulation is not only acceptable, it may be necessary to provide a level playing field for companies with managements that want to do the right thing. The most sophisticated businesses integrate environmental concerns into all aspects of operations and planning—and environmentally aware business planning can create markets or competitive advantages that result in net gains. Indeed, environmental regulations have in many cases improved efficiency and product quality. They have encouraged innovative approaches to package design, raw material accountability, and selection. Increased management oversight of the environmental impacts of operations has, in many cases, led to process improvements that enhance operating reliability and reduces hazards.

Early regulation forced a recognition in many cases that pollution was actually "product" going up the smoke stacks, into the rivers, or onto waste piles, and that capturing this product was often cost effective. So-called "floating roof" storage tanks, for example, designed to minimize hydrocarbon evaporation, often paid for themselves in product that could be sold rather than lost as emissions. However, as smaller and smaller increments are captured, costs may outweigh the benefits.

This book has one overriding theme: Good environmental management techniques benefit everyone. They help protect the environment. They make managers' jobs easier. They even save companies money, although some of these savings may not appear in the short term. Most important, environmental management, like employee relations management, is not optional. A company that does not make the effort to manage its environmental affairs well will manage them badly. If you are responsible for environmental management at your company, it is in everyone's interest for you to do as good a job as possible. Hopefully, the suggestions in this book will help you do that job.

In this edition of the book, I have particularly tried to include references and comments that can be helpful to the smaller company. A smaller company, for example, needs assistance in finding a laboratory that will provide accurate data. I have now included a reference to a detailed analysis of this issue. [2] Although they face essentially the same civil and criminal liabilities as major corporations, smaller companies simply cannot have the resources in house to digest the extensive and constantly changing laws and regulations discussed in this book. Responsible officers and employees of smaller companies can, however, do enough reading to stay abreast of major developments and identify areas in which they must exercise special care or seek outside advice. [3] Many local and industry-specific trade associations and chambers of commerce publish newsletters dealing with state and local matters and legislation and regulations. [4] The agencies themselves often have specific booklets and publications to help small businesses deal with specific compliance issues. (See also discussion of legislation and regulation in Chapter 4.) The criminal liability exposure section of this book is particularly important reading because many criminal prosecutions are against smaller companies and smaller company officers.

The book now also contains a variety of appendices, including EPA and Department of Justice policies, a sample monthly report, and a new appendix dealing with international standards. I have expanded the book to add material on total quality management, job descriptions, and developing corporate objectives and strategies.

If you are new to environmental management, I hope you enjoy the field as much as I do. I can think of few areas that present greater challenges, because few areas demand creative solutions to complex technical and legal problems in the context of complex social policies. In addition, one of the most pleasant aspects of this field is that those who have been in it for a long time generally know one another and, whether we represent industry, government, or citizen groups, we all talk to one another. Although there are now more environmental professionals than I thought possible 20 years ago, just as there are more laws and regulations than I would have dreamed of, I hope you will be fortunate enough to experience the professional interactions and creative challenges that make this field so exciting. I think I can safely predict that the complexities, at least, will be with us for quite some time.

Notes to Chapter 1

1. B. Smart, Beyond Compliance–A New Industry View of the Environment (1992).

2. *See* Ploscyca, *Choosing an Environmental Laboratory*, Hazmat World, Oct. 1992, at 59.

3. A basic library for this purpose might include the following references. The deskbooks published by the Environmental Law Institute on subjects such as RCRA, CERCLA, the Clean Air Act, and the Clean Water Act, as well as the *Environmental Law Reporter*, provide an excellent basis for understanding the intricacies of federal law. The RCRA Deskbook, Superfund Deskbook, Clean Air Deskbook, and Clean Water Deskbook are $85.00 each. The *Environmental Law Reporter* with monthly updates is $995 for the entire looseleaf service and $795 for only the monthly *News & Analysis* and *UPDATE*, published three times a month. *The Environmental Forum*, an excellent bimonthly magazine, is sent to all members of the ELI Associates Program. Annual dues are $75 (public interest, government, and academic rate $50), of which $40 is designated for the subscription. Dues in excess of $40 and all contributions are deductible from federal taxable income. ELI Associates also derive the benefit of discounts on ELI publications and knowledge of various continuing management and legal education programs. The above publications are available from the Environmental Law Institute, 1616 P Street, NW, Washington, D.C., 20036. Examples of other basic publications include *Inside EPA* (subscription rate: $790/yr. in U.S. and Canada) and Inside EPA's *Environmental Policy Alert* (subscription rate: $485/yr. in U.S. and Canada), both available from Washington Publishers, P. O. Box 7167, Ben Franklin Station, Washington, DC. 20004, and the management newsletter *Environment, Health & Safety Management*, available from The Environment Group, Inc., P. O. Box 1269, Wainscot, NY 11975 (subscription rate: $397 in North America).

4. There is now a nonprofit organization in Southern California called the Environmental Compliance Support Association (9150 Flair Drive, P.O. Box 5968, El Monte, CA 91734 (818) 572-0397), which is designed to help small business in complying with complex and overlapping federal, state, and local environmental regulations.

Chapter 2:
Historical and Future Perspectives on Environmental Management

I t may appear to be the prejudice of a legally trained manager to begin a book on environmental management with an extensive discussion of the historical development of the laws and regulations that drive the field. Regardless of whether a manager's training is technical or legal, however, basic environmental management requires an understanding of the development of these laws and regulations, together with a perspective on the phenomena driving that development. [1] Indeed, I hope this historical perspective will help relieve the frustration of the technically trained manager who would like to be free of some of the legal and regulatory constraints to developing technical solutions to problems. These constraints grow out of yesterday's legal and technical compromises. I may be the bearer of bad tidings by focusing on the legal basis for constraints on managers, but these constraints are reality.

Few corporate activities have been influenced by law as much as those in the environmental, health, and safety area. As managers, we try to avoid legal issues by finding technical solutions to problems. We focus on eliminating an effluent or hazardous waste, for example, in order to avoid the requirement of obtaining a permit. However, we cannot ignore the fact that legal issues are driving corporate programs in this area. This is a relatively recent phenomenon.

Until the early 1970s, there was virtually no significant role for lawyers in environmental management. Most state and local laws imposed limited environmental, health, and safety requirements, such as mandatory air and water sampling and permitting, that could be handled by technicians. For the most part, these issues did not require senior management attention. They were considered very limited parts of operating activities, and responsibility for them was usually lodged at lower management levels. Moreover, confrontation between industry and regulatory agencies was not the rule. Since laws and regulations frequently were not specific, differences were settled primarily by technical negotiation. While industry sometimes developed environmental protection mechanisms that went beyond legal requirements, these steps, such as odor control, were largely influenced by concern for local public relations.

While the period of the 1960s was a time of long, stable economic growth, it was also a time of anger and frustration. College graduates saw a questionable future, including the possibility of serving in a Vietnam war that did not seem understandable. The "system" was not responding to their concerns, and, for many, the only answer was taking to the streets in protest. Hopes for a decent future seemed equally bleak in the area of environmental pollution, which slowly began to be recognized as a social problem.

Public awareness of pollution, along with general dissatisfaction with government and the quality of life, greatly increased public social consciousness. Interest in pollution control grew as the public recognized that pollution might endanger public health, as well as fish and wildlife. For years, conservationists had cared about wildlife and natural preservation, but often seemed to care more for trees than people. The activist of the 1960s, the new environmentalist, was in many respects of a different breed. Concern over visible industrial pollution and over the issues raised in Rachel Carson's *Silent Spring* and in John Kenneth Galbraith's *The Affluent Society* culminated in Earth Day in 1970 with a call for new initiatives to resolve environmental problems.

This concern also culminated in the federal environmental "revolution" of the early 1970s, which produced a vast outpouring of federal legislation. [2] There was a general belief that government could manage the economy and solve the country's social problems by concentrating on redistribution of wealth and improving the quality of life. This belief increased what had once been only a limited emphasis on the law as a tool for social change. Moreover, the relative emphasis on the role of the federal government increased. The new environmental laws were based on the assumption that the states needed federal prodding to ensure that pollution would be controlled in a uniform manner. [3] The theory was that there should be no pollution havens. This preference for federal control was not limited to environmental legislation; the expanded federal role in what President Lyndon Johnson called the "Great Society" reached to address a wide variety of social ills, including race discrimination and poverty.

Lack of trust in states and corporations was a prime force behind much of the early environmental legislation, and it was assumed that only the federal government would be tough enough to prod those institutions. [4] While there previously had been some limited federal presence in the environmental area, federal enforcement powers had been weak. [5] For example, before enactment of the Clean Air Act (CAA) of 1970, the federal government's air pollution enforcement activities consisted of the monumental effort of cleaning up one chicken rendering plant and one small phosphate rock defluorinating plant. [6]

Federal environmental legislation of the early 1970s presented new challenges for industry on two levels. First, at the enforcement level, these statutes, like many of the new regulatory laws in other fields, expanded the enforcement powers of both the federal government and the public. There had been very little environmental litigation prior to passage of the new statutes. Some of these statutes, such as the air and water laws, not only encouraged citizen suits both in rulemaking and in direct enforcement when the federal government failed to act, but also specifically provided for attorneys fees against the federal government. [7] This was "part of a broadly based effort to open up the regulatory process to others than regulated industries." [8] Even statutes that did not provide for attorneys fees against the federal government were interpreted to allow such fees against private parties when a citizen group won a victory, even a partial victory. [9] The attorney fee provisions encouraged lawsuits.

The new statutes generated considerable work for environmental lawyers by allowing private individuals and citizen groups to enforce permit requirements and other regulatory standards. Offensive projects could also be blocked under the National Environmental Policy Act (NEPA) with proof that possible (and, in some cases, improbable) impacts had not been considered adequately in environmental impact statements, which NEPA requires for all "major Federal actions significantly affecting the quality of the human environment." [10] The fact that private individuals and groups could significantly impact government and corporate decisions began to be grudgingly accepted as a fact of life. This recognition came, however, only after some initial efforts by the government and industry to argue that some citizen groups did not have "standing" to bring a case. The doctrine of "standing" requires plaintiffs in lawsuits to prove they have suffered "injury"—or are threatened with injury—to legally protected interests. In the context of environmental litigation, however, courts define "injury" very broadly, and injuries to only aesthetic or recreational interests generally suffice. Some environmental groups discovered that the standing doctrine does have limits, however, and lost cases in which they failed to include as plaintiffs members of their organizations who might be injured by the actions challenged. [11]

The wave of federal environmental legislation was built on the foundation of social consciousness laid in the 1960s. The concerns of the 60s helped dictate the choices of employment for young graduates with broadly based social and environmental concerns. Their options included the Department of Justice, other government organizations, and new public interest groups. Creation of the Environmental Protection Agency (EPA) in 1970 also provided employment opportunities for many new graduates. The enforcement theory of these new regulators was that the "mule," namely industry, needed to be hit over the head with a large two-by-four (regulation or enforcement) to get its attention. Indeed, there were some mules for which a two-by-eight might have been insufficient.

The new federal statutes were heavily regulatory. In many instances, they did not simply provide general guidelines, but were the virtual equivalent of regulations, [12] establishing detailed standards without the benefit of peer review or even practical experience. Congress wrote highly specialized legislation for the same reason it promoted private civil lawsuits: it distrusted not only states and industry, but federal agencies as well. The political nature of hearings prior to passage of legislation, plus the confrontational atmosphere between the lobbyists for industry and those for citizen groups, precluded peer review of technical issues.

In addition to establishing regulatory standards, the new environmental legislation engendered significant rulemaking. While the rulemaking did not require formal Administrative Procedure Act (APA) hearings, it was subject to notice and comment requirements of the APA and similar statutes. Environmental organizations began to see the value of formal comments on proposed regulations. They soon felt that they had as much power as industry, and indeed more, considering the environmental orientation of the new regulators. In any event, EPA soon learned that failure to document the basis for its regulatory decisions could lead to reversal by the courts. The relationship between the regulators and the regulated community grew strained as the regulators saw themselves less as technical experts than as mediators between warring factions. As regulations became more specific, regulated industries found themselves in a more adversarial position, with little room for resolving issues by negotiation.

Recognition of the dual presence of the government and citizen groups did not mean that industry would accept every regulation or lawsuit without a fight. Corporate managers, accustomed to dealing with engineering and science, understood "scientific truth" but not "regulatory truth," which, while purportedly based on science, is strongly influenced by political factors. For example, it is a scientific truth that public health specialists rarely have enough information to specify a threshold below which exposure to carcinogens is entirely risk-free. Regulators responded to this scientific truth by creating a simplified, regulatory truth that any exposure to a carcinogen, no matter how trivial, results in a quantifiable risk which should be measured and minimized or eliminated. Confrontations arose because "regulatory truths," which were administered by people who did not understand corporate managers' businesses and who in many instances were hostile to corporations, began to bite financially. This classic clash of two cultures generated an ideal climate for litigation.

Industry challenges to regulations usually were not motivated by attempts to gain competitive advantage. Few companies attempted to submit comments on regulations that would give them economic advantages over their peers or raise substantially different issues from those raised by trade association comments, which, by the nature of trade associations, generally are consensus-based lowest-common-denominator products. The level of sophistication required to attempt to obtain competitive advantage by influencing regulation was rare except when one company already was meeting higher standards and was anxious for the rest of its industry to catch up. Many industries, such as the steel industry, however, saw the new regulations as a threat to their very existence. No one knew the actual economic impact of the new laws, and all factions were extremely skeptical about the others' estimates of that impact. Industry's credibility was not helped by overstatements of economic impact, which were common. Conversely, EPA's credibility was not helped by gross understatements of that impact, which were equally common.

Lawsuits challenging regulations often named 10 or more trade associations as parties. [13] The trade associations took the lead in broad challenges to provisions of the new statutes, but they were joined by individual company members participating as separate parties, if for no other reason than to avoid attacks on standing analogous to those made when environmental organizations failed to name individual members as parties in their lawsuits. [14]

With some justification, industry perceived the regulators as attempting to stretch broad language in the new statutes as far as the courts would let them. Industry felt it had no choice but to attack virtually all regulations as they were promulgated. On the other side, citizen groups uniformly attacked regulations on the grounds that they were not tough enough. These were not just blind attacks by both sides, but attempts to obtain clear regulatory interpretations that were not forthcoming from the regulators. Sometimes, early interpretations were unobtainable, even after rulemaking and appeals. For example, under the CAA, a company even now is in the dubious position of either complying with the law or challenging a specific enforcement action, at its peril, while it seeks court review of the underlying regulations. [15]

It was particularly difficult to challenge a scientific interpretation by

EPA. The burden of proof was on the plaintiff, and no matter how strong the plaintiff's case, EPA could probably win as long as the record provided some basis for its interpretation. [16] Courts give great deference to an agency's interpretation of a statute, particularly in its area of expertise. [17] While principals of administrative law placed a difficult burden on industrial plaintiffs, who argued that EPA regulation had gone to far, activist courts—notably the U.S. Court of Appeals for the District of Columbia Circuit (D.C. Circuit)—often placed a less stringent burden on environmental groups who argued that Agency decisions were not pro-environmental enough. The U.S. Supreme Court soon reminded these courts that the rule of deference to agency expertise cuts both ways, and that the courts could not substitute their judgment for EPA's if EPA had a rational basis for its decision on a technical issue or if its interpretation of a statute in its area of expertise was rational. [18]

Appropriate responses to the legal issues raised by the government and citizen groups required new approaches by industry. These were not always forthcoming. In counseling their clients, many traditional company lawyers failed to understand that environmental legislation was social legislation and would be broadly interpreted. However, as vague statutory provisions and the regulations implementing them became subject to definitive rulings by the courts, different company policies emerged. Many companies began to realize that there was a new regime and that old ways of doing business had changed. These companies began to look for individuals who understood these changes so they could develop environmental, legal, and technical policies that responded to the changes, but still allowed cost-effective management.

Enlightened attitudes at first were not widespread. I recall being asked to give a speech to a group of oil company attorneys on the new CAA of 1970. The title chosen for me was "Ecology in Gasoline Marketing." The impacts on gasoline marketing and petroleum refining of the new legislation and resulting regulation were obvious: costs were going to increase significantly, and the industry would have to radically change its air pollution control strategies. About half of my audience took these messages back to their managements and began to prepare their companies for the coming changes. The other half could only have been described as incredibly hostile, arguing that as an industry newcomer with a governmental bias, I had to be wrong in predicting extensive and expensive regulatory changes.

Efforts to convince some of my own management were also not entirely successful. There was considerable resistance to making many necessary changes in the operations of Oxy's Philadelphia refinery, for example. I raised the appropriate legal issues, but many of the old-line managers still perceived that conditions really weren't that bad. Some felt that the odors emanating from the refinery "smelled like money." Finally, out of frustration, I wrote a memo quoting my then three-year-old daughter: "I don't like Daddy's refinery. It doesn't smell too good." The fact that the need for change was obvious to a three-year-old finally helped get local management attention and helped senior management change the culture.

In today's context, the need to take such an antagonistic (perhaps even foolhardy) approach seems incredible, but in the early days of environmental law and management, traditional executives could not believe that they would have to radically change the way they operated.

As these attitudes changed, corporate attention began to focus on the dollars being spent and possible means of reducing expense. Many corporate executives were frustrated because these issues generally could not be resolved nor costs reduced using standard rational engineering and financial procedures. As discussed above, the statutes did not give agencies broad discretion to "fill in the blanks," but rather were written as regulations, unaided by the practical operating experience and scientific input of the regulatory and regulated communities. Moreover, even when they had discretion, most agency staffs had little understanding or concern about economic impacts. Traditional problem-solving tools such as engineering and financial analysis were less effective in this tight regulatory situation.

Management continued to struggle with the real differences between "regulatory truth" and "scientific truth." This struggle was particularly frustrating for many well-meaning corporate executives who looked mostly at economics and science and did not understand the regulatory and political concerns that overwhelmed their economic and scientific perspectives. Perhaps those who gave advice as attorneys rather than as scientists had some advantage, for the difference between "technical truth" and "regulatory truth" was more easily swallowed by lawyers than by scientists.

During this pressurized and confusing period, major corporations used their new technical and legal staffs to give sophisticated advice to management and to resolve environmental issues. These people became the core of today's environmental profession. Corporations also upgraded the importance of these professionals in terms of both compensation and internal reporting structure. The professionals' increased significance to the corporations required shorter lines of communication and reporting to high levels of management.

The first "pioneers" to move from the public to the private sector were both suspicious of the industry regime of which they were now a part, and ill at ease with colleagues who had remained in the public sector. As a U.S. Department of Justice attorney in the 1960s, about the last place I expected to consider working was an oil company. That would have been the ultimate "sellout." However, I was approached by the then general counsel of Atlantic Richfield, an experienced Washington lawyer who was specifically looking to recruit government attorneys to work on environmental and civil rights issues. His attitudes surprised me: he strongly appreciated and supported the social developments that had radically changed the country. [19] The fact that the atmosphere at the Department of Justice had changed under Attorney General John Mitchell, who was indirectly an excellent recruiting agent for private industry, also influenced my decision to take a chance on working for the "enemy." Moreover, the role of an advocate for environmental concern in a corporation during those early years was clearly defensible. In 1971, having crossed this line from the public to the private sector, I described the philosophy of this new breed:

> Basically, his [the corporate attorney's] position is that of educating the corporation to the vast changes that have taken place in recent years in terms of new laws, regulations, and public attitude. Corporate insensitivity and lack of familiarity with these changes can be expensive. Yet, too many corporations either lack the required knowledge or attack these changes with the standard blanket condemnation (perhaps with a little more subtlety than in the past) which has characterized industry's response over the years to new pollution laws and regulations. Indeed, this "cry of wolf" is largely responsible for many of industry's difficulties. If the claim is continually made that new laws or regulations are unworkable when, in fact, industry is able to comply with these laws and regulations, clearly no regulatory official is going to accept industry's argument when a problem does arise. The war on pollution has its own credibility gap; which, I submit, can be closed by a more realistic response. I suggest that the best means of improving industry's reputation for veracity is compliance with these new laws and regulations. If nothing else, economic self-interest should dictate this conclusion, since today all industries are regulated industries in the environmental area. [20]

Twenty years ago it was also necessary to argue that compliance was needed and that credibility was invaluable.

> Credibility is the most important asset for this new breed of corporate lawyer. Government agencies and environmental groups are sophisticated enough to understand the difference between form and substance, and the attorney who is not sug-

gesting reasonable positions will not be believed. If the attorney cannot establish credibility, his value is lost and he would be considered simply a company spy. [21]

Most corporate environmental work at that time was in the "fire-fighting" mode. Permits were delayed, litigation was threatened, and environmental organizations assumed the worst from companies. The skills of the new breed of environmental professional were put to the test, and opportunities to plan for the future and ensure cost-effectiveness were extremely limited. Gradually, as they gained more experience, corporations became able to manage environmental issues rather than fight them.

Senior management was not interested in environmental problems per se, but rather in their impacts to operational planning and costs and, more importantly, in the action plans for resolving them. This focus required environmental managers to use all their abilities to develop solutions to problems that at first seemed insoluble. For those who understood the concerns of regulatory agencies and environmental groups, the task was easier. But it still was difficult to explain control plans to senior managers unaccustomed to the type of problem resolution that was required. It was often particularly difficult to adequately describe the political and social implications of recommended actions.

The "public to private" pioneers, together with forward-thinking realists already in the private sector, focused corporate interests on the new trends, helping to avoid costly siting decisions and other pitfalls. Energy projects, for example, that might otherwise make economic or technical sense, might not make sense if stalled for several years by litigation over impact statements. To many "traditional" corporate executives, these judgments looked astounding, but the environmental professionals were simply realistically examining the signs of the times. The increasing influence of this new group affected not only individual business decisions, but the overall corporate approach to broad environmental issues. For example, companies began to realize that the "Petroleum Club" syndrome of talking only to each other in the industrial sector did not provide the necessary grasp of the political and social situations in Washington, D.C., and the states.

Throughout the era of modern environmental law, legislation and regulation has reflected public perceptions of a variety of events. Well-known environmental episodes such as Love Canal, the Bhopal and Chernobyl disasters and, most recently, the Exxon Valdez oil spill in March of 1989, all had profound impacts on environmental legislation, regulations, and policies. Interest groups used these events to press for legislation, arguing that new laws were needed to prevent similar incidents in the future and to force slow-moving industry to respond. Thus, the discharge of kepone to the James River was a major impetus for the passage of the Resource Conservation and Recovery Act of 1976 (RCRA), which regulates hazardous waste. Alleged health impacts to residents of Love Canal, a toxic waste disposal site near Niagara Falls, New York, were the catalyst for the 1980 Superfund law (the Comprehensive Environmental Response, Compensation and Liability Act, or CERCLA), which requires remediation of waste sites and embodies the concept that the "polluter pays," regardless of fault. The death of thousands of people in Bhopal, India, from an accidental (or possibly, sabotage-related) release of an acutely toxic chemical, methyl isocyanate, resulted in increased focus on safety and general concern about chemicals. It also led to the 1986 passage of the Emergency Planning and Community Right to Know Act, which requires disclosure of information about potentially dangerous chemicals and development of local response plans. The strong public response to the Exxon Valdez incident, which released some 11 million gallons of oil into Alaska's Prince William Sound in March, 1989, was a major factor behind Congress' enactment of the Oil Pollution Act of 1990.

The close call at the Three Mile Island nuclear power plant in Pennsylvania in 1977 resulted in many changes in regulations governing U.S. nuclear power operations, most of them requiring closer monitoring of operations and additional worker training and qualification requirements. The 1986 Soviet nuclear disaster at Chernobyl, the worst release of radioactive materials ever, apparently resulted in thousands of deaths and significant long-term effects on surrounding areas in the former Soviet Union. Chernobyl has greatly increased the public's concern about nuclear power and contributed to its general distrust of industrial development although the Chernobyl reactor's design—standard for Eastern Europe—is very different from that of reactors in the West.

Management in the 1990s

In the 1990s, we must be prepared to manage environmental issues within a different framework. This is now recognized even in the academic arena. In 1987 there were no environmental management courses in business schools. Today, "30 business schools are teaching elective courses on environmental management and approximately 70 business schools are actively integrating environmental management into their core curricula."[22] Top management is now more aware of environmental costs and generally is also aware that potential regulatory constraints require different approaches. Much of the capital required to make technological changes required by standards mandated throughout the 1970s has been, or soon will be, expended. Issues regarding compliance with existing environmental regulations, including those relating to previous hazardous waste disposal, should by now be identified and action plans should be under way. Resolution of the remaining issues will still require substantial effort, but we can and should begin to focus now on longer range planning.

Modern industrial businesses recognize that environmental laws are largely the product of ideas and social forces whose time has come. Sophisticated businessman know that enforcement of these laws is important as a matter of public policy and to prevent competitive advantage for those who ignore the law. They also recognize that the public and the environment cannot be asked to bear all the risks associated with scientific uncertainty and that industry sometimes must accept controls before all the scientific evidence is conclusive. The public is their customer, and they have to satisfy their customer even when they think the customer is wrong. Perhaps the ability to accept this attitude towards uncertainty provides one measure of a company's social responsibility.

Progressive companies recognize that they need to move beyond compliance. Dupont Chairman and Chief Executive Officer, Edgar Woolard, who is also DuPont's chief environmental officer, calls for an ethic of "corporate environmentalism." Woolard has stated that he has not "hesitate[d] to describe what he sees as the shortcomings of industry's historic approach to environmental issues" and "that improved performance was the only way that industry could hope to earn and keep public good will on environmental matters." [23] The former chairman of the Chevron Corporation, George Kellogg, noted in 1987, "At Chevron, we're very proud of a corporate environmental policy that says we comply fully with the letter and spirit of all laws affecting our operations. But [a]s long as our environmental philosophy is framed by the concept of compliance, we won't get much credit for our positive actions. Compliance means that the moral initiative lies elsewhere outside of industry." [24] The time had come, he added, for the industry to move beyond compliance. Of course, the way some laws and regulations are structured, i.e., with vague requirements, we cannot be confident that we have achieved compliance before going beyond compliance.

Today there are many examples of companies moving beyond compliance, such as ARCO's innovations in producing less polluting fuels; widespread reductions in reported releases under the Toxic Release Inventory; waste reduction programs of Dow, 3M, and Chevron; plastic labeling and recycling; massive energy conservation efforts that reduce power generation-related emissions; and development of lower-impact forestry practices. Important industry-wide efforts such as the chemical industry's and efforts to improve the international environment, such as the Global Environmental

Management Initiative and the International Chamber of Commerce's principles of Sustainable Development, as well as U.S. corporations' efforts to maintain the functional equivalent of operations, are discussed in Chapter 4, Worldwide Management Initiatives to Promote Excellence.

Today, environmental issues are being rapidly integrated into business decision-making. They are considered as important to business as finance, tax, employee relations, and other functions that are traditionally part of the management process. Business is driven by costs, and the costs of dealing with environmental issues simply cannot be ignored. Unfortunately, however, the effort to focus on business planning on long-term issues is impeded by an incredible increase in technically complex regulations. Today's environmental manager is frustrated by the need to read hundreds of new pages of small type in the *Federal Register* and equally complex regulations on the state level. Businesses require an increased number of professionals and technicians to monitor compliance and manage the flow of burdensome, legally required paperwork that limits the ability to focus on anything but day-to-day operations. For example, Occidental has estimated that new fugitive emission regulations required by the CAA Amendments of 1990 will require from 1.4 to 7 million data entries to establish and implement a system for monitoring approximately 150,000 potential emission points at five Occidental petrochemical plants. This problem will continue as scientists find means of measuring concentrations of pollutants at increasingly lower levels. The California South Coast Air Quality Management District, in commenting on EPA's CAA operating permit regulations, indicated that in a best-case scenario, permit applications alone would fill about one half mile of shelf space. This does not include monitoring and other reports that regulated companies would also have to file. [25]

The "regulatory truth" that almost any detectable level of pollution must be analyzed and regulated unbalances the primary role of today's environmental manager—reducing risks. The scientifically trained manager is frustrated by the lack of time and resources to deal effectively with more significant issues in reducing risk. An article in *Science* noted:

> Advances in low-level risk detection threaten to engulf us with information. Regulators typically respond to each newly highlighted risk, whether painstakingly uncovered through scientific investigation or divulged with fanfare by the media, on an *ad hoc* basis. This response makes it hard to relate disparate risks to the overall risk level and impedes intelligent risk reduction, which must consider the costs and benefits involved. Efficient risk management requires decisions not only about what to regulate and how stringently, but also about the appropriate

> division of labor among the agents influencing risks. These
> agents include individuals, whose potential contributions too
> often are overlooked, corporations, and government.[26]

This reality is something we all have to live with, but it still does not make the job any easier.

The immense complexity of the regulatory system creates broader problems. Complying with the *substantive* requirements is immensely difficult and cost is, of course, one of industry's major concerns. These concerns, however, are dwarfed by uncertainties in the regulatory system relating to permit issuance and compliance. This uncertainty is a major problem even for those with sophisticated corporate programs and extensive familiarity with the regulatory process. Thus, many in industry believe that it is time to begin a dialogue with EPA and state and local agencies addressing some carefully chosen existing rules that may require scrutiny, not because they were developed in error, but because new laws and rules may have made them obsolete. This dialogue should focus on the effect these mechanisms have on corporate environmental management and the allocation of corporate and agency resources.

This suggested review is not a retreat from any deadline or currently mandated levels of control. A review of the regulatory process will show program overlaps or pollution controls that no longer make sense. Indeed, EPA's own analysis[27] and the Agency's emphasis on risk-based regulatory priorities imply that some substantive rules should be changed. EPA and industry need to eliminate obstacles to compliance, particularly regulations and attitudes that discourage pollution prevention. They need to encourage pollution prevention that goes beyond mere compliance, and redirect resources so that more environmental regulators will know that they are contributing to environmental quality and not just pushing paper—and taking an unnecessary ration of abuse at that. To get the best performance, and in particular to foster innovation, those in industry who are assigned to environmental matters also need to know that they are involved in a process that makes a difference.

Although EPA has made attempts to incorporate more efficient market mechanisms into environment regulation, under the current statutory framework, such mechanisms can only address the thin, uppermost layers of a massive and rigid structure. That structure, much of which is imposed directly by statute, relies heavily on "command and control" regulation— an attempt to control pollution by bureaucratic fiat rather than by providing incentives for development of creative solutions. Indeed, the 1990 CAA Amendments added to the command and control aspects of the air pollution control program. Aspects of that Act reduced the availability of market mechanisms and really only embraced new, more efficient approaches in provisions designed to control acid rain. Thus, despite EPA's good intent, it may be difficult to achieve broader use of market approaches. [28]

EPA has given no indication that it will oppose pending legislation to impose percentage reductions in releases or generation of waste without giving adequate consideration to those companies that have gone beyond mere compliance. EPA has touted its voluntary "33/50" program, designed to reduce certain pollutants by 50 percent by 1995. While many companies are participating in this program, the reductions are primarily in solid and liquid waste, mainly because early reduction of air emissions may backfire if reduced emissions are used as a baseline for mandatory reductions in the future. If corporate environmental departments urge corporations to make reductions, as they have, and regulators punish them for it, they will not long retain credibility and effectiveness within their organizations. Indeed, many of us are wondering, as we attempt to encourage such responsible behavior, if agencies have taken the view that "no good deed goes unpunished."

EPA's approach to regulation must be substantially restructured if the challenges of complying with the requirements that EPA and Congress will be imposing over the next few years are to be met. The challenges are not simply the costs of regulation that flow directly from the control or reduction of pollutant releases and exposures. Nor are they the paperwork burdens that are simply costly and wasteful. The requirements that create the greatest risks of driving industry off shore are those that make it impossible to operate certain types of businesses or operate in certain areas, no matter how willing to comply a company may be.

Many of the industries that hold out the best promise for preservation and future growth in the manufacturing sector depend on an ability to respond to technological change at a pace dictated by competition, not by regulatory processes. These growth industries include electronics, advanced materials, aerospace, custom and specialty chemicals (including pharmaceuticals), and even automotive manufacturing. Many of these are the prime targets of foreign competition. They cannot wait for regulatory processes that take years when their products can go through their entire life cycle in 18 months. Certainty is the key word. If companies cannot obtain permits under environmental statutes in an expeditious manner, or at least know that they will obtain permits and about how long it will take if they perform the appropriate studies and provide the appropriate data, they will not operate efficiently or economically. If the time frame for obtaining a permit is too far in the future, a company has no choice but to seek alternatives elsewhere, no matter how good its planners are. This is not a pro- or an anti-environmental decision, but simply a business decision taking into account the leveraging impact of time and uncertainty on the business decision. This uncertainty must be addressed if this country is to remain competitive and keep manufacturing jobs in the United States.

Perhaps the best analogy is the Grimms' fairy tale of Cinderella. Her wicked stepsisters told Cinderella that she could go to the ball if she performed a variety of impossible tasks. After performing all these tasks she still did not receive permission. Industry often feels it is in the same position as Cinderella. The situation may be "grim" but it is no fairy tale! It threatens even companies, such as those in the oil and gas production and commodity chemical industries not typically under the intense pressures of time and foreign competition faced by many "down stream" industries. The health of these companies is tied to that of downstream companies, who are their customers. [29] In fact, the industries that must change quickly, and thus are most likely to trigger some regulatory requirement tied to change, both use products produced by energy and chemical companies and dominate those listed as developing critical technologies for the future.

It is also important to address those aspects of regulatory programs that create unpredictability and personal legal risk that cannot be reduced to manageable proportions, no matter what a company's intentions are and no matter how sophisticated its planning and quality management programs may be. As discussed below, the criminalization of environmental law poses a real risk of driving talented managers from the field.

The coming years may seriously undermine environmental improvement if regulatory behavior is demonstrably harmful without benefit. As we (meaning all of us whose job is regulation of the environment) tighten the laws, we increase society's ability to achieve environmental goals. But we also have to be aware that those aspects of the environmental laws that are being tightened have served, in effect, as important safety valves that have mitigated the amount of evident economic damage caused by environmental controls.

For example, the 1990 CAA Amendments accelerated the regulation of hazardous air pollutants by increasing the universe of regulated chemicals and setting a low threshold for what is a "major source." Amendments to the Act's nonattainment program, which applies in areas of the country that missed deadlines for meeting national standards for concentrations of certain pollutants in ambient air, expanded the geographic scope of the nonattainment controls. The amendments also made the nonattainment program more stringent by requiring that more emission reductions from existing sources offset the emission increases that invariably result from new or expanded economic activity, and changed the definition of "major source" to reduce the threshold of emissions that cause sources to be subject to regulation under EPA's nonattainment program. The two programs overlap, because many hazardous air pollutants are also related to nonattainment problems. In the past, a plant that had to make changes quickly could do so because its emissions either were not federally regulated (as was the case with many air toxics) or it could avoid delay by "netting," making reductions that kept its net emissions increase to less than the regulatory threshold. I am not attacking either the change in the major source definition or the new nonattainment provisions when I simply observe that the new law provides far fewer opportunities for facilities to find ways to stay in compliance even if they cannot tolerate delay or cannot accommodate new controls triggered by changes.

This phenomenon is not limited to the CAA. Expansion of RCRA's programs and definitions, addition of new Federal Water Pollution Control Act (FWPCA) requirements, and other changes in the regulatory system raise similar issues, and the prospect is for more legislative pressure in this direction. Recognizing the progressive loss of the pressure relief valves in environmental laws does not mean that we should try to go back to the old, less rigorous laws. It does mean that we have to deal jointly with the potential for economic damage that the rigidity of the new laws pose.

Many environmental laws today employ a sort of averaging; that is, to assure that excess risks (however defined in the particular statute) in all instances are eliminated, the law accepts overregulation in some cases. For example, RCRA imposes similar regulatory standards on entire categories of facilities and chemicals, although individual facilities vary dramatically in the relative degrees of risk they pose. The CAA applies maximum available control technology (MACT) controls to all major sources, even if it can be shown that the risk posed by a particular source is negligible. Thus, the process we see today inevitably will make what are in effect mistakes in particular cases. For those cases, the result is economic damage unaccompanied by benefit.

An example is worth mentioning. A company uses local drinking water as non-contact cooling water. However, once water goes into the plant facility, the plant is responsible for its water quality, and the chlorine in this drinking water violates local standards. As would be required for the use of drinking water in a fish tank, the company reportedly has had to employ a water softener.

The price of meeting the environmental goals we have set as a country will be a certain amount of economic damage—the issue is whether or not the damage will occur against a backdrop of regulatory behavior that is seen as prudent and sensible as well as effective. A regulatory system that produces seemingly arbitrary economic pain could be very harmful to the consensus that we now have in favor of environmental controls. Accordingly, both the regulated community and EPA should preserve and look for opportunities to expand state and EPA discretion—the ability of agencies to accept solutions that address the practical needs of specific situations. The most fruitful area for our attention would not be discretion that allows EPA or a state to relax substantive control requirements, but rather discretion to relax implementation elements that force delays or unnecessary complexity that is not clearly mandated by law.

The cost of complying with our current tangle of federal, state and local laws is staggering. That cost, for 1992, has been estimated at upwards of $130 billion dollars. [30] From 1975 to 1987, total capital investment for environmental benefits was between $25 to $35 billion per year, and rose to $43 to $46 billion per year between 1988 and 1992. [31] At Occidental Petroleum, which is typical of other large chemical and natural resource companies, environmental costs in 1991 totaled $227 million, including $98 million in capital expenditures. Reserves for remediation, or clean-up costs, totaled an *additional* $149 million. Occidental's profits for 1991 were $460 million. Thus, environmental costs were 82 percent of profits and its environmental capital costs were 21 percent of profits. Chevron Corporation, with annual sales of $42 billion, has announced that it will spend $2 billion in the next five years to meet new environmental regulations, a large portion of which will go to upgrading its refineries to comply with the 1990 CAA Amendments. Union Carbide estimates that its environmental capital expenses were $59 million, or 16 percent of total capital expenditures, in 1990, up from $39 million and 9 percent in 1989. Its environmental capital costs for 1990 were 31 percent of its total profits of $188 million. Monsanto estimates that its 1990 environmental capital costs were $80 to $100 million (up from $60 million in 1989), without a percentage of total capital (making its environmental capital costs 18 percent of its total profits of $546 million). Monsanto's total environmental expenditures in 1990 were $376 million, equal to 69 percent of total profit.

Clearly, if these expenses were reduced, profits would somewhat reflect the savings. A recent article in *Science* magazine noted:

> On 20 January, the Democrats became sole heirs to a phenomenon of regulation gone amok. In April 1992, 59 regulatory agencies with about 125,000 employees were at work on 4,186 pending regulations. The cost during 1991 of mandates already in place has been estimated at $542 billion. The fastest growing component of costs is environmental regulations, which

amounted to $115 billion in 1991 but are slated to grow by more
than 50 percent in constant dollars by the year 2000. [32]

EPA estimates that total annual environmental expenditures in the United
States have risen from $74 billion in 1988 to $114 billion in 1992 and are
expected to reach $160 billion by the year 2000. [33] From 1985 to 1987, total
capital investment for environmental benefits was between $25 to $35
billion per year, and rose to $43 to $46 billion per year between 1988 and
1992. [34] EPA has not broken the capital expenditures down, but it did look
at different program areas such as mobile sources (bureaucratese for cars
and trucks), radiation control, water pollution, Superfund remediation, and
underground storage tanks. It has been estimated that the energy industry
may spend up to 20 percent of new plant capital on environmental controls
and technology. Total pollution control costs in the United States may reach
$250 billion in the year 2000. [35] A recent survey by Resources for the Future,
an independent Washington-based environmental and economic research
group, estimates that the total (not just industry) cost of compliance with
hazardous waste regulations alone will be $32 billion by the year 2000. [36]
Professor Dale Jorgensen of the Economics Department at Harvard estimates that the minimum total cost of the new Clean Air Act provisions will
be $24 billion (in 1990 dollars) by the year 2005, although regulatory
agency interpretations of the law could push that number much higher. [37]
According to *Forbes,* [38] every American pays, on average, about $450 more
in taxes and higher prices annually as a result of pollution controls. An
EPA-funded study cited in *Forbes* "estimates that real GNP in 1990 has
already been depressed by no less than 5.8 percent below where it would
have been without federal clean air and water regulation." [39]

Much of the increasing cost of pollution control can be traced to regulations designed to reduce the last increments of pollution. Many of the most
cost-effective steps to control pollution have already been taken. As efforts
continue to control smaller and smaller increments of air and water pollution, costs generally increase. For example, a total expected price increase
of eight cents per gallon can be attributed to past and future changes required
in fuels. It is always easier and cheaper to control the first 90 percent rather
than the last 10 percent.

The above-mentioned amounts are designed to show the order of magnitude of the costs. It is likely that some of the lower estimates grossly
underestimate the projected costs of the Clean Air Act Amendments of
1990. Some of us estimate that the cost of the Clean Air Act's new operating
permit regulations alone will be in excess of $3 billion per year, far higher
than government estimates.

In 1972 roughly 61 percent of total U.S. expenditure on the environment was borne by the private sector. EPA expects that the figure increased in 1992 to about 63 percent. Many people outside EPA believe these estimates are very low, particularly taking into consideration the projected costs of the Clean Air Act Amendments of 1990. One reason that industry's share of costs tends to increase from year to year is that the government finds it easier to use "off budget" financing by charging industry for costs (through fees, etc.) than to increase taxes. In an international market, however, it is not clear how many of those costs can be passed through to the consumers.

Clearly, there are countervailing benefits in pollution controls. The purpose of this discussion of costs is not to argue that the costs of environmental controls outweigh the benefits. The discussion does, however, illustrate the importance of these costs in management analysis and planning. The magnitude of expense is enormous under any estimate. No effectively managed company can ignore such costs.

In addition to tightening expensive control requirements, Congress is giving EPA and state regulators power to intervene into virtually every aspect of product development, content, and production. When bureaucracies have the power to intervene, they intervene often. Virtually inevitable political pressures make intervention the path of least resistance. Without new thinking to forestall the abuse of this power, the growing support among industry managers for continuous environmental improvement will not only stop—it is likely to reverse. Indeed, there are signs that this is already happening. This in the long run could be even more unfortunate than the loss of profits without environmental benefit, even though profits are the fuel on which environmental improvement ultimately depends.

The core premise to examine in the 1990s is that some approaches to environmental (and health and safety) regulation encourage good environmental management and some either discourage it or divert government and industry resources away from activities that have the potential for more beneficial environmental impact. Agencies tend to overlook the normal and predictable behavior of corporations and their employees, failing to recognize that it is usually not in an individual's or company's best interest to risk serious civil or criminal liability for improper actions. "Games" will not be looked on favorably in a permit renewal or enforcement proceeding. However, agencies sometimes insist on prior review of industry actions even when it would not be in the interests of corporations to take the chance of trying to "game" the system. EPA's enforcement would be far more effective if the Agency focused its power on making it costly for those who do try to avoid controls that clearly apply and making it more likely that such parties will be caught.

EPA and state agencies should consider a process that asks questions of program officers instead of imposing answers on them. The new process would ask for an analysis of the incremental benefit of each layer of implementation machinery, such as setting the standard (with the potential for stiff enforcement), requiring state permit review, requiring EPA review of state decisions (with the concomitant lack of flexibility that results from federal citizen suit authority, inflexible comment periods, and mandatory delays), and requiring EPA review of state actions between permit reviews for generic classes of changes, even if no new control requirement is triggered. Someone needs to ask how much additional control is achieved by each increment of these measures. In some programs, it would also be beneficial to establish a review of how changes in one part of the program (e.g., factors that determine which substances are controlled) will affect the costs, flexibility, and value of other program elements (e.g., facility standards or permitting requirements).

If such reviews demonstrate that certain program elements do not provide a benefit when seen in context, then the staff will be less inclined to construe the law in a way that requires pointless expenditure of effort. Such an approach might even get the sympathy, if not the overt concurrence, of citizen groups.

EPA's and industry's pollution prevention efforts are undermined by restrictions that will penalize companies that make reductions too soon. EPA has shown little interest in using its discretion under the law to assure that companies that make early reductions are not disadvantaged relative to those that fail to reduce or even increase pollution. [40] Rather, its provision of credits for such reductions has been rather grudging, apparently based on a fear that someone might get credit for a reduction they would have made anyway. EPA has given no indication that it (and its professional staff) would oppose, let alone strenuously lead the opposition to, legislation that would impose percentage reductions in release or generation of waste without giving adequate consideration to those who have gone beyond mere compliance. EPA staff have shown little understanding of what it means to set baselines for determining credits in the future—this truly makes it difficult to justify making reductions before the baseline is determined. If managers in corporate environmental departments urge their operations to make reductions, as they have, and the companies are punished for it, the managers will not long retain credibility and effectiveness within their organizations. Thus, when efforts to reduce emissions or reduce waste result in increased permitting difficulties, under the theory that "no good deed goes unpunished," such desirable programs will suffer major setbacks. [41]

The ability of both government and industry to keep the system operating is threatened. When the system cannot operate as it is nominally intended to, unpredictable holes appear that provide opportunities to those who take their environmental responsibilities less seriously and those who want to do the right thing are undercut. Our ability to work cooperatively to achieve environmental goals is threatened. We in industry want the system to work. Government and citizen groups want the system to work. We should be able to work together to make it happen now and for the future.

New Mechanisms to Assure Environmental Accountability—Life Cycle Analysis, Sustainable Manufacturing, Full Cost Accounting, and EPA Leadership Program

The ability of regulators and industry to work together will be even more critical in the future as new management techniques such as life cycle analysis, sustainable manufacturing, and full cost accounting are developed to further refine environmental management. At present, there are no existing or proposed regulations in the United States that incorporate such cradle-to-grave analyses, with the exception of New Jersey's Pollution Prevention Act. [42] That act requires companies to perform "a comprehensive financial analysis for each source or production process, of the costs of using hazardous substances, generating hazardous substances as nonproduct output, and releasing hazardous substances" as part of a required pollution prevention plan. [43] The plan must include "a comprehensive financial analysis of the costs or savings realized by investments in pollution prevention options compared to the costs of using hazardous substances, generating hazardous substances as nonproduct output, and releasing hazardous substances." [44] The intent is to require that project financial evaluations take into account the full range of costs and savings, both direct and indirect, tangible and less tangible. This will require a systematic analysis of conventional capital and operating costs items *plus* those items often omitted from conventional project financial evaluation. It is not clear how rigorous these requirements will be in practice.

The Society of Environmental Toxicology and Chemistry (SETACO) Life Cycle Analysis (LCA) Advisory Group argues that "the procedure [life cycle analysis] is too premature to apply, at least not outside the secure confines of a company's own R&D department." [45] Conversion of this useful analytical technique to a regulatory requirement converts a variable scale of benefits versus costs to an ever more rigid *bright line* of minimum elements, with potential enforcement jeopardy and analysis without respect to benefit. Nonetheless, incorporation of the concept into regulation is developing rapidly in Europe, appearing in the British Standard Institution's new environmental management specifications (BS77520) (see discussion of the environmental management specifications in Chapter 5 under Self

Evaluation and Verification), which indicate that companies should address effects "arising at all stages of the life cycle."[46] Other efforts to codify the use of LCA are found in Denmark's new Environmental Protection Act,[47] the European Community's new eco-label award, which is intended to "promote the design, production, marketing and use of products which have a reduced environmental impact during the entire life cycle"[48] and the European Community's proposed law on packaging, which "sets high sorting and recycling targets for all materials in the waste stream, which can only be modified if scientific research, or any other evaluation technique, such as eco-balances, prove that other recovery processes show greater environmental advantages."[49] Attempts have been made to define lifecycle inventory, lifecycle impact analysis, and lifecycle improvement analysis.[50] The appeal of this analysis may be to better understand the full environmental cost of production[51] and to provide useful data for internal and external purposes.

Ladd Greeno of A. D. Little divides uses for life cycle analysis into "internal" and "external" uses.[52] Internal uses include product design improvements, shifts to more environmentally sound raw materials, process improvements, improvements in product use instructions, and improvements in product distribution profiles (which analyze the different impacts associated with selling into certain market segments).[53] External uses include: positioning products, supporting marketing claims and labels, launching counterattacks on products of competitors, demonstrating a proactive environmental stance, and communicating environmental progress.[54]

An example of an "external use" of LCA comes from the recent controversy about cloth versus disposable diapers.[55] One analysis asserted that when you compare the greater use of water and detergents required for cloth diapers with the disposal costs and use of paper products, etc. in disposable diapers, disposable diapers are of less concern to the environment.[56] Although some environmental groups take issue with its methodology, that analysis apparently has been very helpful to Proctor & Gamble, which has included the study in its packages of disposable diapers.[57] Similarly, the use of such analysis suggests that polystyrene containers threaten less overall impact to the environment, although the political pressures to change to paper by fast food companies such as McDonald's are overwhelming (see discussion of the McDonald's/EDF study in Chapter 7). Because LCA is complex and leaves ample room for debate about methodologies and underlying assumptions, such studies do not eliminate controversy. Both cases demonstrate that LCA that is responsive to a political challenge takes place in a context that is not neutral. It must be rigorous enough to overcome a presumption of environmental insult. Indeed, the danger of the use of life cycle analysis is to provide a vehicle for assuring the "political correctness" of a product and, in turn, assuring greater governmental intervention in the production and marketing of products. The concept makes sense, but the "devil is in the details."

Sustainable manufacturing is similar in concept to life cycle analysis. "Product life-cycle analysis defines environmental impacts for the life of the product, but does not address management strategies or worker health and safety issues." [58] The concepts of determining sustainable manufacturing address materials selection, [59] production, [60] Market and After-Market [61] and cost accounting. [62]

EPA has published a notice of intent in the *Federal Register* [63] requesting comment on the creation of an environmental leadership program, which would employ some of the concepts discussed above. A corporation would sign a "Statement of Environmental Principles," and individual facilities within a corporation could become part of a "Model Facility Program." The potential value of participating in the "Model Facility Program" is the recognition of a "green" facility and presumably value in marketing a company's products. EPA has not yet defined what will be in the "Statement of Environmental Principles," but apparently will be looking for risk reduction goals, means of measuring progress, public accountability, planning mechanisms, environmentally sound business practices, community and employee involvement, and compliance. How each of these mechanisms will be used or measured remains to be seen. We do know that EPA is looking at "life cycle assessment" (life cycle analysis) and "environmental cost accounting" (full cost accounting) as examples of good business practices. Pollution prevention would be measured primarily by the Toxics Release Inventory (TRI) mandated by the Emergency Planning and Community Right-To-Know Act (See also discussion in Chapter 4, Environmental Policies and Corporate Responsibility), but could include energy efficiency goals and voluntary reduction of greenhouse gas emissions as part of setting and measuring national risk reduction goals. Toxics use reduction and some form of verified environmental performance assessment are likely to be included.

In looking at public accountability, EPA is considering whether companies should disclose factors responsible for significant changes in the level of emissions at any of their facilities and to furnish TRI-equivalent emission data for their facilities located outside the United States. Disclosure of non-TRI data may also be required. Many environmental professionals are concerned by the oversimplification inherent in EPA's TRI and Environmental Leadership programs. For example, one company's pollutant may be another's product. Many toxic materials are produced that are incorporated into innocuous or beneficial products. Does EPA intend to condemn all such use? Does it make sense simultaneously to urge a company to eliminate the use of a toxic material but to acknowledge the producer of the material as an "environmental leader?" EPA is also seeking comment "on whether the Environmental Leadership Program should contain elements aimed at empowering labor/management committees and/or workers, and, if so, how the Program could achieve that goal without being unduly prescriptive." [64]

"Participating companies could be asked to pledge to make available to the public an annual summary of governmental and citizen environmental enforcement actions, including penalties and fines paid, involving their facilities," [65] irrespective of fault.

Compliance seems to be critical for acceptance into the program, including environmental compliance management systems which would include the components listed in EPA's 1986 Auditing Policy Statement and the Department of Justice July, 1991 policy on criminal prosecution for environmental violations (which are reproduced as Appendix C and F of this book) as well as other criteria as they are developed from voluntary industry standards. Criteria for compliance would also be closely evaluated, audits would be required, and certifications of compliance would have to be signed. While third-party audits would not be mandated, the notice does "solicit comments on other appropriate means of assuring participant's ongoing compliance status." [66]

If violations are discovered, EPA claims that it "has long recognized that a self-discovered, self-reported compliance problem that has been promptly corrected may warrant an enforcement response that differs from the Agency's response to other types of violations." [67] This statement may be greeted with more than a little skepticism from the regulated community. EPA is requesting comment on how the government should respond to such self-discovered violations. Moreover, while compliance naturally has to be the threshold, the program has to accommodate the fact that the number and complexity of requirements that apply to an industrial facility virtually assure that no facility, let alone any whole company, can be in 100 percent compliance.

Removal from the program can occur as a result of a criminal indictment by a facility on a company's top corporate officers "based on their personnel actions at a facility under their control." [68] More significantly, a federal or state civil judicial enforcement action, a major administrative action, or violation of any federal or state order or decree can result in removal or suspension. However, EPA has asked for comment as to "whether the initiation of an enforcement action, the issuance of an indictment, or evidence of significant noncompliance should trigger removal from the program." [69]

This is a real issue affecting all of EPA's enforcement policies, which in turn drive state use of enforcement resources, namely, what kind of noncompliance is trivial? When everyone is in violation, what is a *real* violation? Industry would say that violations that did not involve, or at least suggest, significantly excessive releases can be forgiven, but EPA might object. Their view is that recordkeeping, monitoring, and reporting violations can be very important and they may, in fact, mask more substantive violations.

Industry has to be concerned that entry into the program actually would invite more enforcement difficulty. A routine enforcement action could become a high profile issue if the company or facility was in the program. The threat of losing membership in the program would also greatly affect companies' ability to negotiate with enforcers and could even be used by citizen groups who often bring enforcement actions in cases considered marginal by enforcement officials in order to make a policy argument. Would EPA or state enforcement officials find that threatening a company's status in the program would be an irresistible bargaining tool? This concern may not be serious in our expectation, but it is real to many in industry, and the notice does not address or even acknowledge it.

While EPA's concept of encouraging good environmental management practices is admirable, the agency relies heavily on practices that still are primarily in the conceptual stage, such as life cycle analysis, sustainable manufacturing, and full cost accounting. These concepts hold promise, but there are many issues that need to be resolved. Senior officers of corporations, proud of their programs and seeing a marketing/public relations value in being considered outstanding corporate citizens, should consider the operation of such programs in practice. If there is marketing/public relations value in signing on to the program, the downside of backing out or being removed from the program seems far worse. (See also the discussion of the CERES (Valdez) Principles in Chapter 4, Environmental Policies and Corporate Responsibility which raise many analogous concerns.)

Audits can be useful, but EPA has previously reviewed the issue of mandated third-party audits and decided that they are generally no better, and can be less revealing, than internal audit programs. Toxics use reduction is recognized as a tool for limiting releases, but the concept is not developed enough to address basic problems—like when the pollutant is a company's product, the questionable listing of some materials as "toxic," international competitiveness problems, and the basic question of whether or not there is a prospect for exposure, let alone harm.

We have found in the past that when we take too broad an approach to the issue of toxics, without adequate regard to whether there is really any significant risk, we misplace our resources. (See, e.g., EPA's 1987 report *Unfinished Business.*[70])

An even greater concern is the apparently wide-spread belief in Congress and in the agencies that anything that is a good idea if "voluntary" is even better if made mandatory. Thus, "voluntary" programs have a tendency to become mandatory. All of us in this field should encourage good environmental management programs, but it remains to be seen if the bells and whistles in the EPA "voluntary" program are worth the limited rewards, as opposed to the potential significant restraints on management. The key concerns of industry would be that independent environmental audits and mandatory source reduction (i.e., toxics use reduction) would quickly move from being simple evidence of excellence to minimum elements of acceptable environmental behavior.

In summary, the program strongly suggested by EPA's January 1993 notice could impose excessive disincentives for entry into the ranks of "leadership" that divert attention from pollution reductions to ancillary activities (such as planning and disclosure of releases not covered by current reporting requirements) that could create competitive disadvantages for participants, increase costs without commensurate release reductions, disrupt existing management structures and approaches that are working, and expose companies to added enforcement jeopardy. This will discourage participation to such a degree that it calls the entire effort into question.

Although EPA resources may not be at risk, we should not be inviting industry to expend resources that do not address the most important problems first, simply because they will get "points" in this program. OSHA, in developing its STAR Program to recognize safety excellence, asked industry advice on what makes for strong programs and attempt to "base its program on the characteristics of the most comprehensive safety and health programs used by American industry."[71] In addition, sites accepted into the program "are not expected to be perfect, but they are expected to effectively protect their workers from the hazards of the workplace through their safety and health programs."[72] The EPA notice seems to dictate (or at least strongly signal) what EPA wants or assumes are strong programs or perhaps perfection. It is little wonder that this proposal is being greeted with skepticism.

Both pollution prevention and sustainability raise a fundamental issue: Is EPA, as part of its leadership program, going to judge entire *lines of business* in terms of the product being made or, perhaps, the use served by that product? If sustainability were a criterion, for example, could any fossil fuel company qualify? If environmentalists and state regulators are given an effective veto, will their disapproval of certain lines of business become *de facto* federal policy?

Criminal Liability Exposure—The New Concern for the Environmental Manager

In the 1990s, continued vigilance in the environmental area is particularly important because of the specter of potential criminal prosecution.[73] As former Attorney General Richard Thornburgh stated, "Criminal enforcement is one of the most radically expanding areas of environmental law, with the use of criminal sanctions becoming one of the most effective means of deterring deliberate non-compliance."[74] It is important for today's environmental manager to recognize that you no longer have to be a "bad person" to be prosecuted, and "deliberate" can also mean purposely attempting to avoid knowledge.

The number of federal prosecutions is increasing dramatically. Between 1982, when the U.S. Department of Justice formed its Environmental Crimes Section, and the end of fiscal year 1989, the Department has netted more than 430 pleas and convictions—imposing fines of more than $26 million and jail terms adding up to 270 years. About half of the fines and close to one-fourth of the convictions took place in fiscal year 1989.[75] EPA announced that for the fiscal year that ended on September 30, 1991, it had obtained $14.1 million in criminal fines and that defendants convicted of environmental crimes had served a total of 963 months in prison. The statistics also revealed 104 indictments and 82 convictions during the year.[76] In 1991, under the Clean Water Act and the Safe Drinking Water Act alone, EPA assessed almost $29 million in civil penalties, along with criminal fines of over $5 million.[77] U.S. executives spent a total of 346 months in jail for environmental crimes during fiscal year 1991.[78] Civil penalties levied represented an increase of 61 percent from 1990 levels. In 1991 the agency referred 81 criminal cases to the U.S. Department of Justice and recovered a total of $73 million in civil penalties, both all-time records.[79] In fiscal year 1992, the Justice Department obtained 191 indictments, a new record, 104 guilty pleas or convictions and, yielded a record $163 million in criminal penalties.[80] These statistics do not include the extensive list of state and local laws, ordinances, and regulations that have resulted in criminal penalties.

There has also been a significant increase in the number of government employees involved in criminal enforcement. EPA now has 53 criminal investigators devoted full-time to environmental crimes, and the Environmental Crimes Section at the Environment and Natural Resources Division of the Department of Justice has grown to 25 attorneys. The Pollution Prosecution Act of 1991 [81] increased the number of criminal investigators to 200 by fiscal year 1995, with an additional 50 civil investigators by fiscal year 1992, indicating that institutional requirements mandate a large number of prosecutions. Perhaps most significantly, 150 of the FBI's agents have at least one environmental criminal case on their investigative agendas. [82]

Growing emphasis on criminal enforcement appears to be a permanent trend. There are several bills before the Senate Labor Subcommittee to increase criminal sanctions under the OSH Act. [83]

If you can't find the "bad guys," you can find those formerly subject to civil penalties by expanding the scope of criminal liability. There is strong pressure for prosecutors to give in to what Dan Riesel calls the "Bonfire of the Vanities syndrome"—go after a high-profile white collar defendant on what amounts to almost strict liability under RCRA or the CAA. This certainly beats trying to prosecute a "nickel bag" heroin dealer. The criminal system has not yet gone over the brink, although there are too many individual horror stories, but, as indicated by a former chief of the Environmental Crimes Section, "there is now a machine and the machine must be fed." [84] How that machine is fed will make a major difference in the future of environmental management and law.

Most senior enforcement officials admit that the larger companies are not usually the major enforcement problems. They have too much at stake to try to avoid the system and, thus, have systems in place to help assure compliance. Small companies and their principals, however, playing financial brinkmanship, can be a major concern. But like the pickpockets in London who had their best days earnings during the hangings of other pickpockets, they are not going to be deterred by such penalties. They know that an individual playing fast and loose with recordkeeping, etc., is difficult to find, and they are more concerned with financial survival.

Ambitious state and local district attorneys are also looking for cases. Besides the various federal environmental statutes, [85] which all have criminal penalty provisions, note the broad scope of the criminal side of state statutes dealing with environmental issues. For example, various transportation, storage, and disposal activities are now punishable as felonies under the California Health and Safety Code. [86] In addition, *any* violation of California hazardous waste laws and regulations and any related "permit, rule, standard or requirement" is punishable as a misdemeanor. [87] New Jersey has used a statute adapted from a European law that was designed primarily to protect against fires and avalanches to impose potential criminal liability on any person who "purposely or knowingly unlawfully causes an explosion, flood, avalanche, collapse of a building, release or abandonment of poison gas, radioactive or any other harmful or destructive substance."[88] The Pennsylvania Solid Waste Management Act[89] imposes liability regardless of fault for criminal misdemeanor violations in §6018.606(i). The New Jersey Criminal Code imposes second degree criminal liability upon anyone who purposely or knowingly unlawfully causes a hazardous discharge, a release, or abandonment of a hazardous waste or toxic pollutant.[90] A person who has been convicted of a second degree offense in New Jersey faces a presumption in favor of incarceration for a term of 7 years, which can be lowered to a minimum of 5 years or raised to a maximum of 10 years depending on the court's evaluation of the aggravating and mitigating factors.[91] The presumption in favor of incarceration applies unless the sentencing court "is of the opinion that the [defendant's] imprisonment would be a serious injustice which overrides the need to deter such conduct by others."[92] The New Jersey Supreme Court has repeatedly indicated that this language must be given very narrow and limited reading.[93]

It has become increasingly important that the U.S. Department of Justice have some form of centralized oversight of prosecutions by U.S. Attorneys around the states, many of whom lack expertise in environmental law and are unfamiliar with established civil and administrative options for environmental violations. Indeed, whether a violation is treated criminally, civilly, or administratively can be more a function of what type of investigator first learns of the infraction and in which judicial district it occurs, rather than its environmental severity.[94] As noted in a recent article:

> Following usual bureaucratic practice, the Justice Department, the EPA, and Congress keep score through a "body count." In return for augment appropriations, the congressional oversight committees expect increases in the number of cases brought, the amount of penalties, and the number of people sent to jail. The Justice Department and the EPA promote the success of their respective enforcement programs through the use of such statistics. Unfortunately, this creates a false metric for evaluating the success or failure of an environmental enforcement program.[95]

Whether you are concerned with federal or state law, it is vital to recognize that "in today's enforcement climate, no one, not even those remotely responsible for environmental compliance, is immune from criminal prosecution."[96]

As a general rule, environmental statutes do not require the government to prove that a defendant purposefully violated the law. Rather they establish crimes of *general intent* where the government's burden is limited to demonstrating that an *act* took place with the knowledge of the defendant. Generally, the government need not prove knowledge by the defendant of that the act was prohibited by law. The familiar refrain—ignorance of the law is no excuse—controls. [97]

According to one commentator, a recent case, *United States v. Dee,* [98] "summarily approved a remarkable set of instructions permitting the jury to infer willful blindness and, therefore, the requisite degree of knowledge on the part of corporate officials based on their respective positions of responsibility in an organization." [99] In an Ohio prosecution, a facility manager of a hazardous waste site was held to have constructive knowledge of the RCRA guidance documents, [100] literally several feet of documents.

In addition to the broad definition of "knowledge," managers should also consider the reporting requirements specified in several environmental statutes. The FWPCA, RCRA, TSCA, and particularly the CAA Amendments of 1990 have a vast array of self-reporting requirements. Failure to report can result in civil or criminal liability. There are simply too many potential civil and criminal penalties for failure to notify under various statutes to ignore these requirements. "The environmental laws are about as close as you can get in a criminal context to strict liability," and knowing failure to meet a reporting requirement is particularly dangerous from the standpoint of potential criminal exposure. [101]

The government has also taken the position that "corporate management can, in certain circumstances, be held criminally liable as individuals for environmental violations even where those managers did not personally participate in, or direct, each of the actions which gave rise to criminal liability." [102] The policy of the Justice Department "has been, and will continue to be . . . to conduct environmental criminal investigations with an eye to identifying, prosecuting, and convicting the highest ranking truly responsible corporate officials." [103] In the context of RCRA enforcement, the government "attempts to hold corporate officers and chief executive officers (CEOs) criminally accountable for the actions of their employees and subordinates, even when those top executives did not have *actual* knowledge of their employees' illegal conduct." [104] This theory is known as the "responsible corporate officer doctrine." [105]

There appears to be a trend toward relaxing the traditional requirements of *mens rea* and willfulness. "One does not have to *be* bad to *do* bad when it comes to environmental crimes. The 'black heart' requirement commonly associated with other criminal activity is not necessary to sustain a conviction." [106] The government's position on what is "knowing" and "willful" is suggested in *United States v. Protex*:

> In the context of *public welfare* offenses, courts have repeatedly held that "knowingly" requires only that one act voluntarily, with knowledge of one's actions. It does not require knowledge of the law or a specific intent to break the law. . . . Willfully is viewed similarly, as not requiring or denoting specific intent or evil purpose. [107]

In the RCRA and FWPCA context, the concept that environmental statutes are "public welfare" statutes has been upheld by three U.S. Courts of Appeal. [108] As noted by the Fifth Circuit and quoted with approval by the Eleventh Circuit, RCRA "is undeniably a public welfare statute, involving a heavily regulated area, with great ramifications for the public health and safety." [109]

The Fifth and Sixth Circuit also indicated that "knowing" for purposes of RCRA does not require specific knowledge of a regulation:

> "Knowingly" means no more than that the defendant knows factually what he is doing—storing, what is being stored, and that what is being stored factually has the potential for harm to others or the environment, and that he has no permit—and it is not required that he know that there is a regulation which says what he is storing is hazardous under the RCRA. [110]

The *Baytank* court specifically distinguishes *United States v. Johnson & Towers, Inc.*, [111] which does appear to require specific knowledge of a regulation and appears to reject the "public welfare" concept. [112]

The following analysis of the *Exxon Valdez* case, previously published in *Environment, Health & Safety Management*, is instructive.

> The Exxon Valdez prosecution was settled last year for $250 million, the largest criminal fine in American history, in addition to nearly $1 billion in civil penalties.
>
> Even with $125 million forgiven because of Exxon's earlier cleanup efforts, no other criminal fine has been greater. But it could have been much worse. The Exxon Valdez case provides some insight into the Department of Justice's current aggressive approach, even though it was settled before the government's theories were tested by the court.
>
> The government reached deep into its arsenal of weapons, bringing charges under not only the Clean Water Act, but also under the Refuse Act and Migratory Bird Treaty Act.

The latter two statutes do not govern oil spills directly, but do provide a means of holding a defendant liable for criminal violations of environmental statutes without regard to intent or fault.

Under the Refuse Act, it is a criminal misdemeanor to discharge any refuse from any vessel into the navigable waters of the United States. The Migratory Bird Treaty Act makes it a criminal misdemeanor to kill "by any means" any migratory bird protected by certain international conventions.

Onto this strict criminal liability theory, the government grafted an agency theory, under which Exxon was to be held liable for the acts of its wholly owned subsidiary. By alleging that Exxon itself was liable for the acts of its separately incorporated subsidiary, the government sought to "pierce the corporate veil" and make Exxon's treasury answerable for the liability assessed in the case, in addition to the treasury of its shipping subsidiary.

The ramifications of this approach are disturbing. It attacks the limited liability protection of the traditional parent-subsidiary corporate structure, and by doing so, adds an entirely separate defendant to the case. This doubles the maximum amount of fines that can be assessed: Exxon Corporation and Exxon Shipping Company each could have been fined independently.

The government added a *coup de grace* to its prosecution by invoking the Criminal Fines Improvements Act. Under this federal law, a court can assess a fine of the greater of two amounts — either the amount that the defendant gained from the crime, or the amount that a third party lost because of the crime.

In the Exxon Valdez case, the potential liability was staggering. Based on Exxon's payments in excess of $350 million to settle civil damage claims from the oil spill, it could have faced an additional $700 million in fines under the Criminal Fines Improvements Act.

Moreover, because the Exxon Corporation and its shipping subsidiary could have been assessed separately, the total fine could have amounted to $1.4 billion.

It's no wonder that Exxon settled with the federal government. When contrasted with a potential $1.4 billion criminal fine, the $125 million settlement appears to be favorable indeed. In this context, the country's largest criminal fine ever looks like a good deal for the company.

Because the Exxon Valdez case was settled before trial, we don't know whether the government's legal theories and tactics would have withstood judicial scrutiny.

Certainly, they were an effective weapon in forcing Exxon to the bargaining table at a substantial disadvantage. And the message to the regulated community at large is clear: Growing public concern about the environment has caught the Department of Justice's attention, and the Department is willing to take Draconian steps to enforce the law. [113]

Certain recent case law, however, gives some comfort to the executive. It is argued, based on this case law, that "the government must prove *actual* knowledge (and effective consent) of the prohibited conduct, even for 'responsible corporate officers.'" [114] It remains to be seen whether these cases, which seem to distinguish environmental law issues from the "public welfare" cases (cases addressing such issues as food and drug safety that have been cited to support imposing strict criminal liability in the environmental area [115]), will be generally followed.

The concept of broad criminal liability is carried further in the Clean Air Act Amendments of 1990. For purposes of criminal liability under these Amendments, the term "operator" includes any person who is senior management personnel or who is a corporate officer. [116] However, the person actually responsible for the operation of the equipment can only be subject to criminal liability if the violation was "knowing and willful," a relatively low threshold of knowledge under public welfare statutes. There is also a presumption of continuing violation once EPA has established one day of violation and that the condition or events giving rise to the violation are likely to have recurred or continued past the date the violator was notified of the violation. Actual knowledge is required that an individual placed another person through a release in imminent danger of death or serious bodily harm, but circumstantial evidence can be sufficient, including evidence that a defendant took affirmative steps to be shielded from knowledge of a release. [117] Note that a major stationary source owner is required to submit certification of the compliance status of the source with the Act's requirements. EPA will also now have the authority to require emission source owners to adopt compliance audit procedures for a single instance, periodically, or on a permanent basis. The compliance certification is extremely broad. With potential criminal and civil liability, many managers will be reluctant to sign such certifications, even if they complete substantial due diligence.

The CAA significantly limits the actual operator's liability and focuses on managers, including officers and directors. [118] The U.S. Sentencing

Commission Guidelines Manual includes a specific "environmental offenses" category. [119] "In what used to be a highly subjective process, the rules remove nearly all discretion that judges have traditionally enjoyed at the sentencing stage. Now it is more a matter of making mathematical computations." [120] The U.S. Sentencing Commission has apparently recognized that environmental crimes are more complex than other crimes and is undertaking a thorough review prior to applying them to corporations and before instituting new individual sentencing guidelines. The Commission has released new draft sentencing guidelines for corporate violators of environmental laws. They are, however, very controversial, and it is not expected that the Commission will promulgate them in final form soon.

One source points out, for instance, that release of a chemical under one statute may be considered a major offense, but another statute may deem the same release less serious. Another source argues that even unwitting environmental crimes may cause significant damage and suffering, and that in these cases, restitution for victims may be more important than punishment of offenders. [121]

As two commentators noted,

> While the sentencing commission did not explain its decision formally, the exclusion of environmental crimes from the provisions dealing with fines apparently reflects a determination that such crimes, and their consequences, are fundamentally different from other crimes subject to the guidelines. The commission may have acted in response to comments, particularly from federal law enforcement agencies, that the guidelines' benefit-loss calculus would neither simplify the sentencing of organizations convicted of environmental crimes nor improve deterrence. [122]

The Federal sentencing guidelines for corporations (other than for crimes relating to the environment, export controls, product safety, food and drug, and national defense crimes), did become effective on November 1, 1991:

> The guidelines greatly restrict a judge's discretion in sentencing corporations convicted of federal crimes committed after the effective date and, in most cases, require the imposition of multi-million dollar fines. They may also require imposition of a probation period during which the corporation's operations and records would be subject to governmental review. The guidelines further provide, however, for a reduction in the potential penalties for corporations which have in place a compre-

hensive and effective compliance program to detect and deter criminal violations. [123]

Fines may be as high as $300 million. [124] Aggravating factors that raise the "culpability" score include a corporation's prior criminal record and the level of personnel involved in the criminal conduct. Mitigating factors include self-reporting, cooperation with the government, acceptance of responsibility, and—most significantly—the corporation's implementation of an "effective program to prevent and detect violations of the law." [125]

In summary,

> [m]any states sanction corporations criminally only for the acts of management. By contrast, federal courts have adopted a broadly defined doctrine of imputed liability that permits the criminal conviction of a corporation for acts of its low-level employees or outside agents. A corporation can be convicted of federal crimes even if its employees and agents act without management's knowledge or approval and even if management has specifically prohibited the offensive conduct and taken reasonable steps to prevent it. [126]

This criminal law is critical in the context of environmental assessments or audits. As has been noted by George Van Cleve, former Deputy Assistant Attorney General for the Environment and Natural Resources Division of the U.S. Department of Justice, "[t]he United States has used audit results to good effect in criminal prosecutions to prove that corporate management was aware of the existence of environmental violations and did not act to correct them when it could have done so," [127] and "[t]he United States has consistently refused to limit access to audit results for criminal enforcement purposes." [128] Mr. Van Cleve also notes that "[i]n deciding whether to voluntarily adopt an audit program, a company will likely take a series of factors into account. Among them certainly should be a consideration of whether the liability resulting from uncorrected violations is likely to be manageable." [129] While he does note that there may be a benefit in performing an audit rather than running "the risk of prosecution without knowing in any detail what the risk actually looks like," [130] he cautions that the Department of Justice will look closely at claims of attorney-client privilege. Of course, the threat of criminal prosecution, which has to be made indirectly and artfully, also can be used as leverage to "facilitate" civil settlements. With the increasing realities of potential civil and criminal penalties, there is a tendency up and down the line, particularly if there is a perception that management doesn't care or will not back the employee, to document alleged problems so that the next person up the line will also have liability exposure and to limit the exposure of the person lower down. Management programs that don't have the safety valve of a corporate commitment to dealing with significant issues will find many of these memoranda in their files when there is a civil or criminal prosecution.

EPA and the Department of Justice have recognized the value of environmental audits, but ordinarily reserve the right to obtain such material.[131] Indeed, in a Catch-22 determination, the agencies desire to encourage these programs by holding out the carrot of possible limits on criminal prosecution if the audit and entire management program are sufficiently comprehensive. Thus, on July 1, 1991, the Department of Justice issued its policy to limit the use of information developed in environmental audits and other voluntary compliance efforts in criminal prosecutions under environmental statutes. However, the following excerpt from that statement indicates that the audit and compliance program must be very comprehensive and broad-based in order to secure any form of consideration:

> The attorney for the Department should consider the existence and scope of any regularized, intensive, and comprehensive environmental compliance program; such a program may include an environmental compliance or management audit. Particular consideration should be given to whether the compliance or audit program includes sufficient measures to identify and prevent future noncompliance, and whether the program was adopted in good faith in a timely manner.[132]

Compliance programs may vary, but the following questions should be asked in evaluating any program:

- Was there a strong institutional policy to comply with all environmental requirements?
- Had safeguards beyond those required by existing law been developed and implemented to prevent noncompliance from occurring?
- Were there regular procedures, including internal or external compliance and management audits, to evaluate, detect, prevent, and remedy circumstances like those that led to the noncompliance?
- Were there procedures and safeguards to ensure the integrity of any audit conducted?
- Did the audit evaluate all sources of pollution (i.e., all media), including the possibility of cross-media transfers of pollutants?
- Were the auditor's recommendations implemented in a timely fashion?

- Were adequate resources committed to the auditing program and to implementing its recommendations?
- Was environmental compliance a standard by which employee and corporate departmental performance was judged?

For a more detailed analysis of environmental auditing, see *infra* Chapter 5.

A facility convicted under CAA or FWPCA criminal provisions is barred from government contracting until the condition of noncompliance is corrected. The policy memorandum issued on November 13, 1991, by the EPA Acting Assistant Administrator for Enforcement significantly increases the requirements for removal and what violators must do to be removed from the list. [133] The memorandum specifically addresses the requirement for a proper corporate attitude toward environmental compliance before an environmental violator will be deemed to have corrected the condition giving rise to the listing. Most of these requirements are similar to the seven-factored steps [134] for an effective compliance program listed in the sentencing guidelines for corporations.

Whether under federal or state law, the environmental lawyer or manager is faced with the problem that "[t]here's no bright line that determines whether a case will be administrative, civil, or criminal." [135]

Zero Levels of Pollution

With the passage of time, we have also become more sophisticated in understanding the causes and effects of pollution, and we can detect pollutants in increasingly small amounts and concentrations. When the original Clean Water Act of 1972 indicated a goal of zero pollution, pollutants could be detected at the parts-per-million level. Today, we can in some instances detect pollutants down to parts per quadrillion. Many regulators are privately sorry that these new sophisticated instruments of detection are available because they create regulatory problems. The public often doesn't recognize the difference between harmful quantities and detectable quantities. The mere presence of a carcinogen or hazardous pollutant is sufficient to cause concern. Large numbers of the population will only accept "zero," or at worst, "background" levels.

With such pressures for control of toxics and hazardous wastes to "background" or "zero" levels, future emphasis will be on regulation of these materials. With corporations closely reviewing costs, emphasis will also be on reduction of operating costs. These goals can be complementary: if toxics and wastes can be eliminated, operating costs can be reduced. The watchword in management today seems to be "cost-effective." However,

American industry needs to seek not just cost-effective, but *more* effective ways of managing environmental programs.

A major objective is to have senior management recognize two things. First, environmental management can be a "profit center." It provides opportunities to reduce both present and future costs. Second, compliance is only a small portion of good environmental management. Resolution of compliance issues frees managers from spending time on environmental concerns, allowing them to focus on the business itself. On the other hand, reduced emphasis on compliance could lead financially oriented managers to curtail or reorient the environmental function. Thus, the challenge for the environmental manager is to keep staffing and costs "lean and mean" while maintaining an organization fully capable of dealing with environmental management challenges.

Whether you are now a member of the cadre of environmental, health, and safety managers or are planning to join it shortly, and whether your background is as a regulator or as a general manager, this book will help give you the tools to develop a strong, socially responsible environmental program and related safety and health programs that are cost-effective and that minimize regulatory and enforcement concerns.

Technically trained managers may take some solace in the possibility that some day in the future, a book about environmental management will not have to start with an extensive description of legal developments. Although compliance with law will always be necessary, the search for solutions to environmental problems may move from the realm of law to that of technology. To some extent, this movement has already begun. As the early federal environmental statutes—NEPA, the CAA, and the FWPCA—were promulgated, there was an initial flurry of primarily legal work. Although these statutes still provide considerable work for lawyers, the emphasis has now shifted to technical analysis. Implementation of the more recent hazardous waste statutes is now intensely focused on legal actions; in time, this emphasis hopefully will also shift to technical solutions that protect health and the environment.

I am by no means predicting or advocating unemployment for environmental lawyers. There will always be considerable legal work in this area, but it cannot continue to grow at its present rate. Nor should it—our goal as professionals is to resolve environmental problems, not merely to litigate or study them. We are beginning to solve these problems less as lawyers and more as managers. Hopefully, this book will advance that process.

Notes to Chapter 2

1. *See generally* Friedman, *Corporate Environmental Programs and Litigation: The Role of Lawyer-Managers in Environmental Management*, 45 PUB. ADMIN. REV. 766 (1985), from which a portion of this chapter is adapted. Adapted with permission from PUBLIC ADMINISTRATION REVIEW, © 1985 by The American Society for Public Administration, 1120 G Street NW, Suite 500, Washington, D.C., 20005. All rights reserved.

2. R. KAGAN & E. BARDACH, GOING BY THE BOOK: THE PROBLEM OF REGULATORY UNREASONABLENESS (1982).

3. This assumption has not changed very much in recent years.

4. Ward, *Reflections*, ENVTL. F., Nov. 1984, at 2. *See also* R. MELNICK, REGULATION AND THE COURTS: THE CASE OF THE CLEAN AIR ACT 5-13 (1983). Although they relied on the federal government to control states and corporations, environmentalists distrusted various elements of the federal government as well. Melnick notes that the specificity of many of the early regulations resulted from the bureaucrats' suspicions about the commitment of the Nixon administration to environmental issues and was an attempt to "protect their initiatives from executive branch sabotage." *Id.* at 8.

5. J. QUARLES, CLEANING UP AMERICA: AN INSIDER'S VIEW OF THE ENVIRONMENTAL PROTECTION AGENCY (1976).

6. Bishop Processing Co. v. Gardner, 275 F. Supp. 780 (C.D. Md. 1967), 287 F. Supp. 624 (C.D. Md. 1968), *aff'd*, 423 F.2d 469 (4th Cir. 1969), *cert. denied*, 398 U.S. 904 (1970).

7. For a complete discussion of the availability of attorneys fees against the federal government and the statutes specifically allowing such fees, see Alyeska Pipeline Serv. Co. v. Wilderness Soc'y, 421 U.S. 240, 5 ELR 20286 (1975). *See, e.g.,* Federal Water Pollution Control Act (FWPCA) §1365(d), 33 U.S.C. §1365(d), ELR STAT. FWPCA §505(d); Clean Air Act (CAA) §307(f), 42 U.S.C. §7607(f), ELR STAT. CAA §307(f).

8. MELNICK, *supra* note 4, at 9.

9. The Supreme Court has ruled that a party must be victorious on at least one substantive claim on the merits in order to obtain attorneys fees. Ruckelshaus v. Sierra Club, 463 U.S. 680, 682, 13 ELR 20664, 20665 (1983).

10. NEPA §102(2)(C), 42 U.S.C. §4332(2)(C) (1982), ELR STAT. NEPA §102(2)(C).

11. To achieve standing, "a party must demonstrate that the challenged action has caused him 'injury in fact' and that the injury was to an interest within the zone of interests protected by the applicable law." Schwartz & Hackett, *Citizen Suits Against Private Industry Under the Clean Water Act*, 17 NAT. RESOURCES LAW. 327, 332 (1984) (citing Sierra Club v. Morton, 405 U.S. 727, 733- 34, 2 ELR 20192 (1972)). "In short, a plaintiff may not rely on an interest, no matter how strongly

felt, to attain standing unless he can demonstrate a specific interest that has been injured by the defendant's action." *Id.* at 333.

12. MELNICK, *supra* note 4, at 9.

13. See, for example, the litigation concerning EPA regulation of prevention of significant deterioration (PSD) under the Clean Air Act, Alabama Power Co. v. Costle, 606 F.2d 1068, 9 ELR 20400 (D.C. Cir. 1979). Plaintiffs included the American Petroleum Institute, the National Coal Association, the Mining and Reclamation Council of America, the American Iron and Steel Institute, the American Paper Institute, the National Forest Products Association, the Manufacturing Chemists Association, the American Mining Congress, the Montana Coal Council, and more than 30 power, chemical pipeline, mineral, and coal companies, as well as the Sierra Club and the Environmental Defense Fund.

14. *Sierra Club v. Morton*, 405 U.S. at 727, 2 ELR at 20192; *Ruckelshaus v. Sierra Club*, 463 U.S. at 680, 13 ELR at 20664.

15. *See* Union Electric Co. v. EPA, 427 U.S. 246, 6 ELR 20570 (1976).

16. *See* Leventhal, *Environmental Decisionmaking and the Role of the Courts,* 122 U. PA. L. REV. 509 (1974).

17. Udall v. Tallman, 380 U.S. 1 (1969).

18. Vermont Yankee Nuclear Power Corp. v. Natural Resources Defense Council, 439 U.S. 519, 8 ELR 20288 (1978). On January 27, 1985, the *Washington Post* reported that the Burger Court overturned more D.C. Circuit cases in one year than the Warren Court did in a decade.

19. Almost 20 years later, many more corporate executives exhibit this kind of social conscience. The man who was my boss for may years at Occidental Petroleum, for example, was a former attorney in the Civil Rights Division of the U.S. Department of Justice and the author of a moving account of his representation of those who suffered in the tragic failure of a mine slurry dam. G. STERN, THE BUFFALO CREEK DISASTER (1976).

20. Friedman, *Corporate Responsibility and the Environment,* 1 NEW PRIORITIES 37 (1971).

21. *Id.*

22. *Environmental Education in U.S. Business Schools*, ENVIROLINK, Summer 1992, at 1.

23. B. SMART, BEYOND COMPLIANCE–A NEW INDUSTRY VIEW OF THE ENVIRONMENT 188 (1992).

24. *Quoted in* SMART, *supra* note 23, at 102.

25. EPA's final regulations, 57 Fed. Reg. 32250 (July 21, 1992), are still subject to litigation.

26. Zeckhauser & Viscusi, *Risk Within Reason*, 248 SCIENCE 559 (May 4, 1990).

27. ENVIRONMENTAL PROTECTION AGENCY, UNFINISHED BUSINESS: A COM-

PARATIVE ASSESSMENT OF ENVIRONMENTAL PROBLEMS, OVERVIEW REPORT (1987).

28. F. Friedman and E. Rosenberg, *The Managers' Dilemma—Is There Any Good Advice in Preparing for Compliance with the Clean Air Act of 1990*, ABA, Section on Natural Resources, Energy, and Environmental Law 22nd Annual Conference, Mar. 11-14, 1993, at tab 2; S. Rubalca, *RECLAIM: South Coast Air Quality Management District Embarks on a New Direction in Air Quality Regulation*, ABA Section on Natural Resources, Energy, and Environmental Law 22nd Annual Conference, Mar. 11-14, 1993, at tab 18.

29. Occidental is not a refiner. Refiners do have to evolve their products and production processes rapidly to accommodate different market demands and crude oils, as well as to meet the challenge of the fuels programs in the amended Clean Air Act.

30. Alan Carlin, Paul F. Scodari, & Don H. Garner, *Environmental Investments: The Cost of Cleaning Up*, ENVIRONMENT, Mar. 1992, at 12.

31. *Id.* at 12, 17.

32. Philip H. Abelson, *Editorial*, 259 SCIENCE 159 (1993).

33. Carlin et al., *supra* n. 30, at 12, 17.

34. *Id.*

35. *See id.*

36. ENVTL. POLICY ALERT, Nov. 13, 1991, at 15.

37. ENVTL. POLICY ALERT, Sept. 18, 1991, at 42.

38. Peter Brimelow & Leslie Spencer, *You Can't Get There From Here*, FORBES, July 6, 1992, at 59.

39. *Id.*

40. *See* E. Lynn Grayson, *The Pollution Prevention Act of 1990: Emergence of a New Environmental Policy*, 22 ELR 10392 (June 1992).

41. *See id.*

42. N.J. ADMIN. CODE tit. 7, §1K-4.3(b)(6) (1993).

43. *Id.*

44. Although the Part II cost analysis is referred to in the Act as a "full-cost accounting," DEPE has decided to use the phrase "comprehensive financial analysis . . ." for both Part I and Part II because it is a more descriptive phrase and is less easily confused with other concepts.

45. *Europe Leaping Ahead on Life Cycle Regulations*, ENV'T, HEALTH & SAFETY MGMT., Nov. 23, 1992, at 1.

46. *Id.*

47. The Minister of the Environment is given "sweeping authority to issue bans,

limits, or other restrictions on raw materials or substances in products in order to promote cleaner technology." In deciding what measures are actually necessary, "the whole cycle of substances and materials must be considered 'with a view to minimizing wastage of resources.' " *Id.* at 3.

48. *Id.*

49. *Id.*

50. "James Fava of Roy F. Weston, Frank Consoli from Scott Paper Co., and Richard Denison of the Environmental Defense Fund, prepared a paper on LCA applications for a workshop held in Leiden, the Netherlands, last year. They defined terms of the trade, which are important to distinguish:

> *Lifecycle Inventory* - An objective, data-based process of quantifying energy and raw material requirements, air emissions, waterborne effluents, solid waste, and other environmental releases incurred throughout the lifecycle of a product, process or activity.
>
> *Lifecycle Impact Analysis* - A technical, quantitative, and/or qualitative process to characterize and assess the effects of the environmental loadings identified in the inventory component. The assessment should address both ecological and human health considerations, as well as other effects such as habitat modification and noise pollution.
>
> *Lifecycle Improvement Analysis* - A systematic evaluation of the needs and opportunities to reduce the environmental burden associated with energy and raw materials use and waste emissions throughout the whole lifecycle of a product, process, or activity. This analysis may include both quantitative and qualitative measures of improvements, such as change in product design, raw materials use, industrial processing, consumer use and waste management."

Id.

51. *See* Popoff and Buzzelli, *Full-Cost Accounting*, CHEM. & ENG'G NEWS, Jan. 11, 1993, at 8.

52. *Product Life-Cycle Concepts, A Wider View of The Environment*, remarks made at Conference Board Advisory Council on Environmental Affairs, Jan. 14, 1993 [hereinafter *Product Life-Cycle Concepts*].

53. *Id.*

54. *Id.*

55. *See* Popoff and Buzzelli, *supra* note 51, at 9.

56. *Product Life-Cycle Concepts, supra* note 52.

57. *Id.*

58. *See* ENV'T, HEALTH & SAFETY MGMT., Jan. 1993, at 10.

"What some have called an important 'sleeper' development at last

June's worldwide Earth Summit in Rio de Janeiro was the creation of the new U.N. Commission on Sustainable Development."

"Sustainability means 'meeting the needs of the current generation without compromising the needs of future generations.' "

"Sustainable manufacturing (SM) applies the sustainable development concept to manufacturing operations. 'SM is a comprehensive business strategy that aims to incorporate environmentally proactive thinking into every step of the manufacturing process,' according to Mitchell L. Kennedy, president of Pollution Prevention Consultants, Inc., Cambridge, Massachusetts. 'This requires attention at all levels of the manufacturing process, including those that may not initially be related to the product itself.' "

"Sustainable manufacturing is a larger concept than other pollution prevention ideas, such as design for environment (DFE), toxics use reduction (TUR), or product life-cycle analysis. DFE revolves around the product only and does not include the work environment, factory and machinery design, or overall corporate environmental policy. TUR focuses on internal and external chemical risks at the process and worker level, but does not take into account such areas as packaging, energy use, or end product disposal. Product life-cycle analysis defines environmental impacts for the life of the product, but does not address management strategies or worker health and safety issues."

Id. See generally NATIONAL WILDLIFE FEDERATION CORPORATE CONSERVATION COUNCIL, BUILDING THE SUSTAINABLE CORPORATION (1992) [hereinafter BUILDING THE SUSTAINABLE CORPORATION]. *See also, Agenda 21, Adoption of Agreements on Environment and Development*, U.N. Conference on Environment and Development, U.N. Doc. A/Cont.151/1 (Parts I-IV).

59. Materials can be selected to minimize use of virgin materials and maximize use of recycled materials, decrease waste, decrease the energy required to produce the product, and decrease the per piece manufacturing time. The product can be designed so that finished dimensions are close to the incoming feed stock to reduce the need for excessive materials removal. Toxic materials can be avoided. BUILDING THE SUSTAINABLE CORPORATION, *supra* note 58.

60. Production:
   • Optimize production using P2 [Pollution Prevention] and TUR [Toxics Use Reduction] strategies.
   • Conserve energy. Many of the electric motors used to drive production machinery could be made 20 percent to 30 percent more efficient.
   • Redesign processes to eliminate worker health and safety risks and potential for operator error.

BUILDING THE SUSTAINABLE CORPORATION, *supra* note 58.

61. Market and After-Market:
   • Reduce packaging, use recycled materials in packaging, use environ-

mentally nondemanding printing inks, and use returnable/reusable packaging.
 • Design products for repair and replacement of components, rather than disposal, and for easy disassembly for recycling.
 • Reduce product persistence in the environment by design for recycling and reuse or for degradability of materials that can't be recycled.

BUILDING THE SUSTAINABLE CORPORATION, *supra* note 58.

62. Cost Accounting:
 • View wastes as materials that could be recovered for recycling or reuse and account for them as lost raw materials.
 • Consider as potential revenue sources all costs associated with the treatment and disposal of process wastes, permit fees, and materials taxes.
 • Consider as lost revenue costs associated with not recycling wastes and not conserving energy or materials.
 • Include costs of training workers to safely handle toxic chemicals and of liabilities for spills and mishandling of toxic chemicals.

BUILDING THE SUSTAINABLE CORPORATION, *supra* note 58.

63. 58 Fed. Reg. 4802 (Jan. 15, 1993).

64. *Id.* at 4808.

65. *Id.*

66. *Id.* at 4811.

67. *Id.*

68. *Id.*

69. *Id.*

70. Environmental Protection Agency, UNFINISHED BUSINESS: A COMPARATIVE ASSESSMENT OF ENVIRONMENTAL PROBLEMS, OVERVIEW REPORT (1987).

71. Voluntary Protection Programs, Occupational Safety and Health Admin., Dep't of Labor, Draft *Federal Register* Notice, Apr. 22, 1992, at 7.

72. *Id.*, at 2.

73. For an extensive and well-written discussion of the criminal implications of environmental law see Riesel, *Criminal Prosecution and the Regulation of the Environment*, 1991 A.L.I./A.B.A. COURSE OF STUDY—ENVTL. L. 375, 379, 421-23.

74. *Cited in Moretz, The Rising Cost of Environmental Crime*, OCCUPATIONAL HAZARDS, Mar. 1990, at 38.

75. *Id.* at 39.

76. OFFICE OF ENFORCEMENT, ENVIRONMENTAL PROTECTION AGENCY, EN-FORCEMENT ACCOMPLISHMENTS REPORT FY 1991 3-4, 3-2 (1992).

77. Office of Enforcement, Environmental Protection Agency, ENVIRONMENTAL ACCOMPLISHMENTS REPORT FY 1991 (1991).

78. *Id.*

79. *Id.*

80. Baker & McKenzie, ENVTL. UPDATE, Fall 1992, at 2.

81. Pub. L. No. 101-593, tit. II, 104 Stat. 2962 (1990).

82. Charles A. DeMonaco, Assistant Chief of the Environmental Crimes Section of DOJ's Environment and Natural Resources Division, discussed enforcement trends in an address at the February 1992 ALI/ABA conference. He stated that the FBI has designated environmental crime as a priority and that the FBI is shifting agents from Cold War activities to the environmental area. Charles A. DeMonaco, Remarks at American Law Institute/American Bar Association Conference (Feb. 14, 1992), *quoted in Criminal Enforcement Action No Longer Limited to "Midnight Dumpers," Lawyer Tells Conference*, 32 Env't Rep. (BNA) 2406 (Feb. 21, 1992) [hereinafter *Criminal Enforcement Action No Longer Limited*].

83. S. 445, 102nd Cong., 1st Sess. (1991); S. 2154, 101st Cong., 2nd Sess. (1990). *See also* H.R. 4050, 101st Cong., 2nd Sess. (1990). The current penalty for a willful violation of the OSH Act causing death to any employee is 6 months in prison and/or a fine of no more than $10,000. OSH Act, 29 U.S.C. §666(e) (1982). The proposed Occupational Safety and Health Administration Criminal Penalty Reform Act would increase the penalty to 6 months to 10 years in prison and/or a fine of up to $250,000. The bill provides for a fine of up to $500,000 if the defendant is a corporation. *See* Arnett, *Risky Business: OSHA's Hazard Communication Standard, EPA's Toxics Release Inventory, and Environmental Safety,* 22 ELR 10440 (July 1992).

84. Address by Judson Starr, A.B.A. Section of Natural Resources, Energy, and Environmental Law Annual Conference, Keystone, Colo. (Mar. 15-18, 1990).

85. *See* NICHOLSON, CRIMINAL PROVISIONS IN FEDERAL ENVIRONMENTAL STATUTES, A COMPILATION (Cong. Res. Serv. 1989).

86. CAL. HEALTH & SAFETY CODE §§25189.5-25192. Note also the California Corporate Criminal Act of 1989, adopted in 1990. CAL. PENAL CODE §387 (West 1990) (section 387 was added by A.B. No. 2249 §2, 1990 Cal. Adv. Legis. Sev. 166). The Act provides criminal liability for a corporation or business manager who (1) has actual knowledge of a serious concealed danger subject to regulatory authority and associated with a product or business practice and (2) knowingly fails to provide notice thereof to Cal-OSHA and affected employees in writing unless the corporation or manager knows that such notices already have been given. The notices must be given immediately if there is an imminent risk, otherwise within 15 days, unless the condition is abated within those timeframes.

87. CAL. HEALTH & SAFETY CODE §25190.

88. N.J. STAT. ANN. §2C:17-2.

89. 35 PA. CONS. STAT. ANN. §6018.101 *et seq.* (Purdon 1990). Gerald Krovatin of the law firm of Lowenstein, Sandler, Kohl, Fisher & Boylan in Roseland, New Jersey, supplied me with the material in this note and notes 90 through 93.

90. *See* N.J. STAT. ANN. §2C:17-2(a)(2).

91. *See* N.J. STAT. ANN. §2C:44-1(d).

92. *Id.*

93. *See, e.g.,* State v. Roth, 95 N.J. 334, 471 A.2d 370 (1984).

94. Gaynor & Bartman, *Frontier Justice,* ENVTL. F., Mar./Apr. 1991, at 24. The Department of Justice recently amended the environmental crimes provisions of the U.S. Attorney's Manual making it clear that the Environmental Crimes Section must approve virtually all environmental crime prosecutions made by U.S. attorneys. The amended provisions specifically define environmental crimes that may only be prosecuted after approval by the Department of Justice headquarters. *Amended Environmental Crime Procedures for U.S. Attorneys Manual Released by DOJ,* 23 Env't Rep. (BNA) 2488 (Jan. 22, 1993). Vicki O'Meara, the Acting Assistant Attorney General for Environment and Natural Resources was quoted as noting "that courts had made conflicting decisions and DOJ needed to consider prosecutions on a national level. 'We are sending people to jail here. We are talking about people's lives,' she added." *Id.*

95. Starr, Block & Cooney, *Prosecuting Pollution,* LEGAL TIMES, May 31, 1993.

96. Starr & Kelly, *Environmental Crimes and the Sentencing Guidelines: The Time Has Come and It Is Hard Time,* 20 ELR 10096, 10104 (Mar. 1990).

97. SECTION OF NATURAL RESOURCES, ENERGY, AND ENVIRONMENTAL LAW, AMERICAN BAR ASSOCIATION, 1990 THE YEAR IN REVIEW 213-14 (1991) [hereinafter 1990 THE YEAR IN REVIEW].

98. 912 F.2d 741, 21 ELR 20051 (4th Cir. 1990).

99. 1990 THE YEAR IN REVIEW, *supra* note 97, at 215; *Dee,* 912 F.2d at 745-46, 21 ELR at 20053.

100. State of Ohio v. Stirnkorb, No. 85-CR-5240B (C.P. Clermont County July 19, 1989).

101. Richard M. Hall, Remarks at American Law Institute/American Bar Association Conference (Feb. 14, 1992), *quoted in Criminal Enforcement Action No Longer Limited, supra* note 81, at 2406. *See* Moore, Dabroski & Ballbach, *Why Risk Criminal Charges by Performing Environmental Audits?,* 6 Toxics L. Rep. (BNA) 503 (Sept. 18, 1991).

102. *See* Van Cleve, *The Changing Intersection of Environmental Auditing, Environmental Law and Enforcement Policy,* 12 CARDOZO L. REV. 1215, 1226-27 (1991) (citing United States v. Int'l Minerals & Chem. Corp., 402 U.S. 558 (1971), United States v. Dotterweich, 320 U.S. 277 (1943), and United States v. Johnson & Towers, Inc., 741 F.2d 662, 14 ELR 20634 (3d Cir. 1984)).

103. Habicht, *The Federal Perspective on Environmental Criminal Enforcement*, 17 ELR 10478 (Dec. 1987).

104. Onsdorff & Mesnard, *The Responsible Corporate Officer Doctrine in RCRA Criminal Enforcement: What You Don't Know Can Hurt You*, 22 ELR 10099, 10100 (Feb. 1992) (emphasis in original).

105. Starr & Kelly, *supra* note 96, at 10101-04.

106. *Id.* at 10104.

107. United States v. Protex, No. 87-CR-115 (D. Colo. Mar. 4, 1988), *cited in* McAllister, *Trial of the Criminal Environmental Case: Defense Point of View*, CRIMINAL ENFORCEMENT OF ENVIRONMENTAL LAWS 252 (A.L.I./A.B.A. 1990) (emphasis in original). *See generally,* Barber, *Fair Warning: The Deterioration of Scienter under Environmental Criminal Statutes*, 26 LOY. L. A. L. REV. 105 (1992); Smith, *No Longer Just a Cost of Doing Business: Criminal Liability of Corporate Officials of Violations of the Clean Water Act and the Resource Recovery Act*, 53 LA. L. REV. 119 (Sept. 1992).

108. United States v. Brittain, 931 F.2d 1413, 1419, 21 ELR 21092, 21094 (10th Cir. 1991); United States v. Baytank (Houston), Inc., 934 F.2d 599, 613, 21 ELR 21101, 21107 (5th Cir. 1991); United States v. Hayes Int'l Corp., 786 F.2d 1499, 1503, 16 ELR 20717, 20718 (11th Cir. 1986).

109. *Hayes*, 786 F.2d at 1503, 16 ELR at 20718.

110. *Baytank*, 934 F.2d at 613, 21 ELR at 21107. The Sixth Circuit in *United States v. Dean*, 969 F.2d 796, 22 ELR 21296 (6th Cir 1992) affirmed the conviction of the manager of a Tennessee metal plating plant for four RCRA violations and conspiracy to violate RCRA. The court said it could see no basis on the face of the RCRA statute to require knowledge of the permit requirement as an element of the crime. The court also observed that the force of RCRA's statutory scheme would be significantly weakened if anyone who claimed ignorance of the permit requirement was exempt from prosecution. Note that in the context of the Clean Water Act "knowing endangerment" means protection of U.S. water and although certain conduct, according to the court, "was utterly reprehensible" in endangering employees, it did not meet the specific statutory requirement. United States v. Burowski, (1st Cir., No. 90-2133, October 7, 1992).

111. *Johnson & Towers*, 741 F.2d at 662, 14 ELR at 20634.

112. *Id.* at 669, 14 ELR at 20638; *Baytank*, 934 F.2d at 613, 21 ELR at 21107. In *United States v. Hoflin*, 880 F.2d 1033, 1037-38, 19 ELR 21140, 21142 (9th Cir. 1989), the Ninth Circuit also declined to follow standard set forth in *Johnson & Towers*.

113. Klingon, *Justice Department Pulls Out All the Stops*, ENV'T, HEALTH & SAFETY MGMT, Aug. 31, 1992, at 1, 3 (reprinted with permission).

114. Aufhauser, *Crime and Punishment*, SONREEL NEWS (ABA Section of Natural Resources, Energy, and Environmental Law), Jan./Feb. 1992, at 2 (emphasis in original), *citing* United States v. MacDonald & Watson Waste Oil Co., 933

F.2d 35 (1st Cir. 1991), United States v. White, CR 90-228-232-AAM (E.D. Wash.
Mar. 28, 1991) (government precluded from arguing in RCRA prosecution that a
responsible corporate officer is liable for acts that he "should have known of").
See also Onsdorff & Mesnard, *supra* note 104, at 10104.

Charles A. DeMonaco, Assistant Chief of the Environmental Crimes Section of
the U.S. Department of Justice's Environment and Natural Resources Division,
recently stated that the Justice Department intends to follow the approach of the
First Circuit in United States v. McDonald & Watson. This approach requires that,
before an individual can be found guilty, there must be proof that he or she had
actual knowledge of the criminal wrongdoing. However, he said, "managers
cannot defend their inaction by saying that they did not know about the non-compliance." DeMonaco, Remarks, *supra* note 82, at 2407.

115. *See* United States v. Park, 421 U.S. 658 (1975); *Dotterwiech*, 320 U.S. at 277,
cited by Van Cleve, *supra* note 102, at 1227 n. 36. *See also* Aufhauser, *supra* note
113 (discussing *Park* and *Dotterweich*). For a detailed discussion of the entire
"public welfare" issue and criminal law issues generally, see Riesel, *supra* note
73; Barber, *supra*, note 107 and Smith, *supra*, note 107.

116. CAA §113(h); 42 U.S.C. §7413(h); ELR STAT. CAA §113(h). Section
113(c)(6) of the CAA also provides that for enforcement purposes, the definition
of "person" specifically includes "any responsible corporate officer." 42 U.S.C.
§7413(c)(6), ELR STAT. CAA §113(c)(6).

117. *See* Friedman, *Environmental Management for the Future: Environmental
Auditing Is Not Enough*, 12 CARDOZO L. REV. 1314, 1324-25. *See, e.g.,* CAA
§113(c)(5)(B), 42 U.S.C. §7413(c)(5)(B), ELR STAT. CAA §113(c)(5)(B). *See also*
United States v. Lanza, 790 F.2d 1015, 1021-22 (2d Cir. 1986), *cert. denied*, 479
U.S. 861 (1986) (upholding charge of conscious avoidance of knowledge in fraud
case even though underlying substantive offense was not charged), United States
v. Rothrock, 806 F.2d 318, 323 (1st Cir. 1986) ("The purpose of the willful
blindness theory is to impose criminal liability on people who, recognizing the
likelihood of wrongdoing, nonetheless consciously refuse to take basic investigatory steps." *Id.* at 323.), Illinois EPA v. Citizens Utilities Co., No. 79-142 (Ill.
Pollution Control Board, Jan. 12, 1984) (holding knowledge element fulfilled
where major equipment and operational failures are due to an operator's ignorance
of plant design and failure to investigate).

118. CAA §113(h), 42 U.S.C. §7413(h), ELR STAT. CAA §113(h).

119. U.S. SENTENCING COMMISSION, FEDERAL SENTENCING GUIDELINES §2Q,
reprinted in 18 U.S.C.A. app. 4 at 271 (1992 Supp.) [hereinafter GUIDELINES].

120. Starr & Kelly, *supra* note 96, at 10096. See McGregor, *Sentencing Program
Permits Flexibility*, HAZMAT, Nov. 1992, at 61, for discussion of the use of the
guidelines in a specific case involving individual sentencing for "six counts of
knowingly dredging a canal and discharging fill materials into wetlands in violation
of the Clean Water Act."

121. *Federal Commission Drops Tougher Environmental Penalty Plan Pending Study*, INSIDE EPA, Jan. 3, 1992, at 1.

122. Zornow & Reed, *Guidelines Don't Fit Federal Cases*, NAT'L L.J., Mar. 2, 1992, at 19 (citations omitted).

123. Marshall & Roth, *Federal Sentencing Guidelines Now in Effect for Corporations*, McCUTCHEN UPDATE, Dec. 18, 1991, at 1. Under the Guidelines, mandatory fine ranges are determined using a "base fine" and a "culpability score." The base fine is calculated on the basis of which will be greatest: "i.) the amount in the offense level table (all federal crimes have been assigned numerical offense levels), ii) the pecuniary gain to the organization from the offense (either in revenue or cost savings), or iii) the pecuniary loss caused by the offense to the extent the loss was caused intentionally, knowingly, or recklessly." Miller & Kritz, *New Developments in Corporate Criminal Liability: The Benefits and Risks of Compliance Programs*, MORRISON & FOERSTER, Feb. 1992, at 4 (citing GUIDELINES, *supra* note 119, §8C2.4, at 526). An effective corporate compliance program to prevent and detect violations can reduce the maximum fine "to below the minimum fine for the very same offense committed without such a program." Miller & Kritz, *supra*, at 5.

A compliance program must be "effective" to merit a reduced culpability score. It is not sufficient that the policy is in writing and distributed to all relevant employees. Due diligence, the "hallmark" of an effective program, requires *at a minimum* that the organization must:

> 1) establish standards and procedures to be followed by its employees and other agents;
>
> 2) assign oversight responsibility to "specific individuals within high-level personnel";
>
> 3) use due care not to delegate substantial discretionary authority to individuals who the corporation should have known had a propensity to engage in criminal activities;
>
> 4) effectively communicate its standards and procedures to all employees and agents;
>
> 5) utilize monitoring and auditing systems to detect criminal conduct and a reporting system that effectively eliminates fear of retribution;
>
> 6) consistently enforce disciplinary mechanisms; and
>
> 7) respond appropriately to detected offenses and take steps to prevent further similar offenses.

Miller & Kritz, *supra*, at 5-6 (citing GUIDELINES, *supra* note 119, §8A1.2 note 3(k), at 523. The Guidelines and "mandatory disclosure statutes such as California Penal Code Section 387 put company executives in a difficult position by requiring or encouraging disclosure of the criminal conduct to the government." Miller & Kritz, *supra*, at 7. Note also that while the sentencing guidelines don't directly cover environmental crimes, they do indirectly become involved in probation issues.

124. Marshall & Roth, *supra* note 123, at 1; GUIDELINES, *supra* note 119, §8C2.4, at 529.

125. GUIDELINES, *supra* note 119, §8C2.5, at 531-32.

126. Giuffra, *Sentencing Corporations*, AM. ENTERPRISE, May/June 1990, at 85.

127. Van Cleve, *supra* note 102, at 1227.

128. *Id.*

129. *Id.* at 1228.

130. *Id.*

131. *See* EPA Environmental Auditing Policy Statement, 51 Fed. Reg. 25004 (July 9, 1986), reprinted as Appendix C of this volume, and discussion of that policy in Chapter 5.

132. Factors in Decisions on Criminal Prosecutions for Environmental Violations in the Context of Significant Voluntary Compliance or Disclosure Efforts by the Violator, ELR ADMIN. MATERIALS 35399 (Dep't of Justice 7/1/91). The policy is reprinted as Appendix F of this volume.

133. EPA Policy Regarding the Rule of Corporate Attitude, Policies, Practices, and Procedures, in Determining Whether to Remove a Facility From the EPA List of Violating Facilities Following a Criminal Conviction, 56 Fed. Reg. 64785 (Nov. 13, 1991).

134. *See supra* note 123.

135. Judson Starr, *quoted in* Simon, *Upping the Ante*, FORBES, May 14, 1990, at 121. (See Chapter 5 and the section on Legal Exposure for suggestions on minimizing criminal liability exposure.)

Chapter 3:
Establishing the Basis for a Strong Environmental Management Program

I f you have recently become an environmental manager, the difficulties you will face depend partly on your background. If you were previously a general manager, merely learning the jargon of environmental management may seem an overwhelming task. If you have had environmental experience as a manager or a lawyer, you may find the problems of organizing an effective program within the context of the corporate organization and its specific culture equally overwhelming. This book should be helpful regardless of your background. It introduces some of the jargon that you will need to know, and it outlines an approach to developing an environmental program within your corporate culture.

This book should also be helpful to the experienced environmental manager. If nothing else, it can serve as the basis for a cross-check against your existing programs. It may also help bolster your case to senior management for implementation of certain programs by explaining the value of these programs in detail.

One key prerequisite of successful environmental management is effective staffing. This chapter discusses staffing issues, including staff size and the potential for "turf wars." The chapter then summarizes various useful management tools. Chapters 4 and 5 will cover these tools in detail.

Staffing and Turf Wars

In my experience, the greatest obstacle to effective and cost-effective environmental programs is "turf." Even with the strongest management support, a program simply cannot succeed unless turf issues are minimized. I will discuss turf and staffing issues in detail because of their significance.

Divisional managements have a deep distrust of corporate bureaucrats, whom they view as interfering with their business and, even worse, not understanding it. This reaction is in far too many cases well justified. Many corporations either were or are even now overstaffed, and staff members have to justify their existence by at least showing they are doing something. Many companies are now trying to pare back corporate controls and allow divisions greater management freedom. This, in turn, generates an almost "revenge" mentality, a strong desire to "get back at Corporate," which may have made divisional life miserable, by ignoring corporate staff whenever possible. Cost pressure to reduce divisional staffs also blurs the lines of environmental responsibility.

Hostility between corporate and divisional staff is one problem; inefficient staff management at both levels is another. Obviously, bloated staffs in either corporate or divisional headquarters are to be avoided. Even with reduced staff, however, old tendencies die hard, and there is still too much management by committee. Committee meetings may be smaller, since there are now fewer people to attend, but it would be far better to grant broader authority and encourage risk-taking rather than to tie up scarce resources in needless paperwork and meetings. How can these problems be avoided in environmental management?

Peter Drucker and other management experts maintain that the key to management today is managing information. [1] Information management does not necessarily require large staffs. But many companies, even those with large staffs, still do not have mechanisms to ensure that significant information is received at corporate headquarters and is immediately made available to decisionmakers. This unavailability of significant information is exacerbated by many companies' efforts to decentralize. While decentralization is useful in reducing decisionmaking time and encouraging entrepreneurship, care must be taken that it does not deprive corporate headquarters of vital information.

The corporation in today's regulatory and litigation climate must learn of potentially significant issues at the earliest possible time to avoid major problems. The underlying assumption for effective environmental management must be: What you don't know *will* hurt you. Obtaining and effectively using the necessary information can be accomplished with a minimal staff, provided barriers to obtaining significant data are eliminated or reduced. Occidental has accomplished this by operating as a decentralized organization with a centralized information base. Information management is discussed in detail in Chapter 4.

Occidental was fortunate in avoiding turf and staffing problems from the beginning. It is a relatively new company without a history of overstaffing or "staff wars." When Dr. Armand Hammer, Oxy's former Chief Executive Officer, took over the company in 1957, its net worth was only $100,000. The company expanded primarily through domestic acquisitions in a wide variety of areas, together with rapid growth in the international oil and gas area and limited growth in domestic oil and gas operations. Occidental now includes a number of "industry groups." As used here, "industry group" means a subsidiary or group of subsidiaries in a particular line of business, such as chemical production or oil and gas operations. While independent in many ways, Occidental's industry groups function as if they were divisions of the company for environmental management purposes. For the sake of simplicity, this book uses the term "division" to include both actual divisions and industry groups.

Throughout Occidental's expansion, corporate headquarters functioned as the equivalent of a holding company with a very small staff. The divisions had substantial leeway, with limited reporting to corporate headquarters, and were encouraged to keep staff size down.

Perhaps the most significant factor allowing a small staff to function effectively is smallness itself—the absence of overstaffing throughout the entire corporation. As previously discussed, in some large companies, too much time is spent justifying activity in order to justify jobs. Management experts today consider the concepts of "simple form, lean staff" and a "bias for action" key attributes of successful management. These concepts argue for combining thin staffing with short lines of decisionmaking. At Occidental, for example, comments on new procedures and approaches to regulations and legislation can be produced quickly, simply because very few people are required to make such decisions. Thus, thin staffing must be combined with decisionmaking authority for the system to function effectively.

Corporate staff must be sensitive to divisional needs. The "iron fist" approach in dealing with operating management or divisional environmental staffs simply does not work. All organizations have learned to resist pressures from the top. The dismal experience of new administrators of federal agencies who try to change policies and means of control from the top down, rather than gaining the confidence of the civil service, is a good example of the impossibility of achieving change without cooperation and trust. Professionals must work collectively at both corporate and divisional levels to develop strong programs.

As discussed below, Occidental increased its emphasis on good environmental management in 1978. Because the divisions had been operating semi-autonomously in the environmental area with effective staffs, the mandate for improved environmental management did not mean the growth of a massive corporate staff. Instead, growth consisted of the addition of one professional at headquarters. Corporate staff looked toward ensuring that there were capable environmental professionals in the divisions, where the basic work was being—and should be—done. The role of corporate staff is to assist rather than replace or direct the efforts of division staff. The result is that jealousies and "turf wars" are rarely problems. Indeed, the corporate staff clearly is not large enough to take over for the divisions even if it wanted to. Instead, the corporate staff focuses on ensuring that the divisions and facilities have tools and personnel capable of doing the job. Corporate procedures provide corporate staff with authority to review and comment on appointments of senior divisional environment, health, and safety personnel. If divisions have competent personnel, the corporate role is easier. Moreover, the corporate role in approving appointments helps assure environmental professionals in the divisions of a direct functional line of communication with corporate staff that will help them obtain necessary resources. Under this arrangement, divisional managements know that the Board of Directors and corporate management place a high priority on good environmental management.

Another means of minimizing "turf" wars is to integrate key staff functions. Battles among staff groups can be just as counterproductive as fights between divisional and corporate staff. As discussed subsequently, the line between environment and safety is becoming increasingly vague. These two functions should report to the same manager in order to minimize potential problems. The medical function is also closely tied to environment and safety, as is industrial hygiene; therefore, it makes sense to also have the same line of reporting for these two functions. A line that is even harder to identify is the line between safety and risk engineering. The risk engineering group is normally concerned about fires and explosions to the extent that they impact on property losses. However, fires and explosions obviously risk personnel safety. The answer is to assure that both functions have the same reporting structure to maximize the value of both functions and eliminate any gray areas. Of course, many of these issues, such as sudden releases, also have environmental implications.

Occidental has also found that it makes sense to have the legislative and regulatory function with respect to environment, health, and safety be on the same reporting line. This does not mean that this reporting structure should include the traditional lobbyists in your Washington, D.C., office, but rather, as discussed in more detail in Chapter 4, individuals with technical and legal skills who can have credibility with key regulatory and legislative officials, because of their specific knowledge and at times, drafting expertise, should sometimes become involved in lobbying efforts although they may report to environment and safety managers.

A more difficult question is the integration of the legal function. Interaction with lawyers is discussed in more detail in Chapter 8. Obviously, in my own case, as an active practicing lawyer as well as a manager, the integration of the function was relatively easy, particularly since I reported to an Executive Vice President who was also Occidental's Senior General Counsel and Secretary. The environmental counsel reported to me on a strong dotted-line relationship and, because of many years of working together when that individual was at EPA and on various bar committees and other activities prior to his coming to Oxy, there was no real friction. The danger of reporting through the legal department in most companies is that there is a tendency to view these functions as legal, rather than operational. We were very careful at Occidental to make my department separate from the Legal Department.

As the environmental area has become more legally oriented and more experienced lawyers have moved into the senior environmental position, this issue of distinguishing between a legal and a management position has become more of a concern. If the Legal Department has a "turf" mentality, it may feel threatened with a lawyer in charge of the environmental function. Consequently, that individual needs to tread lightly on his or her legal skill when dealing with the Legal Department.

Communication between corporate and divisional staffs is also critical. At Occidental, corporate staff maintain continuing dialogues with divisional managements to ensure that those managements understand that they are not being undercut. Corporate staff also have a mandate that allows full discussion with interested individuals in the divisions without the interference of a rigid chain of command.

Occidental has grown rapidly over the years with the acquisition of IBP (beef and pork slaughtering, subsequently divested), Cities Service (oil and gas), and MidCon (gas pipelines)—each with a different corporate "personality." After each decision to merge and before actual closing, corporate staff met immediately with counterparts in these organizations to acquaint them with Oxy's programs and, above all, to assure both operating management and environmental staff that Occidental did not have a bureaucratic corporate staff that would interfere with divisional management. The results were that by the time of closing, transitions had been completed, and the mentality of working together without turf problems in this area was cemented.

Developing Management Controls in a Strong Environmental Program

The following discussion outlines a variety of techniques that Occidental Petroleum has used to develop a strong environmental management program at minimal cost, together with the context in which these controls were developed. Of course, the context will be different for every company. The context for Occidental included traumatic experiences on the Niagara frontier of New York. Such experiences may at least be useful in raising a company's awareness of these issues and inspiring efforts to avoid future problems. Indeed, many strong programs in other corporations (Allied Chemical and Union Carbide, for example) have been encouraged as a result of traumatic experiences that caught management's attention, increased understanding of potential problems in the divisions, and galvanized support and funding for broader based programs. Such situations foster broader cooperation, which may not always be available in corporations that have not had traumatic experiences. In any event, Occidental's experience in developing broad-range programs to avoid future problems, to deal with past problems effectively, and to do both cost-effectively with small staffs may be useful to others. Chapter 4 discusses the application of these programs in both centralized and decentralized organizations.

Occidental Petroleum's headquarters-level efforts to develop corporate-wide environmental programs began in September 1978 with the appointment of a director of health and environment. Divisional programs, of course, had commenced long before. Between September 1978 and May 1981, significant progress occurred in developing and carrying out a range of environmental programs. These programs included informal assessments, reporting on significant issues and the status of permits, and limited identification of upcoming regulatory and legislative issues. Divisional staffing was upgraded to carry out corporate requirements. Progress accelerated with additional staff and resources. A corporate environmental attorney position was created in May 1981. Between June and October 1981, the corporate staff was expanded to add a vice president, a records administrator, a manager of assessments, and a manager of external affairs (now director of external affairs and compliance). Senior management's involvement continued and expanded. During 1980 and 1981, following an SEC settlement and creation of an Environmental Committee of the Board, [2] the Board and top management gave the corporate environmental department a mandate to develop and maintain systems that would independently determine the status of compliance and independently ensure that the company was properly addressing environmental concerns.

Today that staff is still very small by most corporate standards. Two individuals are in charge of, respectively, environment and safety, and industrial hygiene. In 1990 the Risk Engineering Department (then consisting of four professionals and now composed of two professionals with another professional in a divisional position) was added to the group in recognition of the close interrelationship between personnel safety and loss prevention. Oxy's environmental counsel was based in Washington, D.C.

(although he has been transferred to the chemical division in Dallas), along with two individuals handling legislation and regulation, one of whom doubled as the Director of Environmental Affairs and is now my successor. A manager of health, safety and environmental programs was added in Los Angeles late in 1992. While the Environmental Committee of the Board always concerned itself with safety and health, in 1989 its name was changed to the Environmental, Health, and Safety Committee to reemphasize these concerns. In addition, a third outside director was added to the Committee.

The policies, procedures, and controls implemented by the Occidental Health, Environment and Safety Department are not unique. The combination of programs and the overall corporate philosophy, history, management support, and flexibility embodied in these programs may well be unusual, however. As in so many other management systems, the key is management commitment. Direct involvement of an Environmental, Health, and Safety Committee of the Board of Directors is a powerful incentive for corporate and divisional staff. A strong environmental policy signed by the Chief Executive Officer and the involvement of other senior officers in environmental program development also clearly send the right message.

Obviously, environmental managers have to deal with the corporate culture as they find it. However, while Occidental's corporate culture and management and Board awareness have substantially aided its ability to develop strong divisional and corporate programs, these programs need not be unique to Occidental. Most of them should be transferable to others in the environmental corporate community. The basic objectives of a good program are

- regular, timely, and uniform reporting from the operating line through senior management to the board of directors;
- prompt identification and resolution of environmental issues;
- establishment of preventive programs and procedures; and
- identification of developing issues or trends.

The key elements of the program are

- a computerized, centralized information system (whether in a centralized or a decentralized management system);
- a facility assessment program;
- an internal planning document and timetable;
- a capital expenditure review system;
- a willingness to address problems once they are discovered; and
- a legislative and regulatory action program.

Note that each element of the program ties into at least one objective.

In these cost-conscious times, it has been my experience that these programs can save a corporation substantial sums while keeping both corporate and divisional staffs to a minimum size. Keeping staff to an absolute minimum is essential. To do this, it is necessary to continually review job functions and program needs, consolidating functions and eliminating unnecessary positions. In addition, development of broad-based procedures and guidelines that can be monitored on an exception basis rather than on day-to-day performance allows corporate personnel to concentrate more effectively on longer range planning, program development, and compliance. A computerized database and the general use of computer-based techniques allow for effective, efficient use of data, facilitate understanding of issues, and free the staff to concentrate on broader issues.

The Occidental approach to environmental management has several key characteristics:

- Top corporate management is strongly committed to and involved in the company's environmental management programs, as is perhaps best demonstrated by the Board of Directors' taking the relatively unusual step of establishing an Environmental Committee composed of Board members.
- Both corporate and divisional staffs are committed to maintaining a high level of professional expertise encompassing a range of essential disciplines and backgrounds.
- The underlying administrative or procedural systems essential to carrying out the substantive programs are in place and operational. These systems and programs include environmental assessments; management by exception; awareness of liabilities, legislation, and regulations; a computerized environmental database; objective indices of performance; and reporting of significant matters to allow close headquarters monitoring by a small corporate staff.
- Turf problems among staff groups and divisions are minimized, primarily by having the entire corporation thinly staffed and focused on the primary concern of getting a job accomplished. Decisionmaking is largely free of bureaucratic constraints. [3]

Integrating the Safety and Risk Engineering Functions With the Environmental Function

Traditionally, environmental issues have been handled separately from safety and risk engineering. This is no longer advisable. Safety programs have been primarily concerned with various programs to reduce injury or illness without focusing on process reviews that could avoid major injuries or loss of life. Risk engineering has in the past focused more on inspections than on broader range process analysis. Conversely, today many environmental departments are beginning to look closely at the problems of sudden and massive releases, and the resultant threats to the environment. All of these areas need to come together to cope with and hopefully prevent events that create major environmental issues, impact on personnel safety, and damage property. Regulatory agencies have begun to focus on the importance of integrating these functions because of a string of explosions involving chemical facilities.

On October 23, 1989, a polyethylene plant in Pasadena, Texas, belonging to Phillips Petroleum exploded and burned, killing 23 people. In the review of the accident, EPA, as a part of its Chemical Accident Prevention Program, conducted a chemical safety audit of the Phillips complex. Other agencies participated:

> [T]he purpose of this audit was to assess the facility's chemical emergency preparedness and prevention procedures and to determine the potential for and consequences of releases that have a potential impact off site. Detailed information on the facility was collected from documents provided by Phillips and through discussions with company staff. This information included a description of the physical characteristics of the site, emergency preparedness and planning activities, community emergency response planning, public alert and notification procedures, safety and loss prevention activities and accidental release investigations. A list was compiled of the hazardous chemicals at the site and the procedures for handling and processing these chemicals were reviewed. Systems for monitoring the operation of the process and equipment and for mitigating the effects of process upsets were also reviewed. Recommendations were developed for emergency response planning, equipment for monitoring hazardous substance releases, reporting and notification procedures for chemical releases, alarm equipment, and employee evacuation training. [4]

This Chemical Accident Prevention Program arises out of the Emergency Planning and Community Right-To-Know Act of 1986. [5] In this law (also known as Title III of the Superfund Amendments and Reauthorization Act, or SARA), Congress directed EPA to conduct a review of emergency systems for preventing, detecting, and mitigating accidents and alerting the public. That review has been the keystone of EPA's accident efforts. The resulting report, issued in 1988, stated that prevention of accidental releases requires a holistic approach, integrating technologies, procedures, and management practices at all stages in the life cycle of a facility. It also emphasized that site, process, and chemical-specific hazards dictate the choice of technology and techniques at specific facilities. [6] EPA is conducting audits "to identify both problematic and successful practices and technologies for preventing and mitigating releases." [7] Thus, EPA's traditional role as an "environmental" agency has now been greatly extended into the safety area.

While EPA, as noted above, is calling for more process safety efforts, OSHA now requires such reviews. As part of its review of the Phillips incident, OSHA made the following finding: "A process hazard analysis or other equivalent method had not been utilized in the Phillips polyethylene plants to identify process hazards and the potential for malfunctioning and human error and to reduce or eliminate such hazards." [8] Phillips was cited for willful violations under the general duty clause of the OSH Act for failure to complete such analysis. OSHA planned to issue a draft rulemaking requiring such reviews:

> The rulemaking was to consider a number of possible risk reduction steps including measures requiring employers to
>
> (1) set up a management system (in writing), understand, and correct the hazards involved in the use, storage, manufacturing, handling and movement of highly hazardous materials;
>
> (2) communicate that information to employees;
>
> (3) conduct hazard analyses;
>
> (4) establish and implement procedures to accommodate changes in plant equipment and technology;
>
> (5) develop and implement operating procedures including emergency and shut-down procedures;
>
> (6) train employees in those procedures;
>
> (7) implement a preventive maintenance program that includes testing and inspection of critical equipment;
>
> (8) implement a hot-work permit system;
>
> (9) establish a workplace facility emergency action plan; and
>
> (10) insure that contractors working at the facility are aware of the hazards associated with their work at the site and of the applicable safety rules and actions to be taken during an emergency. [9]

Basically, OSHA's intent was to codify established good industry practices as advocated by the American Association of Chemical Engineers, the Chemical Manufacturers Association, and the American Petroleum Institute. The proposed requirements, which were issued in the *Federal Register* on July 17, 1990,[10] and issued in final form on February 24, 1992,[11] follow OSHA's original assumption. The Clean Air Act Amendments of 1990 create a new Chemical Safety and Hazard Investigation Board, similar to the National Transportation Safety Board, to investigate chemical accidents. EPA is required to promulgate rules to prevent accidental releases of toxic pollutants. In addition and of particular importance, EPA rules will require hazard assessments at facilities handling a broad range of chemicals. The new law includes extensive detailed requirements for the content of these assessments.[12] However, OSHA's proposed process hazard management regulations[13] apply not only to manufacture and use of these chemicals, including ammonia and chlorine, but also to storage of more than a certain amount of them. The OSHA regulations are management oriented, while EPA regulations are expected to be technically oriented. To understand the probable EPA approach, it is useful to examine EPA's comments on the OSHA draft regulations. EPA objected to the OSHA proposed regulations on the basis that they were not sufficiently detailed. EPA indicated that the process safety amendments "appear to be disjointed and should be interrelated into a comprehensive system tailored to the needs of the facility."[14] EPA has suggested that employers complete the hazard evaluation first and then build from the results of the evaluation. EPA has "questions and concerns about the methodologies used for listing chemical substances, the toxicity values used, the substance hazard index methodology, and threshold determination."[15] The opportunity for EPA to encroach on the traditional areas of OSHA's jurisdiction is obvious, with the resulting implication for EPA regulation of facility operations.[16]

A review of OSHA's regulations[17] indicates that OSHA has done an excellent job in meeting its goals. The rule requires that many facilities conduct process hazard analyses. Employers will also be required to

(1) compile process safety information and data on toxicity levels;

(2) maintain and communicate to employees safe procedures for process-related tasks;

(3) train workers so they understand the nature and causes of problems that might arise and increase their awareness of specific hazards;

(4) ensure that contractors onsite work safely and that contract employees are properly trained and informed;

(5) perform periodic inspections of equipment;

(6) issue "hot-work permits";

(7) establish and maintain written procedures prior to implementing changes in technology or equipment;

(8) use a team of experts to investigate potentially major incidents;

(9) develop emergency action plans; and

(10) conduct compliance safety audits at least every three years to assess the effectiveness of the process safety management program.

However, it is clear that EPA and OSHA are now developing a close working relationship. As the press release announcing its report on the Phillips explosion states, OSHA is committed to working "with the [EPA] to develop a joint investigation strategy for catastrophic chemical accidents which affect both plant workers and people in the surrounding community." [18] EPA and OSHA have agreed to coordinate programs to protect employees and those who live near industrial sites. The agencies will conduct joint inspections and training as well as exchange information on violations. EPA and OSHA have issued a Memorandum of Understanding that provides instructions and guidelines for cooperative enforcement efforts, mutual cross-training programs, information/data sharing, and other jointly agreed upon activities. [19]

If EPA and OSHA can work together, it is equally imperative that the industrial counterparts in company environment and safety departments also work together. While many companies complete Hazard and Operability Reviews (Haz Ops) (detailed reviews of the process for failure modes) they probably require expansion. Such reviews, together with the means of reducing the hazards identified, need to be prioritized for existing facilities on the basis of potential exposure, from both property or production loss (risk engineering) and potential risk to workers and the surrounding community (safety and environmental). Such reviews probably also need to be expanded in scope. These reviews should normally be done on a plant level by a team from operations, maintenance, and engineering with overview by safety, risk engineering, and environmental personnel.

Another means of assuring integration is to examine existing job descriptions. In general, it is useful to keep job descriptions updated to assure that they are consistent with the present objectives of your organization. (See discussion of Long Range Planning in Chapter 4.) It is also a useful vehicle for educating your human resources department, which probably doesn't fully appreciate the rapid changes in this area and the effect on finding and appropriately compensating competent personnel. However, the exercise of reviewing the descriptions, particularly if it is done as a team effort with the environment, safety, and process risk management (risk engineering) personnel, is an excellent vehicle for allowing your staff to fully appreciate the scope of each other's work and the necessary overlaps, as illustrated by the following examples from my time at Occidental. When the overlaps are recognized, the ensuing discussion helps eliminate "turf" problems and encourages teamwork.

POSITION TITLE	POSITION SUMMARY	OVERLAPPING ELEMENTS
Vice President, Health, Environment and Safety	Provides corporate-wide strategic direction for the protection of health, safety, the environment, and company assets and their impact on the preservation and enhancement of shareholder value.	Develops corporate policies and implementation procedures for Occidental Petroleum Corporation (OPC) and its Industry Groups/Direct Reporting Divisions (IG/DRDs) necessary to protect human health and the environment and to comply with applicable laws, rules, and regulations.
Director, Environmental Affairs and Technical Support	Provides corporate-wide strategic direction for the protection of human health and the environment and to assure the development of environmental management systems that provide for compliance with corporate policy and all applicable regulations; contributes to the effective management of environmental risks and liabilities; and preserves and enhances shareholder value.	Establishes management system(s) for evaluating and ensuring implementation of OPC policies and procedures in coordination with the other functional directors of Health, Environment, Safety, and Process Risk Management (HESPRM).

Assesses IG/DRD compliance with applicable OPC policies and procedures; communicates findings to IG/DRD management, OPC management, and the Environmental, Health and Safety Committee of the Board of Directors (ECOB) as appropriate.

Supports issues identification and OPC position development and strategy for involvement in legislative and regulatory issues relating to the environment; assists in the areas of human health and safety; and provides technical, legislative, and regulatory advocacy and support to IG/DRD on environmental matters as requested by the Director, External Affairs and Compliance Support.

Assures integration of environmental programs with business strategies within OPC and the IG/DRD. |

POSITION TITLE	POSITION SUMMARY	OVERLAPPING ELEMENTS
Director, Safety, Environmental Health and Assessment Programs	Provides corporate wide strategic direction for the protection of health and safety, regulating compliance in the health and safety field and preserving and enhancing shareholder value. Serves as the corporation's focal point for health, environment, safety, and process risk management (HESPRM) assessment programs.	Develops corporate policies and implementing procedures related to the protection of health and safety (H&S) and HESPRM assessment programs for OPC, its industry groups and IG/DRDs. Oversees implementation of OPC policies and procedures related to H&S and HESPRM assessment programs. Assesses IG/DRD compliance with applicable OPC policies and procedures and regulatory requirements; communicates findings to OPC, IG/DRD management and ECOB as appropriate. Provides technical and regulatory direction for HESPRM assessment efforts, H&S programs, and organizational development corporate wide.
Director, Process Risk Management	Provides corporate-wide strategic direction for process risk management.	Assesses integration of H&S programs and business strategies within OPC and IG/DRD. Develops OPC policies that provide: 1) protection from catastrophic losses arising from episodic events, 2) plant reliability and process integrity, and 3) the data necessary to integrate appropriate risk factors into business decisions. Assess IG/DRD compliance with OPC's Policies and Procedures, and regulatory requirements and provides results to OPC and IG/DRD management and to the ECOB as appropriate. Integrates OPC's process risk management programs with the health, environment, and safety programs and assists with the administration of those programs. Assures integration of process risk management programs with OPC & IG business strategy.
Director, External Affairs and Compliance Support	Provides strategic direction for the OPC HESPRM legislative and regulatory programs.Provides an external perspective on OPC and industry group HESPRM programs and policies.	Identifies possible impact of HESPRM legislation and regulations on OPC and IG/DRD business strategies in coordination with directors of functional HESPRM areas.

Total Quality Management

Total Quality Management (TQM) is an increasingly popular management concept that needs to be integrated with all other aspects in order to improve decisionmaking.[20] Many companies, whether they use the term TQM or not, are beginning to apply these concepts to environmental management in the same way that they are applying them to production quality control and other more traditional aspects of general management. I view much of this as common sense: attempting to constantly improve your performance and trying to measure it. This book makes a variety of suggestions to achieve these goals, but I have not phrased it in TQM terms. If a term is necessary to identify good business practices in order to improve quality and responsiveness to customers, the public, and regulatory agencies, then TQM is a good vehicle.

In applying the TQM concept, it is assumed that "when businesses apply total quality to environmental management they reap three basic benefits:

- an alignment with business strategy,
- continuous improvement with measurable results, and
- a customer and supplier alignment."[21]

As discussed throughout this book, it is important for environmental management to be accepted as an integral part of all levels of management. TQM assumes that by integrating environmental aspects of business as part of total quality throughout business, environmental management can become part of a company's strategy on how to conduct its business. The very same tools and strategy that apply to production, sales, and distribution can be applied to specific environmental programs. Environmental management then speaks the same language as the rest of the business and crosses a real historical hurdle of being viewed as an outsider to basic business strategy.[22]

Continuous improvement, another dogma of TQM, is a concept with which we all can agree. "Success in TQM is measured by continuing quality improvement. Achieving continuing quality improvement depends on good organization, management and environmental policy, and good acceptance of that policy throughout the corporation."[23] But placing numerical assumptions on matters other than those that easily lend themselves to statistics such as waste reduction, excursions, and citations may be difficult[24] and could be counterproductive. For example, failure to recognize that "soft dollar" savings in terms of regulatory changes, etc., can be just as important as "hard dollars" could be detrimental.

Much of TQM is focused on the customer (defined broadly, looking at "the corporation as the supplier of environmental behavior and the community and the general public as the customers" —perhaps "corporate constituencies" better captures the idea [25]). "Meeting customers' needs is the driving force behind the entire quality revolution in the United States." [26]

In summary, a commitment to quality, however phrased, is critical to good management, including environmental management. As discussed throughout this book, "the major barriers to quality superiority are not technical, they are behavioral. The root cause why we have not moved further faster is the intractability of many organizations in the face of change." [27]

It is increasingly recognized that continuous, measurable improvement in environmental performance is a core element of corporate management and governance. There is, however, a potential problem with excessive reliance on quantifiable measures of environmental performance. In such a system, what is not quantified—or quantifiable—is often treated as something that does not exist. Some risks may not be quantified because of the inherent weaknesses in methods of quantifying related to unanticipated releases. The value and benefit of such quantification should be compared on a case-by-case basis to the liability that might be created by such quantification. Such liability may be far out of proportion to the actual expectation of the likelihood and magnitude of potential incidents. Note that this may sound like the kind of risk that insurers are only now becoming aware of and do not yet fully insure. Moreover, it is a far different matter to quantify risk for a particular risk at a particular facility than to quantify a category of risks for a category of facilities. It is also difficult to quantify performance in preparing for future requirements or future liabilities. Beyond measurable parameters, a corporate program needs to have appropriate incentives and disincentives, so that the program can encourage good long-term planning and preparation. Effective planning and preparation will, in turn, reduce long-term costs, refine product design and product development, and revitalize marketing activities. Such a system of incentives and disincentives will work to maintain the corporation's influence over rules and laws that might have a dramatic impact on its economic health.

An excellent piece entitled What's Wrong With Total Quality Management [28] lists the following "quality mistakes" in implementing TQM:

- 1 "Focus on Changing Culture vs. Changing Behavior." "Too often we hear executives, managers and employees talking the vocabulary of Total Quality without even knowing what the words mean in terms of behavior."

- 2 "Failing to Fully and Accurately Define Performance Requirements."

- 3. "Failing to Perform a Gap Analysis and Develop a Strategic Quality Plan Prior to Implementing TQM."

- 4. "Failure to Establish a Functioning Executive Quality Council."

- 5. "Failure to Establish Key Quality Measures and Goals for Every Level of the Organization, Linked to Organization-Wide Requirements for Market Leadership."

- 6. "Failure to Change Compensation Systems to Hold Senior Executives and Middle Managers Responsible for Quality Leadership and Achieving Quality Results."

- 7. "Failing to Restructure to Place Managers, Supervisors and Employees Physically and Emotionally Close to the Customers They Serve."

- 8. "Relying Upon Training and/or Quality Improvement Techniques as THE Way to Implement TQM."

- 9. "Failing to Do 'Just-In-Time Training' and to Provide Follow-Up Coaching to Ensure That Skills Taught in the Training are Immediately Applied On the Job."

- 10. "Seeking Short Term Breakthroughs vs. Long-Term Continuous Improvement."

The authors also note that in the 1990s "quality is becoming a base expectation for American consumers" and that "quality is becoming the price of admission to the marketplace. [29]" The promise and reality of TQM in the 1990s is "continuous improvements; not sudden breakthroughs; and retention of profits and market share rather than significant gains." [30] If your company has major problems and "you need to get $20 million out of your operating costs in six months, TQM isn't the answer. Instead you are probably going to have to close plants, lay off workers, shut down product lines, and do all of the other traditional things you might do to get those $20 million worth of savings. Once you have made and executed those tough decisions, then turn to TQM for the future." [31]

Recruiting Environmental Professionals

You may be the best general manager and be prepared to adopt the best system of management controls, but without adequate staff you simply will not be able to accomplish your mission. There are several excellent sources for competent personnel. Before you can take advantage of them, however, you may have to argue with your employee relations department, which may not fully understand how important it is to hire staff who can operate independently in the environmental area. Too many companies still employ technicians rather than managers, and employee relations departments can usually point to "comparable" staff in other companies. They may not recognize that "comparability" is not what you need, particularly if the allegedly comparable organization has a very large staff and each individual has limited responsibility. My response to the "comparability" argument is that I would rather have one swan than two turkeys working for me, and as a manager, I would rather manage programs than a large staff. If you can hire first-rate people who can function independently, you will be able to perform your tasks in the most cost-effective manner. Writing your job description to indicate that the recruit must be able to function independently and deal with a wide variety of people both inside and outside the company will help touch the magic bases with the employee relations department.

Assuming that, using your management and sales skills, you have had job descriptions and compensation schedules approved that will allow you to recruit first-rate people, you next face the assumption that you should, if possible, recruit from within the organization. If you are fortunate enough to have capable people within your company whom you can place in your environmental organization, this clearly may be the best source of talent. It always takes substantial time for a new person to understand the corporate culture and learn whom to call and whom not to call to initiate action. If you are able to find a person who combines knowledge of the organization with sensitivity to environmental issues and the social policy behind legislation and regulations, together with the sales ability that any successful staff person must have, you will be fortunate. In one of Oxy's divisions, for example, several senior environmental managers had both technical skills and broad sales experience in the company before assuming their present positions.

"People skills" may be even more important than technical understanding in environmental management. A person need not be a professional environmental manager to function in an environmental position, although the best manager usually combines broad understanding of the corporation with professional environmental skills. An operating manager who can speak the language of other operating managers can also be helpful in implementing and "selling" a program. However, the former operating manager needs to step back and think conceptually in order to engage in more than a fire-fighting operation. This is particularly important in longer range planning and budgeting, where immediate payout for expenditures may not be readily apparent.

Unfortunately, too many corporations use "hiring from within" as an excuse to find slots for managers who have outlived their usefulness in some other department. These corporations are not giving the environment, health, and safety functions proper priority, and usually have these functions reporting far too low in the organization to get attention. The way around this concept of placing "rejects" is to have particular individuals in mind and readily available to fill positions.

If you are recruiting from outside, and if you have spent your entire career in a corporation, your first inclination will be to look for managers within other corporations. Trade associations are another good source of employees. Trade association work can help build contacts and establish networks. It also allows you to identify competent people in other companies or on the trade association staff whom you may be able to recruit for your operations.

Government agencies are another excellent source of potential employees. Many people with strong technical and legal skills begin their careers in government agencies because they recognize that the level of responsibility and challenge given to junior personnel in government usually far exceeds what is available in industrial settings. Moreover, many people committed to an environmental ethic assume that government is the only place to work. A person who has had broad responsibility in a government agency and has a strong environmental commitment can be an ideal candidate for an environmental position in industry. Obviously, the bureaucrat who is uncomfortable with decisionmaking and who shows no signs of creativity is not an ideal candidate. However, we have all seen the bright engineer or lawyer who finds holes in our arguments or who, when we are right, is willing to take a position supporting us. The tough but bright and rational regulator can make the transition to industry and make a major contribution.

I recall about 14 years ago hiring a young lawyer out of the U.S. Department of Justice, which, like EPA, is an excellent source of talent. He had recently won a major victory against an industry by developing a strong technical knowledge of that industry and then creating legal arguments to bolster his position. The decision against the industry came down shortly before he gave notice and came to work for me. About a week later, I had him sit in for me on a trade association meeting that included representatives of that industry. Their initial reaction at seeing this individual was sheer horror, until they realized that he had beaten them fair and square and without ideological malice. They also recognized that the same scientific and legal talent that had won a victory for the government would be useful in the industry setting.

The first challenge in recruiting a government employee is to show him or her that a person can be strongly committed to an environmental ethic in an industrial setting. [32] Indeed, a good environmental manager develops a compliance program that is far stronger than any that could be developed by a regulatory agency, simply because he or she knows what can be done and knows how to motivate the personnel responsible for completing the job. A good environmental manager is also aware of agency sensitivities and develops programs that will minimize regulatory exposure.

If you plan to hire government employees or any other environmental professionals, it is important to recognize that you must be serious about your program. Environmental professionals are committed to resolving problems once they are discovered. If your company does not recognize the legal and moral implications of dealing with issues and dealing with them credibly, you will have a hard time attracting environmental professionals, whether from other companies or from the government.

Finally, an individual working for a national citizens group, such as the Natural Resources Defense Council, the Environmental Defense Fund, or the Sierra Club, should not be ruled out. Individuals in these organizations have obtained broad experience that is transferable to industry. Many of the points made above regarding government employees also apply to public interest group employees.

Notes to Chapter 3

1. Peter Drucker is a renowned economist, management consultant, and expert in the field of corporate management. *See generally* P. Drucker, MANAGING FOR RESULTS: ECONOMIC TASKS AND RISK-TAKING DECISIONS (1964); P. Drucker, THE PRACTICE OF MANAGEMENT (1954); P. Drucker, TECHNOLOGY, MANAGEMENT & SOCIETY (1970).

2. In May 1981, a resolution adopted by the Board of Directors authorized implementation of a variety of recommendations concerning environmental issues. The recommendations included reaffirmation of the corporate policy to make required disclosures of environmental matters in a full and timely manner, and establishment of an Environmental Committee of the Board of Directors, which later became the Environmental, Health, and Safety Committee, to oversee corporate programs and reports. The recommendations arose from the settlement of a July 1980 Securities and Exchange Commission order, which, in turn, arose from Occidental's efforts to acquire the Mead Corporation in 1978. Occidental agreed to designate a director, an environmental official, and an independent consulting firm to prepare a report that would "recommend procedures to the full Board of Directors to ensure that Occidental will be in a position to disclose, in accordance with the federal securities laws on a complete, timely and accurate basis, all required information relating to environmental matters." *See* In the Matter of Occidental Petroleum Corporation, Exchange Act Release No. 16950 (July 2, 1980).

Other recommendations included preparation of a book on laws, obligations, and liabilities; revision of corporate policies and procedures, including separation of environmental policies from other policies; dual-path reporting, e.g., to the Health, Environment and Safety Department and the Legal Department; development of a computerized database; preparation of an annual report; annual review of procedures; preparation by the divisions of policies and procedures; submission of reports on capital and operating costs; preparation of a collection of federal and state laws and regulations applicable to each facility; and establishment of training programs.

3. There are other ways to describe the basics for strong environmental management programs. Arthur D. Little, a large consulting firm that does many environmental audits, uses the following elements to describe a state-of-the-art environmental management program:

1. Clearly defined, broadly communicated policies and procedures.
2. An environmental, health, and safety program congruent with organizational structure.
3. Day-to-day management systems.
4. Formalized long-range planning program.
5. A formal risk management system.
6. Regulatory surveillance.
7. Management information systems.
8. Project and program reviews.

9. Issue-specific programs.
10. Oversight and control.

In addition, they view environmental management in three stages—problem solving, managing for compliance and, the highest level, managing for assurance. ARTHUR D. LITTLE, INC., STATE OF THE ART ENVIRONMENTAL, HEALTH AND SAFETY PROGRAMS: HOW DO YOU COMPARE? (1990). A checklist for rating environmental management programs was recently suggested. Manchen, *Rating Your Environmental Department*, POLLUTION ENG'G, Apr. 1990, at 81.

Union Carbide also has developed its own formulation in rating environmental management programs, focusing on five different levels. Level 1 is no programs at all. Level 2 is reaction (damage control). Level 3 is compliance (laws and regulations). Level 4 is prevention (compliance plus) which "is where most of the environmentally leading edge companies are today. Such companies have extensive environmental training and audit programs and are often looking to reduce the level of waste they generate through comprehensive waste minimization programs. They anticipate problems with company standards that are often more stringent than those imposed by the government." *Union Carbide: Moving Beyond Compliance*, ENVTL. MANAGER, June 1990, at 6. Level 5 is leadership, which includes showing management how good environmental, health, and safety programs can add to a corporation's bottom line such as "through the development of new technology, customer-focused marketing and services and advertising." *Id.*

4. OCCUPATIONAL SAFETY & HEALTH ADMINISTRATION, U.S. DEP'T OF LABOR, THE PHILLIPS 66 COMPANY HOUSTON CHEMICAL COMPLEX EXPLOSION AND FIRE 18 (Apr. 1990) [hereinafter OSHA REPORT].

5. Pub. L. No. 99-499, 42 U.S.C. §§11001-11050, ELR STAT. EPCRA §§301-30 (Oct. 17, 1986).

6. OSHA REPORT, *supra* note 4, at 18.

7. *Id.* at 19. EPA conducted 33 audits in 1989 and expected to complete 40 in fiscal year 1990.

8. *Id.* at 23.

9. *Id.* at 34.

10. 29 C.F.R. pt. 1910; 55 Fed. Reg. 29150 (July 17, 1990).

11. 57 Fed. Reg. 6356 (Feb. 24, 1992).

12. *See* SENS. CHAFEE & BAUCUS, STATEMENT OF SENATE MANAGERS, S. 1630, THE CLEAN AIR ACT AMENDMENTS OF 1990, 136 CONG. REC. 16933 (daily ed. Oct. 27, 1990).

13. 55 Fed. Reg. 29150 (July 17, 1990).

14. *See* 20 O.S.H. Rep. (BNA) 899 (Oct. 24, 1990).

15. *Id.*

16. For a detailed discussion of these regulations and their interrelation to the Clean Air Act Amendments of 1990, see Friedman, *The Overlap Between the Clean Air*

Act and Proposed OSHA Process Hazard Management Regulations, HAZARDOUS WASTE & TOXIC TORTS L. & STRATEGY, Jan. 1991, at 1.

17. 29 C.F.R. pt. 1910, 57 Fed. Reg. at 6356, *supra* notes 10 and 11.

18. U.S. Dep't of Labor, Press Release No. 90-207, at 3 (Apr. 26, 1990).

19. U.S. Dep't of Labor, Press Release No. 90-622 (Nov. 28, 1990).

20. The Global Environmental Management Initiative, which is discussed in Chapter 4 of this volume, organized an extensive conference on TQM as it applies to environmental management. The numerous papers delivered at this conference were published in a volume entitled PROCEEDINGS—CORPORATE QUALITY/ENVIRONMENTAL MANAGEMENT: THE FIRST CONFERENCE (Washington, D.C., January 9-10, 1991) [hereinafter PROCEEDINGS]. It is far beyond the scope of this volume to deal with TQM in detail, but papers are found in the Proceedings on such subjects as organizing a TQM program; its use in engineering services and use in federal agencies; environmental problem solving; competitive benchmarking; and tracking information. It also includes tools such as statistics and variation; fishbone diagrams (a cause and effect diagram "because it looks like the skeleton of a fish, with the head being the effect or problem to be resolved and the causes and sub-causes forming the bones of the skeleton," Leskovian, *Use of Causes and Effect Diagrams and Pareto Charts for Environmental Quality Management,* PROCEEDINGS, *supra,* at 77), and pareto charts ("a major factor(s) make up the subject being analyzed. It is the search for significance, for the vital few versus the trivial many." Leskovian, PROCEEDINGS, *supra,* at 79).

21. Carpenter, *GEMI and the Total Quality Journey to Environmental Excellence,* PROCEEDINGS, *supra* note 20, at 3.

22. *Id.*

23. Bowers, *What Is Total Quality Management?,* PROCEEDINGS, *supra* note 20, at 135.

24. Union Carbide claims that it has an effective system for measuring compliance and the effectiveness of corporate systems. *See* Coulter, *Union Carbide's Audit Classification Program,* PROCEEDINGS, *supra* note 20, at 177.

25. Carpenter, *supra* note 21, at 3.

26. Sands, *Developing Customer and Supplier Relationships at Dow,* PROCEEDINGS, *supra* note 20, at 59.

27. Heilpern & Limpert, *Building Organizations for Continuing Improvement,* PROCEEDINGS, *supra* note 20, at 11.

28. Boyett & Conn, *What's Wrong with Total Quality Management,* TAPPING THE NETWORK J., Spring 1992.

29. *Id.*

30. *Id.*

31. *Id.*

32. For a general discussion, see Friedman, *60s Activism and 80s Realities—We've Come A Long Way*, ENVTL. F., July 1983, at 8.

Chapter 4:
Implementing Strong Environmental Management Programs

C hapter 3 outlined the basic tools and programs necessary for effective environmental management. This chapter discusses these programs and their implementation in detail. Although much of the chapter focuses on decentralized organizations, the programs reviewed are equally applicable to centralized organizations, as discussed at the conclusion of this chapter.

Although each of the elements discussed below is important, the key to implementation is recognition by line managers that strong environmental programs are their responsibility. In any organization, the environmental staff can advise, cajole, and develop basic programs, but unless line management carries out those programs, they cannot be successful. Today's environmental manager must develop good relationships with the line people and must understand the significance of line operations. The environmental manager is in essence a salesman, selling the advantage of his product in a nonthreatening manner to line and staff managers and, in turn, making the field more comfortable by supplying information. The successful manager, particularly in the early stages when he or she is developing credibility, must spend a substantial amount of time on the road with his or her counterparts in the divisions and in the field. For example, if you haven't been in an underground coal mine, you have no credibility with coal miners.

Management Commitment

One critical step in the development of Occidental's corporate support for environmental programs was the Board of Directors' establishment of an Environmental Committee (now the Environmental, Health, and Safety Committee). The existence of such a committee, or a system of reporting to a member of the Board, gives tremendous clout to environment, health, and safety programs, and I highly recommend it as a major element of an effective environmental management program. This concept has also been helpful in building the programs at Allied-Signal and the new programs at Union Carbide. If nothing else, it is a symbol of management commitment. The fact that members of the Board of Directors will be aware of significant issues is also a major incentive for fixing what is wrong and avoiding impending problems. Many times, my simply indicating that I would like to advise the Environmental Committee that something was being done to eliminate an issue ensured that, in fact, action was taken. The Committee has also required periodic review of and annual reports on environmental matters, including costs, the status of implementation of recommendations, identification of "unascertainable" matters,[1] and long-range plans to en-sure that the Board is fully informed of significant environmental matters.

Another aid to good environmental management is preparation by the corporate staff of a monthly report for corporate management and the divisions. At Occidental, that report consists of a summary letter on issues of interest; a fact sheet giving statistical information on "excursions,"[2] citations, penalties paid, and assessments conducted; and detailed informa-tion on legislative/regulatory affairs. An example of such a report is in-cluded as Appendix B. Thus, independent analyses of environmental issues are broadly and frequently circulated throughout the corporation. Those analyses help avoid surprises.

Interrelationship With Divisions—Policies, Procedures, and Programs

Definition and Allocation of Corporate and Divisional Responsibilities

In either a centralized or a decentralized organization, corporate environ-mental protection staff must provide leadership in carrying a strong envi-ronmental policy throughout the corporation. A corporate staff should be organized to step back and look toward longer range planning and imple-mentation. Divisional staff, by their nature, must be more attuned to day-to-day problems as well as the specific mission of their division. With strong divisional staffs, broad procedures, and a strong database, the pri-mary roles of a corporate group in a decentralized organization should be audit/assessment, longer range problem-solving, and ensuring that the divisions have the necessary personnel and tools to do their jobs.

At Oxy, each divisional environmental department must define areas of responsibility for environmental matters, identify environmental programs and issues, and recommend corrective actions and strategies. The education, training, and experience of divisional staff must be commensurate with the types of environmental issues the organization faces. Ongoing programs must maintain or upgrade the technical expertise of professional and non-professional staffs. Those staffs must maintain active communication with other corporate environmental concerns, either directly or through the corporate Health, Environment and Safety Department.

The Occidental corporate group, through policies, procedures, and guidelines, has developed specific requirements for divisional environmental organizations throughout the corporation. Policies, procedures, and guidelines each perform different functions and it is important to keep the three concepts separate. Policies should be broad-based, outlining the key aspects of an environmental program and establishing the company's commitment to that program. Means of implementing policies should be described separately in procedures and guidelines. Procedures should be mandatory methods of implementing policies. Guidelines should be written when implementation of a policy does not lend itself to specific procedures or when a procedure itself needs additional explanation. Generally, I prefer procedures to guidelines because procedures are tighter. As a company's program matures, it may be practical, and preferable, to substitute procedures for guidelines. For example, Occidental has replaced almost all of its guidelines with procedures. For example, while Occidental has a procedure for review of acquisitions and sales of property, the specific areas to consider vary with the scope of the transaction. Thus, an extensive guideline indicating the areas to consider is more appropriate than a procedure requiring review of all the areas of concern.

Corporate procedures at Oxy define relationships among the corporate Health, Environment and Safety Department and its counterparts in the divisions. They provide for communication of corporate policies and procedures, review and comment on proposed divisional environmental organizations before they are established, and concurrence of the corporate Vice President for Health, Environment and Safety or his designee before appointment of a divisional chief environmental, safety, or health administrator. Procedures also address organization of divisions, response to proposed and newly enacted environmental laws and regulations, monthly environmental reporting, implementation of environmental assessment programs, reporting of environmental matters on a timely basis, and employee awareness and training. Guidelines include requests for substantial expenditures and reporting of "substantial risk" under §8(e) of the Toxic Substances Control Act (TSCA). [3]

Occidental has found that this series of procedures and guidelines adequately covers its needs. None of these procedures is extensive. Other companies' procedures and guidelines generally cover the same subjects, but may differ in scope. In some companies, procedures and guidelines may approach the form of a code with detailed instructions on each aspect of these areas. Detailed instructions and programs for providing awareness and training are common. Other companies may be reluctant to address certain subjects, such as reporting by divisions and maintaining functional equivalents of U.S. levels of protection for foreign operations.

Environmental Policies and Corporate Responsibility

In setting the stage for implementation of environmental programs, it is imperative to establish the company philosophy by promulgating an environmental policy. Most major corporations today have environmental policies. These policies can be vague and meaningless, or they can be the cornerstones of strong environmental programs. If a policy includes, as it should, a commitment to make the expenditures necessary to implement it, it sends an appropriate message throughout the company. If it states, as does one policy of another company, that "where physically and economically feasible" the company will "eliminate or minimize the undesirable consequences of its activity," and that the company "will surpass applicable standards in instances when it is in the Company's interests to do so," it can send a negative signal that the company's commitment is limited.

Ten years ago, environmental policies often were issued by relatively low-level corporate officials. Given the increased corporate and public awareness of the importance of these issues, today they are more appropriately issued by chief executive officers. This sends company personnel the strongest message that there is a commitment from the top.

Management's commitment must be carried throughout the corporation. The best way to emphasize this commitment is to state in the policy that line managers are charged with individual responsibility for the environmental performance of their activities. It may also be helpful for the policy to state, as Occidental's does, that "every employee is expected to carry out the spirit as well as the letter of this policy." In a cover letter accompanying Occidental's policy, Dr. Armand Hammer, former Chairman of the Board and Chief Executive Officer, also stated that he expected "full and complete adherence" to the policy. Dr. Ray R. Irani, the present Chairman of the Board and Chief Executive Officer, in his cover letter to Occidental's new environmental policy, dated June 1, 1991, added, "We recognize the importance, at all stages of our businesses from strategic planning to the ultimate disposal of products, to consider the impact on the communities in which we operate and to use natural resources wisely to achieve a sustainable level of global development."

An environmental policy should include a commitment to conducting all operations, including sale and distribution of products and services, in compliance with applicable environmental laws, regulations, and standards. This commitment must be specific and without loopholes. This is the basic concept—compliance with the law. The program should also adopt appropriate standards to protect people and the environment in cases in which laws and regulations are inadequate or do not exist. This approach should include international operations and should provide for a standard of protection of health and the environment functionally equivalent to that which the company requires at U.S. locations. (See the section "International Environmental Review" in this chapter.) It is crucial for today's corporations to be committed to using modern control methods, procedures, and processes that are technically sound and economically feasible and that minimize waste generation and releases. This commitment can also save money in the long run, because pollution control equipment that is optional now may be mandatory in the future. Retrofit installment of pollution control equipment is generally more expensive and less cost-effective; it is easier to design the equipment as part of a project than to shoehorn in changes later, or better still, not generate the pollutant at all.

An environmental policy should provide the basis for an internal compliance system. Internal compliance systems are neutral. They should remain constant regardless of changing political attitudes. The bottom line is that they make economic sense. Under a good internal compliance system, if it makes economic sense to have stricter environmental and health standards than the law requires, those standards will be in place. Conversely, legal standards will be challenged (although not as part of the compliance system) if they do not make economic sense and there are legal bases for challenge. Whatever the standards, the internal compliance effort should provide for an assessment program to ensure that each operating facility knows and is meeting its obligations and responsibilities under law.

The environmental policy should require each division to develop a self-monitoring environmental assessment program to ensure compliance. (I prefer the term "assessment" to the term "audit" since, unlike a financial audit, there are still few specific standards to audit against. See "International Environmental Review," *infra.*) However, this book uses the terms "assessment" and "audit" interchangeably for the sake of simplicity.) A broad-based assessment program guidance document helps divisions establish the program and specifies a protocol for implementing it. The assessment program ensures routine, daily compliance and provides an overview of day-to-day operations. Assessments also help in environmental strategic planning, identifying areas where compliance costs can be reduced or risk avoided, environmental training of assessment team members, and developing greater environmental awareness throughout the corporation. Chapter 5 discusses the assessment program and guidance document in detail. As assessments generate specific follow-up recommendations, a tracking system should allow both the division and the corporate group to ensure that each division carries out those recommendations. Occidental uses a computerized database (see the section "Computerized Management Information Systems" in this chapter) to track the recommendations.

The environmental policy should also establish programs of self-monitoring and reporting through multiple organizational channels. Any large company, because of its size and diversity, will never be absolutely positive that it is always in compliance, but that certainty is a goal worth pursuing. Thus, policy commitments to training employees to identify issues of environmental concern, emphasizing individual responsibilities, and teaching actions to be taken to protect the environment are critical. These commitments help emphasize line management responsibilities. Line responsibility for employee training is equally important in the safety area. Perhaps one reason that environment, health, and safety often are combined in a single corporate department is that very similar corporate management techniques are used to deal with these issues.

The policy should also encourage process innovations and fundamental research, including development of means to reduce waste generation and discharges of contaminants into the environment. Here, too, sound environmental policy and economics can coincide. There is economic justification to reduce waste generation as disposal and compliance costs increase. Perhaps the situation is analogous to energy conservation. Several years ago, when oil cost $3.50 a barrel, the incentive to reduce energy costs was not terribly significant. But at $18 to $20 a barrel, the economic incentive greatly increased.

Finally, the policy should include a commitment to providing adequate funds to carry out a strong environmental program. Providing stable funding is not always easy, particularly in troubled economic times, and if this commitment is not included in the policy, it can be ignored. Funding limitations put a strain on managers, both line and staff, and programs of excellence may be difficult to achieve. However, at a minimum, compliance with laws and regulations must be maintained. Responsible corporations pursue this goal even during recessions. Commitment to a strong corporate environmental program will build credibility with the government, making it willing to listen to suggestions. A company is then in a good position to assist in development of equitable and effective environmental rules and regulations.

Corporate environmental policies and corporate responsibility need to be placed in context. Modern and progressive environmental programs are designed to protect the environment and achieve regulatory compliance while minimizing corporate exposure to long-term and short-term capital requirements and operating expenses. While there is a tendency to focus on the regulatory issues because of the pervasive nature of regulatory regimes, it is also important to recognize that corporations desire to be responsible. Thus, Occidental's corporate environmental policy states in part:

> Life and health are precious and must be safeguarded. If we are to sustain worldwide development, we must accept the world's natural resources are finite and are to be conserved and protected. Environmental protection is good for the community and is good business. Therefore, the protection of human health and the environment is one of Occidental's highest priorities.

In the context of a company's entire risk management program, strong environmental management programs provide for effective loss prevention and loss control, although quantifying the effectiveness of a program in terms of loss control can be difficult. They also provide for "compliance." However, compliance on one day may not be compliance on another day. In essence, an organization must be *capable* of compliance. The Vice President, Operations Compliance at Occidental's OxyChem Division, David Willette, defines the *conditions* for compliance as follows:

- The organization and facilities must be capable of compliance.
- Compliance must be a natural end point of the way work is performed.
- Resources must be focused by priority.
- Measurement systems must be focused on precursor events.
- The Capital budget must be adequate to meet needs.

Meeting compliance, therefore, calls for a strategy which uses a total incident concept to:

- Capture and track *any* unwanted event or condition.
- Focus on root cause issues.
- Focus resources using findings.

Although a company may also intend its risk management program to demonstrate "social responsibility," this goal may be elusive. The basis for generic assumptions as to social responsibility should be considered carefully. For example, the break-up of the tanker, the Exxon *Valdez*, is perceived by many members of the public as being traced to Exxon's environmental program. The primary issue in that instance was not related to the environmental program but to the competence of the tanker captain and other members of the crew. The strengths or weaknesses of the environmental program are irrelevant to the breakup of the tanker. Union Carbide has been castigated by the public for the tragic death of thousands of people in Bhopal, India, as a result of an accident in a chemical plant involving an acutely toxic chemical. However, Carbide claims strong evidence of sabotage by a disgruntled worker who took the valve off a tank and added water to contaminate product in the tank not knowing that the chemical reaction would result in a toxic cloud.

Some environmental organizations, in their efforts to measure program effectiveness, have focused on the number of sites subject to remediation under federal and state cleanup statutes such as the Comprehensive Environmental Response, Compensation, and Liability Act (CERCLA or Superfund). [4] But the number of sites undergoing remedial actions is not a reliable indication of today's management programs or social responsibility. Most of the sites subject to remediation resulted from practices that occurred at least 20 years ago. Also, today's remedial sites are not accurate gauges of the social responsibility of past practices, since companies are often held responsible for practices that were legal, "state of the art," and not viewed as damaging to the environment at the time under statutes that provide retroactively for joint and several liability without fault for those past actions.

Environmental organizations also attempt to evaluate program effectiveness by quantifying the amount of so-called toxic materials that are released. This data is readily available for a variety of materials released by certain manufacturing operations that must be reported under the Emergency Planning and Community Right-To-Know Act (EPCRA). [5] However, these gross numbers do not tell you anything about these releases in relation to the effectiveness of process controls or in relation to the levels of production. DuPont, for example, is castigated by these organizations because of the levels of releases but, as the largest U.S. chemical company, it also, for obvious reasons, shows the largest amount of total releases.

Some companies have been able to show significant reductions in releases in recent years. Others have not. However, in some instances, the large recent reductions were easy changes that should have been accomplished years ago. A company may not show significant recent reductions because it has had a program in place for many years and had made the easy reductions early on.

Some companies have also begun to publish "green reports," annual reports on the environment, which are designed to show the public that the company is environmentally progressive. However, after browsing through the pretty pictures in the report (which is, of course, printed on recycled paper), the reader quickly notices the report's limitations. Much of the information in that report is already publicly available (such as the data on toxics required under the EPCRA [6]) or would have to be disclosed under the U.S. Securities and Exchange Commission (SEC) rules if it is "material."[7] The SEC's interpretative release of May 1989 concerning the disclosure required in Management's Discussion and Analysis of Financial Condition and Results of Operations (MD&A) in SEC filings states that once management knows of a potentially material environmental problem, "it must disclose it unless it can determine that the problem is not reasonably likely to cause a material effect, either because the event is not likely to happen or if it does happen, the effect is not likely to be material."[8] It must also disclose "the material effects that compliance with environmental laws may have on the capital expenditures, earnings and competitive position of the registrant and its subsidiaries."[9]

These green reports also list a variety of environmental accomplishments which, again, usually do not give any real basis for comparison. Many of the public-spirited gestures are, on closer inspection, not completely altruistic. For example, a company that needs authorization for a specific project will often make such gestures to obtain goodwill from the local public or permitting authority. Television and radio commercials attempting to show the caring nature of the company should also be examined objectively.

I do not mean to imply that green reports should not be published. Publishing a green report can be very valuable to a consumer-based company, simply because such a report will help sell the company's products. It may also be valuable for a company in an area such as waste management, which requires extensive and controversial permitting, to publish such detailed reports. However, the value for commodity companies with little public dealings is very limited, particularly since publishing extensive reports is very expensive, and the money could be better spent on specific efforts to improve environmental operations. Clearly, such a company should list some of its significant accomplishments and other significant environmental issues and costs in its annual report or in a separate report, but the weight of the evidence of a company's environmental responsibility and its loss prevention and loss control programs should not be weighed by the size of its green report.

Can only a company that manufactures ice cream be considered environmentally responsible, with good loss prevention and loss control programs? I find it ironic that a chemical company, such as OxyChem, that recycles the plastic containers used by the ice cream company might not be deemed "environmentally responsible" as easily as the ice cream company would.

The best means of measuring the effectiveness and social responsibility of programs in the environmental area (and the related areas of safety, process safety, and risk engineering) is to examine the scope of a company's entire management program. This is, of course, the purpose of this book, to provide a guide to good environmental management practices.

Recently, a coalition of environmental, church, and environmentally concerned investment organizations published a set of principles designed "to encourage companies 'to make a public accounting of the planet's ecological problems—and to pledge to do better.'" [10] These principles, developed by the Social Investment Forum and its Coalition for Environmentally Responsible Economies Project (CERES), were originally known as the Valdez Principles, after the massive oil spill resulting from a tanker accident in Valdez, Alaska. The principles deal with the following issues:

- Protection of the biosphere;
- Sustainable use of natural resources;
- Reduction and disposal of waste;
- Wise use of energy;
- Risk reduction;
- Marketing of safe products and services;
- Damage compensation;
- Disclosure;
- Environmental directors and managers; and
- Assessment and annual audit. [11]

One advocate for the principles has described them as follows:

> In a nutshell, the principles provide a non-governmental third-party system for evaluating annual corporate progress in ten areas of environmental performance, from waste reduction and wise use of energy, to board level representation and environmental audits. The idea, in part, is to cite exemplary corporate performance in each of these categories, hoping to "raise all boats" to these improved levels of operation. [12]

The original principles were not signed by any major corporation. The corporate sector criticized them, particularly because they did not reflect today's sophisticated environmental management programs and they failed to articulate terms that would distinguish truly progressive companies from those that are still recalcitrant in protecting human health. [13] Indeed, there was no corporate input when the original principles were drafted, although the drafters made an effort to involve corporations in developing guidelines to the principles. An additional problem with the principles is that

> [it] is unlikely that any grading system will change the public opinion of who the corporate 'black hats' are. For example, companies providing services—such as retailing, insurance, and air travel—fare better in public opinion polls on environmental

image than utilities, natural resource extractors, and manufacturing concerns. Realistic implementation can only be a long term proposition, not an overnight matter. [14]

While I have been critical of the original Valdez Principles, and of some other means of measuring social responsibility, what CERES has attempted is very difficult. "CERES's issuance of the Valdez Principles has prodded new thinking and reassessments of behavior. This is all to the good. No one doubts that we can do better—and many of us are committed to doing so." [15] Indeed, Occidental specifically adopted two concepts from the Valdez Principles, revising its environmental policy to indicate a commitment to sustainable development, and is completing a simple annual report for stockholders on the environmental issues concerning the company.

In an effort to address industry concerns, the principles were significantly revised in April 1992. [16] They have been renamed the CERES Principles. Perhaps the most significant change is the elimination of the immediate requirement of using outside environmental auditors. The CERES Principles instead require that companies annually complete an open-ended environmental questionnaire, which is perhaps more comprehensive than necessary in requiring data that industry people may consider questionable. The title of Principle Number 9 has been changed from "Environmental Directors and Managers" to "Management Commitment." Instead of requiring that companies "have one board member qualified to represent environmental interests," [17] Principle 9 now requires that companies consider demonstrated environmental commitment as a factor in selecting board members. [18] The language dealing with compensation for environmental damages has been revised to require more attainable commitment from companies. A broad disclaimer has been added stating that these "principles are not intended to create new legal liabilities, expand existing rights or obligations, waive legal defenses, or otherwise affect the legal position of any signatory company in any legal proceedings for any purpose." [19]

The questionnaire has been initially distributed, and it is too early to tell if the changes in the principles and the accompanying questionnaire will result in many major companies signing them. The Sun Company endorsed the principals in 1993 "as a generic code of conduct applicable to business behavior throughout the world," although Sun will continue to operate its business under its own set of principles (which CERES has recognized is consistent with its goals). The revised Principle Number 6, dealing with manufacturing, still appears to be of major concern to chemical manufacturers and manufacturers of other products that may be looked on unfavorably by certain groups. [20] In any event, there clearly has been a good faith effort to address industry concerns.

One additional failure of the Valdez Principles, namely, that they were strictly a domestic effort, is being addressed by industry efforts to develop a world-wide code of conduct, discussed in the section on International Environmental Review. Other issues concerning environmental auditing are discussed in Chapter 5.

The Investor Responsibility Research Center, Inc. (IRRC) attempts to provide institutional investors with "impartial" information about the environmental performance of major U.S. corporations. However, it is difficult to compare one company to another. There are too many differences in product mixes, ages of facilities, and level of enforcement in different areas of the country to provide meaningful data. When you have a company that is involved in a variety of fields, it is further complicated and totally meaningless when the classification is incorrect. [21]

In short, while I am not attacking IRRC's concept of trying to provide "impartial information," that organization and those who look at the ratings need to look closely at the assumptions behind any rating system or "impartial information" to understand a company's level of performance.

Now that the basic corporate policy is in place, the next step is implementing its programs. The following sections discuss means of implementation.

Reporting—Management-by-Exception

As discussed in Chapter 3, perhaps the most critical concept in environmental management is that what you don't know *will* hurt you. In an effort to stay informed, however, a corporate department can overreach and require data on virtually everything, to the annoyance of division and field personnel. A better approach recognizes divisional sensitivities while ensuring that critical information is available to those who need to deal with it. The concept is that you do not need all information, only information that is significant and that concerns exceptions to the day-to-day routine. If you have that information, you can intervene when necessary. A specific reporting procedure implements this "management-by-exception" approach.

Occidental has institutionalized the management-by-exception concept by requiring reporting on its mainframe computerized system of "significant matters," "excursions," and "reportable incidents." This system implements the premise that all groups throughout the corporation must use a common database to ensure consistency of information and records. The system provides common data for the Environmental and Legal Departments. In addition, it provides follow-up and updating capabilities, with a complete history of any changes. The system results in complete and timely reporting of "significant matters" to corporate headquarters. It is extremely useful as a follow-up system for such items as action plans based on environmental assessments, and it allows easy identification of multiple excursion areas and causes. [22]

"Significant matters" are events or situations that have resulted or may result in

(a) deviations from environmental standards or requirements affecting facilities or operations;

(b) adverse publicity or adverse community relations regarding a specific company action or operation;

(c) notices of violation or advisory actions by regulatory agencies regarding environmental control matters or permit compliance;

(d) legal actions either by or against a division;

(e) identified risks to the environment;

(f) interference with continued production or marketing of any product because of environmental considerations;

(g) substantial incremental expenditures or loss of business related to events or situations caused by environmental considerations;

(h) any problem for which the existing technical solution would impose a significant financial burden threatening the financial viability of the facility or operation; or

(i) any problem for which the staff cannot identify either remedial technology or cost of correction.

Any legal action under (c) or (d) above and any item under (b), (e), or (i) is considered "significant" without regard to potential costs and liabilities. An event or situation meeting any of the other criteria above is considered "significant" if it may result in capital expenditures or potential costs exceeding $1 million. Other cut-off points may be appropriate for other corporations, depending on their size.

A "significant matter" arising from an accident or an incident must be reported *immediately* to corporate headquarters, while any other "significant matter" must be reported as soon as possible during working hours. The corporate environmental department then may make recommendations to the division and can advise corporate management of the item and the recommended action if necessary.

"Excursion" is defined as "any emission, discharge, or other release of material outside the parameters established in an agency-issued permit which limits the amount of such materials that can be discharged. This includes releases determined to be excursions based on measurements by official test procedures and reported to the agency. Excursions recorded by other means and which are not reported to the agency should be separately identified and reported." Occidental does not make any distinction as to seriousness of excursions. The goal is to develop a state of mind that recognizes that excursions can be precursors to citations and should be avoided as part of normal operations.

Some of the status information also includes "reportable incidents." These are defined as including "any emission, discharge, or other release of material which is outside parameters established by any regulation or standard, other than a specific permit, which is reported to a government agency. This does not include those items covered by spill or Superfund reports." Items covered by spill or Superfund reports are reported as "significant matters."

Developing Information Systems

The preceding section discussed management of risk through a management-by-exception concept, which is designed to allow corporate and division staff immediate (or real time) access to information on potential environmental problems. This section takes the concept of managing information a step further and discusses the computer as a management tool. The section addresses the use of personal computers (PCs) and the use of a computerized management information system (MIS). It also discusses ways to determine the necessary scope of both environmental MISs (which are designed to facilitate management-by-exception of significant matters) and environmental database systems (which are designed to maintain detailed information on permits, effluent, waste, etc.). Finally, it discusses ways to "sell" both systems within your organization.

Use of Personal and Lap-Top Computers as Management Tools

At the outset, it is important to look at the computer as a management tool. While this may appear to be an obvious point and I have hesitated to keep the following section in this book, I am still surprised at the number of managers who fail to recognize this fundamental idea. Far too many managers, including some engineers with doctorates, still are inherently afraid of computers or feel they are only useful as number crunchers or word processors. Many managers also assume that it is beneath them to use computers and that such use should be strictly for the technical support and clerical groups. This is equally true of many lawyers. These beliefs are groundless. PCs not only save time, they can improve work product.

First, one does not have to be a computer expert to use a computer effectively. I am not talking about programming or even using a wide variety of programs. Simple word processing and working with spreadsheets are just not that difficult. My own knowledge is rudimentary, but sufficient for my needs. Indeed, the test my staff used to determine if a program was "user-friendly" was to let me try it. If I could handle it, it qualified.

Basic word processing and simple spreadsheet programs alone are major timesavers. I prefer for all staff to do their own typing using PCs. This is not to save money on secretaries, but simply because it is more convenient and efficient. Drafting and redrafting are very easy with the simple, user-friendly word processing programs available today. If you dictate material, you have to wait for it to be typed, mark it up, and then get a redraft. Preparing it yourself saves time and greatly improves quality. PCs allow instant drafting and redrafting, with no time lost in retyping.

I make extensive use of lap-top computers in negotiations, where word processing can be particularly helpful. I recall one negotiation, which normally would have taken three days, that was done in a few hours thanks to the capability for instant drafting and redrafting.

I have also made extensive use of lap-tops when reviewing possible acquisitions. They are ideal for taking notes and then placing them onto a spreadsheet to determine potential costs. In addition, you can have a completed assessment on the road and review it without waiting for extensive review and correction of typed material. This is not "high-tech," but a simple means of saving time and labor. This use as a labor-saving device is sometimes lost on those who don't recognize the PC and the lap-top as tools for managers.

In one potential acquisition, a team of Oxy's people and a team from a partner were surveying potential environmental exposure. The Occidental group had lap-tops and were using them extensively. However, one of the partner's representatives called one of my people aside and asked him, "Isn't Frank a vice president at Oxy?" My puzzled staff person replied, "Yes." The partner's representative then asked, "If he is a vice president, why is he doing his own typing?"

This attitude that a manager does not "type" must be overcome. In that proposed acquisition, the fact that all of the managers "typed" allowed us to complete our review and prepare the necessary documentation in probably one-quarter to one-third the time it would otherwise have taken. Indeed, as we completed work over a weekend, I did not bring my secretary in until Sunday, because it was far more effective for me to put what I wanted on a spreadsheet than to give it to my secretary.

Use of desk-top and lap-top computers, especially while in hotel rooms or airplanes, also makes travel time much more productive. There are lap-tops available, particularly for simple word processing, that weigh three pounds and fit easily into a small briefcase. If you are working on a matter in your office, it is very simple to move that material from your PC to the lap-top (download), continue it on the road, then move the revised material back to your PC (upload) and finish it. While traveling, you can also take a small printer with you or simply plug into the nearest printer. Printing capability is available almost everywhere. I recall taking a small lap-top computer to Singapore and Bangkok. After I reviewed environmental issues at several of our facilities, senior divisional management, which happened to be there at the same time, wanted my recommendations immediately. I was able to print these recommendations out using one printer in a hotel in Singapore and another at an office in Bangkok.

Finally, increasing use of PCs by senior managers and lawyers is leading to an interesting phenomenon. Traditionally, junior managers or associates prepare drafts. Now it is easier for a senior manager or partner to prepare a rough draft and let the junior manager or associate clean it up.

Computerized Management Information Systems

After you determine what information you need to avoid environmental "surprises," you need to collect and interpret that information. A computerized MIS is extremely helpful here. Such a system should be the communication mode and database of most of the information needed to achieve environmental objectives such as those discussed in Chapter 3. In particular, it should be capable of including the reportable items previously described, or whatever items you feel should be reportable.

Occidental has developed and uses a computerized management system.[23] This system, which is managed and monitored by the corporate Health, Environment and Safety Department, efficiently tracks all significant environmental incidents, reportable excursions from compliance requirements, and legal actions taken or pending. In addition, it can identify significant items for assessment teams and can track action plans arising from environment and safety assessments. It can provide statistical data for determination of trends and/or analysis of causes. The system has also recently been expanded to include safety and process risk management.

Occidental's company-wide, on-line system resides in the company's mainframe computer. It allows development of a record on any specific event, which can be retrieved only by the responsible facility, the division, and the corporate environmental and legal departments. The system can produce printed or on-line reports. Occidental developed a number of fixed format reports, but reports can also be tailored based on locations, types of issues, and/or specific date intervals. This way, the user gets just the information he or she needs rather than being inundated with computer printout. For special cases, *ad hoc* reports can also be generated.

This system has many benefits. First, as the official company tracking record on identified environmental issues, it ensures that all levels of the corporation have access to, and operate on, the same information base. Second, the system requires managers to identify key information clearly. Third, it requires establishment of a work plan for each issue, including a timetable for completion for each folio. In summary, the whole concept of the system is to force action. As discussed in Chapter 5, the development of action plans together with a computerized follow-up system not only solves problems, it reduces legal exposure. Recent enhancements to the system also increase its utility in trend analysis. By coding events, proposed actions, and final resolution of action plans, management can now identify emerging trends in the types of problems they face and in determination of a broad basis of the most effective types of corrective action.

The system allows a small staff of seven corporate environmental, health, safety, and process risk management professionals in Los Angeles and Washington, D.C., to develop and monitor programs as well as ensure prompt and complete reporting of matters of significance to management. It has been of equal if not greater value to divisional professionals and is flexible enough to be applied in diverse industry groups such as chemical manufacturing; oil and gas exploration, production, and distribution; and coal and non-coal mining. At the facility level, the system has also substantially reduced the time spent generating paper and communicating by telephone. Indeed, the system has been readily accepted by the field largely because it is of value to the field; it is not simply a "black box" into which the field must enter data for corporate use.

Occidental's system is an environmental management system, *not* a database management system. It is not designed to maintain detailed information on permits, emissions, waste, and effluents. Particularly at the divisional or facility level, you may want such detailed information along with an environmental management system. A variety of commercially available systems are capable of performing these database management tasks. [24]

Developing and Selling Computerized Systems

If you acquire or develop an environmental management or database management system, you will want it to be technically advanced, proven, flexible, and appropriate to your level of computer literacy. If the system will be broadly used, it is particularly important that it be "user-friendly."

Rather than developing systems from scratch, you are almost always better off purchasing commercially available products. The various groups involved, however, particularly the MIS group and the confirmed computer hackers in your user group, will lean toward building their own system, because the commercial database is never as advanced as they would like.

No commercial system will meet 100 percent of your specific needs, but the costs in money and time of designing your own system are usually prohibitive, and you will not have the advantage of professional experience, particularly in the never-ending "debugging." As a general rule, if an environmental database management system handles 85 percent of your needs, it pays to implement and then revise it. In view of the margins for error in designing your own system, if a commercial system suits at least 50 percent of your needs, you should still seriously consider buying and then upgrading it. The important thing is getting a system up and working rather than waiting for the perfect system.

If a commercial system does not handle at least 50 percent of your needs, then you might want to consider building your own. Occidental developed its environmental management system because there was no computerized system capable of performing the management tasks needed. I do not know of any other to date.

Your expectations need to be realistic and allow ample margins of error in the assumptions made in building a system. Everyone wants instant gratification, but it takes a significant commitment by personnel to design an application. As a rule of thumb, if the application takes longer than four months to design, it is probably too large and should be further broken down. This breaking down of tasks is one way of limiting cost overruns. Cheops's Rule, namely, that nothing is ever built within time and budget, usually applies to building computer systems. The same rule applies to installing any commercial system, since there are almost always specific "bugs" unique to your operations that will take time and money to resolve.

In developing a system, the obvious first step is to determine what you need. Do you need an environmental management system, a database management system, or both? At Oxy, for example, the corporate group has an environmental management system but has not needed an environmental database management system, although the divisions do have such systems. However, the corporate group has developed a safety and health data management system, which it uses to track Occupational Safety and Health Act (OSH Act) reporting, among other things. The usual goal is to find or design a system that will satisfy all company needs for environmental information and documentation and, if possible, will print out official forms. You may find it more desirable to have several systems than to wait for the so-called universal system that has yet to be designed.

In designing a system, you should recognize up front that they don't last forever. Three to five years is the usual lifetime. The system must therefore be evolutionary in nature, since all your informational and computer needs simply cannot be anticipated. Evolutionary flexibility is particularly important in view of the incredible changes in hardware and software that have occurred in the last few years. Occidental's MIS, for example, has evolved over a seven-year period and is much more flexible and user-friendly than when first designed.

It is also important to determine whether you want the data centralized or decentralized. My experience is that combining mainframe systems with field entry provides the benefits of both centralization and decentralization. If you want to share data, central control of the database is critical, along with a common data specification. Networking, particularly on a mainframe, works quite well. Recognize that both mainframe and nonmainframe systems are diverse. The possibilities include stand-alone systems at a single facility, multiple users at a single facility, or multiple users at multiple facilities. Any of those systems can be designed for exception reporting, as in the Oxy system. While PCs are an option and are almost becoming universal, the opportunities for broad networking are still limited. For example, while floppy disks can be mailed back and forth and local area (LAN) and wide area network (WAN) interfaces are emerging, data reliability and consistency are still questionable. Security is an important issue with PC-based systems, and the importance of backing up data, and maintaining consistency from transaction to transaction, should never be ignored.

It is important to recognize that the quality of the information in your system depends on the input. John Coryell of DuPont has identified "Coryell's Corollary of Instant Data Gratification," which states, "Unless a data entry person gets some quick, positive feedback on the quality of the (just completed) data entry task, the data entry quality is likely to be disappointing." If the person entering the data assumes that it is going into a "black box," cooperation will be limited. Unless the data entry improves that person's quality of life, such as providing useful data or cutting down on paperwork and phone calls, data will not get entered in a timely fashion. A rumbling dissatisfaction with the system will also develop. When you have people with different levels of computer literacy and understanding using a broad-based system, "problems" with the system can easily be considered out of context and can destroy your work in selling that system.

In implementing a system, another key point is to look at existing sources of data. You will want to avoid entering data that are already being entered in another system. Entering data twice is simply inefficient, and the people doing it will not be very happy. You will need to determine where electronically entered data already exist in your organization and whether an electronic interface can be constructed. If you are going to sell a system, you clearly need to make maximum use of existing data.

Note also that when there are many potential users of a system, it is important to check whether the existing computer capabilities can handle the traffic and whether overloading will slow down the practical use of the system, making it frustrating and slow for the person entering the data. In determining whether a system will work for you, it is important to know how many people will use the system and at what time of day.

Your biggest concern in deciding on a system is not the system itself, but its impact on the organization. The political problems in developing such systems can be more difficult than the technical problems. Knowledge is viewed as power, and when a new portion of the organization acquires data, there will be concern about what that group will do with the data. This fear of the misuse (and, in some cases, the use) of data must be addressed. If it is a corporate versus divisional problem, the first rule is to make clear that there will be no sandbagging and that the primary goal of the system is to give the divisions a management tool. All that corporate will do is conduct limited oversight. The divisions must have confidence that when you obtain additional data, you will still give them the opportunity to fix a problem first, rather than running to upper management. Support for such a system needs to be developed, preferably from the bottom up. Top-down pressure will be actively resisted unless it is a command from top management. Even if it is a command from top management, it is very easy to ensure that a system will not work by giving it limited cooperation.

In pursuing the need for a safety and health system, Occidental's management worked first with the divisions, which at various meetings indicated what they were looking for to meet their own needs. Occidental then picked a system, with division input, that took care of most of the divisions' needs and at the same time satisfied corporate needs for oversight and guidance. Subsequently Occidental developed its own system, which not only included mainframe entry but also accepted data input using a customized PC data entry tool. It was important to find a system that was very user-friendly, since the goal was not to add additional people for centralized entry, but to make the system valuable to the field and provide for field entry. Note that computer systems do not necessarily reduce headcounts, but they can help limit increases.

An interesting phenomenon will take place once these systems are instituted. Many people fear technology, particularly new technology. However, if the system is gradually implemented and not oversold, many personnel will wonder what they did without it, particularly as the growing requirements of federal, state, and local reporting become increasingly overwhelming. Indeed, new uses for the system may be found. For example, the Risk Management and Security Departments at Occidental have also used a computerized management system based on the environmental system.

The Planning Document—Short-Range and Long-Range Planning and Goals

When I first came to Occidental, the task of understanding all the critical issues seemed overwhelming. This feeling is common to all of us who either come to environmental management as a new task or change jobs and take over the environmental function in a new company. In order to simplify and prioritize, I used a planning document to track the major issues and concerns within the company. The divisions subsequently found the planning document concept advantageous and integrated their specific issues into the document. Thus, both corporate and division staff used the planning document for their own purposes. The corporate overview assisted in longer range planning and prioritization without interfering in the divisions' tasks. [25]

The planning document that I used was a simple compilation of items considered important based on assessment findings; entries in the environmental management system; and identified issues emerging in the legislative or regulatory arena, the press, or the opinion of staff experts. It was not computerized, although the items could easily have been entered into the computerized environmental management system.

The format included the objectives to be achieved, the approaches to be taken in achieving them, and the responsibilities and target dates for both the division(s) and the corporate groups involved. No item under any heading was more than 25 words in length. Most were 5 or 10. The document was updated and circulated for review and comment by the divisions approximately twice a year. Since it was included in reports to senior management and the Board of Directors, this clear statement of identified longer-term issues and goals developed into a major lever forcing prompt action.

As the programs matured, this kind of detailed analysis became less significant. While the planning document approach can be very helpful in simplifying and prioritizing, there is a need today to move toward more sophisticated approaches. Corporate and the divisions continue to be involved in planning, but Occidental is now looking more at the broader concepts involved in total quality management and developing strategic goals, strategic plans, and tactical plans as well as following up on the broader issues raised in program reviews (see the section on "Corporate Program Review" in Chapter 5, *infra*). Oxy has substituted this approach for its original planning document.

The planning program is a major element of Occidental's environmental program, since it contains the essence of the company's long-term (five-year) and short-term (one-year) environmental strategies. Its primary objective is development of preventive programs and procedures based on identified issues and trends. This preventive strategy is especially important when minimization of liability is a goal. Many companies still have programs that simply react to regulations and problems as they arise. It is more effective, however, to take a proactive approach, in which emerging issues are identified and programs are implemented to correct or avoid problems.

Long-range strategies and goals are integral to a company's (and a division's) assessment program, and should be included in the planning document. Long-range objectives are defined as those realized more than one year in the future, typically in the three-to-five-year time frame. These objectives should include

- compliance with existing and yet-to-be-promulgated regulations;
- maintenance of existing environmental programs;
- resolution of issues that have technical, factual, or legal uncertainties;
- performance of environmental activities that will enhance the company's public image; and
- identification of procedures needed for developing timely information required for new products, facilities, and permits (for example, PSD/National Pollutant Discharge Elimination System (NPDES) application data, and premarket notification under the Toxic Substances Control Act).

The long-range strategies and goals program should include the following:

- a long-range objectives statement reflecting the environmental goals of the company (or division);
- specific objectives, to be accomplished within a five-year time frame, that apply to all divisions and facilities;
- a description of the method by which objectives will be monitored for completion;

• a description of the method for reporting progress toward satisfying these long-range strategic objectives; and
• a description of environmental research and development activities that will be conducted to solve environmental compliance problems or to further the state of the art in specific areas.

Long-range planning helps you focus clearly on your program's requirements. Perhaps even more significantly, it lets senior corporate and divisional management know that you are actually managing, not "fire-fighting." Long-range planning also places environmental management in the context of general management with its goals, objectives, etc.

Oxy's chemical subsidiary, OxyChem, developed an excellent spreadsheet formula that is quite useful as a means of showing logic flow and as a follow-up system in implementing long-range plans. Its format is as follows:

• Column 1—Corporate goals.
• Column 2—Industry group or division objectives. These are the "evergreen" corporate goals adopted by and restated appropriately for the industry group or division.
• Column 3—Industry group or division results. These are strategic or conceptual statements describing the "how to" programs that will support the corporate goals over the next five years.
• Column 4—Industry group or division goals. These are tactical statements reflecting what must be accomplished this year to achieve the long-term results. They must be definitive and measurable.
• Column 5—Industry group or division action plans to accomplish the goals. These include action plans arising from assessments (including plans relating to plant compliance issues), plant goals (such as excursion goals), and individual performance measures and job responsibilities, as well as compliance-related programs to be implemented by corporate staff.

Note the importance of individual plant action in meeting the long-range goals. Planning is not merely a function of corporate and division staff; facilities are specifically involved in determining how they will meet the goals. Defining the first year's goals and action plans generally seems easy. Identifying longer range programs and plans takes more thought.

Long range planning, in today's total quality management environment, should start with an overall corporate objective, a mission statement, followed by strategic objectives and methods of implementation. For example, Occidental set as its corporate objective: "Continued support of management at all levels in achieving corporate goals and positioning Occidental Petroleum Corporation (OPC) to seize and maintain competitive advantage in order to maximize shareholder value." The departmental mission is "to provide the corporation guidance and assurance in its efforts to enhance the quality of life for current and future generations through continuous improvement in the protection of human health and the environment and the safe conduct of all activities." Strategic objectives are: "(1) Continuous improvement in the protection of company assets, human health, safety and the environment, (2) Management of all activities consistent with OPC requirements (including verification of compliance with all governmental requirements), and (3) Identification and support opportunities for the integration of health, environment, safety and process risk management (HESPRM) into OPC business planning and management process." Methods to meet these objectives are: "(1) Support OPC senior management in communicating their ongoing commitment and expectations to protect human life, the environment and company assets to all levels of the corporation and the public, (2) Identify and support opportunities for HESPRM to contribute to OPC business planning and management processes and programs, (3) Provide direction for the integration of management within the HESPRM functions and activities, and (4) Measure HESPRM contribution to the businesses of the corporation." This could also be summed up by the following chart [26] which explains this process in total quality management terms (see also discussion of Total Quality Management in Chapter 3):

Occidental Petroleum Corporation (OPC) HESPRM Management System

→ GOAL: Protect human health and the environment; provide a safe workplace for employees; and effectively manage allocation of resources (capital, human, etc.) to address HESPRM.

↓

→ OBJECTIVE: Ensure/verify continuous improvement in HESPRM; ensure/verify consistency with OPC HESPRM policies & procedures; and identify opportunities for HESPRM integration with business objectives/strategies.

↓

→ STRATEGY: EH&S human resource development; systems evaluation/program reviews; consultancy to industry groups (IG) on as needed basis; data trending/analysis; communication with OPC management, reporting to Environment, Health and Safety Committee of the Board of Directors (ECOB); EH&S planning; and legislative/ regulatory trending for compliance and planning.

↓

→ COMMUNICATION: Reporting to and meeting with ECOB; Administrators' meetings (heads of environment, safety and risk engineering departments in the divisions); monthly reports to management; and external affairs activities, etc.

↓

→ IMPLEMENTATION: Assessment participation; IG program reviews; IG project consultancy; and leg/reg analysis; etc.

↓

→ MEASUREMENT: IG measurement data (as appropriate to attain objective); assessing compliance with legal requirements; costing info. (e.g. contingent liabilities tracking); Other (value-added measures based on IGs programs' effectiveness in managing Oxy's risks and measures related to OPC management opportunities for HESPRM integration).

↓

FEEDBACK

←

Procter & Gamble has developed the following clear and concise objectives for their environmental program: [27]

- Cost avoidance through superior performance.
- Robust environmental and safety management systems.
- 100 percent deployment.
- Trained people in place.
- Superior performance as measured by annual audit.
- Compliance.
- Statistically in-control and capable systems.
- Deployment of a multi-media pollution prevention system.
- Business driven [looking for savings].
- Includes energy and all releases.

Another means of determining long-range strategy is to ask the following questions, posed by Sara McGee: [28]

- What are the most important two or three things you want to get done for the company?
- How are goals set in the company?
- How does the company communicate its goals?
- How does the company manage the regulatory dynamic and rate of change?
- What mechanisms are used to institutionalize the company's environmental position?
- Are there some basic concepts you manage by?
- How does the company decide which programs to initiate?
- Do you have a well-defined environmental strategy?

The answers should also be helpful in forcing longer-range planning and, in turn, more effective management. In summary, the exercise of long-range planning is extremely helpful in focusing programs beyond the present to meeting longer range goals and objectives that will not only strengthen the environment, health and safety programs, but strengthen the corporation.

Capital Expenditure Review

Capital expenditure review is another example of a proactive approach. At Occidental, review of the environmental effects of all Authorizations for

Expenditure (AFEs) is a preventive measure aimed at ensuring compliance with regulatory requirements and minimizing liability. AFE requests cover expenditures for construction of new facilities, modification of existing facilities, and acquisition or sale of existing assets. The review policy thus helps not only to take care of identified issues, but to avoid future problems.

Occidental's AFE policy requires the requester to conduct a health, safety, and environmental review of any capital expenditure request requiring Board of Directors approval. The policy is now being expanded to include reviews of AFEs approvable at lower levels by divisional staff. Corporate legal and technical staff also review AFEs before they are presented to the Board. These staffs have considerable experience in Occidental's industries and can either assess a project's health, safety, and environmental considerations or know enough to discuss the project with the appropriate division people, requesting elaboration of the comments or modification of the project as appropriate.

Extensive checklists should be prepared for AFE review, particularly regarding acquisitions. [29] It is important to tailor these checklists to your specific needs. Not every AFE requires review of most of the elements of the checklist. Indeed, even in a major acquisition, it is impossible to review all of these elements in detail. Rather, the checklist is designed to ensure that some specialized concern is not overlooked in a capital expenditure or property acquisition or sale.

The reason for requiring review of AFEs is that spending money, particularly on plant expansion or equipment changes, and selling assets can have environmental and legal consequences that must be considered. The start of construction or any modification or addition of equipment can trigger a variety of permit requirements. For example, air emissions from an existing process may be permitted or "grandfathered," but a process modification can trigger a status review and create potential retrofitting expenditures. Another process change might generate a new waste stream. This could greatly exacerbate existing permitting problems, or an agency could require cleanup of existing wastes as a condition for permitting the new stream. Using the modification to resolve any earlier environmental problems and ensuring that the modification includes measures to protect the environment, such as proper diking and secondary containment, can help minimize these difficulties. If there is going to be new construction and a crew doing a substantial amount of work, it is usually cheaper to perform other retrofit work at that time. AFE review helps focus attention on these issues.

AFE review is also a useful vehicle for pressing necessary expenditures to avoid future environmental problems. For example, an environmental assessment may recognize that a facility manager does not have authority to spend the funds necessary to make an environmental improvement, but may still find that improvement necessary. The facility manager can request the funds through the AFE procedure, and submission of an AFE would be an action plan. Review and comment authority provides an excellent vehicle to support the expenditure. This kind of review also helps develop awareness among operating management of environment, health, and safety issues, which helps avoid future problems.

Finally, the review of asset sales ensures that permitting and exposure issues are considered. For example, if you sell a portion of an existing plant but keep the portion that includes water pollution control facilities, you may face permitting problems if the purchaser starts discharging new effluent streams into those facilities. The buyer faces similar concerns if the seller changes its effluent streams. Of course, the biggest concern in selling assets is potential exposure resulting from previous waste disposal practices. Many states require notification from the seller if there are hazardous wastes or substances on site, and New Jersey requires cleanup of sites prior to sale. AFE review helps focus attention on exposure issues, which are discussed in detail in Chapter 6.

Occidental has used AFE review successfully in connection with major acquisitions and planned construction projects and in catching major problems with relatively small projects. For example, several years ago, an industry group that had little experience with hazardous waste problems submitted a proposal to purchase a piece of property. The property had earlier been the site of a Navy facility, a tank farm, and an asphalt production plant. Needless to say, following AFE review, that purchase was not made.

AFE review should not, however, be a major source of paperwork or result in the equivalent of massive environmental impact reports (EIRs) or statements (EISs). Normally, the requester simply provides a statement that the environmental, health, and safety implications of the project have been considered, or a brief statement laying out those implications and the actions to be taken. If AFE review becomes the equivalent of the EIS process, it will lose its effectiveness and encourage sniping at divisional and corporate bureaucracies.

International Environmental Review

Internal Programs

International operations are undergoing increased scrutiny in major corporations. There was a growing recognition before the Bhopal tragedy that safety and environmental issues associated with international operations could subject a corporation to potential liability. Bhopal brought this recognition to the forefront for senior management. Many major companies have extended their health, safety, and environmental assessment programs to their international operations. Many have also found that, in completing these assessments, it does not pay to make any significant distinction between the standards demanded for domestic and those demanded for international facilities. While this consciousness developed after Bhopal for companies with chemical operations and other manufacturing operations susceptible to potential major catastrophes or catastrophic releases, other companies have only recently begun to recognize the potentially significant environmental issues in their overseas operations.

If you have had long experience in dealing with environmental issues in a domestic industry context, these recent discussions with your international management, local representatives, and local governments have been, in the words of Yogi Berra, "deja vu all over again." Concerns are expressed that certain environmental groups are getting active in a country, inciting local people and causing concern from the government. The government does not want to deal with these people, since under the local law they do not have to. Moreover, they view these people as unwanted activists and outside agitators. The local representatives cannot understand how these people could have political influence. How could some underfunded local group aided by "outside agitators" stall a development plan or interfere with a concession or other agreement involving a multinational giant?

Environmental issues now impact areas that could not have been foreseen 20 years ago. International and local managements, as well as local governments, may be finding it difficult to understand how environmental issues may impact them. Their operations may be affected by outside constituencies that are not part of the traditional permitting and operational context. They may also find it difficult to anticipate the economic and political implications of the cost of changes in operation.

All of these discussions, which many of you are now having, bring back virtually identical discussions that occurred when I first joined industry more than 20 years ago as a young former Department of Justice attorney at the beginning of the environmental revolution. (see *supra* Chapter 2). While in the United States we have had more than 20 years of learning to work with stringent environmental laws that impact business decisions and governmental and nongovernmental bodies that may have even greater impact, we are asking our own people (local management and expatriates on site) and local government officials in a very short period to absorb and be comfortable with major changes that affect how they operate.

While we understand and sympathize with this instant cultural change, we must be certain that our own people and our host governments can adjust to these changes if we are to continue to be successful. Indeed, the pressure may be greater in other countries and changes will certainly take place in a more compressed time period than they have in the United States. The political and economic history of some of the host countries and their perception of the history of industry and manufacturing is helpful in understanding the significance of this concern.

Our country has had a history of due process of law from its inception. Unfortunately, very few other countries can make similar claims. For many, due process has been only a recent phenomenon and for too many it is still a limited reality. We have assumed (whether in reality or as a national myth, depending on your political views) that we are a classless society, or at least we have the opportunity to change our class. If nothing else, we have a long history of a large middle class. In many other countries, there have traditionally been only two classes—peasants and aristocrats. Only now is there the beginning of a middle class and there is still limited opportunity, if any, for a peasant to move into relative prosperity. While the history in the United States of stringent environmental laws is only over the last 20 years, it is still long enough for a whole generation to accept the reality of strict regulation of the environment. These same laws have also provided the safety valve of citizen suits: the right of the individual to challenge actions that might be viewed as environmentally unacceptable. Before the importance of environmental protection was recognized in the United States, many industries performed in a manner that today's observers would characterize as environmentally unacceptable.

Outside the United States, the history of industry recognition of environmental concerns and compliance with environmental regulations is far worse. In many countries, the issue of compliance with environmental regulations is moot, since such regulations did not exist. For anyone who has spent time in Eastern Europe or the former Soviet Union, it is easy to understand why many of these citizens are very suspicious about claims of "clean" industry. Operating practices in many cases have not been what we would consider "prudent operations" by any stretch of the imagination. With the history of pollution (and particularly with some industry-real dangers of illness and disease as a result of virtually unregulated operations), it is easy to see why industry may not be met with open arms. When the perception of uncontrolled pollution is added to the assumption that it will not benefit an individual's lifestyle sufficiently to consider additional pollution from a cost-benefit standpoint, opposition will grow. If such development, for example, is near areas such as rain forests, which support an incredibly diverse variety of plant, animal, and insect species and which may have already been exploited by locals, or as in the former Soviet Union or Eastern Europe, where there can be an almost mystic attachment to the land, opposition becomes a real possibility.

It is also hard for those not involved to understand the growing "green" movements throughout the world. Politicians of all types have understood that the environment is a good issue, particularly when, unlike in many instances in the United States, the concerns are real. The issues that made non-political people in the United States environmentalists in the 1960s and 1970s are even more of a concern in many of the countries where you operate or may plan to operate.

In this context, international environmental groups such as the Natural Resources Defense Council, Defenders of Wildlife, and Greenpeace are rapidly becoming involved, allying themselves with local groups, national-ist movements, and opposition parties. The environmental groups are very effective in raising issues that have appeal in local politics. In many instances they do not have to try hard to find issues. Thus, it is reported that a local environmental organization in Indonesia has filed a suit against five government agencies and a national company for failure to comply with the environmental impact assessment laws, [30] that a group in the Philippines has brought a class action suit on behalf of future generations of Filipino children seeking damages resulting from the government's timber licensing practices, and that in Korea, a water supply contaminated by industrial waste has led to criminal charges against top corporate officials. I am personally aware of efforts to have the Valdez Principles (a set of principles of environmental conduct developed by U.S. environmental organizations that include mandatory outside audits (discussed above)) adopted as law in Thailand. We are seeing the equivalent of environmental impact statements being required in a wide variety of countries.

Some environmental organizations are becoming more sophisticated in distinguishing between the "black hats" and the "white hats." Robert F. Kennedy, Jr., of the Natural Resources Defense Council, raised significant concerns over what he viewed as dubious environmentalist success in forcing Conoco to withdraw from oil development in Ecuador and Scott Paper to withdraw from a project in Indonesia, only to be replaced by what he viewed as less responsible developers. [31] He noted, "There are many times, of course, when companies deserve bashing. But platitudes will not save the world's remaining rain forests. We need a more sophisticated approach, one that will allow us to negotiate with those corporations willing to commit themselves to the highest environmental standards. The problem, after all, is not caused by U.S. corporations, but by government decisions driven by a complex cycle of debt, poverty and growing populations." [32]

The World Bank now looks actively at a country's environmental policies and specifically requires an environmental impact study before it will give any development grants. The World Bank has indicated it will aggressively assess environmental impacts of many of its development projects and add "environmental components" to existing and new projects when appropriate. It is conducting a study of 20 countries to better assess environmental concerns at the macroeconomic level. It now also requires that prospective borrowers consult affected groups and make the results of the assessments available to them. This policy in turn will increase pressures on governments to be more open with respect to internal development or industrial projects and their potential environmental impact. [33] The World Bank

> is also involved in a special environmental program to support projects in developing countries that benefit the global environment and that developing countries could not fund on their own. The program, called the Global Environment Facility (GEF), is a joint venture among national governments, the World Bank, the United Nations Development Programme, and the United Nations Environment Programme. The GEF is funded with $1.5 billion, earmarked for projects to reduce and limit greenhouse gas emissions, preserve biological diversity and maintain natural habitats, control pollution of international waters, and protect the ozone layer from further depletion. [34]

This program also increases pressure on projects that could interfere with this broad-ranged program.

The U.S. Agency for International Development (AID) has a department that focuses on environment, with local representatives in many countries of interest. The United Nations Centre on Transnational Corporations is looking at means for ensuring sustainable development and has been examining corporate environmental programs, looking toward international codes of conduct. It has now published a paper which indicates the role of corporations which is envisioned as a result of the Rio Declaration on Environment and Development and Agenda 21, the principles of action. That paper is included as Appendix G, to more fully illustrate the international pressures that are growing on corporations. These are just a few of the trends that are important.

Thus, in an international context, the impact of your operations has to be considered from an environmental standpoint in an entirely different political context. Changing government attitudes, required operational responses, active and informed opposition, and culture clashes complicate the industrial equation throughout the world.

Many companies now believe that, as the primary means of minimizing impacts in host countries, they must adopt standards of operation that are equivalent to their standards in their home operations. This protestation is usually greeted by, at best, a polite yawn from environmental organizations, because such a policy, unless it is clearly explained and implemented, is meaningless. The critical path is to document the basis, including specific numerical standards and specific operating practices. At Occidental we used the term "functional equivalent" to make clear that what we were talking about is the standard of protection for health and the environment equivalent to that which the company maintains at its U.S. locations. Today, the rapid changes in local laws and attitudes make such a policy an imperative.

In a growing number of instances there is little, if any, difference between domestic and foreign laws and regulations. The European Community has adopted strict air and water quality standards, and most European countries heavily regulate disposal of hazardous waste. In many South American and Asian countries, laws and regulations are rapidly changing to closely approximate U.S. standards. Enforcement has not yet caught up with the laws and regulations in many of those countries, but when the laws are enforced, they will usually be enforced against foreign-owned facilities.

In many instances, facilities are not completely aware of existing laws and regulations because of the lack of enforcement. The first step in implementing a "functional equivalency" policy is to complete research on the local requirements. When these requirements are placed in tabular form next to the requirements for a representative facility in the United States, the differences are usually minimal. It is hard for a facility to argue that it should not at least meet the requirements of the host country.

Above all, and regardless of the legal requirements, a corporation should be guided by the simplistic principle established in a popular commercial for an oil filter: "Pay me now or pay me later." If laws or regulations will eventually require retrofitting, it is appropriate to make the necessary changes *now* rather than to spend much more later on.

Therefore, the best means of avoiding future problems is to establish an international policy with a standard of protection for health and the environment equivalent to that which the company maintains at its U.S. locations. [35] Such a policy does not require slavish copying of all U.S. laws and regulations. There is ample evidence that equivalent means will protect health and the environment just as adequately as some of these laws and regulations, particularly those that are technology-based. However, where existing or proposed control requirements or procedures would be inconsistent with those followed in the United States, it is critical that a responsible expert, either in-house or out-of-house, documents in the permanent records of the corporation the basis for the conclusion that these requirements or procedures afford equivalent protection compatible with the intent of the policy. In most instances, this documentation requirement will produce an interesting phenomenon: the number of requests for exceptions to the policy will be minimal.

Most environmental controls do not require large and expensive equipment installations, but rather consist of tighter practices and procedures. Even where equipment is involved, environmental controls may result in sufficient savings in reduced loss of product, raw material, etc., that they are good business in simple economic terms. In other instances, equipment and installation actually cost substantially less than in the United States, although the amount saved is difficult to quantify. This is not because the actual hardware costs less, but because extensive administrative costs (including costs of technical consultants, lawyers, and prolonged paperwork with regulatory agencies) that are endemic in the United States are much less prevalent in other countries. For example, an incinerator that would not be cost-effective in the United States may be cost-effective overseas because its cost in the United States is greatly increased by the cost and delay of obtaining permits. In addition, the normal design of most U.S. plants includes basic pollution control, and in many instances it is easier to use off-the-shelf design than to redesign purposely to eliminate pollution control devices. On the other hand, some aspects of good environmental management may be more difficult overseas. [36] For example, in many parts of the world there are no hazardous waste disposal areas that environmental professionals are totally comfortable with in terms of long-term exposure.

The international environmental program needs to include a system for prompt follow-up and action on any identified issues. This system will usually be part of the regular environmental assessment process. The program must also include a reporting procedure and timetable for its implementation.

In developing its international environmental program, Oxy followed a procedure developed by its chemical subsidiary, OxyChem. This procedure establishes the following milestone steps:

☐ *List local standards for discharges to all media.* In many cases, no numerical local standards exist, and you must establish standards on a site-by-site basis through interpretation and discussion with local officials.

☐ *Determine typical U.S. standards for discharges to all media.* In many cases no single "typical U.S. standard" exists. Standards for water are normally based on the capabilities of technology. Air emission standards are usually based on ambient air quality.

☐ *Formulate "equivalent" standards using professional expertise.* Use the local and typical U.S. standards to develop "equivalent" standards. If local standards are more demanding, they will govern. If typical U.S. standards are more demanding and are scientifically sound, they will govern. It is vital to document the logic you use in setting "equivalents." In this regard, it is helpful to identify the intent of the U.S. standards.

☐ *Establish "equivalent" standards with the plant, considering site-specific conditions.* Once "equivalent" standards are formulated, the plants must review and agree to the numbers, just as a U.S. plant does in negotiating a permit with a U.S. agency. In most instances there is little room for negotiation, but the plant may raise factors that would make compliance with a particular standard unnecessary. The basis for such variances should be documented. Similarly, plants will often need to conduct sampling and analysis, perhaps on a seasonal basis, before they can determine whether they can meet particular standards. Sampling and analysis requirements, too, are in line with U.S. practices. "Impossibility" is not an acceptable argument when the discharge would result in an unacceptable adverse environmental or health effect.

☐ *Develop sampling/analytical protocols for the "equivalent" standards.* Even when a plant has agreed to "equivalent" standards, sampling or analytical procedures must be established. For example, for a parameter as simple as Ph, the frequency and type of measurement (e.g., continuous versus daily/weekly grab sampling) must be resolved and the necessary procedures established. Remember that if the procedures that would ordinarily be used are sophisticated EPA or state procedures, the required equipment may not be readily available to service the foreign locations.

☐ *Monitor and report against the "equivalent" standards.* Although monitoring and reporting should be routine, it does take time to collect meaningful data, and it should be expected that some monitoring will show exceedances of "equivalent" standards. When this occurs, corrective action should be considered and documented.

☐ *Where necessary, establish and track to completion action plans to correct exceedances of "equivalent" standards.* It may take some time, possibly several years, to complete the engineering design, AFE preparation, equipment purchase, construction, and start-up necessary to achieve compliance.

Notwithstanding such commitments, discussed above, companies attempting to invest in Eastern Europe and the former Soviet Union may be faced with extensive difficulties in building new facilities. Pollution from existing operations is severe, and there is extensive pressure by the "greens" (including direct involvement of U.S. environmental organizations) to prevent new operations until existing operations are better controlled. In many cases, they have successfully prevented new construction. Many of us would argue that this strategy is counterproductive, since the new operations will be bringing in the newest technologies and funds as well as operational ethics that will be necessary in the long run to improve environmental controls. However, the "greens" believe that U.S. companies are "exporting" pollution. This perception is extremely difficult to overcome, since these people have never seen how a well-controlled industrial operation can function. They only know what they have seen, and in many instances what they have seen is not acceptable. A "functional equivalent" policy may help to overcome their skepticism, but this will be a long-term process.

If there is active environmental involvement in a country, it is also quite likely that the appropriate ministries are receiving offers from these governmental and non-governmental entities to assist in the drafting of national and local environmental regulations. If you do not get involved, rest assured that you may see the worst command-and-control regulations in place. However, if you have a clearly articulated functional equivalence policy, you are in a good position to offer credible assistance to the ministry with sound, technically based requirements that protect the environment. If you do nothing, you have no basis for complaint.

Finally, the confusion of the local representative is shared by the governmental ministries and the local national company, which may be a partner. In many countries today, the environmental regulations are handled by an industrial ministry, but there are growing trends to create local environmental protection agencies that will control the bulk of environmental permitting. This is analogous to the sharing of regulatory authority between our EPA and state governments (national and local regulation) and the Department of the Interior and EPA (resources and permitting). Basic industrial rules will still be controlled by the industrial ministry, but air and water permitting, etc., will be controlled by the new EPA. Such an agency has a different constituency than an industrial ministry. While it may not prevent operations, there can be extensive delays in permitting as the new agency raises concerns, enforces, or tries to enforce new regulations and deals with the local environmental community who now believes it has a specific governmental voice.

The local national company is also in a quandary over these changes. Its mission is development, and it usually does not fully understand and appreciate these new trends. While local environmental organizations are suspicious of international companies, they usually reserve their particular wrath for the national company. Many of these national companies are now hiring environmental professionals who are in turn gradually educating their managements to the importance of these issues. However, these national companies and the government ministries, although deeply suspicious about these environmental issues and their impact on development and cost, also recognize the importance of defending your position to the public and the press. For them, like many corporations' international operations, it is difficult to adjust to major changes in operation without the long history of such struggles in the United States.

Dealing with environmental issues in today's political climate is not easy, but if we do not recognize concern for environment worldwide as an idea whose time has come, opportunities for continued investment and growth in industry will soon diminish.

An international program as protective as a domestic program is not developed or implemented overnight. It is usually easier to maintain high standards in the safety area than in the environmental area, although constant vigilance is necessary in areas where, for example, local customs do not normally include wearing hard hats, safety glasses, respiratory masks, safety shoes, and other safety equipment. In addition, local customs or religions sometimes include a fatalistic attitude or a "macho" attitude that must be overcome in improving safety awareness. Finally, while people in the United States are commonly familiar with mechanical equipment and vehicles, a country moving from a simple agrarian economy to one involving sophisticated equipment or vehicles faces major problems of training and awareness. U.S. companies should set the highest standards for personnel safety. Industrial hygiene sometimes suffers because of lack of suitable testing equipment and of local personnel capable of completing appropriate monitoring. However, in most instances this is not a major problem.

In summary, the basic and overriding objective in international operations is that no operation, activity, or product, when properly conducted or handled, should cause a significant or permanent adverse effect on health or the environment. Where adverse effects are foreseen or occur, ameliorative action must be taken to avoid or correct them.

Worldwide Management Initiatives to Promote Excellence

Recently, approximately 15 U.S. companies with international interests, including Occidental, joined in an effort known as the Global Environmental Management Initiative (GEMI). This effort, which is being undertaken jointly with the International Chamber of Commerce and the United Nations Environmental Programme (UNEP), is designed to develop guidelines for international business; to promote, assemble, and create worldwide critical thinking on environmental management techniques, systems, and results; and to share this thinking with the public.

A variety of needs resulted in the formation of GEMI. It was felt that without industry leadership to establish expectations of responsible and effective corporate environmental behavior, other groups such as consumers, governmental agencies, and others will set the standards for industry. As discussed throughout this book, changes and evolution in corporate behavior are most effectively driven internally to the corporation. [37] Moreover, there are no accepted or understood tools or measurement systems to gauge or judge the effectiveness of environmental performance. Corporate goals and management systems to track health and safety performance need to be revised and, where appropriate, made applicable to the environmental area. Similarly, state of the art "codes of conduct," such as the chemical industry's Responsible Care, need to be shared with and adapted to the needs of multi-national and multi-sector industries. All of these efforts need to be synergized for greater effect.

In this vacuum, particularly lacking guidance toward a global environmental ethic from a specific center for corporate leadership and thought on environmental management, GEMI was formed. If this effort is successful, it can raise the level and effectiveness of environmental performance and management by business worldwide through the examples and leadership of corporate thought leaders, as well as develop a comprehensive industrial ethic for environmentally sound development.

This effort will welcome contributions from all sources, including the developers of the Valdez Principles. It is only through joint efforts worldwide that this consciousness raising can be effective.

In May 1990, the International Chamber of Commerce in Bergen, Norway, announced that world business will create a "charter for sustainable development" as a guideline for the environmental management of world business. This charter was unveiled at a conference in Rotterdam in April 1991. [38] GEMI was an active participant in this effort.

Joint Ventures

Implementing the principles discussed above regarding health, safety, and environmental policies is difficult in itself, and is much more difficult when your company is not the sole owner and operator of the facility. There are no easy ways to implement such policies in joint ventures, particularly when the partner is a host state or state-controlled quasi-corporation and has a significant minority or even a controlling interest.

There are arguments against entering joint ventures where there could be substantial liability if your company cannot adequately control potential harmful exposure of workers and the surrounding public. This is not a common leveraging factor in business decisions, but it should not be ignored. However, the usual situation requires convincing either a governmental or private joint venture partner that a company's domestic health, environment, and safety policies should be implemented. The easiest way is to establish those policies as part of the basis for the joint venture. Tying actions to company policies protecting health, safety, and the environment, rather than to compliance with U.S. laws, avoids offending local sensibilities and national pride (by avoiding perceived insults to local laws and regulations).

Sophisticated local private investors may be persuaded by the "pay me now or pay me later" concept, and, indeed, that specific language can be an effective sales tool to demonstrate the cost-effectiveness of an environmental policy. This concept also helps mitigate the potential resentment of other corporations that are unwilling to adopt more stringent internal regulation. Gradual introduction of certain health and safety concepts sometimes eases their acceptance such as use of hard hats and safety shoes in tropical climates.

Many countries provide criminal penalties for injuries and fatalities. In these countries, when the joint venture partner is a government entity, it is particularly important to document requests for improved safety practices and programs in the corporation's permanent records, in case the partner's refusal to approve implementation leads to an unfortunate accident.

Legislation and Regulation

This section addresses the handling of legislation and regulation as a staff function. It discusses internal staffing and gives general hints for dealing with agencies. Chapter 8 discusses the use of engineering and legal personnel in dealing with federal agencies and legislative bodies. Chapter 9 discusses specific issues in dealing with federal, state, and local agencies and citizen groups.

The first problem in government relations is simply making sure that you identify and obtain all the information you need, and channel that information to the proper places in your organization. I do not know of any organization, either decentralized or centralized, that is satisfied with its handling of government relations in this regard, particularly on the state and local levels. Merely keeping everyone up-to-date on key changes in federal legislation and regulation requires a sizable staff. Many law firms publish newsletters as services to clients; if reviewed by in-house counsel to ensure that they are correct, these can be effective substitutes for your own newsletters regarding general legislative and regulatory developments.

Most organizations, including Occidental, do not have the staff to write memos detailing the specific impact of these developments on facilities. Centralized or decentralized organizations with large corporate staffs may devote more time to these matters. However, continuous memos on these issues are really not necessary if you establish a network of key lawyers and managers to track them. This approach succeeds if field personnel trust that the specialists know what they are doing and are sufficiently experienced to spot issues that may cause problems for facilities or divisions. If the specialist identifies such an issue, it is assumed that he or she will contact the division or field expert to confirm the problem and start developing a solution.

It is even more difficult to obtain and effectively process information on government issues at the state and local levels. At the federal level, a limited staff in Washington can at least keep track of important developments. Information gathering is less formalized at the state and local levels. Unless a company has a full-time staff person or consultant doing this job, it can miss important issues. There are trade association newsletters and computerized services that will allow you to keep some track of legislation and regulations, but there is still that sinking feeling that something important may be missed. This is particularly problematic if communication between corporate and field management is inadequate. If a plant or facility attempts to follow legislation and regulations without a fair level of sophistication in both the political process and environmental law, it is quite likely to miss an issue. Conversely, if the local people are not following a state or local issue, the corporate group could miss the issue's significance to the plant. Open lines of communication are therefore critical to the "network" approach discussed above. Corporate specialists can only help divisions and plants if they understand their situations and concerns.

After obtaining the necessary information on governmental issues, your company must decide how to address them. The proper handling of legislative and regulatory issues has not been given enough attention. Many industry representatives trying to cope with these issues either handle them ineffectively or simply give up in frustration. These patterns can be changed if a company focuses not on defending its current practices, but on resolving problems and identifying probable future requirements early. Trained professionals can accomplish these goals. Unfortunately, however, while management of environment, health, and safety issues has in general been turned over to professionals, the same cannot be said of specialized advocacy concerning environmental legislation and regulations. Far too few companies effectively coordinate their Washington, D.C., efforts with their environmental professionals to reconcile regulatory and legislative needs and realities.

In many companies, this failure is primarily a result of unnecessary and counterproductive "turf" wars between traditional government affairs offices and the new breed of technical and legal professionals. Traditional government affairs offices often feel threatened by these specialists, who are now becoming more and more active in the government affairs offices' territory: the arcane world of Washington, D.C. Government affairs offices are less concerned about dealings with regulatory agencies, recognizing that they do not have specialized expertise in this area. They are primarily concerned about the legislative arena, in which their expertise has previously been unquestioned.

This discussion is not a denigration of traditional lobbyists. In most Washington, D.C., offices they have been and can continue to be effective. However, in regulatory agencies and in Congress, experienced technical and legal staff now handle much of the work in the health, environment, and safety area, including preparation of conceptual papers and drafting. This is also true of environmental organizations, which recognize the critical importance of government staffs and employ highly knowledgeable individuals in their efforts to match the skills of those staffs.

In contrast, few companies have specialized, professional, Washington-based environmental staffs with equally high qualifications. Industry representatives, in order to be effective, must be viewed as skilled professionals attempting to resolve problems, rather than just as advocates. Most industry representatives are not so viewed, which is a major factor in the success of the environmental organizations. Many industry representatives simply do not have the specialized skills or personal credibility to deal effectively with the skilled government and environmental group staffs. Even companies with highly qualified staffs may limit their flexibility to negotiate rapidly, effectively, and credibly. Moreover, most companies are not organized to respond immediately to instant drafting requests by legislative and regulatory agencies.

The new environmental specialists in industry can be effective in dealing with government staffs. Indeed, they normally deal exclusively with staff rather than directly with members of the House of Representatives or the Senate. Because of the complexity of this area, members of Congress are almost at the mercy of staff, with little time to understand all the ramifications of much of the new legislation being promulgated. It is therefore critical to convince the staff, which often is hostile to industrial interests, of the utility and social value of your position. If traditional lobbyists work together with specialists, personally introducing them to members of Congress or staff, both groups can be maximally effective. Problems occur, however, when the government affairs office tries to keep specialists from contact with members of Congress or staff or assures the home office that there is no problem, without considering the fact that social policies and, with them, the ability to influence legislation have radically changed. (*See* Chapter 2.)

The two groups have to work together, and they have to realize that "we will fight them on the beaches" is not a successful philosophy in dealing with environment, health, and safety legislation. There are many concepts that may not make much sense from a traditional industry perspective—or, for that matter, from a technical or logical perspective—but, rightly or wrongly, they are ideas whose time has come. The successful industry advocate today recognizes that the goal is usually to minimize impact, working in the interstices of such legislation, rather than fighting the statutes in toto. This approach will do his employer the most good.

It is not easy to obtain effective representation that produces imaginative, cost-effective, and environmentally acceptable solutions to environmental issues. However, it does not require a large budget—merely close coordination of the environmental professionals, the traditional Washington staff, and divisional staffs, as well as trust and mutual recognition of skills. Even the best representation will not always be effective, but one beneficial change in a regulation or proposed statute can pay for a specialized staff.

Occidental had two environmental representatives in Washington, D.C. One is Oxy's Director, External Affairs and Technical Support, who has strong legal and technical skills, as well as extensive EPA experience. The other was Director, Environmental Affairs and Technical Support, who has a strong technical background as well as federal and state agency experience and subsequently became my successor in Los Angeles. Since these Washington representatives had expertise in the key areas, as well as credibility with government agencies and congressional staffs, they did not have to spend time on briefing the home office or returning for decisions on every point. They also effectively used the governmental and legislative expertise of the other representatives in Washington, D.C. Occidental found that this staff combination was extremely productive and effectively used the broad variety of skills available within the company to resolve environmental issues. Awareness of social and political values and possessing the legal and scientific skills are the critical factors in producing consensus and viable solutions. Short lines of communication also allow for rapid turnaround, which is vital to productive work in this area.

Anyone attempting to obtain legislative and regulatory changes must maintain good relations with government agencies. Some ethical questions have been raised about the "revolving door" policy that allows people who leave a government agency to represent private parties before that agency. Obviously, there can be abuse. However, the primary advantage of an ex-regulator is not some kind of arcane knowledge of government procedures or of specific government actions, but rather a recognition of how government works, along with basic credibility with government personnel. If you work with people for years and establish a reputation for competence and credibility, you need not lose that reputation because you now represent a different party.

You should be aware, however, that

> there is a heavy burden on the former regulator now representing the private party. He [or she] cannot compromise credibility for the sake of a one-shot gain by the client. The environmental community is small, and that one-shot gain will quickly deteriorate to a long-term loss. Quick decisions pro or con on issues and willingness to work with an individual rapidly evaporate, and the opportunity to effectively represent the private client will quickly vanish. In essence, government agencies and environmental groups understand the difference between form and substance, and the corporate representative who is not suggesting reasonable positions cannot succeed. [39]

The same cautions apply to any environmental manager or lawyer attempting to build a long-term relationship with an agency.

The former regulator or public interest representative also has learned that neither regulatory agencies nor environmental groups are omniscient. Some regulatory schemes are poorly developed by inexperienced regulators, and some solutions are more costly than necessary. It is not a sin against the environment to consider costs among other priorities in achieving a goal. It is also important to work with agencies to improve their understanding of the application of new technologies. "Technology forcing" sometimes can go too far; simply because technology has worked on a bench scale does not mean it will work in practice. Industry tends to look for "off the shelf" technology, but sometimes agencies appear to push for technology that is "off the wall." Usually, the best answer lies in between.

Finally, if you are frustrated at your lack of confidence in your company's handling of the legislative and regulatory process, remember that this frustration is endemic to environmental management. In times of limited resources, however, staffs simply will not be increased to the point where we all have a high level of confidence regarding governmental issues. These staffs were usually the first ones cut in earlier recessions, and management is not about to encourage restaffing. Such staffs are also difficult to justify in "hard dollars." Thus, in this area of management, as in all others, the key is developing lines of communication between the field and headquarters. If this is done, either a decentralized or a centralized organization can implement an effective program. We must take our corporate cultures as we find them, but within those cultures, we can provide the necessary lines of communication. Budget limits need not pose insurmountable problems. Obviously, with an unlimited budget anyone should have an effective program. Few managers have that luxury, nor is it necessary. It is hoped that this book will help you design not only effective, but cost-effective programs.

Training and Education Programs

A strong environmental management program depends, in large part, on continuing awareness of the current status of, and trends in, environmental management and technology as developed by regulatory agencies, policy-makers, scientists, and engineers. [40] This awareness is achieved through a continuing program of education and training that addresses the various needs of hourly employees, supervisors, environmental specialists, assessment team members, division managers, community residents, and local community officials. The scope and detail of these programs vary with the corporate culture. Some companies use elaborate films; others bring people together for long training programs. Others, while not using complicated systems, develop an ethic that makes training easier. Many of the better programs are modeled on or combined with safety awareness programs, which have a longer history of implementation and acceptance. In general, to ensure that personnel maintain a high level of environmental awareness, training and education programs should cover

- environmental awareness and compliance policies;
- supervisory responsibilities;
- corporate liabilities;
- environmental technology updates;
- working with regulatory agencies;
- community support needs;
- emergency response plans; and
- impacts of new legislation and regulations.

One specialized training program should be directed to members of individual facility assessment teams. The membership of these teams is likely to vary, especially in larger companies with many divisions or facilities subject to the assessment process. Multiple teams may be necessary, and team membership may change from one facility to another. Starting with personnel who possess the requisite knowledge of environmental regulations, facility operations, and division plans, this training should emphasize how to conduct the assessment in an effective and timely manner.

If a corporate staff is small, it is more difficult to establish strong training and awareness programs, but if there is good cooperation and interest in the divisions, the corporate staff can do its job by ensuring that the divisions have good programs. Sometimes an organization with a small staff may need consultants to help implement such programs.

Decentralized Versus Centralized Organizational Structures

The programs discussed in this chapter were designed for the decentralized organization with a small corporate staff. Obviously, I am not hiding my bias for that form of organization. However, the programs discussed are equally beneficial to centralized organizations or decentralized organizations with larger staffs. All organizations need systems for reporting to senior management and the board of directors, including strong policies, procedures, and programs that prevent surprises by ensuring reporting of significant matters. In addition, all organizations need to encourage planning by vehicles such as planning documents. Systems for reviewing capital expenditures, acquisitions, divestments, legislation, and regulations are equally important. Implementation of these programs, however, may be somewhat different in centralized than in decentralized organizations.

In a centralized organization, virtually all specialized work is done at headquarters, with limited work in the field. One advantage of a centralized program is uniformity. This may be important in establishing plant parameters or specific policies for dealing with agencies. Centralization may also work well when facilities are too small to require full-time environment, health, and safety staff, and the limited services of centralized specialists are sufficient. An example of a strong centralized program is 3M.

Many organizations are decentralized in name, and to some extent in function, but still have large centralized staffs. These staffs may provide expertise, but they also spend substantial time collecting or, in some instances, prying information from the field. Such organizations do try to have more expertise available at the plant level than centralized organizations do. Large decentralized organizations may also have centralized groups that do nothing but training or program planning and have sizable budgets to deal with these issues. General Electric is a good example of such an organization. It has both a strong decentralized program and a sizable central staff performing broader functions.

Centralization, which assumes that corporate staff, rather than field personnel, will do most of the environmental work, does not eliminate "turf" problems or difficulty in obtaining information on significant issues. Nor does it necessarily ensure that corrective action is taken. While centralized organizations normally are designed to handle most of the major permitting activities, and perhaps to coordinate contacts with government agencies, they often do not have timely access to critical data. Like decentralized organizations, they must develop their relationships with local plant managers in order to avoid long memo-writing exercises. As in the decentralized organization, the human factor cannot be overemphasized. Neither centralized nor decentralized management can be done from behind a desk.

In both centralized and decentralized organizations, primary environmental responsibility should rest with line managers. In centralized organizations, many field managers assume that the corporate center bears this responsibility. The manager of the centralized organization must overcome this assumption. While the centralized organization may provide uniform guidance and specialized expertise, the best manual of policies and procedures is of no value unless it is read and followed. Lack of responsibility and sufficient expertise in the field can lead to major problems. For example, if field managers allow sloppy practices between corporate environmental audits, it is quite possible to have major problems with poor spill control and tank testing. Plant awareness is even more critical to strong programs in the safety area.

Some companies take the position that the centralized staff is providing services for which facilities should be charged. The experience of many managers in such organizations is that they spend considerable time fighting with the field over billing matters, which detracts from their primary management functions. More significantly, requiring divisions to pay for services creates a disincentive for them to seek advice when they may need it, which is counterproductive to a program. Frankly, I am convinced that this charging for services is primarily a paper exercise and does very little, if anything, to reduce cost. If an individual performs specific services for a division on a regular basis, this can be budgeted, but charging for services performed on an ad hoc basis discourages use of the staff specialist when needed. If the staff group also performs audit functions, it can be particularly galling for a division to pay for its own audit.

Notes to Chapter 4

1. Occidental procedures define "unascertainable" matters as "relevant and unresolved legal, factual, or technological questions or problems which render remedial actions, costs, or actual or contemplated claims or proceedings uncertain." Examples would be possible uncertainties arising from new regulations or new interpretations of existing regulations.

2. Occidental procedures define an "excursion" as "any emission, discharge, or other release of material which is outside the parameters established in an agency-issued permit which limits the amount of such materials which can be discharged. This includes releases determined to be excursions based on measurements by official test procedures and reported to the agency. Excursions recorded by other means and which are not reported to the agency should be separately identified and reported."

3. 15 U.S.C. §2607(e), ELR Stat. TSCA §8.

4. 42 U.S.C. §§9601-9675, ELR Stat. CERCLA §§101-405.

5. EPCRA §313, 42 U.S.C. §11023, ELR Stat. EPCRA §313.

6. *Id.*

7. "Material" is not specifically defined but the test, according to the U.S. Supreme Court, is based on a "balancing of both the indicated probability that the event will occur and the anticipated magnitude of the event in the light of the totality of the company activity." Basic, Inc. v. Levinson, 485 U.S. 224, 229 (1988). For legal proceedings, Item 103 of Securities and Exchange Commission (SEC) Regulation S-K specifically requires disclosure if (a) such proceeding is material to the business or financial condition of the registrant; (b) such proceeding involves primarily a claim for damages or involves potential monetary sanctions, capital expenditures, deferred charges or charges to income and the amount involved, exclusive of interest and costs, exceeds 10 percent of the current assets of the registrant and its subsidiaries on a consolidated basis; or (c) a governmental authority is a party to such proceeding and such proceeding involves potential monetary sanctions, unless the registrant reasonably believes that such proceeding will result in no monetary sanctions, or in monetary sanctions, exclusive of interest and costs, of less than $100,000; provided, however, that such proceedings that are similar in nature may be grouped and described generically. *See* Archer, McMahon & Crough, *SEC Reporting of Environmental Liabilities*, 20 ELR 10105 (Mar. 1990); Rabinowitz & Murphy, *Environmental Disclosure: What the SEC Requires*, Envtl. Fin., Spring 1991, at 31.

8. Archer et al., *supra* note 7, at 10107.

9. *Id.* at 10106.

10. *See generally* Berz, *Keep Risk Reduction Decisions in the Board Room*, Envtl. F., Mar./Apr. 1990, at 32.

11. The entire Valdez Principles are:

1. *Protection of the Biosphere*—We will minimize the release of any pollutant that may cause environmental damage to the air, water, or earth. We will safeguard habitats in rivers, lakes, wetlands, coastal zones, and oceans, and will minimize contributing to the greenhouse effect, depletion of the ozone layer, acid rain, or smog.

2. *Sustainable Use of Natural Resources*—We will make sustainable use of renewable natural resources such as water, soils, and forests. We will conserve nonrenewable resources through efficient use and careful planning. We will protect wildlife habitats, open spaces, and wilderness, while preserving biodiversity.

3. *Reduction and Disposal of Waste*—We will minimize waste, especially hazardous waste, and wherever possible recycle materials. We will dispose of all wastes through safe and responsible methods.

4. *Wise Use of Energy*—We will make every effort to use environmentally safe and sustainable energy sources to meet our needs. We will invest in improved energy efficiency and conservation in our operations. We will maximize the energy efficiency of products we produce or sell.

5. *Risk Reduction*—We will minimize the environmental, health, and safety risks to our employees and the communities in which we operate by employing safe technologies and operating procedures and by being constantly prepared for emergencies.

6. *Marketing of Safe Products and Services*—We will sell products or services that minimize adverse environmental impacts and that are safe as consumers commonly use them. We will inform consumers of the environmental impacts of our products or services.

7. *Damage Compensation*—We will take responsibility for any harm we cause to the environment by making every effort to fully restore the environment and to compensate those persons who are adversely affected.

8. *Disclosure*—We will disclose to our employees and the public incidents relating to our operations that cause environmental harm or pose health or safety hazards. We will disclose potential environmental, health, or safety hazards posed by our operations, and we will not take any retaliatory personnel actions against any employees who report on any condition that creates a danger to the environment or poses health or safety hazards.

9. *Environmental Directors and Managers*—At least one member of the board of directors will be a person qualified to represent environmental interests. We will commit management resources to implement these principles, including the funding of an office of vice president for environmental affairs or an equivalent executive position, reporting directly to the CEO, to monitor and report upon our implementation efforts.

10. *Assessment and Annual Audit*—We will conduct and make public an annual self-evaluation of our progress in implementing these

principles and in complying with all applicable laws and regulations throughout our worldwide operations. We will work toward the timely creation of independent environmental audit procedures which we will complete annually and make available to the public.

12. Doyle, *Protecting Planet and Portfolio*, ENVTL. F., Mar./Apr. 1990, at 37.

13. *See generally* Friedman, *Don't Sign the Valdez Principles*, ENVTL. F., Mar./Apr. 1990, at 32.

14. Meyers, *Business' New Ten Commandments*, ENVTL. F., Mar./Apr. 1990, at 33.

15. Friedman, *supra* note 13, at 42.

16. The entire CERES Principles are:

Introduction—By adopting these Principles, we publicly affirm our belief that corporations have a responsibility for the environment, and must conduct all aspects of their business as responsible stewards of the environment by operating in a manner that protects the Earth. We believe that corporations must not compromise the ability of future generations to sustain themselves.

We will update our practices continually in light of advances in technology and new understandings in health and environmental science. In collaboration with CERES, we will promote a dynamic process to ensure that the principles are interpreted in a way that accommodates changing technologies and environmental realities. We intend to make consistent, measurable progress in implementing these Principles and to apply them in all aspects of our operations throughout the world.

1. *Protection of the Biosphere*—We will reduce and make continual progress toward eliminating the release of any substance that may cause environmental damage to the air, water, or the earth or its inhabitants. We will safeguard all habitats affected by our operations and will protect open spaces and wilderness, while preserving biodiversity.

2. *Sustainable Use of Natural Resources*—We will make sustainable use of renewable natural resources such as water, soils and forests. We will conserve nonrenewable natural resources through efficient use and careful planning.

3. *Reduction and Disposal of Wastes*—We will reduce and where possible eliminate waste through source reduction and recycling. All waste will be handled and disposed of through safe and responsible methods.

4. *Energy Conservation*—We will conserve energy and improve the energy efficiency of our internal operations and of the goods and services we sell. We will make every effort to use environmentally safe and sustainable energy sources.

5. *Risk Reduction*—We will strive to minimize the environmental, health and safety risks to our employees and the communities in which we operate through safe technologies, facilities and operating procedures, and by being prepared for emergencies.

6. *Safe Products and Services*—We will reduce and where possible eliminate the use, manufacture, or sale of products and services that cause environmental damage or health or safety hazards. We will inform our customers of the environmental impacts of our products or services and try to correct unsafe use.

7. *Environmental Restoration*—We will promptly and responsibly correct conditions we have caused that endanger health, safety or the environment. To the extent feasible, we will redress injuries we have caused to persons or damage we have caused to the environment and will restore the environment.

8. *Informing the Public*—We will inform in a timely manner everyone who may be affected by conditions caused by our company that might endanger health, safety or the environment. We will regularly seek advice and counsel through dialogue with persons in communities near our facilities. We will not take any action against employees for reporting dangerous incidents or conditions to management or to appropriate authorities.

9. *Management's Commitment*—We will implement these Principles and sustain a process that ensures that the Board of Directors and Chief Executive Officer are fully informed about pertinent environmental issues and are fully responsible for environmental policy. In selecting our Board of Directors, we will consider demonstrated environmental commitment as a factor.

10. *Audits and Reports*—We will conduct an annual self-evaluation of our progress in implementing these Principles. We will support the timely creation of generally accepted environmental audit procedures. We will annually complete the CERES Report, which will be made available to the public.

Disclaimer—These Principles establish an environmental ethic with criteria by which investors and others can assess the environmental performance of companies. Companies that sign these Principles pledge to go voluntarily beyond the requirements of the law. These Principles are not intended to create new legal liabilities, expand existing rights or obligations, waive legal defenses, or otherwise affect the legal position of any signatory company, and are not intended to be used against a signatory in any legal proceeding for any purpose.

The revised Principles were adopted on April 28, 1992. They are on file with the Coalition for Environmentally Responsible Economies, 711 Atlantic Ave., Boston MA 02111.

17. Valdez Principles, *supra* note 11.

18. CERES Principles, *supra* note 16.

19. *Id.*

20. *Compare* CERES Principle Number 6, *supra* note 16, *with* Valdez Principle Number 6, *supra* note 11.

21. IRRC's 1992 publication incorrectly classified Occidental as an "integrated domestic oil company." It is a commodity chemical company, an oil and gas exploration and production company, a natural gas pipeline company, and a coal company (scheduled for divestiture). Thus, the company's operations and consequently its performance are not adequately reflected. Another example of an inconsistent comparison was found in the area of mine safety and the data presentation in the 1992 IRRC report regarding Mine Safety and Health Act (MSHA) penalties. Since the alleged citations listed under MSHA are essentially all in coal mining operations, the correct comparison of Oxy's coal company would be against the coal industry's MSHA penalties. In comparing indices within the coal industry, the type of mining (surface mining or underground mining) conducted and the varying levels of agency enforcement in different parts of the country also affect these comparisons. Occidental was involved predominantly in underground mining, which traditionally has received greater agency scrutiny. IRRC provided Occidental with a MSHA penalty index of 35.3 (three-year average) for the coal industry. The Occidental penalty index for the same averaged time period was 34.3, demonstrating that Occidental's performance was better than the industry average. However, the IRRC data, without correction, showed Occidental as substantially worse than the other "integrated domestic oil compan[ies]."

22. General internal procedures for reporting environmental matters are discussed *infra* in Chapter 5; procedures for recordkeeping are discussed in Chapter 5 as well. Occidental's computerized system is discussed later in this chapter. The importance of including policies and procedures in environmental assessment protocols is discussed in the section on "Environmental Policy and Organization" in Chapter 5.

23. Occidental is now making this system, the Oxy-EAS,[TM] commercially available.

24. These systems are discussed in detail in Rich, *Environmental Software Review 1988*, POLLUTION ENG'G, Jan. 1988, at 40.

25. The following discussion is derived in part from Friedman & Giannotti, *Environmental Self-Assessment*, in LAW OF ENVIRONMENTAL PROTECTION §7.05 (S. Novick ed. 1987).

26. Prepared by Catharine DeLacy, Vice President, Health, Environment and Safety, Occidental Petroleum Corporation.

27. Personal communication with George Carpenter, Director, Environment, Energy & Safety Systems, Proctor & Gamble.

28. S. McGee, *Creating an Environmental Department*, ENVTL. MANAGER, Nov. 1992, at 3-4.

29. These checklists are included as Appendix D.

30. *Land Use and Environmental Law Briefing*, MORRISON & FOERSTER, Aug. 1991, at 1.

31. Robert F. Kennedy, Jr. *Amazon Sabotage*, WASHINGTON POST, Aug. 24, 1992, at A17, col 1.

32. *Id.*

33. *See* Scott, *Making a Bank Turn*, ENVTL. F., Mar./Apr. 1992, at 21, 22.

34. *World Bank Strengthens Environmental Requirements for Major Project Funding*, POLLUTION PREVENTION NEWS, July 1991, at 5.

35. Note that your actions abroad may also have implications in the United States:

> If the plaintiff's lawyers had filed suit in Texas for the Union Carbide incident in Bhopal, India, I believe the litigation would have remained in Texas and not sent back to India. In a 1990 case styled *Dow Chemical Company v. Domingo Castro Alfaro*, 786 S.W.2d. 674 (Texas Supreme Court 1990), the highest court in this state declared that foreign plaintiffs bringing a cause of action against a Delaware corporation authorized to do business in Texas to recover damages for physical and mental injuries sustained after they handled pesticides in a foreign country could bring suit in Texas. This decision was based upon an 1985 treaty between the United States and Costa Rica granting each citizen of the other reciprocity to the other's court system. The mere fact that all of the action took place in Costa Rica had no effect on the Texas Supreme Court in permitting the lawsuit to be brought in Texas. Your company's future may wind up in a Texas court—in a town you never saw on a map before, in front of a jury that "hates big business." Even though you reside in a state or country outside Texas, you may well be required to defend your company and/or your actions in this state. Texas is not a good place for a defendant to try its lawsuits. It is a nice place to visit but not as a witness.

Hartline, *Legal Consequences of Plant Failures - After the Smoke Clears,* paper presented at First International Conference on Improving Refineries and Chemical and Natural Gas Plants, organized by Gulf Publishing Company and Hydrocarbon Processing, Houston, Texas, Nov. 10-12, 1992, at 18.

36. *See also Environment Is Reaching "Take-Off" Point in Europe*, ENVTL. MANAGER, June 1990, at 12:

> Some forward-looking U.S. companies have sought to implement the same environmental standards in their facilities around the world, even if local laws aren't being enforced. This isn't always so easy.
>
> "It's a difficult thing to do in practice, particularly when foreign rules aren't clear," says [Turner] Smith [an American environmental lawyer based in Brussels]. Still, companies are better off setting global standards than doing nothing, he says. They will be better able to defend a civil suit down the road.

Id.

37. *See generally* Berz, *supra* note 10, at 34. "The necessary corporate ethic to protect the environment must come from within, not from outside groups like CERES." *Id.*

38. The following are the principles proposed by the International Chamber of Commerce and endorsed by GEMI:

(a) *Corporate priority*: To recognize environmental management as among the highest corporate priorities and as a key determinant to sustainable development; to establish policies, programmes, and practices for conducting operations in an environmentally sound manner.

(b) *Integrated management*: To integrate these policies, programmes, and practices fully into each business as an essential element of management in all its functions.

(c) *Process of improvement*: To continue to improve corporate policies, programmes, and environmental performance, taking into account technical developments, scientific understanding, consumer needs and community expectations, with legal regulations as a starting point; and to apply the same environmental criteria internationally.

(d) *Employee education*: To educate, train, and motivate employees to conduct their activities in an environmentally responsible manner.

(e) *Prior assessment*: To assess environmental impacts before starting a new activity or project and before decommissioning a facility or leaving a site.

(f) *Products and services*: To develop and provide products or services that have no undue environmental impact and are safe in their intended use, that are efficient in their consumption of energy and natural resources, and that can be recycled, reused, or disposed of safely.

(g) *Consumer advice*: To advise, and where relevant educate, customers, distributors, and the public in the safe use, transportation, storage, and disposal of products provided; and to apply similar considerations to the provision of services.

(h) *Facilities and operations*: To develop, design, and operate facilities and conduct activities into consideration of the efficient use of renewable resources, the minimization of adverse environmental impact and waste generation, and the safe and responsible disposal of residual wastes.

(i) *Research*: To conduct or support research on the environmental impacts of raw materials, products, processes, emissions, and wastes associated with the enterprise and on the means of minimizing such adverse impacts.

(j) *Precautionary approach*: To modify the manufacture, marketing, or use of products or services or the conduct of activities, consistent with scientific and technical understanding, to prevent serious or irreversible environmental degradation.

(k) *Contractors and suppliers*: To promote the adoption of these principles by contractors acting on behalf of the enterprise, encouraging and, where appropriate, requiring improvements in their practices to make them consistent with those of the enterprise; and to encourage the wider adoption of these principles by suppliers.

(l) *Emergency preparedness*: To develop and maintain, where significant hazards exist, emergency preparedness plans in conjunction with the emergency services, relevant authorities, and the local community, recognizing potential transboundary impacts.

(m) *Transfer of technology*: To contribute to the transfer of environmentally sound technology and management methods throughout the industrial and public sectors.

(n) *Contributing to the common effort*: To contribute to the development of public policy and to business, governmental, and intergovernmental programmes and educational initiatives that will enhance environmental awareness and protection.

(o) *Openness to concerns*: To foster openness and dialogue with employees and the public, anticipating and responding to their concerns about the potential hazards and impacts of operations, products, wastes, or services, including those of transboundary or global significance.

(p) *Compliance and reporting*: To measure environmental performance; to conduct regular environmental audits and assessments of compliance with company requirements, legal requirements, and these principles; and periodically to provide appropriate information to the Board of Directors, shareholders, employees, the authorities, and the public.

39. Friedman, *60s Activism and 80s Realities—We've Come A Long Way*, ENVTL. F., July 1983, at 8, 11.

40. The following discussion is derived in part from Friedman & Giannotti, *supra* note 25, §7.05.

Chapter 5:
Environmental Auditing and Environmental Management

Responsible environmental management recognizes that "what you don't know *will* hurt you." Auditing is only one aspect of this management, but it has received considerable attention as a means of reducing EPA inspections and ensuring legal compliance.[1] This focus on auditing alone, without other strong programs and procedures, is misplaced. Auditing can provide only limited control and awareness of potential issues. An audit is merely a "snapshot" of existing controls at a facility. Without other management systems, the audit is a very limited part of modern environmental management.

Indeed, the term "auditing" itself confuses the issue. I prefer the term "assessment" (although, for the sake of simplicity, this book uses the two terms interchangeably). Environmental auditing is not like financial auditing, which is conducted under formal procedures pursuant to rules and standards that allow comparisons and judgments of compliance.[2] Environmental regulations are not always specific, and vary considerably both by location and by industry. It is not always clear whether particular regulations even apply to a facility. As two former EPA officials have recognized, "environmental auditing is too new, too fluid and too diverse to support a structured program approach,"[3] although this is changing (see Certified Professionals and Auditing Standards in this chapter). While many law firms and consulting organizations are in fact suggesting this structured approach, many of us with both law and management backgrounds raise caution flags in terms of effectiveness and cost-effectiveness.

This is not to say that audits are not beneficial. An environmental assessment program constitutes an integral part of a general management system, assisting a company in organizing and managing effective environmental programs. An environmental assessment program also provides other benefits relating to financial planning, Securities and Exchange Commission (SEC) reporting, personnel development, public and employee relations, expansion planning, legislative and regulatory strategy development, and evaluation of acquisitions and divestitures. It is possible to achieve the benefits of environmental assessments without encountering the problems posed by a structured approach to those assessments. This discussion focuses on establishing standards that promote internally consistent evaluations and provide a basis for comparisons to other programs.

To be an effective management tool, which should be its purpose, auditing must be examined in the context of responsible management. As discussed in the preceding chapters, the management goals are

- Development and implementation of corporate-wide policies, programs, and guidelines providing independent assurances that the corporation is properly addressing environmental concerns. "Independence" does not require certification by outside counsel or auditors. If staff groups not directly involved in operations implement the reviews and controls, this normally will provide the necessary independence. [4]
- Implementation of a system for promptly identifying problems and advising management of those problems and the steps being taken to solve them.
- Maintenance of a system for independently determining the environmental compliance status of all facilities and subsidiaries and for ensuring that any required actions are taken. Again, the whole purpose of auditing and other management programs is to ensure that the corporation is responding quickly and effectively to issues and concerns.
- Development and implementation of mechanisms for identifying emerging and future environmental issues as well as for coordinating planning for responses to issues involving more than one division.
- Minimization of the liability exposure of the corporation, its officers, and its employees.

An audit program should be designed to further these goals. The basic criteria for judging the quality of a program are "top management support; an audit manager or team independent of production responsibilities; a structured program with written audit procedures; a system for reporting audit findings to senior management; and a corrective action program." [5] The environmental assessment program, when managed at the corporate level, helps ensure that effective systems for managing environmental risk and liabilities actually are in place, understood, and followed.

Some advocate an audit system that incorporates exhaustive facility reviews, using a large team and extensive checklists and record inspections. [6] While facility reviews are clearly necessary, many of us believe that they should be management-system oriented. [7] Massive reviews are appropriate at the initiation of a program in order to ascertain facilities' basic problems, and in other exceptional cases. Otherwise, many companies, such as Occidental Petroleum, focus their audits on systems and on major flaws, although in response to detailed regulatory requirements and an enhanced appreciation of the importance of compliance, these audits are becoming increasingly detailed. Once facilities understand their basic environmental mission, the facility audit is merely a cross-check to determine that the systems are performing adequately. This allows auditing on a more frequent and, in my judgment, a more cost-effective basis. Occidental also has internal financial auditors check records and permits as part of their financial audits. This allows a spot check on recordkeeping without burdening the environmental system review.

Within Occidental, each division must maintain its own assessment program. The corporate department has produced an assessment program procedure, which it updates with additional guidance memoranda. Divisional assessments must meet at least the minimum criteria specified in the document as updated. An assessment program, procedure, or guidance document may also detail the basics of an entire environmental program. While this may be convenient, it is not necessary as long as your program is documented and that documentation is easily accessible.

In addition to helping shape and improve assessment programs, the corporate department's responsibilities include critiquing all assessment reports, observing select on-site reviews, reviewing site schedules, and ensuring that recommended follow-up systems are in place and working. On occasion, Oxy's corporate personnel visit facilities for informal reviews apart from the normal assessment process. Problems have been observed on some of those visits and corrective actions initiated. Further, an independent view of operations by experienced personnel has frequently identified program or procedural modifications that can make compliance more economical.

Environmental assessments are reviewed by staff not associated with manufacturing operations and are critiqued by the corporate group. These procedures provide that degree of independence without which a system cannot function. (The issue of independence is discussed in detail in the next section of this chapter.) Corporate review helps ensure that internal environmental management procedures are followed and potential problems uncovered before they surface in regulatory agencies or the media.

The Environmental, Health, and Safety Committee of the Board; the Executive Vice President and Senior General Counsel and Secretary (who is also a director); and the Executive Vice President and Senior Operating Officer review environmental assessments and the corporate group's critiques. This high level of review is a great advantage. Far too often, a company assumes that it has resolved many of its problems simply by having an assessment program. However, the assessments are circulated only to lower middle-level management, and no recommendations are made and/or no actions are taken. Of course, the moment a facility has major enforcement problems, its assessment report will surface (usually even if attempts are made to protect it legally), and the company will have major difficulties explaining why no responsible manager took action to correct the deficiencies or why action was postponed. This is *not* a hypothetical situation. Experienced environmental lawyers and managers can cite too many examples of otherwise responsible companies that simply did not provide the management controls to ensure follow-up on their assessments. These companies would find this lack of follow-up inexcusable in a financial or an operational context.

The following discussion provides general information on the significant elements that an environmental assessment program should include, outlines the benefits of such a program, and describes the significant elements that an environmental assessment procedure should include.[8] The discussion also includes some additional details on general reporting systems. Note that the environmental assessment program should make no distinctions between domestic and international operations. The advantages of such a program are equally applicable to international operations, as discussed in detail *supra* in Chapter 4.

Controversies as to What Is "Independent" Review[9]

A continuing and growing potential conflict exists between corporate personnel charged with environmental auditing responsibilities and outside consultants. There is also a potential conflict between in-house and outside counsel.

There is a perception among the public and some legislators that an environmental audit cannot be "independent" unless performed by an outsider. Many suspect that this perception is encouraged by outside consultants and lawyers. This suspicion is also encouraged by some of the maneuvering on the "Valdez Principles," discussed previously in Chapter 4 and later in this chapter. I was advised by a consultant retained by the proponents of the Valdez Principles that their requirement on auditing, which has been amended in the CERES Principles, was developed by environmental consultants and plaintiffs' environmental lawyers. Similarly, many law firms are touting their expertise in performing full-scale auditing of a company's environmental compliance. While there may be times when both outside consultants and lawyers are necessary, particularly where in-house staffs are not sophisticated or may have been compromised, or where there is "a realistically high potential of uncovering significant irregularities," [10] this is an area for potential abuse.

An example of the bias toward "outside" auditors is the Office of Technology Assessment's (OTA's) suggestion that a program be established for certifying public environmental auditors:

> who could attest to the quality of site and cleanup data and reports. . . . Responsible party studies and cleanups would have to use certified public environmental auditors. Governmental agencies and groups receiving EPA Technical Assistance Grants would also be required to use certified public environmental auditors to the extent that the work was conducted by nongovernmental contractors for onsite investigation and engineering activities. The basis for certification would be meeting a set of criteria established by EPA after discussions with a number of organizations representing professional engineers, consulting engineers, hazardous waste professionals, and EPA's Science Advisory Board. [11]

Congress would direct EPA to establish a certification program expeditiously.

The tenth principle of the CERES principles states:

Audits and Reports
> We will conduct an annual self-evaluation of our progress in implementing these Principles. We will support the timely creation of generally accepted environmental audit procedures. We will annually complete the CERES Report, which will be made available to the public.

Note that the guidelines assume that outside firm review will eventually be required. Many will, therefore, have significant misgivings about this portion of the CERES Principles. Parenthetically, if the concept behind the CERES Principles is a financial audit, the usual language of such audits is quite general and broad. Some members of the CERES coalition are assuming eventual broad access to all kinds of findings. [12]

Of course, this latter view as to "public availability" may be counterproductive and might limit the audit to identifying only the most obvious issues, rather than providing detailed reviews and issue identification, which are extremely helpful in program implementation.

Good environmental audits are not mere "check-lists"; they are operational reviews. As long as there is a commitment to assure that problems surfaced are addressed, this program review can and should be done by qualified in-house people who are "independent" of production responsibilities. An in-house individual, familiar with the operations and credible to the facility being audited, can determine far more about what is right or wrong with a facility than an outsider. The bottom line is not to find mislabeled drums, but to determine why the program allowed for mislabeling in the first place.

The narrow interpretation of the value of an environmental assessment is further revealed in some of CERES's specific recommendations. An apparent focus of the audit guidance is to identify "all sites of contamination." This indicates a lack of understanding of environmental management. The purpose of an environmental assessment is not merely to locate contaminated sites, but to address any ongoing threats to workers or the community; not all threats relate to contamination and not all contamination poses a threat. The guidelines also seem to imply that all facilities would need to be audited annually. This would divert needed resources to low-risk facilities at the expense of more productive audits at potentially high-risk facilities.

Certified Professionals and Auditing Standards

There has been continued discussion as to whether individuals engaged in environmental auditing should be certified and even greater controversy as to the scope of such certification and what specific requirements such certification would entail. (See also a discussion of state involvement in environmental audits under "Effects on the Regulated Community" later in this chapter.) An industry group called the Association of Environmental Consulting Firms (AECF) is attempting to establish a certification process for environmental auditors on the assumption that "if a more exact environmental assessment requirement is developed for parties attempting to use the [CERCLA innocent landowner] defense, [13] a more standardized audit process will be needed to maintain consistency and ensure fairness across the board. . . ."[14] The brochure of another organization, the American Institute of Environmental Property Auditing, states that the Institute looks forward to certification because at present there are "no standards or criteria for the knowledge and expertise to be possessed by property transfer auditors." (See also discussion of "verifiers" in International Environmental Auditing Standards in this chapter.)

A Code of professional conduct has been developed by the Board of Certified Safety Professionals.[15] A similar code has been developed by the Institute of Internal Auditors.[16]

An environmental committee within the American Society for Testing & Materials has given its approval to a set of standards which would aid those seeking protection under Superfund's innocent landowner defense. The standards would define a minimum level of environmental due diligence a future land owner would have to follow in order to use the innocent landowner defense. The ASTM committee on Environmental Assessments approved both the Phase I site assessment and the transaction screening standards on October 29 1992. The set of standards have been in development for more than three years and are awaiting the approval of the full ASTM committee, which is expected in January [1993]. [17]

The standards are divided into two separate actions . . .—the phase I environmental site assessment and the transaction screening process. [18]

The phase I assessment is to be used primarily for sites that are believed to have a high risk of contamination and contains four components: a review of existing records of the site, a site inspection, interviews with current owners and local government officials and a final evaluation and report. The standard also mandates that the assessment be conducted by an environmental official. [19]

The transaction screening process consists of a host of questions that are posed to owners of the property and local officials regarding the condition of the properties in question and unlike the phase I assessment the screening process does not require that it be conducted by an environmental official. [20]

Among the questions asked are "Is the property or any adjoining property used for an industrial use? Is the property or any adjoining property used as a gasoline station, motor repair facility, commercial printing facility, dry cleaners, photo developing lab, junkyard or landfill, or as a waste treatment facility? [21]

If the answer is yes to any one of the questions, the prospective purchaser must perform a phase I assessment. [22]

Two private organizations in the United States and Canada are working on standards. The Canadian Standards Association (CSA) is working on standards and the Environmental Auditing Roundtable has completed standards which are included in Appendix G. NSF International and CSA are cooperating in the development and co-publication of voluntary North

American documents in the fields of environmental management systems and environmental auditing, in conjunction with the Environmental Auditing Forum, the Environmental Auditing Roundtable, and the Institute for Environmental Auditing.

In many ways, this call for certification is analogous to efforts to create a specialty certification for environmental lawyers. The American Bar Association's Section of Natural Resources, Energy, and Environmental Law, which is the base for most of the more experienced lawyers in this field, has opposed such certification. The field is simply too diverse to lend itself to easy characterization. Perhaps another analogy is also appropriate: Mr. Justice Stewart in a Supreme Court obscenity case noted that he could not define obscenity, "but I know it when I see it."[23] Perhaps a listing of individuals holding themselves out as professionals, together with accessibility to credentials, references, and experience, is the only easy way. In environmental law, too many individuals are obsessed with specific regulations or narrow areas of statutes. The days are past when some of us old-timers felt that we were environmental lawyers with at least a passing familiarity with the whole spectrum of environmental law. But even as the field becomes more complex, there is still the basic judgment factor. While we may not know the specific answer, experience tells us that there is a potential problem, and that either we should explore it or we should call in an expert.

In the same way, an environmental auditor need not be expert in every area, but he or she should have broad experience and judgment to recognize, for example, a potential groundwater problem, without being a hydrologist. Environmental auditing courses that are being developed on many campuses can assist in the basics, but they do not in themselves teach judgment. There seems to be a need for more training courses, particularly in the fundamentals of the technical bases for environmental auditing. This expertise can be gained, providing the individual has a solid professional base. If not, environmental auditing becomes a rote exercise.

Thus, the future of environmental auditing will rest on the ability to recognize the broader issues and to enforce the implementation of long-term programs such as waste minimization, particularly on a multi-media approach, rather than on narrow expertise and utilizing checklists. There is real concern that environmental auditing and environmental law should not become so specialized that the larger picture is lost. Environmental auditing must be part of the decisionmaking process if it is to be used effectively. This is the joy and the intellectual challenge of the work.

Use of Financial Auditors

Another concept that will grow in the 1990s is the use of internal financial auditors to perform some environmental audit functions. While the early environmental audits have progressed from limited checklists to program reviews, there is still a need for basic documentation checking. I submit that it is a waste of experienced environmental personnel to spend substantial amounts of time on record reviews. I have found that using the financial auditors for detailed checks during their visits to facilities (which are not as frequent as the environmental audits) has been extremely helpful. They are very thorough and require extensive documentation as part of their normal auditing process. With some limited training and access to environmental professionals for specific questions, they can perform these review functions adequately. If they have questions, environmental professionals are available to answer them. Occidental has prepared an extensive control questionnaire and complementary audit program for their use in their reviews (reproduced as Appendix E to this volume) with the following objectives:

- To ensure that all company policies and procedures regarding environmental and safety issues are being adhered to.
- To ensure that proper documentation exists for areas of concern noted in the most recent assessments and that any other identified issues have been addressed and corrective action has been properly taken.
- To ensure that documentation of all applicable regulations, training, and required reporting is maintained.
- To ensure that compliance with all permit and regulatory requirements is properly and adequately documented in the environmental and safety records, and to ensure that these files are maintained in an organized fashion.
- To ensure that all work-related injuries and illnesses are recorded.

If environmental auditing is to grow in stature, we must assure that we are not perceived as the equivalent of junior financial auditors, but rather as experienced professionals with broad environmental skills, an integral part of environmental management. This increased use of internal financial auditors will free us to look at more important issues. As discussed subsequently, if our programs at this stage are merely compliance-oriented, we are not positioned for the 1990s. Our reviews today should be program oriented and include recognition of risk reduction and safety-related issues such as process hazard reviews and waste minimization programs. In addition, such program reviews should examine the interrelationship of such programs and the effective use of resources. It should include organization, planning, guidance, communication, documentation, monitoring, measurement of accomplishments, and having the management systems in place to assure effective coverage of the overlapping areas of the several disciplines involved.

Corporate Program Review

A final check in determining the adequacy of environmental programs is to complete a periodic review of their adequacy. This step is often overlooked and is perhaps the most important step in assuring adequacy of loss prevention and loss control programs.

In large corporations, the staff in health, environment, safety, and, in Occidental's case, risk engineering (HESRE) programs, tends to be "compartmentalized"; that is, specific functional units may be responsible for individual functional areas. The individual units may not recognize overlaps and the need for adequate coordination and communication. Basic program management issues can go unnoticed. A "Program Management Review" can be used to show how the company's HESRE programs are integrated; how they compare with corporate policies, procedures, and guidelines; and how they attain their stated intent. Identifying program deficiencies, so long as they are immediately corrected, does not generate the legal problems related to facility audits because of self-reporting requirements. Most significantly, identifying the program deficiencies will help cure specific problems that are occurring at facilities primarily because of program deficiencies.

Often assessment or audit programs are facility specific. They review the performance of the facility's implementation of HESRE programs. However, periodically it is important to focus on the broader-range integrated HESRE management issues that drive the quality of the HESRE performance. To accomplish this, a program review can be initiated that is not limited to verifying action plans. A program review will assist in identifying specific program element deficiencies, implementation inconsistencies, and inconsistent management criteria and execution. In other words, such a review can aid in identifying the root causes of problems, including common management deficiencies that decrease the effectiveness of efforts to comply with policies, procedures, and regulations. Generally, a broad and integrated valuation of HESRE programs as implemented can provide senior management valuable information that can positively affect the corporation's future performance and profitability.

Such reviews can also be effective in testing the adequacy of a corporate program. They may help managers identify issues relating to quality control and quality assurance mechanisms that need to be addressed in individual corporate programs.

There are three stated purposes of a program review. One purpose is to determine if the division's HESRE programs are consistent with corporate policies, procedures, and guidelines. Another purpose is to evaluate these programs relative to their stated intent. Finally, the review provides an opportunity to capitalize on identified improvements.

It is important to keep such reviews as unbiased and non-judgmental as possible. The critical point is not what occurred in the past or what is occurring now, but rather to determine if appropriate and necessary management systems are in place and functioning; if adequate resources are provided to assure the systems' continuation and effectiveness; and if appropriate measures are executed to measure the quality of program performance, including the means to meet future challenges. Additionally, reviews may need to extend beyond HESRE components and include ongoing business management systems. Integration of HESRE into business decisionmaking may be critical for continued success of the program.

To start a program review, a 'desk top' review of existing written documents is required (for example, examining policies, standards, procedures, guidelines, directives, principles, and assessment reports). The documents can provide a framework for the review as well as an understanding of the management and operating infrastructure for divisions and where the HESRE "accountability" resides. There is a tendency in business to place all HESRE accountability at the plant level. Clearly, the plant manager should have the primary responsibility for assuring compliance with the laws and company policies, procedures, and guidelines, but those more senior in management and in appropriate staff functions should share that accountability and responsibility. Therefore, assurance to provide adequate funding and resources is a critical element to review. Company or division cultures can play a critical part in understanding how the commitment of resources to HESRE issues is accomplished. A program review can assist in this effort. An examination of accountability would include HESRE function descriptions, job descriptions and assignment of responsibility/accountability for functions to various line managers, requests and approval of funds, and performance and practices of human resources, as well as maintenance and operations.

A significant part of the initial 'desk top' review includes the issues of program quality control/quality assurance. These include description, charge and management support, and commitment of assessment programs, copies of third-party assessments, action plan reviews, follow up and documentation of quality control/quality assurance measures and activities built into HESRE programs, and policies and procedures, etc. This last provides an opportunity for action by division management and staffs to explain quality assurance/quality control as it applies to their HESRE efforts. The document review should not be limited to headquarters. Similar reviews of documentation should take place at all levels of management, including the facility level.

Interviews with appropriate and key operating and staff personnel are necessary to gain a true understanding of how the management systems and staff view and fulfill their responsibilities with respect to environment, health, and safety. Additionally, facility visits are a critical element of a program review. By participating in and conducting facility visits, trends in HESRE performance and implementation that may not have been obvious may emerge. The program review needs to go beyond traditional assessment reviews in order to assure that there is more to an organization's efforts than a book of procedures.

The program review, therefore, needs to check on the overall implementation, communication, supervision, monitoring, and enforcement of company policies. The policies should require compliance with the law and should establish a program to assure that every employee will be able to report a violation of the policy in a confidential manner and without fear of retribution throughout the chain of supervision or, if the employee believes that such a report would be ineffective under the particular circumstance, reporting to a designated corporate compliance officer should be available. However, the primary responsibility for compliance should rest on the chief executive officer of each division, not on a designated corporate compliance officer. The divisions need to develop and document appropriate programs to ensure that all current and proposed facilities, equipment, products, and procedures comply with the policy. They should also ensure that prompt action is taken as may be required, develop and document reporting procedures, and develop and document a timetable for implementing the programs. A review of these programs is, obviously, a part of the program review by corporate, but periodic reports to the corporate environmental department are also helpful.

It is probably better to have the designated corporate compliance officer outside of the normal chain of command in the environmental area. If that officer is in the chain of command, it might be argued that although the corporate environmental department needs to provide guidance and interpretation of the policy requirements and review all programs and reports for compliance, there is no outside check and confirmation on the performance. It is, therefore, probably preferable for the compliance officer to be a senior level management person whose principal responsibilities as compliance officer will be to provide a means, when necessary, for any policy violation to be reported directly to the corporation and to maintain constant standards for policy enforcement. This person should of course be backed up by counsel, and it seems advisable to appoint a compliance counsel to deal with the legal issues. Thus, the primary responsibility for compliance rests on the actual operations, but at the same time means are developed for maintaining compliance with the policy and with laws and regulations at the corporate level. This technique also has the advantages of providing another vehicle for understanding environmental issues at senior levels of management and for communicating their importance.

As stated previously, the program review should also consider operations, maintenance, and capital issues. In times of lower profits, there can be a tendency to change operating practices and reduce preventive maintenance more than is appropriate. These trends, if specifically looked for, can show up in a program review, particularly after a variety of personnel interviews and facility visits. A close review also should be undertaken of the capital expenditure process. The written process may show that capital will always be found for compliance; however, there can be underlying problems. Perhaps determinations are made not to seek capital for compliance expenditures until too late in a given situation or decisions are made at an inappropriate level within an organization, or such requests, particularly when made late in the budget process, may not be viewed favorably by the higher levels of management and will be deferred. Here, again, the issue of management accountability is important. The decisions concerning HESRE issues should not be left solely with facility managers. All levels of management are accountable and should be held responsible for their part in making HESRE decisions.

All of the HESRE areas should go beyond the traditional costs of doing business and should be reviewed in a manner integral with all other management functions. If such reviews are thorough and complete, management and operational problems can be identified and remedied at the appropriate levels of management.

Besides being an excellent management tool, in the United States the program review also helps provide an important additional safeguard. The July 1, 1991, U.S. Department of Justice policy (discussed in the "Criminal Liability Exposure" section in Chapter 2) to limit the use of information developed in environmental audits and other voluntary compliance efforts in criminal prosecutions under environmental statutes indicates that the audit and compliance program must be comprehensive and broad-based in order to secure any form of consideration.

This encouragement of a comprehensive program, although in a criminal penalty context, does highlight the weakness of many environmental programs—they are facility specific and do not address the broader issues that are part of Total Quality Management. Such issues must be addressed if a company is to be certain that it is addressing the important issues as early as possible and thereby reducing its costs.

Self-Evaluation and Verification

There are a variety of techniques to assure that the value created by a program review is not lost. Perhaps the best technique is to use a self-evaluation tool to help assure continued concern. There has been considerable publicity recently on certain evaluation programs. (See discussion of Valdez and CERES Principles in Chapter 4, Environmental Policies and Corporate Responsibilities, and industry efforts in Chapter 4, Worldwide Management Initiatives to Promote Excellence.) Many of these efforts are at least partially the result of environmental critics' claims that there are no "hard numbers" to evaluate a company's programs. I suggest that, if this is the rationale for adopting such a program, it is naive and a waste of money. Whatever numbers are generated will be subject to criticism. Some programs are important to some companies and others are not. This distinction will undoubtedly be lost on industry critics, particularly those who are more concerned about a company's products than its management systems. Even comparing different divisions with separate product lines is difficult.

It will also be difficult to establish a verification system that will assure the critics of the uniformity and validity of the data. The Global Environmental Management Initiative (GEMI) (discussed *supra.* in Chapter 4, Worldwide Management Initiatives to Promote Excellence) has released a standard assessment tool[24] which it will distribute worldwide. The tool translates the International Chamber of Commerce's Business Charter for Sustainable Development into "digestible corporate activities needed to attain the goals."[25] Note that there are other efforts, particularly in Europe, to find standardization. These include the British Standard Institute (BSI), the Canadian Standards Association (CSA) and American National Standards Institute (ANSI). Each are members of the ISO92. All of these efforts have the same fundamental failings discussed with the GEMI efforts, namely the difficulty in maintaining meaningful data for *outside* audiences or comparison of product lines or companies with each other.

The foregoing is not meant to be a criticism of the GEMI efforts, which Occidental participated in and supported. I am concerned that "international standards" will become a procrustean bed ("one size fits all") that will limit creativity and growth in environmental programs. If these standards are not adopted completely, a company might be concerned that its program is incomplete or perceived by the "public" as incomplete.

There is, however, considerable *internal* value in self-assessment programs to assist in continuous improvement following or preceding a program review. They should not be used as a measure for comparing the status of one division against another, but as a means to measure progress toward program goals in each division. Stated simply, you should not be hung up on numbers.

As discussed subsequently, the GEMI efforts and some of the European efforts should be looked at as useful guides for developing your own company's index of areas for evaluation. Thus, the GEMI technique (a four step process for internal use) can be modified to the following three steps:

- Level 1—Developmental
- Level 2—Attainment
- Level 3—Assurance

A large variety of elements have been identified and will also be valued in accordance with importance:

- A—Very Important
- B—Important
- C—Less Important

Note that this system is *not* limited to environmental issues or international or national principles but includes health, safety and "process risk management" (which is a more appropriate description than "risk engineering") as well as internal corporate objectives. This system allows divisions to measure the progress of the implementation of programs in a way that is easily understandable to management and gets "corporate off their backs" by minimizing the corporate role of *verification* that the necessary programs are in place and working.

International Environmental Auditing Standards

Much of the European effort on environmental auditing is based on the fact that, unlike U.S. laws, most European laws do not provide for self-monitoring and the various enforcement agencies, therefore, are struggling to obtain data. [26] Many companies in the pursuit of "quality" and the recognition of such efforts by the British Standards Institute have adopted the management system principles contained in ISO 9000, developed by the British Standards Institute, as the European and internationally recognized quality system. Certification as being in conformance with ISO 9000 improves export possibilities since many foreign companies either prefer or require that suppliers be certified as complying with ISO 9000. European efforts to develop environmental auditing standards as well as certification under ISO 9000 may have a profound impact on environmental auditing programs in the United States.

The British Standards Institute has now prepared a comprehensive system for environmental management which went into effect on March 16, 1992.[27] "Compliance with a British Standard does not of itself confer immunity from legal obligations. This British Standard is issued subject to review by the technical committee responsible for drafting no later than September 1, 1993 to facilitate pilot application. At the time of the review changes will be made where required in the light of the experience gained or to reflect changes to the draft European Community Eco-Audit Regulation (Version 3, December 1991) in the intervening time from publication of this standard."[28]

Besides calling for the kind of review and systems discussed in this book, it also calls for, under Section 4.11:

> *Environmental management reviews.* The organization's management shall, at appropriate intervals, review the environmental management system adopted to satisfy the requirements of this standard, to ensure its continuing suitability and effectiveness. The results of such reviews shall be published if the organization has a commitment to do so.
>
> Management reviews shall include assessment of the results of environmental management audits (see 4.10).

This is equivalent to the program review previously discussed. Annex A of the standard contains a "Guide to Environmental Management System Requirements." The Annex states:

> The environmental management system should be designed so that emphasis is placed on the prevention of adverse environmental effects, rather than on detection and amelioration after occurrence. It should
>
> a) identify and assess the environmental effects arising from the organization's existing or proposed activities, products or services;
>
> b) identify and assess the environmental effects arising from incidents, accidents and potential emergency situations;
>
> c) identify the relevant regulatory requirements;
>
> d) enable priorities to be identified and pertinent environmental objectives and targets to be set;

e) facilitate planning, control, monitoring, auditing and review activities to ensure both that the policy is complied with, and that it remains relevant;

f) be capable of evolution to suit changing circumstances.

The European Community Eco-Audit Regulation was adopted in March 1993. [29] Although this scheme is "voluntary," as is compliance with ISO 9000 and the Environmental Management Standard, there will be strong pressures to adopt such standards as a part of "quality" standards. The regulations require the following under Annex I, Section D, "Good Management Practices:"

1. A sense of responsibility for the environment amongst employees at all levels, shall be fostered.

2. The environmental impact of all new activities, products and processes shall be assessed in advance.

3. The impact of current activities on the local environment shall be assessed and monitored, and any significant impact of these activities on the environment in general, shall be examined.

4. Measures necessary to prevent or eliminate pollution, and where this is not feasible, to reduce pollutant emissions and waste generation to the minimum and to conserve resources shall be taken, taking account of possible clean technologies.

5. Measures necessary to prevent accidental emissions of materials or energy shall be taken.

6. Monitoring procedures shall be established and applied, to check compliance with the environmental policy and, where these procedures require measurement and testing, to establish and update records of the results.

7. Procedures and action to be pursued in the event of detection of non-compliance with its environmental policy, objectives or targets, shall be established and updated.

8. Cooperation with the public authorities shall be ensured to establish and update contingency procedures to minimize the impact of any accidental discharges to the environment that nevertheless occur.

9. Information necessary to understand the environmental impact of the company's activities shall be provided to the public, and an open dialogue with the public should be pursued.

10. Appropriate advice shall be provided to customers on the relevant environmental aspects of the handling, use and disposal of the products made by the company.

11. Provisions shall be taken to ensure that contractors working at the site on the company's behalf apply environmental standards equivalent to the company's own. [30]

The European Community Eco-Audit Regulation requires the employment of "an accredited environmental verifier" who "must be independent of the site's auditor" [31] and who is required to check

a. whether the environmental policy has been established and if it meets the requirements of Article 3 and with the relevant requirements in Annex I;

b. whether an environmental management system and programme are in place and operational at the site and whether they comply with the relevant requirements in Annex I;

c. whether the environmental review and audit are carried out in accordance with the relevant requirements in Annex I and II; [and]

d. whether the data and information in the environmental statement are reliable and whether the statement adequately covers all the significant environmental issues of relevance to the site. [32]

The function of the accredited environmental verifier is to certify:

–compliance with all the requirements of this Regulation, particularly concerning the environmental policy, and programme, the environmental review, the functioning of the environmental management system, the environmental audit process and the environmental statements;

–the reliability of the data and information in the environmental statement and whether the statement adequately covers all the significant environmental issues of relevance to the site.

The verifier will:

in particular, investigate in a sound professional manner, the technical validity of the environmental review or audit or other procedures carried out by the company, without unnecessarily duplicating those procedures.

Further:

the verifier will operate on the basis of a written agreement with the company which defines the scope of the work, enables the verifier to operate in an independent professional manner and commits the company to providing the necessary cooperation.

The verification will involve examination of documentation, a visit to the site including, in particular interviews with personnel, preparation of a report to the company management and solution of the issues raised by the report.

The documentation to be examined in advance of the site visit will include basic information about the site and activities there, the environmental policy and programme, the description of the environmental management system in operation at the site, details of the previous environmental review or audit carried out, the report on that review or audit and on any corrective action taken afterwards, and the draft environmental statement.

. . . . The verifier's report to the company management will specify:

a) in general, cases of non-compliance with the provisions of this Regulation, and in particular;

b) technical defects in the environmental review, or audit method, or environmental management system, or any other relevant process;

c) points of disagreement with the draft environmental statement, together with details of the amendments or additions that should be made to the environmental statement. [33]

It is not clear what the verifiers will verify since there are no protocols or standards. Thus, through the back door, regulators will be able to obtain the data that they presently have difficulty obtaining under law.

European Standard EN45012, which deals with accreditation standards, must be taken into account. That standard seems to favor some form of accounting training or background. Note that:

In 1993, a bill will be submitted to the Dutch Parliament to make compulsory the preparation by companies of an annual environmental report, based on the findings of an environmental audit. It is recognized that these reports will have to be verified. It has been suggested that this task should be undertaken by an "environmental accountant"—defined by the Minister of the Environment as "an external expert who controls and certifies the quantitative results of the measurements and records of an environmental report." [Note that this definition is more limited than for environmental verifiers in the draft Eco-Audit Regulation].

"Environmental accountants" are not the same as financial accountants, since they would require broad environmental expertise. But one possibility being mooted is that they would be a legally-recognized branch of the accountancy profession. Many accountancy practices are gearing themselves to take on the new work, and an Association for Environmental Accountants has recently been established.

Environmental NGOs have expressed doubts about the accountancy profession's capacity to take on environmental work. [34]

The U.N. Business Council for Sustainable Development requested the International Standards Organization to undertake a broad environmental standardization effort in preparation for the 1992 U.N. Conference on Environment and Development in Brazil. This resulted in the establishment of the Strategic Advisory Group on the Environment (SAGE) in September 1991. Under the terms of the treaty establishing the European Economic Community (EEC), environmental standards must be developed and implemented. Many member countries would prefer that ISO standards be adopted by the European Community (EC), rather than standards that may already exist in some countries in the Community.

SAGE superseded an ISO group formed in 1990 to address international standardization for eco-labelling. SAGE's charter is to:

1. assess the needs for future international standardization to promote worldwide application of the key elements of sustainable industrial development, including, but not limited to consumer information and eco-labelling; the use and transport of resources, in particular raw materials and energy; and environmental effects during production, distribution, use of products, disposal and recycling;

2. recommend an overall ISO/IEC [International Standards Organization and International Electrotechnical Committee] strategic plan for environmental performance and/or management standardization; including primary objectives, proposed new work items, timing needs and guidance for the inclusion of environmental considerations in product standards and test methods within the existing ISO/IEC technical committee system;

3. report its recommendations to the ISO and IEC Councils.

The SAGE formed workgroups to perform its function. These are:

–Environmental Labelling (Canada as convener)

–Environmental Auditing (Netherlands as convener)

–Environmental Management Systems (British Standards Institution as convener)

–Standards for Environmental Performance Evaluation Standards (USA as convener)

–Life Cycle Analysis (Denmark as convener)

–Environmental Aspects of Product Standards (Germany as convener)

There is a U.S. Technical Advisory Group for SAGE developed by the American National Standards Institute (ANSI).

Some of the SAGE workgroups have begun to develop drafts of standards. ANSI, representing the United States in this matter, believes that this is beyond the scope of the SAGE and submitted a protest letter to the ISO in the spring of 1992. [35] The protest was acknowledged, but no action has yet been taken by the ISO to halt this work. ANSI wrote ISO again in July 1992 on this matter. [36]

The British have an interest in their own agenda. [37] BSI already has an environmental management standard, and is involved in making recommendations to ISO through SAGE for international environmental management systems. They have a significant head start.

Not only will BSI make a lot of money on the worldwide sales of standards documents, but British companies already certified under BS-7750 will have an early edge in international trade. [38]

A proposal to form an ISO Technical Committee (TC) in the area of environment has been circulated to the SAGE subgroups. Such a TC would formalize the activity under ISO rules. The U.S. Technical Advisory Group (US/TAG) for SAGE has made a preliminary decision that a TC should be approved, and that the United States should seek the Secretariat of the TC. If a TC is formed, they will receive the work of SAGE, but are not bound to accept any of it. As the work is proceeding, the effort is mostly driven by Western Europe. A TC would be required to have broader international representation.

EPA is considering a so-called "environmental leadership program," a "voluntary program" which may eventually mandate an outside auditor concept and complex environmental auditing similar to the European schemes, in return for recognition as a "green facility." (See discussion in Chapter 2—New Mechanisms To Assure Environmental Accountability—

Life Cycle Analysis, Sustainable Manufacturing, Full Cost Accounting and EPA Leadership Program.)

The Environmental Assessment Program in General

No single environmental assessment program can apply to all companies, or even to diverse businesses within one company. However, an assessment program should have certain standard characteristics:

- the basic elements of the program should be consistent throughout all divisions (even if the procedures differ);
- the format for developing an assessment program document should be consistent; and
- definitions and terms should be used uniformly in assessments and compliance activities.

An assessment program and its documentation should be considered an ongoing process. Events such as changes in personnel or their responsibilities, changes in regulations, and acquisition of new facilities require updates, revisions, or modifications to procedures. In keeping current, the program not only maintains its effectiveness but also creates an accurate awareness of the current environmental status of all operations and reduces the potential for undesirable surprises.

Description of the Company

The assessment program document should begin with an overview of the company's major characteristics. This description should be detailed enough to provide a clear picture of the company's overall organization, products, and business areas. For a company with only one or two facilities, this could be a facility description. The purpose of the section, however, is to provide an overview of the whole company, by division if appropriate, from a headquarters perspective. It is not a facility-by-facility accounting. Like the rest of the document, this section is designed for basic information and use by the environmental assessor. It should not be so detailed as to preclude easy use. This documentation should also be helpful as part of general environmental management.

The description should include the following information:

- location and description of corporate and divisional headquarters;
- major products or business areas;
- major departments or divisions;
- number and location of facilities;
- corporate organization chart, including the environmental

department, showing lines of responsibility (*see* Appendix A); and

- a table listing each facility by name, principal business area or product, and person responsible for the facility.

Environmental Policy and Organization

The key to a successful assessment program is top-level management support, which is reflected in a formal company policy, as discussed in Chapter 4. In turn, each division of the company should establish a policy consistent with the company's policy.

Each division should also establish an organization to handle environmental matters. The diversity and size of the business areas will dictate the structure of the organization, which should be uniquely tailored to the characteristics of each division.

An environmental organization chart should show the reporting and responsibility relationships of all key environmental staff, including the relationship of the senior environmental person to the line organization. [39] Position descriptions setting forth the roles and functions of key environmental staff should accompany the organization chart. These usually need to be updated regularly. The chart and position descriptions should be included in the assessment program guidance document.

Environmental Categorization of Facilities

The company and its divisions should have a procedure for categorizing facilities with respect to potential environmental impact. Key factors and evaluation criteria may include

- geography (domestic and foreign locations);
- function (for example, major processing facilities, warehouses, and waste disposal facilities);
- operating status (including present, past, and future sites);
- ownership (whether the company owns or only operates the facility);
- age and general condition of the facility;
- pollutant excursion incident history;
- type and quantity of material processed, stored, and disposed;
- past operations or practices;
- proximity to environmentally sensitive areas;
- sensitive local or community factors; and
- presence of environmental staff at the site.

A classification system can then be developed that ranks the facilities according to their potential for creating negative environmental impacts.

After the facilities are categorized, a plan must be developed that specifies how often site visits should be conducted. These plans vary depending on the number of facilities, their categorization, and the resources available to conduct site visits. Each division should develop a plan suiting its own particular requirements.

For example, facilities categorized as posing few or no environmental problems might be listed for review once every three years, or whenever a significant change occurs in a process or in the condition or status of the facility. Facilities categorized as having a low potential for environmental problems could be assessed at least once every two years, or whenever a significant change occurs. Facilities that have potentially serious environmental problems and that could present significant liabilities if they are not reviewed more frequently could be assessed at least once every year. Facilities with the greatest potential for environmental liability should be assessed not more than once every six months, but not less than once every year. This last category rarely applies. A facility might fall into this highest-risk category because of the nature of its processes, operating conditions, or wastes, or because of the perceptions of regulatory authorities or the general public.

Most major facilities should be assessed annually, particularly in view of liability exposure and changing regulatory requirements; less significant facilities can be assessed less frequently. Note that a small facility can still be significant in terms of exposure.

Internal Procedures for Reporting Environmental Matters

As previously discussed (see "Reporting—Management-by-Exception" in Chapter 4), the company should establish internal policies and procedures for reporting significant environmental issues, regulatory activities, and legal actions. These policies and procedures should be included in the environmental assessment procedure. Each division should also establish internal policies and procedures that facilitate compliance with company requirements and ensure timely notification of division management on significant matters. The Oxy procedures previously discussed provide for compliance and timely notification.

The policies and procedures for reporting significant environmental matters should be consistent with other company reporting requirements. The procedures should provide for multi-path reporting to the environmental and legal departments as well as to the finance department, which must account for capital, operating, and maintenance expenditures for environmental projects. The reporting system should flow from the facility level to the division level and then up to company headquarters or, as at

Oxy, through the division and corporate headquarters simultaneously for "significant matters," using the computerized management system.

This type of reporting procedure promotes prompt and complete reporting with appropriate review at all levels of the company and provides reassurance that all legal and environmental departments are using the same database. It also gives management the opportunity to seek legal review at the earliest possible opportunity. This can help the attorney use attorney-client and work-product privileges effectively in investigating possible noncompliance issues. All levels of company management should receive appropriate guidelines on how to request legal advice and how to handle information to ensure the creation of, and maximum protection by, a privilege, although such privileges are very difficult to create and maintain. [40]

The establishment of company-wide internal reporting procedures is also essential if the company is publicly held. The procedures must ensure timely and accurate reporting to the SEC.

Internal Procedures for Recordkeeping

Permits, monitoring reports, corporate policy statements, and other related records are key documents in an effective environmental management program. Well-organized maintenance and ready accessibility of these documents facilitate day-to-day environmental management and help ensure that the needs of the company and the requirements of various statutes and regulations are met. Therefore, the company and all divisions should develop internal procedures for establishing and maintaining effective and efficient recordkeeping systems. Each division should design a system that is tailored to its individual needs and operations but that also sets minimum standards for facility files in the following five areas.

Types of Records to Be Maintained

Environmental record files should contain all documents essential to managing the facility's environmental program. These documents should include

- copies of laws, regulations, permits, corporate policy statements, and other guidelines applicable to the business of the facility or division;
- copies of important correspondence related to the environmental management program; and
- records of monitoring and inspection activities.

Additional documentation may be included as the division deems necessary. The following is a more complete listing of the types of records that the environmental file should contain:

- local, state, and federal laws and regulations affecting the facility;
- permits in effect and applications pending;
- regulatory agency contacts;
- facility layout and process descriptions;
- air emission records, information on waterborne effluents and outfalls, water monitoring data, descriptions of solid wastes and their disposal methods, and waste monitoring data (including manifests);
- past practice descriptions, water supply descriptions, spill control plans, emergency response plans, and disaster plans;
- pertinent correspondence and company/division policies and procedures; and
- routine and nonroutine reports to government agencies.

Central Facility Environmental File

Records should be kept in a central file at each facility. This standard procedure makes it easier to verify the presence or absence of a record. It also ensures that all essential records are readily identifiable and quickly retrievable. When it is not practical to keep some records in the central file (laboratory books and records, for example), a reference folder can be kept in the central file indicating the location of other files. Note that not all of these records need to be maintained in divisional or corporate headquarters, but they should all be accessible. As previously discussed in Chapter 4, computerized database management and environmental management systems can help keep records easily accessible to divisional and corporate management. Environmental files should be organized consistently throughout the division, although file organization need not be identical at all facilities.

Outdated Records

In general, records should be kept at least as long as required by law, regulation, permit, or corporate policy (whichever requires the longest retention). On the other hand, obsolete records and other documents should not be allowed to clutter the environmental file. A division should establish a computerized procedure for identifying appropriate retention times for generic classes of documents and for determining specific disposition schedules for individual records. All records removed from the active environmental file because they are no longer current or needed should be reviewed for appropriate disposition (archives, retention, return to originator, or destruction).

There is no pat recommendation for disposition decisions. Most people keep too much paper in their files. I limited this excess by following an arbitrary rule of refusing to buy new file cabinets. This automatically forces continual review of files in addition to the reductions required by file retention procedures. This arbitrary rule also accelerated removal of the usual clutter of duplicate documents and out-of-date articles, notes, etc., that are no longer beneficial (and probably never were) and that complicate the search for meaningful material. If material has not been used in three years, it is probably not worth keeping. An assessment should be kept at least until the next assessment is conducted and the documentation on an action plan is completed. I recommend a policy of requiring action plans to be completed within one year.

Custodianship and Review

Since environmental records are important to the continued operation of every facility and to the avoidance of corporate liability, it is prudent to assign responsibility for their safekeeping to a member of the environmental management staff or a qualified records manager. An individual other than the custodian should review the records file periodically to ensure adherence to established policies and standards.

Access and Availability

Integrity of the environmental records file is important to ensure that all essential records are intact and readily available for reference as needed. Access to the file and release of information must be controlled. Therefore, the company and all divisions should promulgate policies on access to environmental records and the release of information.

Individual environmental staff members may need working files containing copies of relevant documents in the central file. The same standards regarding access, release of information, and records disposition must be applied to working files as are applied to central files, and the environmental file custodian should have a record of all environmental working files.

Unascertainable Issues

An "unascertainable" issue or problem is one whose nature and extent are uncertain because of insufficient factual, technological, or legal data. On occasion, a number of unascertainable issues, or issues with unascertainable aspects, may be identified at a company's facilities. Unascertainable issues commonly fall into the following general categories:

- Problems of unknown dimension. For example, monitoring wells may detect potentially toxic materials below a facility, but the extent and severity of any risk to health or the environment, as well as the technological options and costs for treatment, may be unknown.
- Environmental issues for which no adequate present-day remedial technology is known.
- Environmental laws or regulations whose implementation is unclear, existing regulations that are presently in litigation, and regulations under consideration that are not as yet approved or promulgated.
- Environmental issues that will require detailed engineering studies to develop solutions and ascertain ultimate compliance costs.

Including unascertainable issues in an assessment program shows that the company knows the issues it faces. The objective in addressing existing unascertainables, as well as those revealed by future assessments, is to identify those issues clearly and plan their resolution. At Occidental, the Environmental, Health, and Safety Committee of the Board is also continually updated as to the status of unascertainable issues.

The Assessment Team

Assessments of individual facilities should be carried out by an assessment team, operating with the full support and authority of management. The team performs the assessment and prepares the report that is the basis for measuring progress toward environmental objectives and for initiating action plans. The assessment team is the heart of the operations phase of the corporate and divisional environmental assessment program.

The size and makeup of an assessment team depends on the size of the facility, the complexity of the environmental issues, and the period of time since the last assessment. The team must have broad knowledge of applicable environmental regulations, policies, and company operations, as well as an understanding of the individual facility's operation, and must be independent of the facility being reviewed. (For a more detailed discussion of the "independence" issue, see "Controversies as to What Is 'Independent' Review" earlier in this chapter.)

There are several ways to ensure independence. Some companies have a large number of personnel who do nothing but audits and who report either to an auditing department or to the legal department. This structure is not necessary to achieve independence. Moreover, it isolates the audit, impeding its best use: as a management tool for operational improvement. The more removed the audit is from the division and the more indirect the auditors' perceived understanding of the operation, the more difficult it becomes to implement the audit recommendations. The desired independence can be achieved by using a team from the division's environmental department, which is separate from operational control. If divisional personnel do the assessment, it is also important to have a separate procedure to ensure independence and action. The procedure utilized at Occidental, described *supra*, provides for review of these audits by an independent corporate group. This ensures that significant issues surface and that appropriate action is taken.

It is helpful to vary at least one member of the team at each assessment. Continuity and understanding of the operation are important, but a fresh point of view is also beneficial.

While there may be times when an outside contractor or lawyer should control an audit, auditing should not be viewed as a full employment program for either group. Indeed, relatively small corporations can easily handle these programs effectively in house with proper initial guidance.

Attorneys should direct and control assessments in specific limited instances, including occasions when enforcement action or litigation has begun or is reasonably contemplated, or a government agency has asked for information. Some companies prefer to have an attorney manage their entire assessment program. The program described here, however, is not run by attorneys, although it allows for attorney control under special circumstances. In most instances, environmental assessment should be a management tool that is not under legal supervision. An attorney should be available to advise each team, however. It is important in all cases that the attorney participate by ensuring that the team understands its responsibilities, including

- its charter and obligations;
- its operating procedures;
- definitions of such basic terms as "violation," "excursion," and "compliance";
- how to deal with areas that are already the subject of litigation;
- how to write reports and what items to include in them; and
- procedures to follow when potential violations exist.

In addition, the attorney should review the team's preliminary reports before they are issued in final form to be sure that items that are or should be subject to attorney-client or work-product privileges are adequately protected. The attorney should also be sure that a follow-up system is in place that will alert him or her if issues arise that require an attorney's expertise and assistance.

Some companies, particularly those that have determined that attempting to conduct assessments under attorney-client privilege may not be worth the effort, are not sure as to the future scope of attorney involvement. There may also be suspicion from environmental management that the attorneys may want to micromanage the assessment. Similarly, the attorneys may assume that every action by the environmental staff will result in potentially significant legal problems.

A good way of diffusing potential conflict and, at the same time, mini-mizing the concerns of both organizations is to have the attorneys actually participate in some representative assessments. (See also discussion in Chapter 8, Dealing With Lawyers.) It is useful for the attorneys to actually see facilities in operation and understand what is, in fact, being assessed. The interaction in the informal setting and informal dress that climbing around a facility or traipsing around the "back forty" requires helps build confidence and understanding. It also allows the lawyers to develop more responsive guides for the client's needs and allows the client to do its job free of unnecessary restrictions from the lawyers.

Conducting the Assessment

Individual site reviews by an assessment team are central to any assessment program. Site assessments determine the status of compliance with federal, state, and local regulations and with company policies and programs on a facility-by-facility basis. Over time, many staff members may be part of assessment teams. Given the constantly changing makeup of the teams, procedures must be in place to ensure that assessments are conducted consistently and properly. The basic operational steps outlined below will standardize the conduct of assessments. As discussed above, legal counsel should be sought throughout the process, particularly when compliance judgments must be made.

Notify the Facility

The facility should be notified of the impending visit. There is usually little to be gained by surprise visits. The timing of the advance notice can vary, but a sufficient interval must be provided to allow the facility to prepare, to collect data, and to ensure staff availability. For large facilities, a pre-visit questionnaire may be used to prepare the site environmental manager and the assessment team for the visit. The questionnaire helps keep disruptions to a minimum by requesting in advance that the facility identify major environmental issues, make certain files available, and schedule key per-sonnel for interviews. However, care should be taken that the facility does not view the assessment as a "checklist" exercise and recognizes that the review will be operationally oriented.

Review Background Material

The assessment team should review pertinent information on the facility, including the response to the pre-visit questionnaire if used, and the results of any previous assessments. These reviews should be done with an eye toward identifying potentially significant impact issues. In the absence of a completed pre-visit questionnaire or past assessment, the team could review the following categories of information to become familiar with site operations:

- facility identification;
- environmental contacts at the facility;
- topographical map or line drawing of the plant and its environs, including all buildings and structures and their uses, all vents and waste collection points, intake and discharge structures, any existing monitoring facilities, nearby water bodies, nearby wetlands and springs, and all drinking water wells on the property and in the vicinity;
- existing federal, state, or local environmental permits issued to the facility, and pending applications for environmental permits;
- compliance schedules, consent orders, judgments, waivers, or variances related to compliance with any environmental law;
- facility operations subject to citation, fine, or civil or criminal suit for violation of environmental requirements; and
- regulated substances used at the facility and locations of storage, processing, and disposal of each substance.

Team Meetings

The assessment team should meet to discuss the background data received and to identify key areas to be highlighted during the site visit. The team should then meet with the division and facility management staff deemed appropriate by the site's environmental manager. The agenda should include an overview of the assessment concept; a brief description of the site's operations; and an overview of the facility's organization, major environmental concerns, training program, public relations, and anticipated regulatory requirements.

Conduct Interviews and Review Files

During the tour of the facility, the team should observe and evaluate general operating practices, interview site operators, and inspect records. The team should follow corporate or divisional guidelines on assessment protocol and methodology. Protocol requires that the visit be conducted in a constructive, nonadversarial fashion because of its sensitive nature. As in other areas, a nonadversarial approach is generally far more effective in obtaining action. If nothing else, it will usually draw out more information. The facility's management should view the assessment as a vehicle for bolstering requests for needed funding, not as a fault-finding expedition. If it views the assessment positively, more information will be volunteered and the operational nature of the review will be improved.

Divisions should have discretion to develop assessment methodology based on their various operations. Different approaches may be appropriate, including:

- Asking a comprehensive list of "yes or no" questions centered on the requirements of the regulations, leaving the team little flexibility. This approach is usually too restrictive and limits the possibility of operational improvements, which is one of the greatest advantages of assessments.
- Posing a series of more general questions in order to determine the general status of the facility.
- Listing areas for review and leaving the questions and response format up to the team. If you have an experienced response team, this approach usually works best.

Develop On-Site and Off-Site Reports

The team should discuss its observations while conducting the assessment, but should meet on site afterwards to develop its findings before presenting any preliminary results. This session should result in a consensus on the potential weak points of the facility's program. Again, to be effective, an assessment should not just focus on compliance but should also be an operational review. The team should write up its findings as an on-site report. Lap-top computers can substantially assist this process. The team should use this on-site report, with preliminary conclusions, to brief the facility's management before the team leaves. This report then serves as a working paper for the team in preparing the final report.

The team should write the off-site, or final, report within one or two weeks after the audit, and the facility's manager should have an opportunity to comment on the final report. If lap-top computers are used, almost the entire assessment report can be completed on site and action plans can be agreed upon without extensive exchange of drafts and reviews. This speeds up the process and minimizes second-guessing.

Benefits of an Environmental Assessment Program

Ensuring Compliance

In view of the array of possible sanctions for violating environmental laws and regulations, it is critical to develop a method for ensuring compliance, or at least for determining whether potential noncompliance problems exist that need to be addressed. Obtaining this information is an essential step toward avoiding civil and criminal liability. The benefit of ensuring compliance is thus a strong incentive to develop and implement an assessment program. Of course, this benefit is not tied solely to an assessment program, but to an overall management system committed to finding significant issues and resolving them.

An environmental assessment program provides one method for determining the status of compliance. It focuses on ensuring early identification of actual or potential compliance problems, ensuring that management is aware of the status of operations, and ensuring appropriate resolution of problems in ways that reduce the risk of inadvertent violations and agency enforcement actions. It must be action-oriented to ensure that problems discovered are eliminated and that no "smoking guns" remain unattended.

The information developed by an assessment program concerning compliance is important for several reasons discussed in the following sections. [41]

☐ *Avoiding Civil and Criminal Liability.* Virtually all of the environmental statutes provide sanctions for noncompliance. These can include civil penalties, criminal fines and imprisonment, injunctions, citizen suits, other actions, and permit or registration suspensions or revocations. There is a growing trend toward criminal prosecution. [42] In addition to the criminal sanctions in the federal environmental statutes, a number of provisions in the U.S. Criminal Code may impose criminal liability in environmental situations. [43]

The environmental laws apply to "persons." Legally, "persons" includes both corporations and individuals acting for corporations, including directors, officers, managers, and all employees. Thus, both corporations and their employees are subject to civil and criminal liability under the environmental laws.

An employee's knowing act can subject both the employee and the corporation to criminal fines. An individual who did not actually participate in an act can also be held criminally liable if that individual approved of the conduct, or negligently or knowingly failed to prevent the violation. Thus, a corporate officer can be held vicariously liable for the conduct of subordinate employees. Purposeful failure to investigate or "deliberate ignorance" has been interpreted as knowledge for purposes of criminal liability.[44] A major benefit of an environmental assessment system "will be the fact that the corporation will be less apt to be prosecuted criminally and less apt to be subjected to punitive damages when sued by private parties."[45] (For additional discussion of criminal issues, see the section on "Criminal Liability Exposure" in Chapter 2.)

☐ *Ensuring Accurate Certifications.* An assessment may provide the basis for certification by a company official of the accuracy and completeness of a permit application. This is a significant benefit because it is important that these certifications be accurate. Some of the environmental statutes requiring permits, such as RCRA and the FWPCA,[46] provide criminal penalties for making false statements on permit applications. Provisions in the U.S. Criminal Code can also apply.[47]

☐ *Ensuring Accurate SEC Disclosures.* Identification of environmental problems also helps ensure that publicly held companies submit timely and accurate reports as required by the securities and exchange laws and regulations. A finding by the SEC that a company has failed to disclose environmentally related matters, thereby deceiving investors, could jeopardize the company's ability to raise capital through new stock offerings or debt instruments. It could also cause the SEC to initiate costly and time-consuming administrative proceedings, which in turn can give rise to shareholders' class actions and derivative suits. Indirect SEC enforcement of environmental laws and regulations is thus potentially more powerful than direct agency enforcement.

Environmentally related matters that the SEC requires to be reported include

- two-year estimates of capital expenditures for environmental compliance, or estimates for a longer period if they have been developed and failure to disclose them would be misleading;
- particular types of environmental proceedings, as described below; and
- under certain circumstances, as described below, company policies or approaches concerning environmental compliance.

Environmental proceedings that must be reported include all administrative or judicial proceedings that arise or are known to be contemplated under any federal, state, or local provisions regulating discharge of materials into the environment, and that fall into any of three categories. First, any private or governmental proceeding that is material to the business or financial condition of the corporation must be reported.[48] Second, any private or governmental proceeding for damages, potential monetary sanctions, capital expenditures, deferred charges, or charges to income is reportable if the amount involved (exclusive of interest and costs) exceeds 10 percent of the current assets of the corporation. [49] Third, any governmental proceeding must be reported if monetary sanctions (exclusive of interest and costs) will or reasonably are expected to exceed $100,000. [50] Stated another way, an environmental proceeding need not be reported if there is a reasonable belief that the proceeding will result in fines of less than $100,000 and is not otherwise material to the business or financial condition of the company.

It is important to remember that reportable environmentally related proceedings are not limited to those initiated by an agency or private individual. Reportable proceedings can include any action, including any rule challenge or request for administrative hearing, initiated by the corporation alone, by the corporation with another company, or by an industry trade association in which the corporation is a named party, if the action meets any of the reporting conditions.

If a company policy is likely to result in enforcement actions and fines, the company must disclose the policy and an estimate of the fines. Even when disclosure or comments concerning a company's environmental policy are not required, any voluntary statements must be accurate.

The SEC's May 1989 interpretative release concerning the disclosure required in Management's Discussion and Analysis of Financial Condition and Results of Operations (MD&A) in SEC filings further details the scope of disclosure. [51] The "MD&A Release states that once management knows of a potentially material environmental problem, it must disclose it unless it can determine that the problem is not reasonably likely to cause a material effect, either because the event is not likely to happen or if it does happen, the effect is not likely to be material." [52] Thus, in preparing SEC filings, data developed during routine assessments and assessments made for acquisition and sale of properties becomes important. "Individuals preparing SEC filings should also be aware that outside consultants as well as inside departments often prepare cost estimates during due diligence reviews for acquisitions and refinancing." [53] Note also that in preparing documentation of the determinations required under the MD&A Release,

> management should be aware that documents prepared during in-house or outside investigations of environmental problems may not be privileged. Even if certain documents are privileged, the facts they contain may ultimately be discovered. Registrants should be careful not to make admissions of liability in documents prepared to facilitate decision-making regarding SEC filings. [54]

EPA and the SEC have a cooperative agreement that allows the SEC access to EPA data to, in essence, audit the adequacy of the data that a company releases. [55] Under the agreement, the SEC has offered to perform "full disclosures" of any corporation for EPA and EPA allows the SEC access to various EPA files. [56] EPA has agreed to provide the SEC with six categories of information on a quarterly basis. The types of information to be provided are:

(1) Names of parties receiving Superfund notice letters, identifying them as potentially liable for the cost of a Superfund cleanup (source: Superfund enforcement tracking system);

(2) List of all filed (but not concluded) RCRA and CERCLA cases (source: Consolidated Enforcement Docket);

(3) List of all recently concluded civil cases under federal environmental laws (source: Consolidated Enforcement Docket);

(4) List of all filed criminal cases under federal environmental laws (source: Criminal Enforcement Docket);

(5) List of all facilities barred from government contractors under the Clean Water Act and the Clean Air Act; and

(6) List of all RCRA facilities subject to cleanup requirements (source: Corrective Action Reporting System). [57]

In exchange, the SEC stated it would "consider targeting Environmental Disclosures" for its enforcement efforts, according to an EPA source. [58] Representatives of both agencies will continue to work toward a more formal agreement governing the exchange of information between the two agencies. [59]

Other Benefits

Ensuring compliance is one of the most important and useful purposes of an environmental assessment program and good environmental management programs in general. Assessments, along with other environmental management programs, also provide other benefits. Both the risk of liability exposure and the need to develop good management systems should encourage even small organizations to implement some system ensuring that management is made aware of potential problems and is committed to solving them. Moreover, taking care of your problems now, using an environmental assessment program as part of an overall system, is cost-effective, and will reduce longer term liability and environmental costs. Environmental assessments are especially beneficial in the specific areas discussed below.

☐ *Business Planning.* Environmental considerations can play a significant role in a company's business planning, including financial planning; planning for new product lines, new business lines, and modifications or expansions of current operations; and risk management. An environmental assessment program provides both corrective and preventive assistance by identifying potential problem areas and new restrictions that may require immediate or long-term capital or operating expenditures.

New products may be subject to current or proposed regulations that may affect production costs and marketing ability. For example, a new chemical substance may be subject to a TSCA §5(e) order limiting its use or requiring very extensive safety restrictions on its manufacture or processing. [60] A good environmental assessment program would identify these constraints, which would have to be factored into the company's economic considerations.

Environmental considerations are also important factors in acquisitions and divestitures. By helping to identify and evaluate environmental contingencies, an assessment can provide information on which assets should be sold and on whether to buy all or part of another company. Chapter 6 discusses acquisition review in detail.

Modification or expansion of an existing operation can also trigger significant environmental issues. A new facility, whether in an attainment or a nonattainment area, may require extensive preconstruction review under the Clean Air Act, for example. [61] Locating a facility on or near a former waste disposal site may result in expensive and long-term remedial measures. A good environmental assessment program will detect these potential problems. As noted previously, Occidental also keeps track of much of this information through its computerized management system.

As liability insurance becomes increasingly important and difficult to obtain, an environmental assessment program can assist risk management decisionmaking regarding the amounts and types of insurance coverage needed. For example, RCRA requires "financial assurance" from owners or operators of hazardous waste treatment, storage, or disposal facilities to cover closure and post-closure care, as well as liabilities arising from accidents. The assessment program can help provide the information necessary to secure these financial assurances through insurance, bonds, or other methods acceptable to the agencies.

☐ *Employee Development.* Assessments can raise employee consciousness regarding the importance of compliance and the risks of noncompliance. This increased awareness can improve environmental performance. Employees' performance in ensuring and maintaining compliance can also be assessed and used as a factor in evaluating employees for salary increases and promotions. Finally, a clearly identified and implemented environmental program can help employee morale and recruitment.

☐ *Public Relations.* An assessment program can provide the basis for positive public relations when no problems exist, or when problems are found but are promptly and effectively corrected. Indeed, the very existence of an assessment program can be a public relations advantage. A company will also be able to respond promptly to the media in an emergency or crisis arising from an environmental incident, since the assessment program will provide readily available information. Although a public relations effort does not itself solve any environmental problem, it can help improve a bad image resulting from an actual or perceived poor environmental compliance record. A bad image can result in unwanted press and media attention, tie up management time responding to inquiries, and adversely affect sales and stock values.

☐ *Management of Legislative and Regulatory Affairs.* The knowledge environmental assessments provide about a company's operations, including problems and compliance status, can be of great help in evaluating the impact of new environmental laws and regulations. This can enable the company to comment effectively on, or even to challenge, the constant stream of laws and regulations being proposed and enacted.

Legal Exposure

In my judgment, legal exposure is the biggest "red herring" discouraging some companies from implementing audit systems and other management programs that document problems. The "smoking gun" is every attorney's nightmare, but basically smoking guns are problems only if undiscovered or uncorrected. You still have legal concerns after discovery and correction, but dealing with the issue is usually the best way to minimize potential liability and is unlikely to increase that liability. Of course, this means that the decision to implement a program that may disclose problems must also be a decision to do something about those problems. [62]

While initial auditing programs and other information-based management programs should be developed cautiously, the benefits of review in reducing present and future liabilities far outweigh potential legal risks. My experience indicates that significant legal problems rarely arise in assessments, partly because assessments deal with many areas that the law already requires to be reported to agencies, such as permit excursions. Legal problems that do arise can be handled easily if counsel ensures that the assessment team understands its responsibilities, particularly how to deal with areas in litigation, how to write and what to include in reports, and what procedures to follow when potential violations exist. [63] Assessment teams need not run their reports by the lawyers in an effort to create attorney-client privilege or attorney work-product privilege. In many cases it is doubtful that claims of privilege could prevail anyway. [64] The primary concern is to use the reports as management tools, avoiding the possibility "that the Law Department could become a bottleneck, and thus impede corrective action." [65]

Indeed, far from increasing legal exposure, assessment programs can decrease that exposure. Assessments encourage discovery and correction of problems. In addition, as previously discussed, substantial precedent indicates that corporate officers can be held vicariously liable for the conduct of subordinate employees. As mentioned previously, purposeful failure to investigate or deliberate ignorance has been interpreted to be knowledge for purposes of criminal liability. [66] Assessment programs are one way to acquire the information you need to avoid this liability.

There is also a growing trend toward expanding tort liability laws throughout the country to impose what could be called "absolute liability," regardless of fault, for injuries caused by products or exposure to allegedly hazardous or carcinogenic substances. Moreover, EPA is developing a law enforcement program with a special focus on hazardous waste issues and existing consent decrees, and is hiring criminal investigators at headquarters and for each region. These potential legal exposures increase the need for awareness and strong compliance programs.

Note also that,

> as a practical matter, because in-house counsel are frequently called upon to provide business as well as legal advice with respect to matters under investigation, it may be difficult for in-house counsel to establish and maintain the privilege. This problem is exacerbated when information obtained in the internal investigation is shared by in-house counsel with auditors, accountants, underwriters and corporate officials not involved in the defense of the case. Waiver of the privilege is likely in these situations. [67] Moreover, the government is both more alert to the potential for waiver where in-house counsel is handling the internal investigation, and more disposed to press the issue. This point is underscored by the following statement of the Director of the Division of Enforcement of the Securities and Exchange Commission at the time of the 1982 Annual Meeting of the ABA Section of Corporation, Banking and Business Law:

>> The Commission staff will be inquisitive when examining whether the privilege or the work product protections have been correctly established and maintained by house counsel. This curiosity does not reflect disrespect for the important role of house counsel; rather it is a recognition

of the practical difficulties that are inherent in their attempts to establish and to preserve privileged communications and work product materials.

Where a waiver has occurred, counsel could well be sought by the government as a witness in the case. Notes, memoranda and other attorney work product would be subject to production in such circumstances. [68]

Government Involvement in Environmental Auditing—EPA's Policy Statement and State Regulation

Environmental auditing, originally designed as a management tool, is now drawing regulatory attention. After much review and consideration, EPA issued its policy statement on environmental auditing, effective July 9, 1986. [69] In sum, it is EPA policy to encourage regulated entities to use environmental auditing to help achieve and maintain compliance with environmental laws and regulations, as well as to help identify and correct unregulated environmental hazards. The policy statement specifically

- encourages regulated entities to develop, implement, and upgrade environmental auditing programs;
- discusses when EPA may request audit reports;
- explains how EPA's inspection and enforcement activities may respond to regulated entities' efforts to assure compliance through auditing;
- endorses environmental auditing at federal facilities;
- encourages state and local environmental auditing initiatives; and
- outlines elements of effective audit programs. EPA cautions, however, that "the existence of an auditing program does not create any defense to, or otherwise limit, the responsibility of any regulated entity to comply with applicable regulatory requirements." [70]

EPA and Environmental Audits

EPA's policy statement is its first formal endorsement of environmental auditing programs. In defining environmental audits and outlining their many potential benefits, EPA is quick to point out that audits do not replace regulatory agency inspections or activities required by law (such as emissions monitoring). In encouraging audits, EPA specifically states that it will not interfere with or dictate environmental management practices and that it wants auditing to remain voluntary. As discussed *infra* in this chapter, there is a contrary trend in some states. EPA's policy does not rule out the possibility that EPA may request audit reports, but it acknowledges that routine requests would inhibit auditing programs. Thus, EPA will not make routine requests but will use a case-by-case approach instead.

EPA has indicated that it will consider a new policy of its own following the issuance of the Department of Justice Policy on July 1, 1991 (discussed in Chapter 2). It seems likely that EPA will follow the Department of Justice policy, which should not be a major change from EPA's existing policy.

☐ *Standards for Requesting Audit Reports.* What standards does EPA use to determine whether it will request an audit report in a particular case? The policy states that EPA will seek a report "where [it] determines it is needed to accomplish a statutory mission, or where the Government deems it to be material to a criminal investigation." [71] EPA "expects such requests to be limited, most likely focused on particular information needs rather than the entire report, and usually made where the information needed cannot be obtained from monitoring, reporting or other data otherwise available . . . ." [72]

Several "illustrative" examples are set forth:

- audits would be requested if called for by a consent decree or other settlement agreement;
- audits would be requested if a company places its management practices at issue by raising them as a defense; and
- audits would be requested if state of mind or intent is a relevant element of inquiry, as in a criminal investigation.

☐ *Mandatory Auditing.* EPA states that it will not mandate auditing, but there are exceptions to this rule. Specifically, EPA may require auditing as part of a settlement. EPA notes that it is developing guidance for structuring appropriate environmental audit provisions for use in settlement negotiations and consent decrees. [73] According to the policy, mandated auditing is most likely when a pattern of violations can be attributed to the absence or poor results of an environmental management system or when the type or nature of violations indicates that similar problems may exist or occur. [74]

Elements of Effective Environmental Auditing Programs

An appendix to EPA's policy statement identifies seven elements as those most likely to result in an effective program. These elements are as follows:

- explicit top management support for environmental auditing and commitment to follow up on audit findings;
- an environmental auditing function independent of audited activities;
- adequate team staffing and auditor training;

- explicit audit program objectives, scope, resources, and frequency;
- a process that collects, analyzes, interprets, and documents information and is sufficient, reliable, relevant, and useful to achieve audit objectives;
- a process that includes specific procedures to prepare prompt, candid, clear, and appropriate written reports on audit findings, corrective actions, and implementation schedules; and
- a process that includes quality control procedures to assure accuracy and thoroughness. [75]

If properly implemented, the environmental assessment program outlined in this chapter will meet or surpass EPA's standards of effectiveness in all these categories. See also discussion on International Environmental Auditing Standards in Chapter 5 and EPA Leadership Program in Chapter 2.

Effects on the Regulated Community

EPA has stated that an audit program will not result in any agreement to decrease the frequency of inspections, to reduce enforcement, or to give any other incentives. The policy statement does indicate, however, that an audit program should help an entity improve its environmental performance. Improved environmental performance should result in fewer EPA inspections to the extent that this performance is a factor in scheduling those inspections. Also, EPA's enforcement policy considers efforts to avoid and promptly correct environmental problems. If an audit program furthers those efforts, "EPA may exercise its discretion" in making enforcement decisions. [76]

EPA's policy statement thus does not promise less enforcement oversight or fewer inspections, as EPA had contemplated during the developmental phase. However, it does not appear that an entity implementing an audit program will be any worse off than before. The policy is EPA's first formal statement recognizing that an entity with a properly implemented program and good follow-up for identified problems will be in a better compliance position, and that EPA will therefore find fewer problems when it exercises its discretion to look at that entity's operations.

EPA's position that it may seek copies of audit reports only states what has always been the case: that these reports could be subject to EPA inquiry. The policy thus reinforces the importance of making sure that auditors are properly trained, both in the technical aspects of conducting the audits and in report writing, to avoid unnecessary problems caused by unartful drafting. Nothing in EPA's policy reduces the protection afforded by the attorney-client privilege if audits and reports are conducted and prepared so as to be subject to that protection. [77]

The benefits of environmental auditing programs were demonstrated in many businesses before EPA formally sanctioned these programs and EPA's policy does not change these benefits. It seems reasonable to say that EPA's policy statement places a federal imprimatur on environmental auditing, and recognizes the benefits and uses of this environmental management tool.

State Involvement in Environmental Auditing

Recently, the states have shown some interest in environmental auditing. While EPA has recognized that auditing is basically a management tool, some states have viewed it as a new area for regulation.

The State of California has taken the view that if companies are to engage in environmental auditing, they should have qualified people available. The state reasoned that many smaller companies do not have the expertise to determine who is qualified to conduct an environmental assessment. Registration of environmental assessors and publication of their qualifications provide a basis for that determination. However, rather than creating a "consultants' full employment act" by making the use of registered assessors mandatory, the state instead provided for "voluntary registration of environmental assessors." [78] In order to become a registered environmental assessor, an applicant must show through "academic training, occupational experience, and reputation" that he is "qualified to objectively conduct one or more aspects of an environmental assessment." The law recognizes that these qualifications can be found in members of a number of professions, such as, "but . . . not . . . limited to, specialists trained as analytical chemists, professional engineers, epidemiologists, hydrologists, attorneys with expertise in hazardous substance law, physicians, industrial hygienists, toxicologists, and environmental program managers." If an applicant demonstrates the appropriate experience, including five years of full-time experience in his general field of expertise within the last eight years and two years of substantial experience in performing environmental assessments within the last four years, and provides three or more references "who as employers or clients can attest to the accuracy of the evidence provided by the applicant, to the applicant's professional character, or both," [79] the state will register the applicant. The state plans to publish a directory of registered environmental assessors. All of Occidental's corporate environment and safety staff, including myself, were registered environmental assessors in California.

California has basically taken a sensible approach to this issue. It has recognized a core of professionals whom companies are free to use or not to use, but has not gotten in the way of the functional use of assessments. The concern of many environmental professionals has been *mandatory* use of so-called registered or certified assessors as the only assurance of "independent" review. There are clearly ways to ensure independence without requiring the unnecessary expense of hiring an outside contractor who may not be attuned to the best means of solving a problem within a corporate culture, can create unnecessary legal expense, and can interfere with good management practices. Many professionals are concerned that such mandatory use might stop assessment programs in their tracks. If outside contractors will increase companies' costs substantially and cannot really be integrated into the management use of audits, regulation will kill the practice it is trying to protect. EPA and California have specifically recognized this by avoiding mandatory registration and mandatory audits or standards.

Unfortunately, legislation such as that proposed in New Jersey could bring reality to the environmental manager's worst nightmare. The proposed New Jersey Environmental Audit Review Act, A. 1822, would establish a program for examination and certification of environmental auditors. The proposed New Jersey qualification requirements are more restrictive than those in California, but do recognize that in-house personnel can be utilized. The proposed bill would require industrial establishments, as defined by the New Jersey Environmental Cleanup Responsibility Act, [80] to be audited annually by a certified auditor until closed, terminated, or transferred. The bill also mandates the scope of audit and provides for public disclosure. The State of Delaware had a bill pending that will require companies and those that are held out as auditors to pass tests and certain certification proceedings. [81] Environmental managers will obviously be following these developments and the progress of future efforts to mandate auditing and/or use of certified auditors.

Notes to Chapter 5

1. EPA has published a bibliography of articles on auditing and environmental management. The ANNOTATED BIBLIOGRAPHY ON ENVIRONMENTAL AUDITING (Mar. 1988) is available from EPA's Office of Enforcement and Compliance Monitoring. The following discussion is adapted by permission of Clark Boardman Company, Ltd., from Friedman & Giannotti, *Environmental Self-Assessment*, in LAW OF ENVIRONMENTAL PROTECTION §7.05 (S. Novick ed. 1987). All use rights reserved by Clark Boardman Company, Ltd., 435 Hudson Street, New York, New York 10014.

2. Friedman, *Organizing and Managing Effective Corporate Environmental Protection Programs*, ENVTL. F., May 1984, at 40; Kent, *Internal Environmental Review Programs—Pitfalls and Benefits*, J. WATER POLLUTION CONTROL FED'N, Mar. 1985, at 1.

3. *See* Blumenfeld & Haddad, *Beyond the Battleground: A (Non) Regulatory Perspective on Environmental Auditing* (EPA Draft 1983), *reprinted in* ENVIRONMENTAL AUDITING HANDBOOK: A GUIDE TO CORPORATE AND ENVIRONMENTAL RISK MANAGEMENT (L. Harrison ed. 1984); *see also* Kent, *supra* note 2.

4. Occidental has a unique dual system of reporting to an Executive Vice President and to an Environmental Health and Safety Committee consisting of two outside directors who are on the Executive Committee of the Board of Directors.

5. Blumenfeld & Haddad, *supra* note 3.

6. Olin Chemical Corporation, for example, follows this approach.

7. Friedman, *supra* note 2; Kent, *supra* note 2.

8. In addition, it describes some basic documentation that is useful for general management.

9. The following is adapted from Friedman, *Environmental Auditing in the 1990s*, 1 ENVTL. AUDITOR 229 (1990), and Friedman, *Don't Sign the Valdez Principles*, ENVTL. F., Mar./Apr. 1990, at 32.

10. Riesel, *Criminal Prosecution and the Regulation of the Environment*, 1993 A.L.I.-A.B.A. COURSE OF STUDY-ENVTL LAW 565. Such audits "should have significant lawyer participation in the design, supervision and actual conduct of the audit." *Id.* In this instance, legal protection is particularly important and it is argued that "the employment of outside counsel takes the audit out of the scope of an ordinary business endeavor and transforms it into the gathering of facts to support the rendering of legal advice." *Id.* at 564.

11. OFFICE OF TECHNOLOGY ASSESSMENT, COMING CLEAN—SUPERFUND PROBLEMS CAN BE SOLVED, Option 25 (Oct. 1989).

12. This language has been significantly revised in the most recent version of the Principles, which have been renamed the CERES Principles. *See* Chapter 4, notes 11-20 and accompanying text.

Co-op America, an activist group urging "boycotts" and "activist information campaigns" to get corporations to sign the Valdez Principles, indicates that *"Using the Valdez Principles, you and I will now be able to say 'STOP' to corporations who make their profits by raping the Earth."* Its analysis of the audit provisions, sent to its members, is as follows: "Under this plan, each company which supports the principles must agree to undergo an environmental audit every year. Just like a financial audit, an outside, independent professional will measure a company's impact on the environment, and assess how well they comply with the Principles. *These audit ratings will be made public.* That's what makes the Valdez Principles so revolutionary: full disclosure of their environmental record to all of a corporation's stakeholders. Already, the Valdez Principles coalition is working with professionals in the accounting and environmental engineering fields to design these unique audits" (emphasis in original).

13. CERCLA §107(b)(3), 42 U.S.C. §9607(b)(3), ELR Stat. CERCLA §107(b)(3). See discussion in Chapter 6.

14. *Industry Group Seeks New Certification Standards,* Inside EPA Superfund Report, May 9, 1990, at 8.

15. Board of Certified Safety Professionals Code of Professional Conduct:

Purpose
This Code sets forth the principles and standards of professional conduct to be observed by holders of documents of certification conferred by The Board of Certified Safety Professionals.

Principles
Certificants shall, in their professional activities, sustain and advance the integrity, honor and prestige of the Safety Profession by:
1. Using their knowledge and skill for the enhancement of the safety and health of people and the protection of property and the environment.
2. Being honest and impartial, and serving the public, employees, employers and clients with fidelity.
3. Striving to increase their own competence and the prestige of the safety profession.
4. Avoiding circumstances where compromise of professional conduct or conflict of interest may arise.

Standards
Certificants shall:
1. Hold paramount the safety and health of people and the protection of property and the environment in performance of professional duties and exercise their obligation to advise employers, clients or appropriate authorities of danger to people, property or the environment.
2. Perform professional services and assignments only in areas of their competence.
3. Issue public statements only in an objective and truthful manner.

4. Act in professional matters for employers or clients as faithful agents or trustees.

5. Build their professional reputation on merit of service.

6. Strive for continuous self-development while participating in their chosen professional safety discipline.

16. Standards for the Professional Practice of Internal Auditing

1. Assessors must be independent of the facilities and organizations they are assessing and be objective in performing the assessment.

2. Assessments shall be performed with proficiency and due professional care.

3. Assessments shall be conducted by personnel who have the relevant professional experience, technical knowledge and skills in the disciplines needed to perform the assessment.

4. The scope of the assessment shall encompass the examination and evaluation of the appropriateness, adequacy and effectiveness of the organization's management system and the quality of performance in carrying out assigned responsibilities.

5. Assessment work shall include planning of the assessment, examining and evaluating information, communicating results and following up to ascertain that appropriate action is taken on reported assessment findings.

6. Assessment programs shall include quality assurance elements for the evaluation of the conduct of assessments.

17. *ASTM Environmental Committee Ok's Innocent Landowner Standard*, INSIDE EPA SUPERFUND REPORT, Nov. 18, 1992, at 27.

18. *Id.*

19. *Id.*

20. *Id.*

21. *Id.*

22. *Id.*

23. Jacobellis v. Ohio, 378 U.S. 184, 197 (1964).

24. Available from GEMI at 2000 L St. NW, Suite 710, Washington D.C., 202-296-7449.

25. *Environment Today*, July 20, 1992, at 3.

26. *See generally* Gerardo & Wasserman, *Proceedings of 2nd International Conference on Environmental Enforcement*, Budapest, Hungary, (Sept. 22-23, 1992) (closing remarks).

27. The British Standard is available from the British Standards Institute, 2 Park Street, London, W1A 2BS.

28. *Id.*

29. For a detailed analysis, see F. William Brownell, Hunton & Williams, The European Community Eco-Audit Regulation (1993) (unpublished Memorandum, on file with Hunton & Williams, Washington, D.C.).

30. Proposal for a Council Regulation (EEC) Allowing Voluntary Participation by Companies in the Industrial Sector in a Community Eco-Management and Audit Scheme at 15, available as an attachment to F. William Brownell, Hunton & Williams, The European Community Eco-Audit Regulation (1993) (unpublished Memorandum, on file with Hunton & Williams, Washington, D.C.).

31. *Id.* at 4.

32. *Id.* at 4.

33. *Id.* at 20.

34. BAILLIE AND WILKINSON, ACCREDITATION OF ENVIRONMENTAL VERIFIERS IN THE FRAMEWORK OF THE PROPOSED ECO-AUDIT SCHEME, (1992) (published by the Institute for European Environmental Policy).

35. Note, as previously discussed, that the Environmental Management Standard is being developed by the British Standards Institute (BSI). "And it's no coincidence that BSI has also developed a British environmental management standard (BS-7750). But that's where the trouble starts. 'The Americans are saying the British are pushing their own agenda,' according to Steven P. Cornish, program administrator, standards technology secretary, US/TAG-SAGE (ANSI, NY)." Global EHS Standards Setting Gets Political, 3 ENV'T, HEALTH & SAFETY MGMT. 2 (Oct. 12, 1992).

36. *Id.* "According to Cornish, and to some internal memoranda being circulated, US participants felt strongly that the British SAGE group is not only going too fast, but was also exceeding its mandate by actually beginning to write standards. The role of SAGE advisory bodies, they say, is strategic only. At some point, technical standards-writing bodies will be convened for each standard, as has been traditional when ISO develops standards. 'The SAGE subgroups are not properly set up to actually write standards,' Cornish observes." *Id.*

37. *Id.*

38. According to Steven P. Cornish, program administrator, standards technology secretary, US/TAG-SAGE (ANSI, NY), *Id.* at 1, 2.

39. A sample organization chart is included as Appendix A.

40. It is beyond the scope of this book to discuss the attorney-client privilege in detail. Very briefly, the privilege is designed to protect confidential communications between an attorney and a client from forced disclosure, thus allowing a client to confide in an attorney, secure in the knowledge that no information will be disclosed. The privilege does not include everything arising from the existence of an attorney-client relationship. It is an exception to rules requiring full disclosure and therefore will be construed narrowly. The privilege applies to communications relating to facts of which the attorney was informed for the primary purpose of

securing either an opinion on law or legal services or assistance in some legal proceeding.

> Communications between corporate counsel and the company's employees for the purpose of obtaining information relevant to legal matters as to which counsel must advise the company are subject to the company's attorney-client privilege. Upjohn Co. v. United States, 449 U.S. 383 (1981). This principle applies to former as well as current employees of the company. *In re* Coordinated Pretrial Proceedings in Petroleum Products Antitrust Litigation, 658 F.2d 1355 (9th Cir. 1981), *cert. denied*, 455 U.S. 990 (1982). Communications between employees and in-house counsel stand on the same legal footing as those between employees and outside counsel. In re LTV Securities Litigation, 89 F.R.D. 595, 601 (N.D. Tex. 1989).

Bennett, Rauh & Kriegel, *The Role of Internal Investigations in Defending Against Charges of Corporate Misconduct*, CRIMINAL ENFORCEMENT OF ENVIRONMENTAL LAWS 132 (ALI/ABA) (Apr. 1990).

In an extensive article detailing the criminal implications of environmental law, Dan Riesel clearly spells out the very narrow limitations of attorney-client privilege and the work product doctrine, concluding that "[o]nly where counsel conducts an audit to assist him in the defense of a specific case would it appear that the audit is safe from disclosure pursuant to a subpoena duces tecum." Riesel, *Criminal Prosecution and the Regulation of the Environment*, 1991 A.L.I./A.B.A. COURSE OF STUDY—ENVTL. L. 375, 379, 421-23.

Prosecutors argue that the attorney-client privilege is narrowly construed. Mr. Riesel further notes that

> [s]ince the doctrine only applies to legal advice and not to underlying facts, it is contended by the government that the doctrine does not apply to the data on which audits are based or to the fact that management was aware of such data. Thus, the government argues that the privilege should not be considered an umbrella to cover all the information that an attorney acquires in the course of his representation. If the audit was prepared by or for management and is simply transmitted to counsel, it is clear that the doctrine does not apply. Moreover, to the extent that the audit identifies ongoing violations, the audit arguably is evidence of an ongoing crime and thus loses any protection that it might otherwise have.

Id. at 422-23 (citations omitted). *See* Bennett, Rauh & Kriegel, *supra*.

As noted *supra*, it is very difficult to establish this privilege in an environmental assessment context. *See* United States v. Chevron U.S.A., Inc., No. 88-6681, 1989 U.S. Dist. LEXIS 12267 (E.D. Pa., Oct. 16, 1989) *cited in Courts Require Disclosure of Environmental Audits*, ENVTL. MANAGER, Mar. 1993, at 8 (holding that an audit must be disclosed although an attorney was present at the audit because it was not shown that the attorney was present in his capacity as attorney rather than simply as a business advisor). For a detailed description of the privilege, see the references in note 64, *infra*.

41. For specific examples of the potential benefits of environmental audits, see *Benefits of Environmental Auditing: Case Examples* (Dec. 1984), prepared for EPA and available from EPA's Office of Enforcement and Compliance Monitoring.

42. *See generally* Greenhouse, *Responsibility for Job Safety*, N.Y. TIMES, June 25, 1985, at 30.

43. *See, e.g.*, 18 U.S.C. §§2 (Aiders and Abettors), 3 (Accessory After the Fact), 4 (Concealment of Knowledge), 371 (Conspiracy), 1001 (False Statements), 1341 (Mail Fraud), and 1505 (Obstruction of Agency Proceedings).

44. *See* RCRA §3008(f), 42 U.S.C. §6928(f), ELR STAT. RCRA §3008(f) (setting forth special rules for establishing criminal liability for a knowing endangerment violation).

45. Kent, *supra* note 2, at 193.

46. RCRA §3008(d)-(f), 42 U.S.C. §6928(d)-(f), ELR STAT. RCRA §3008(d)-(f); FWPCA §309(c), 33 U.S.C. §1319(c), ELR STAT. FWPCA §309(c).

47. *See, e.g.*, United States v. Johnson & Towers, Inc., 741 F.2d 662, 14 ELR 20634 (3d Cir. 1984), *cert. denied*, 469 U.S. 1208 (1985); RCRA §3008(f), 42 U.S.C. §6928(f), ELR STAT. RCRA §3008(f).

48. 17 C.F.R. §229.103(5)(A) (1991).

49. 17 C.F.R. §229.103(5)(B) (1991).

50. 17 C.F.R. §229.103(5)(C) (1991).

51. 54 Fed. Reg. 22427 (May 24, 1989). For a detailed discussion of this release and SEC reporting in general, see Archer, McMahon & Crough, *SEC Reporting of Environmental Liabilities*, 20 ELR 10105 (Mar. 1990).

52. 54 Fed. Reg. at 22427; *see also* Chapter 4, notes 7-9 and accompanying text.

53. Archer et al., *supra* note 51, at 10107.

54. *Id.* at 10108.

55. Harrelson, *EPA Agrees to Information Exchange with SEC*, INSIDE EPA SUPERFUND REPORT, Mar. 28, 1990, at 2. *See also* Benham, *SEC, EPA Team Go After Polluters*, Investor's Daily, May 29, 1990, at 1; *Companies Tackle Environmental Disclosures*, Investor's Daily, May 30, 1990, at 1.

56. Harrelson, *supra* note 55, at 2.

57. *Id.*

58. *Id.*

59. *Id.*

60. *See* 15 U.S.C. §2604(e), ELR STAT. TSCA §5(e).

61. 42 U.S.C. §§7401-7671q, ELR STAT. CAA §§101-618.

62. *See also Environmental Audits: Not for the Halfhearted*, ENVTL. MANAGER, July 1990, at 3; Kane, *Environmental Auditing: A Sound Risk If Done Right*, HAZARDOUS WASTE & TOXIC TORTS L. & STRATEGY, May 1990, at 1.

63. *See* Giannotti, *Advising the Corporate Client on Environmental Compliance*, 13 A.B.A. CORP. COMPLIANCE INST. (July 9-10, 1983); *see also* Gibson & Farenthold, *New Perspectives on Corporate Risk and Ways to Reduce It*, ENVTL. F., Mar. 1983, at 35, 37-44.

64. *See* WEISS, ISSUES OF CONFIDENTIALITY AND DISCLOSURE IN ENVIRON-MENTAL AUDITING (EPA Office of Standards and Regulations, Regulatory Reform Staffs, Nov. 1983); ABA American Presentations by D.A. Giannotti to the American Bar Association (1983) and to McKenna, Conner & Cuneo (1985); Frost & Siegel, *Environmental Audits: How to Protect Them From Disclosure*, 5 Toxics L. Rep. (BNA) 1211 (1991); Riesel, *supra* note 40, at 422-23.

65. Kent, *supra* note 2, at 192.

66. The Restatement of Torts has adopted the view that "[c]ompliance with a legislative enactment or an administrative regulation does not prevent a finding of negligence where a reasonable man would take additional precautions." RESTATE-MENT (SECOND) OF TORTS §288(c). While the Restatement view is not necessarily the view of many states, it does indicate potential additional exposure.

67. *See, e.g.,* John Doe Corp. v. United States, 675 F.2d 482 (2d Cir. 1982), *cited in* Bennett, Rauh & Kriegel, *supra* note 40, at 132.

68. Bennett, Rauh & Kriegel, *supra* note 40.

69. 51 Fed. Reg. 25004 (1986). The policy is included as Appendix C.

70. *Id.*

71. *Id.* at 25007.

72. *Id.* Note also the Joint Explanatory Statement of the Committee of Conference on the Clean Air Act Amendments of 1990, H.R. REP. No. 952, 101st Cong., 2d Sess. 348:

> Nothing in subsection 113(c) is intended to discourage owners or operators of sources subject to this Act from conducting self-evaluations or self-audits and acting to correct any problems identified. On the contrary, the environmental benefits from such review and prompt corrective action are substantial and section 113 should be read to encourage self-evaluation and self-audits.
>
> Owners and operators of sources are in the best position to identify deficiencies and correct them, and should be encouraged to adopt procedures where internal compliance audits are performed and management is informed. Such internal audits will improve the owners' and operators' ability to identify and correct problems before, rather than after, government inspections and other enforcement actions are needed.
>
> The criminal penalties available under subsection 113(c) should not

be applied in a situation where a person, acting in good faith, promptly reports the results of an audit and promptly acts to correct any deviation. Knowledge gained by an individual solely in conducting an audit or while attempting to correct any deficiencies identified in the audit or the audit report itself should not ordinarily form the basis of the intent which results in criminal penalties.

This federal forbearance may not extend to citizen group litigation or litigation between potentially responsible parties (PRPs) in Superfund or related litigation. Under Superfund, PRPs include: (1) the owner and operator of a vessel or facility; (2) any person who owned or operated any facility at the time of disposal of any hazardous substance; (3) transporters of hazardous substances; and (4) generators of hazardous substances. CERCLA §107(a)(1)-(4); 42 U.S.C. §9607(a)(1)-(4); ELR STAT. CERCLA §107(a)(1)-(4).

73. 51 Fed. Reg. at 25007 (1986).

74. *Id.*

75. *Id.* at 25008-09.

76. *Id.* at 25007.

77. *But see supra* note 64.

78. CAL. HEALTH & SAFETY CODE §§25570-25570.4, as implemented in CAL. ADMIN. CODE 19030-19032.

79. *Id.*

80. N.J. STAT. ANN. §§13:1K-6 TO -28.

81. *Industry Group Seeks New Certification Standards, supra* note 13, at 9.

Chapter 6:
Review of Acquisitions

Reviewing acquisitions is one of the most important responsibilities of today's environmental managers and environmental counsel. Members of both disciplines put their jobs on the line in estimating the environmental exposure of acquisitions. For example, the scope of liability for past disposal actions of any type is extremely broad and the current owner of a facility from which there is a release or threat of release is strictly liable without regard to causation. [1]

The determination of "owner" or "operator" is extremely broad, in some cases vitiating traditional concepts of corporate liability. There is no clear definition of these terms under either the Comprehensive Environmental Response, Compensation, and Liability Act (CERCLA) or the Resource Conservation and Recovery Act (RCRA). One decision by a federal court of appeals held that a corporate officer could not be found liable under CERCLA unless the plaintiff could show, using the traditional corporate veil protection, that the named individuals were the alter ego for the corporation. This ruling came despite the fact that EPA had filed a brief *amicus curiae* urging a contrary determination. [2] Other courts, however, have adopted the Agency's position. [3]

Lenders who foreclose on property do so at their peril. If a bank forecloses on a property, it could be considered in a "contractual relationship, existing directly or indirectly with the defendant" under §107(b)(3) of CERCLA. [4] The lender who forecloses becomes an "owner or operator." [5] CERCLA excludes from the definition of "owner or operator" any "person, who without participating in the management of a vessel or facility hold indicia of ownership primarily to protect its security interest in the vessel or facility." [6] However, that definition has been interpreted as being limited to providing "financial assistance and general, and even isolated instances of specific, management advice to . . . debtors without risking CERCLA liability if the secured creditor does not participate in the day to day management of the business or facility either before or after the business ceases operation." [7]

The 11th Circuit ruled in *United States v. Fleet Factors* [8] that a secured creditor is liable under CERCLA if its involvement with the management of the facility is sufficiently broad to support the inference that it could affect hazardous waste disposal decisions.

> Fleet foreclosed on its interest in some of [the borrower's] inventory and equipment, but not on the real estate. EPA discovered hazardous substances on the site and incurred $400,000 in cleanup costs. EPA sought reimbursement from Fleet, among others. The court denied Fleet's motion for summary judgment, holding that Fleet, by dictating excess inventory prices, shipping schedules, and employment policy, had exercised "pervasive if not complete" involvement. . . . In language that shook the lending industry, the court held that "a secured creditor may incur CERCLA liability by participating in the financial management of a facility to a degree indicating a capacity to influence the corporation's treatment of hazardous wastes. [9]

On April 29, 1992, EPA published a rule attempting to limit the *Fleet Factors* decision as to the range of activities that a secured party may undertake without being considered an "owner or operator" for purposes of CERCLA liability. [10] The following pre-foreclosure policing and workout activities are not considered by EPA as management:

- Requiring the borrower to clean up the facility prior to or during the life of the loan; [11]
- Requiring compliance with applicable federal, state, and local environmental rules and regulations during the life of the loan; [12]
- Securing or exercising authority to monitor or inspect the property, borrower's business or financial condition, or both; [13] and
- Other requirements by which the lender is adequately able to police the loan, provided that the exercise by the lender of such other loan policing activities is not considered evidence of management participation under the "general test." [14]

EPA defines the following workout activities as not being considered "participation in management":

- Restructuring or renegotiating the terms of the security interest; [15]
- Requiring payment of additional rent or interest; [16]
- Exercising forbearance; [17]
- Requiring or exercising rights pursuant to an assignment of accounts; [18]
- Requiring or exercising rights pursuant to an escrow agreement pertaining to amounts owing to an obligor; [19]

- Providing specific or general financial or other advice, suggestions, counseling, or guidance; [20] and
- Exercising any right or remedy the lender is entitled to by law or under any warranties, covenants, conditions, representations, or promises from the borrower. [21]

Note that this rule is an EPA interpretation. Some lenders believe that certainty of protection requires an amendment to the statute. In addition, environmentalists are concerned that the rule will remove any incentive lenders now have to perform environmental assessments of properties or borrowers' waste management practices before approving a loan. Environmentalists are also concerned that the post-foreclosure provisions of the rule may allow lenders to own the property and operate the facility without being liable under Superfund, despite the law's explicit provisions that "owners" and "operators" are liable for cleanup costs. Industry argues that the law grants lenders an exemption as long as they do not "participate in management" of a facility, while the final rule protects them as long as they do not completely divest the borrower of control over a facility, a significant extension of legal exemption that may be challenged in court.

On remand, the *Fleet Factors* district court held that application of the participation-in-management test depends, in part, on whether the defendant met the standard of a reasonable, similarly-situated secured creditor. The court found the lender at issue to be liable. [22]

Once acquired, contaminated property may be difficult to unload. Indeed, even in bankruptcy, a bankruptcy trustee cannot use §544(a) of the Bankruptcy Code to abandon a hazardous waste site in contravention of a state statute or regulation that is reasonably designed to protect the public health and safety from identified hazards. [23] Moreover,

> [A]t least thirty-nine states have enacted their own particular version of CERCLA. Although most of these statutes follow CERCLA, each of these statutes must be examined for their own peculiarities. For example, several state statutes have an "innocent purchaser" defense similar to the one found in Section 107(b) of CERCLA, but many do not. Generally, however, these statutes feature (i) a mini Superfund for state executed cleanups; (ii) abatement and cost recovery provisions; and (iii) superliens. These statutes are generally based on a strict liability concept. New York and New Jersey statues are illustrative of these varying statutory schemes. [24]

Scope and Structure of Review

It is beyond the scope of this book to discuss in detail all of the elements of a site review. The checklist included as Appendix D will give you some indication of how to scope such a review. In addition, several critical items warrant particular consideration.

Before acquiring any property or facilities, or any company that owns property or facilities, it is critical to conduct physical assessments of all sites where present or past operations could conceivably have caused environmental contamination. If you are acquiring a company, you should assess each facility it owns; each facility it leases or operates; and, if possible, each facility it has owned, leased, or operated in the past. These assessments are essential to identify potential liabilities under CERCLA,[25] RCRA,[26] and other federal and state laws.

The assessment process should start as early in the acquisition process as possible in order to ensure completeness. You obviously have to consider the sensitivities of the seller in pressing for time, but since you will rarely have the opportunity to perform on-site testing, you will need ample time for document search and inspection. There is no hard-and-fast rule on how much time is necessary; it depends on the nature of the transaction and the type of asset being purchased. If you are purchasing a facility that you suspect may have groundwater problems, you will want more time than if you are purchasing a piece of property that from time immemorial has been rural farmland (unless you suspect pesticide contamination on the farmland). If the seller is a "deep pocket" and is prepared to give a broad indemnity, the review can be more limited than if the seller has limited assets and the property has been used for industrial purposes since the beginning of the industrial revolution.

While it is important to check permitting and other issues regarding air emissions and effluent discharges, the leveraging impacts will usually come from past waste disposal and potential groundwater contamination. If time and personnel constraints limit physical site reviews, sites with potential liability exposure caused by past disposal and groundwater contamination should have first priority.

It is particularly important to determine whether the site was included in the survey that former Congressman Bob Eckhardt completed during the Superfund debate, requiring major chemical companies to list their disposal of potentially hazardous waste. It is also important to check with state and federal agencies to determine whether the site is listed or is being considered for listing as a site requiring cleanup.

Even if a site is not listed, you should ascertain whether it is covered by any of the various federal and state laws that require cleanup expenditures or otherwise affect the value of the property. For example, the 1984 amendments to RCRA provide that all RCRA permits, including those issued for storage units and for postclosure care, must require "corrective action for all releases of hazardous waste or constituents from any solid waste management unit at [the] . . . facility . . . regardless of the time at which waste was placed in such unit." [27] EPA interprets these provisions as establishing RCRA authority to clean up virtually any contamination at a plant site. Further, EPA contends that its RCRA "interim status" authority extends to releases from solid as well as hazardous waste sites and that it can therefore issue cleanup orders even when an owner or operator closes a facility under interim status. Moreover, in some states, particularly New Jersey, acquisition of a site where industrial activities have previously taken place triggers a variety of state actions. [28] State laws can also significantly affect property valuation. In California, for example, the value of a site can change if it is classified as a "hazardous waste property" or as a "border zone property" that is within 2,000 feet of "significant disposal of hazardous waste." [29]

Physical site assessments should be performed by experts, preferably both legal and technical. Experience and expertise are needed to judge whether a facility requires physical assessment and, if so, how that assessment should be conducted and what it should examine. Experience is particularly useful in reviewing documentation and interviewing personnel; indeed, there is no substitute for experience in determining what has been intentionally or unintentionally omitted from a statement. If you use outside counsel for site assessments, the need for specific expertise may make it advisable to use environmental counsel rather than real estate counsel.

In Occidental's case, corporate and/or division staffs usually conduct site visits when reviewing acquisitions of capital assets that include land or manufacturing facilities. Very occasionally, it uses consultants to assist in field evaluations. When Occidental purchases facilities or whole operating companies, it gives them copies of its checklist before the "due diligence" meetings on environmental matters.

If you use outside counsel or consultants for site reviews, you should question them closely. Outside representatives sometimes tend to "low ball" exposure estimates for fear of killing deals. Similarly, in making your own estimates, you may be concerned about being the "deal killer." The best way to handle this concern is to make your estimates based on best-, median-, and worst-case assumptions, documenting the bases for your positions. Any work in this area should be done through and at the request of the legal department to minimize public access to the analyses.

Whether or not you use outside representatives, it is *your* obligation either as a manager or as counsel to ensure that estimates are realistic. Your role is to make the best estimate possible. It is then up to the business managers to look at this exposure and determine whether it is out of line in relation to the rest of the deal. Avoiding realistic estimates of exposure does no one a service. You should also avoid making overly pessimistic estimates in order to protect yourself on a long-range basis. This kind of approach is not helpful to management, and your credibility is at stake.

Recently, many international companies have been purchasing U.S. facilities. The prices paid for some of those facilities and the subsequent costs of environmental remediation indicate that these companies seem to have particular difficulty understanding the economic and political implications of U.S. laws and potential liability exposure. As with domestic purchasers, documentation of the basis for your opinion and/or the need for in-depth review is important, especially if there is a tendency to downplay the leveraging impact of environmental issues.

Information Reviewed

Certain information should be obtained from the company or facility management before the actual visit. This includes general identifying information, such as facility name and location; a description of the principal operations; copies of all relevant environmental policies, procedures, and guidelines; and a list of all specific federal, state, and local environmental regulations, standards, and guidelines applicable to the facility's operations.

Actual site assessments should begin with reviews of all relevant records and permits. Environmental personnel should also be questioned closely on the scope of the documentation and personal knowledge. The files will often show judgments that are not necessarily the "official" views of the company or facility being acquired and that will be very helpful in making more realistic estimates of exposure. General limitations on file reviews should be viewed with suspicion.

An assessment could also include sampling and analysis of groundwater, soil, physical structures, surface waters and sediment, ambient air, or specifically permitted emission sources, if practical or appropriate. Sampling and analysis should not begin, however, until the review of records and permits has been completed. These documents are essential aids in locating possibly contaminated areas on the property, and the location of these areas is a major factor in planning and executing the sampling and analysis program. Similarly, although preliminary site assessments may be made early in the investigation, a final site assessment should not be undertaken until after completion of the document review.

The following sections discuss some of the most important categories of information that should be reviewed prior to an acquisition. [30]

Licenses and Permits

As previously stated, it is important to review and evaluate the licenses and permits possessed and required by facilities. Any pending applications for environmental permits or licenses should also be examined. The review must consider not only existing requirements, but impending or potential future requirements as well. It should include federal and state permits (for example, permits required by RCRA or the FWPCA), state permits by rule (for example, permits involving underground injection wells, underground storage tanks, or pretreatment standards), and state or local permits required by the Clean Air Act.

In addition to identifying which permits exist or are required, you should consider whether their limitations are achievable and acceptable. Will permit limits allow expansions or modifications of operations and, if so, will more stringent parameters be imposed? What federal, state, or local hurdles exist? Can the permits be transferred or must the new owner or operator apply for new ones? Will "grandfathering" be lost by a change in ownership? What public notice, comment, and hearing procedures would apply? Are new permit programs likely to apply soon? Are "interim program permits" likely to become more stringent or costly in the future, or to lapse altogether?

Regulatory History and Current Status

It is important to determine a facility's history of compliance with regulatory requirements. You should review the facility's management files, concentrating on

- any permit violations, with or without fines or penalties;
- excursions above applicable parameters (in monthly discharge monitoring reports, for example);
- discharges at or near the limit of daily maximums, monthly averages, or other restrictions;
- good management practices (for example, is the facility well managed and run when compared to Department of Transportation, Mine Safety and Health Administration, or OSH Act standards? [31] Or is it just fortunate it has not been inspected?);
- required programs (for example, are RCRA groundwater monitoring programs, OSH Act hazard communication programs, and Spill Prevention Control and Countermeasure Plans in place and well designed?);
- orders, citations, notices of violation, or similar administrative actions;
- civil or criminal actions filed against the company with re-

spect to any facility not in compliance with regulations, standards, or permits;
• threatened or contemplated enforcement actions;
• compliance schedules, consent orders, judgments, waivers, or
variances related to compliance with any environmental program; and
• fines or penalties levied or paid for any of the above matters.

As a rule of thumb, this review should cover the facility's activities for at
least the past five years.

Information on the last federal, state, and local agency inspections that
covered environmental matters should be reviewed, including the dates, the
contents of any reports, the nature of any actions required of the company,
and the current status of any such actions.

All applicable recordkeeping and reporting requirements should also be
reviewed and compared to actual practice at the facility. The review should
include the relevant documents listed above and all information on the
current status of the facility's recordkeeping and reporting. Again, individual interviews should be encouraged since they sometimes supply leads that
may not be in the records. You should also consider the adequacy of the
facility's records. If they are questionable, how many others probably exist
that have not been identified?

You should also contact all regulatory authorities that have jurisdiction.
Note that local regulations may be broad in scope and may be enforced by
agencies that normally do not have broad jurisdiction, such as local fire
departments. While it is advisable to obtain as much information as possible
from the relevant agencies, you will find that many sellers are sensitive
regarding these inquiries. Sometimes the inquiries can trigger dormant
controversies concerning compliance or accelerate agency action to resolve
pending permitting issues. If the seller has told the agency that its funds are
insufficient, the agency may attempt to get involved in the deal to ensure
that its interests are protected.

In general, how do applicable regulatory authorities regard the facility?
As a problem, or as a good citizen? If as a problem, will the authorities be
pleased to see new ownership? Or is the activity or operation unwelcome
per se in that area? Will a new owner receive a fresh start or "clean slate"?
Finally, you should learn ahead of time of any potential additional enforcement actions that could leverage the transaction.

Is the facility the object of local citizen or environmental group attention?
If so, is it favorable or unfavorable? Have there been any citizen or
employee complaints concerning environmental activities at the facility?
(As a rule of thumb, you should investigate any such complaints made

within the last 10 years.) What is their current status? Are movements afoot to close the facility or restrict its operations? Does the facility generate air or water emissions that expose the local population to potential health risks? If so, is there evidence that local public opinion is sensitive to the issue? In general, what is the facility's standing in its community?

This discussion is not all-inclusive. The checklist in Appendix D suggests many other areas and types of data that can be included in the compliance history and current status review.

Prior Ownership and Operations

If the facility is, or ever was, used for operations that could have caused environmental contamination, it is important to reconstruct the past history of the site, including the chain of title. The history should determine what operations were performed at the site during each period, who performed those operations, and whether those parties owned, leased, or merely operated the site. This historical survey should seek both evidence of contamination and the identities of companies responsible for any contamination. The companies may still exist, and could share responsibility for the contamination. This can be particularly important in view of the growing trend toward requiring cleanup (in New Jersey, for example). [32]

The strict construction of the following language exempting an "innocent purchaser" from liability under §107(b) of CERCLA gives little comfort:

> [t]o establish that the defendant had no reason to know . . . the defendant must have undertaken, at the time of acquisition, all appropriate inquiry into the previous ownership and uses of the property consistent with good commercial or customary practice in an effort to minimize liability. For purposes of the preceding sentence the court shall take into account any specialized knowledge or experience on the part of the defendant, the relationship of the purchase price to the value of the property if uncontaminated, commonly known or reasonably ascertainable information about the property, the obviousness of the presence or likely presence of contamination at the property, and the ability to detect such contamination by appropriate inspection. [33]

This language of the statute dealing with "appropriate inquiry into the previous ownership and uses of the property consistent with good commercial or customary practice" creates a difficult burden on a landowner attempting to qualify for an exemption. [34]

Query: Given the broad recognition today of the need to do environmental reviews of property acquisitions, will there be many, if any, cases in the future where a buyer can qualify as an "innocent purchaser" without performing such an assessment? Roger Marzulla, former Assistant Attorney General, Land and Natural Resources Division, U.S. Department of Justice, analogized the Department of Justice view on the scope of the exemption to Diogenes looking for an honest man. If you didn't find the alleged contamination, you didn't look hard enough, and if you did find it, then you were not subject to the exemption.

Often, however, very little of the evidence that you would like to have is available. You simply will not and cannot have engineering certainty in these transactions. At best, even with extensive site reviews, you are dealing with order of magnitude numbers. Your best insurance is to have either strong in-house staff or good consultants who know the general kind of business or site that you are buying and can give you a range of exposure. You may have a sketchy record of the businesses on the site at the turn of the century, for example, but just knowing the nature of those businesses tells you a lot about the kind of chemicals that were probably used. Coupled with general knowledge of disposal practices at that time, this data will give a range of exposure. It has been my experience that when I work with a staff that has a broad range of operating and environmental experience, once we know what is being produced and what was previously produced on a site, there is usually not much difference in the estimated ranges of exposure before and after complete site review.

Potential Off-Site Liabilities

Off-site liability is usually the area where environmental costs leverage transactions. Under RCRA and CERCLA, a facility (or its corporate or individual owner) may have liability at every site where its wastes were ever disposed. Thus, it is essential to compile as complete a list as possible of all the wastes ever generated at a site and of all the sites to which those wastes were shipped. Moreover, some non-waste products, such as "recyclable" materials, electrical transformers, and certain pesticide manufacturing equipment, can lead to off-site RCRA or CERCLA liability. You should also look for these types of items and follow them to their destinations. The historical review discussed previously can suggest possible off-site liabilities that may not yet have been discovered.

Sources of pertinent information include the facility's customer lists, billing files, shipping files, hazardous waste manifests, and state and federal hazardous waste manifest files obtained through the Freedom of Information Act [33] and its state equivalents. Customer lists and, more importantly, lists of "recyclers" and waste disposal sites should be reviewed carefully. Present or future Superfund sites may appear. Here, again, it is vital that you make your own judgment as to the scope of Superfund liability. Companies or facilities being acquired tend to "low ball" exposure estimates, so your judgment is critical.

Insurance Coverage

All of the company's or facility's past insurance policies should be compiled. Any previous owners' insurance coverage should also be identified if possible. Insurance coverage information is very important as a possible defense to potential site contamination, toxic tort, and off-site Superfund liabilities.

Unfortunately, most companies have very poor files on past insurance policies. Although the insurance companies, insurance agents, and brokers should be consulted, their records may not be any better, and their potential liability may make them unwilling to cooperate. State and federal government files can help identify required insurance coverages. Sometimes local attorneys or court files can provide clues to the identity of insurance companies providing past coverage.

Insurance policies that can be located should be analyzed for coverage, exclusions, limits, and terms (for example, "claims made" versus "occurrence"). As much of a historical overview as possible should be constructed.

Possible Risk-Mitigation Mechanisms

Depending on the particular circumstances of each case, including the nature of the potential liability, a number of mechanisms can be employed to reduce risks to some extent, or at least to spread them over more parties.

Structure of the Transaction

The way an acquisition is consummated can in some cases be tailored to reduce risks. For example, it may be possible to purchase a company's physical assets only. From an environmental risk standpoint, an asset purchase is frequently less risky than a stock purchase or a merger. In some states, however, a company that purchases another's assets and carries on its business is considered to have assumed its liabilities, just as with a stock purchase. Purchase of some, but not all, assets of a company may therefore be still less risky. Individual state laws must be consulted on this and related issues.

A variety of subsidiaries and related corporate structures can also reduce risks in some cases. For instance, "A" Corporation could spin off a division as "B" Corporation, a wholly owned subsidiary, for the purpose of acquiring "C" Corporation or a specific asset of "C" Corporation. These creative arrangements have pros and cons from both business and liability standpoints, and those factors should be considered in detail.

Contract Provisions

Contract clauses such as warranties, indemnifications, and specific allocations of future liabilities resulting from past activities or pre-existing
contamination should always be considered and, if appropriate, used in any
acquisition or sale. These contract clauses, assuming they can be bargained
for (and this is a major assumption), can provide 100 percent coverage
against risks—but with two enormous provisos:

- These types of contractual arrangements never bind the government and are unlikely to affect the rights of private third
  parties who may be injured. At most, these clauses give the party
  sued by the government or a private plaintiff an action over and
  against the other contracting party.
- These clauses are only as good as the financial soundness of
  the other party. An ironclad, 100 percent indemnification by a
  defunct or insolvent company is worthless.

There are certain minimum provisions that should be included among the
representations and warranties, including:

- All required federal, state, and local permits concerning or
  related to environmental protection and regulation of the property have been secured and are current.
- The seller is and has been in full compliance with such
  environmental permits, and any other requirements under any
  federal, state, or local law, regulation, or ordinance. This latter
  provision is of increasing importance as many environmental
  requirements are not necessarily reflected in permits, such as
  various reporting requirements. Note that obtaining such a broad
  representation may be difficult, and it is more likely that the
  seller may agree to warrant only "material" permits or compliance, with a schedule attached. The schedule or the contract itself
  will define a standard of "materiality." The schedule may also
  reference any other "baseline" condition and will usually include all permits necessary for operation and/or to be transferred.
  Moreover, in view of the increasing complexity of the area, it is
  quite possible that a seller may balk at any warranty as against
  any "other" requirement of law. It is likely that seller will
  qualify this "to the best of seller's knowledge." Many counsel
  in this area consider that the schedule is the most important
  document in negotiations, as it is the culmination of environmental due diligence review.

- There are no pending actions against the seller under any

environmental law, regulation, or ordinance, and the seller has not received notice in any form of such action or of a possible action.

• There are no past or current releases of hazardous substances on, over, at, from, into, or onto any facility at the property, as those terms are understood under CERCLA as amended by SARA. Again, this warranty may be considered overly broad by a seller.

• The seller is not aware of any environmental condition, situation, or incident on, at, or concerning the property that possibly could give rise to an action or to liability under any law, rule, ordinance, or common law theory. This provision would also probably be subject to question by a seller.

Except when it is clear that the seller (or buyer, as the case may be) is judgment-proof, an effort should always be made to address environmental conditions and apportion liabilities in the purchase contract. Certain "baseline" conditions should also be referenced in the agreement and an allocation scheme should be developed to deal with existing conditions. Sometimes such a scheme is based on sliding scales over certain time periods, e.g., 5 or 10 years. These sliding scales can also include caps on liability. Allocations can be difficult when in future proceedings, seller claims that it is buyer's operations of the facility that are now causing the condition giving rise to indemnity claims.

Every acquisition should be accompanied by written representations by the seller, his attorneys, and his accountants concerning the condition of the property, the compliance status of the facility, and existing or threatened environmental litigation. These representations will form the basis of any necessary future discussions or negotiations of environmental liabilities. In extreme cases, the representations may also serve as a basis of an effort to void the transaction for fraud or misrepresentation.

All of these representations and warranties should survive closing, consider possible statute of limitation concerns and be tied to an indemnification clause, with liability to seller for all resulting liability. Note that the term "liability" should be defined. Sellers usually assume that "liability" applies only in a specific adjudication. However, it is likely that a seller will demand that there be a specific time limit on any representations and warranties and will also limit that indemnification to existing laws and regulations. It is particularly important if you are a seller to specifically limit any representation to existing laws and regulations to avoid any future misunderstandings.

Prior Agreements With Regulatory Authorities

There may be cases when, for business reasons, it is desirable to purchase a facility that is in some degree of difficulty with a regulatory authority. Permit revocation may be threatened, for example, or a facility may be hopelessly behind schedule under a consent order. In such a case, an effort should be made prior to purchase to obtain agreements from the appropriate authorities that a new schedule will be set, that is, that the purchaser will have a fresh start with an achievable schedule. Similarly, if a site is already contaminated, an agreement could be sought outlining a cleanup plan that would satisfy the authorities. [35]

A regulatory authority may be flexible in these matters because the alternative is often that the seller goes out of business, leaving the government to deal with a contaminated site and eliminating a source of employment that is important to the locality. Even if no agreement can be reached, advance discussions with regulatory authorities are invaluable for letting the would-be buyer know what burdens it is assuming.

Insurance Coverage

Finally, insurance can provide significant protection against both site cleanup (on site and off site) and toxic tort liabilities. The purchasing company should have appropriate coverage with adequate limits. The acquired company's own insurance coverage, however, is almost equally significant because "occurrence based" policies can provide coverage for present or future liabilities when the "occurrence" (for example, an act of disposal or a manufacturing operation that caused site contamination or slowly developing personal injuries) happened years earlier under previous ownership. Past policies are especially important now because insurance is usually difficult to acquire, very expensive, and sold on a "claims made" basis.

Notes to Chapter 6

1. New York v. Shore Realty Corp., 759 F.2d 1032, 15 ELR 20358 (2d Cir. 1985) (holding that CERCLA imposes strict liability on the current owner of a facility from which there is a release or threat of release, regardless of causation); Missouri v. Indep. Petrochemical Corp., 610 F. Supp. 4, 15 ELR 20161 (E.D. Mo. 1985) (liability for third-party disposal). *See also Second Circuit Ruling Spells Out Superfund Land Owners' Liabilities,* ENVTL. F., Sept. 1985, at 15; Light, *United States of America v. Thomas Jefferson IV, et al.,* ENVTL. F., Sept. 1985, at 17 (a very clever satire on the broad scope of liability allegedly arising from a "disposal" action by Thomas Jefferson).

2. Joslyn Mfg. Co. v. T.L. James & Co., 696 F. Supp. 222, 19 ELR 20518 (W.D. La. 1988), *aff'd,* 893 F.2d 80 (5th Cir. 1990). See discussion of this case and a contrary determination of a district court, *Kelley v. Arco Indus.,* 723 F. Supp. 1214, 20 ELR 20264 (W.D. Mich. 1989) in JENNER & BLOCK L. NEWS, Winter 1990, at 9. See also discussion in Murhy & Samson, *Corporate Responsibility for Environmental Damages,* WHITE & CASE INSIGHTS, Apr. 1990, at 23, and Riesel, *Environmental Concerns of Real Estate and Business Transactions,* 1990 A.L.I./A.B.A. COURSE OF STUDY—ENVTL. L. 423, 440.

3. U.S. v. Kayser-Roth Corp., 910 F.2d 24, 27, 20 ELR 21462 (1st Cir. 1990), *cert. denied,* 498 U.S. 1804 (1991)

4. CERCLA §107(b)(3); 42 U.S.C. §9607(b)(3); ELR STAT. CERCLA §107(b)(3). See United States v. Maryland Bank & Trust Co., 633 F. Supp. 573, 581, 16 ELR 20557 (D. Md. 1986), vitiating the third-party defense to liability under CERCLA.

5. *See* United States v. Mirabile, 15 ELR 20994 (No. 84-2280, E.D. Pa. Sept. 4, 1985).

6. CERCLA §101(20)(A), 42 U.S.C. §9601(20)(A), ELR STAT. CERCLA §101(20)(A).

7. United States v. Fleet Factors Corp., 724 F. Supp. 955, 19 ELR 20529 (S.D. Ga. 1988), discussed in detail in Riesel, *supra* note 2, at 442-44.

8. United States v. Fleet Factors Corp., 901 F.2d 1550, 20 ELR 20832 (11th Cir. 1990), *aff'g* 724 F. Supp. 955, 19 ELR 20529 (S.D. Ga. 1988), *cert. denied,* 111 S. Ct. 752 (1991).

9. Sellinger & Chapman, *EPA's Proposed Rule on Lender Liability Under CERCLA: No Panacea for the Financial Services Industry,* 21 ELR 10618, 10619 (Oct. 1991), quoting *Fleet Factors,* 901 F.2d at 1557-59, 20 ELR at 20835-36.

10. Final Rule Amending the National Oil and Hazardous Substances Pollution Contingency Plan, 57 Fed. Reg. 18344 (1992) (to be codified at 40 C.F.R. pt. 300).

11. *Id.* at 18383.

12. *Id.*

13. *Id.*

14. *Id.*

15. *Id.*

16. *Id.*

17. *Id.*

18. *Id.*

19. *Id.*

20. *Id.*

21. *Id.*

22. *United States v. Fleet Factors*, 23 ELR 20961 (S.D. Ga. May 12, 1993).

23. Midlantic Nat'l Bank v. New Jersey Dep't Envtl. Protection, 474 U.S. 494, 16 ELR 20278 (1986). For more detail, see Riesel, *supra* note 2, at 442-44.

24. Riesel, *supra* note 2, at 454-55. For an extensive list of specific statutes and statutory terms, see *id.* at 454-57.

25. 42 U.S.C. §§9601-75, ELR STAT. CERCLA §§101-405.

26. 42 U.S.C. §§6901-6992k, ELR STAT. RCRA §§1001-11012.

27. RCRA §3004(u), 42 U.S.C. §6924(u), ELR STAT. RCRA §3004(u). RCRA also requires hazardous waste disposal operations to be noted on deeds. *See* 40 C.F.R. §264.120 (1991).

28. The New Jersey Environmental Cleanup Responsibility Act, N.J. STAT. ANN. §§13:1K-6 to -28, requires state action when any of an extensive list of industrial commercial activities has occurred. *See also* New Jersey Spill Compensation and Control Act, N.J. STAT. ANN. §§58:10-23.11 to .11z, establishing a "super-priority" lien on all property in the state for costs of government cleanup.

29. *See* CAL. HEALTH & SAFETY CODE §§25220-25241. A variance is needed for a wide variety of land uses. CAL. HEALTH & SAFETY CODE §25232.

30. The following discussion is derived in part from Friedman & Giannotti, *Environmental Self-Assessment*, in LAW OF ENVIRONMENTAL PROTECTION §7.05 (S. Novick ed. 1987, 1992). Adapted by permission of Clark Boardman Company, Ltd., from LAW OF ENVIRONMENTAL PROTECTION (S. Novick ed. 1987). All use rights reserved by Clark Boardman Company, Ltd., 435 Hudson Street, New York, New York 10014.

31. 29 U.S.C. §§651-678 (1988).

32. *See supra* note 28.

33. CERCLA §101(35)(B), 42 U.S.C. §9601(35)(B), ELR STAT. CERCLA §101(35)(b). *See also* CERCLA §107(b), 42 U.S.C. §9607(b), ELR STAT. CERCLA §107(b).

34. See Riesel, *supra* note 2, at 440-43, for a detailed analysis of the legislative history, the case law, and the difficulty of qualifying for that exemption.

35. See EPA's prospective purchaser settlements guidance. 54 Fed. Reg. 34235 (Aug. 18, 1989).

Chapter 7:
Waste Minimization

Many companies are now exploring multi-media waste minimization. This concept defines waste very broadly to include all materials released to the environment, on site or off. In essence, it means reducing the amount of air emissions, effluents, and hazardous and nonhazardous wastes generated. If nothing else, a waste minimization program recognizes the growing legal pressure to control remaining sources of pollution. It is easier and probably cheaper to develop your own reduction program than to wait for regulation. Reductions can come from recycling and other beneficial uses of materials as well as from source reductions.

A unique document, a joint report prepared in April 1991 by McDonald's Corporation and the Environmental Defense Fund, deals with the waste reduction recommendations made by a joint task force of both organizations on waste reduction. The task force's overall objective was to reduce the environmental impact of McDonald's operations. The fundamental nature of McDonald's business was recognized, namely "to serve hot, fresh food to a large group of customers efficiently in a limited period of time." [1] The evaluation criteria included (1) consistency with the EPA waste management hierarchy (reduce, reuse, recycle and incinerate/dispose) with a recognition that "changes aimed specifically at reducing solid waste may have other environmental impacts;" (2) magnitude of environmental impacts, both quantitatively and the "public's perception of such impacts;" (3) public health and safety including a recognition that "no options should be implemented that risks the health and safety of its employees, customers or the communities in which McDonald's operates" and that "public health concerns are driven by accurate information and not simply public perception;" (4) practicality, including customer attitudes; and (5) economic costs and benefits, including customer attitudes. [2]

The results of these efforts produced a corporate waste reduction policy and a comprehensive waste reduction action plan.

A major problem noted by the task force was that "[p]ackaging materials used by take-out and drive-thru customers (50-70% of the business, depending on a restaurant's location) cannot easily be collected by in-store recycling programs initiated by McDonald's. For those items, source-reduction steps and design changes that allow packaging to fit into evolving community recycling programs will deliver the greatest environmental benefits." In addition, "[t]he task force concluded that there is no single method for minimizing solid waste at McDonald's. Rather, there are a number of specific solutions that, collectively employed, will achieve significant waste reductions."[3]

There is a misconception that McDonald's decision to replace polystyrene foam clamshells with a "paper" wrap was a "paper vs. plastics" decision. The new packaging material was a three-layered sandwich wrap, which consisted of a layer of tissue inside, a sheet of polyethylene in the middle, and a sheet of paper on the outside. Thus, McDonald's decision to phase out polystyrene packaging and substitute paper-based wraps *cannot* be evaluated as a generic "paper vs. plastic" issue. Instead, the merits of alternative materials emerge only after closely examining the packages involved. The nature of the materials involved, such as mode of production, current rate of recycling, etc., dramatically affects their relative environmental consequences and must be carefully taken into account in comparing the materials. In this case, the potential for recycling problems in collection, processing and marketing[4] were critical factors.

Thus, waste minimization and recycling decisions are not simple and must be examined on a case-by-case basis. (See also discussion of New Mechanisms To Assure Environmental Accountability—Life Cycle Analysis, Sustainable Manufacturing, Full Cost Accounting and EPA Leadership Program in Chapter 1.)

Waste minimization is not a new concept. At least since RCRA was amended in 1984 to require generators to certify that they have minimized their hazardous waste generation, many companies have made efforts to generate less solid and hazardous waste. These minimization programs, however, generally have not included reductions in air emissions or effluent discharges to water, even when the companies have been making those reductions as required by other statutes (such as the Clean Air Act (CAA), which creates constant pressure to reduce emissions of both conventional and toxic air pollutants). The passage of the Emergency Planning and Community Right-To-Know Act of 1986 (EPCRA)[5] has inspired a change in this attitude. EPCRA has put industry on notice that releases at levels once unquestioned will now be subject to public and legislative scrutiny and possible control. This chapter focuses on how to broaden minimization programs to encompass emissions and effluents as well as solid and hazardous wastes.

EPCRA and Emissions Reductions

Even before EPCRA, many companies recognized the importance of knowing their emissions levels and voluntarily required their facilities to report releases internally. Some states also required reporting. Sometimes these efforts led to "good news/bad news" situations. Companies that had started reporting before EPCRA had time to prepare for the effects of their reports and, in some cases, to reduce their releases. However, the reporting programs they had invested in were not always consistent with EPCRA. Moreover, it was sometimes problematic for companies to show that their programs were consistent with EPCRA's requirements, because the bases for previous reporting were not always well documented.

EPCRA contains several related programs for disseminating information on industrial use and release of toxic and hazardous substances. [6] EPCRA §313 requires many manufacturing facilities annually to report routine releases of "toxic chemicals." [7] Section 312 requires most commercial and industrial facilities to report on inventories of "hazardous chemicals" possessed in excess of listed threshold quantities. [8]

When EPCRA became effective, many companies were primarily concerned about how to accomplish the basic tasks of obtaining information and presenting it in a meaningful manner. They were also concerned about how to correctly and consistently determine the amounts they had to report under §313. These determinations still present major difficulties. At industry's urging, Congress refrained from requiring actual measurement of releases, instead allowing companies either to measure releases or to estimate them based on a number of assumptions. Most companies have chosen to estimate and have spent considerable time teaching their personnel the necessary techniques. Estimation of releases is far from an exact science, and different techniques can yield different results. The relevant EPA guidance document tends to lead to overestimation. [9] If a company is primarily concerned with reducing its potential legal exposure for violations of EPCRA's reporting requirements, it can make its estimates "conservative" (that is, high). [10] If the company is more concerned that reporting higher amounts may lead to public concern or to legal exposure under other statutes, it can estimate the lowest defensible values.

Section 313 releases are routine and, before EPCRA, were simply accepted and controlled generically as smoke, particulates, or organics. These releases are now labeled "toxic," even though concentrations beyond plant fence lines may never approach levels that would actually cause health effects.[11] Some companies, however, have been shocked at the size of the figures they have reported under EPCRA, particularly those on fugitive emissions,[12] which are especially difficult to estimate accurately and can be enormous. A calculated release rate of less than 2.5 pounds per hour (such as from equipment leaks) for 24 hours a day will total 10 tons a year. Even with a tiny leak rate, the total estimated emissions from a plant with thousands of flanges, pumps, and valves would be huge.

The likely consequences of EPCRA reporting include increased public concern and regulatory activity regarding toxic releases. From a public relations standpoint alone, release figures need to be reduced. They look immense to the general public. Moreover, legislators have wasted no time in highlighting them. In March 1989,[13] Congressman Henry Waxman (D-Cal.) made public preliminary EPA estimates that U.S. industry releases 2.4 billion pounds of §313 "toxic pollutants" into the nation's air each year.[14] The chemical industry was cited as the largest emitter, releasing an estimated 886.5 million pounds per year. These numbers greatly increased pressures to amend the CAA to reduce emissions of so-called hazardous air pollutants. Indeed, the use of §313 reports by environmentalists and the attendant publicity made enactment of new air toxic controls a foregone conclusion.

EPCRA will also increase the pressure and opportunity for state and local governments to reduce releases, particularly air emissions. Many state and local agencies have sought to establish accurate inventories of hazardous or toxic air pollutants in order to develop regulatory programs. Now that EPCRA has given them the inventories, the agencies will require emitters to establish strategies and timetables for reducing the pollutants, perhaps significantly. The agencies are likely to approach the problem not in terms of reducing specific toxic or hazardous air pollutants, but in terms of reducing particulates (PM_{10}) and volatile organic precursors to ozone, the indicator pollutant for smog. Indeed, the reduction in ozone precursors required to attain the ozone standard under §108 of the CAA[15] will probably be greater than any reduction resulting from additional regulation of the precursors for their own sakes. The potentially large amounts of fugitive emissions identified under EPCRA will be tempting targets for regulatory agencies anxious to further reduce ozone precursors in nonattainment areas.

Voluntary Emissions Reductions

It is imperative that all companies examine their EPCRA figures and develop reduction strategies, ideally as components of overall waste minimization programs.[16] This is true for two reasons. First, as discussed above, changes in federal, state, and local regulation of air emissions are likely to require such reductions. Second, EPCRA offers opportunities for companies to improve their environmental programs. The statute provides incentives to track emissions and to develop good computerized tracking and reporting systems. Both these functions are key to good environmental programs. Indeed, many corporate environmental departments have actually welcomed EPCRA as a way to obtain the emissions inventories that their facilities had been slow to develop. In addition, companies can and should use reporting to trigger waste reduction and potential cost savings. 3M's most recent data indicate a total savings of $530 million through 1991. [17]

By analogy, many progressive companies have achieved substantial hazardous waste reductions as a result of both regulatory and internal concentration on the costs of disposal and product loss in the form of leaks and other waste. For example, 3M Company estimates that its program, Pollution Prevention Pays (3P) has achieved since 1975 savings of $482 million worldwide ($408 million from U.S. operations, $74 million international) as of April 1989. [18] Solid waste pollutants (hazardous and non-hazardous) have been reduced by more than 535,000 tons. [19] The longer term effort (90 percent reduction from a 1987 baseline) will require extensive research and development in order to redesign products and processes. [20]

New uses or markets have been found for materials that once were wastes. The situation today, as the data from the EPCRA reports become widely available, is analogous to the situation after submission of some of the early RCRA reports. Large numbers were publicized, and agencies and the public pressed industry to reduce them. In response, industry examined its practices and found many opportunities for waste reduction and cost savings, either in the traditional sense or in the "pay me now or pay me later" sense. It was cheaper to reduce wastes quickly than to wait for additional regulation. Similarly, economics combined with post-EPCRA regulatory pressure should create opportunities for substantial emissions reductions and potential cost savings. The cost savings may be less in the air pollution area, and all new regulatory programs create new expenses, but intelligent companies can turn EPCRA's requirements into at least limited targets of opportunity.

Voluntary emissions reductions can have substantial benefits in terms of public relations, liability, and costs. Well-publicized voluntary reductions will reduce public pressure against "industrial polluters." Moreover, if a company voluntarily reduces fugitive ozone precursor emissions before regulations require those reductions, it may be able to reduce the cost of control programs. It can do this either by offsetting the reductions against emissions from future new sources or modifications or by selling them to other companies through its state's emissions banking system. Most importantly, if industry does not reduce emissions voluntarily, it can expect to face tighter regulation and increased costs.

Voluntary emissions reductions also have risks, however. First, the future of emissions "banks" is in question. Existing air programs allow sources to "bank" emission credits from shutdowns or reductions achieved beyond those required by law. As state agencies struggle to reduce ozone precursors, they will be tempted to "expropriate" banked credits to get federal reduction credits or to control industrial growth in particular areas. The South Coast Air Quality Management District has already proposed to do this in Southern California. Emissions banks have no deposit insurance; depositors may not recover the costs of their expropriated credits, particularly if they cannot show "vested rights." Second, voluntary reductions may not fully satisfy the federal requirements that are almost sure to come, so additional reductions may prove necessary. Since it is cheaper to add controls to a loosely controlled source than to a tightly controlled one, future legislation could actually penalize companies that have voluntarily reduced emissions. It is therefore very important to keep detailed records sufficient to demonstrate unequivocally both the absolute and percentage reductions your voluntary controls achieve.

Advanced Waste Minimization Programs

Voluntarily reducing your emissions is the first step in establishing a post-EPCRA waste minimization program. The second step is tracking wastes from materials acquisition to product and waste disposition. This tracking, sometimes called product stewardship, is virtually a materials balance. While difficult, it should at least be a goal. [21]

The third step is establishing a waste inventory that distinguishes wastes routinely produced during operations from those produced by nonrecurring events. Your program should focus on reducing recurring waste streams. It is not possible to minimize existing wastes resulting from nonrecurring events. For example, cleanups mandated by either RCRA or CERCLA for past situations usually require specific technologies or disposal methods. Such cleanups may preclude certain forms of disposal that might qualify as waste minimization. Therefore, since you will base reduction plans on your yearly waste total, it is deceptive to add nonrecurring wastes to that total without specific identification. The inventory should also differentiate hazardous from nonhazardous wastes, although both should be reduced.

The ideal minimization program reduces the amount of waste generated. Waste that is not generated does not pose disposal problems or trigger additional air or water permit conditions. In addition, source reduction is the only type of waste minimization credited by regulatory agencies and the congressional Office of Technology Assessment (OTA). OTA defines waste minimization as "in-plant processes that reduce, avoid or eliminate" waste generation. [22] The Pollution Prevention Act of 1990, passed as part of the Budget Reconciliation Act, reads as follows:

> The term "source reduction" does not include any practice which alters the physical, chemical, or biological characteristics or the volume of a hazardous substance, pollutant, or contaminant through a process or activity which itself is not integral to and necessary for the production of a product or the providing of a service. [23]

In many companies, it may be difficult to provide specific justification for increased maintenance and for capital requests in the areas of waste minimization, effluent or discharge reduction, and process hazard reduction in keeping with the expansion of general environmental, health, and safety requirements, without specific regulatory requirements.

In other companies, there may be authorizations for expenditures approved that have little or no economic justification but are based on environmental, health, and safety concerns. However, this may not be widely known at lower levels of the company. It is important that the environment, health, and safety staffs assure the people in the divisions that they should not hide behind the "our management won't give us the money" excuse. Recognizing the normal, healthy conflict between environmental, health, and safety and financial needs, it is important that you assure that these issues are surfaced and critically reviewed high enough in the organization that the concerns noted above are not valid.

One possible solution to this problem is to have all environmental, health, and safety projects that may have questionable economic justification reviewed by the appropriate division environment, health, safety, or risk engineering staff. The fact that this channel is available should be publicized at the process development, engineering, and facility levels.

Some examples of items that might be included in special justifications are:

- Time value of operating capital not invested in inventories.
- The value of extending the life of natural resources as well as the value of reduced by-product (produced water, refuse or slime, and gypsum) disposal costs in the extractive industries when improved recovery is effected.
- The value of allowable banking or sale of emission reduction rights in nonattainment areas.

- Reduction in monitoring and permitting costs for pits and underground tanks removed from service.
- Reduction in disposal costs through waste minimization.
- Reduction in costs by avoiding foreseeable regulatory procedural compliance requirements.

While some of these may be included in justifications, others are not since they are considered "soft dollars." Others may not be quantifiable, but will be applicable in complying with pollution reduction and risk minimization requirements. Additional intangible benefits are minimization of the possibility of enforcement actions or third party claims, and provision of support in expediting permit approvals by demonstrating corporate sincerity.

One strong caveat should be considered in developing a pollution prevention program. [24] The existing federal regulatory structure may create strong disincentives to such a program. For example, proposed EPA permit regulations under the Clean Air Act Amendments of 1990 provide that if a facility changes its feedstock from "toxic" chemical A to another listed chemical B, even if *less* toxic, this change may constitute a modification and could subject an entire facility to new source maximum available control technology (MACT) requirements and permitting delays. Moreover, the new thresholds for preconstruction review are so low (in some cases 10 tons per year—less than three pounds an hour in *potentially* increased emissions) that virtually any change at a facility may trigger new source review and lengthy permitting requirements.

If new materials or controls alter the amount or nature of waste generated, RCRA requirements such as permits and reporting may be triggered, along with associated liabilities. Should a company use a recycling or recovery system such as a distillation column to minimize or eliminate the need for off-site disposal, that unit and/or material may be subject to RCRA part B hazardous waste permitting, corrective action, and other requirements at the facility. Recovery or removal of a toxic constituent from waste waters before discharge may constitute hazardous waste treatment under RCRA and thereby trigger RCRA part B permitting. Air permitting may also be triggered by this change.

Of course, FWPCA (Clean Water Act) implications cannot be ignored. Any process change or modification that alters the constituent profile of a water discharge will require a modification of the NPDES permit. The FWPCA has an "anti-backsliding" provision. Reductions in effluents or their toxic constituents may therefore become a cap. If a facility opts to reduce emissions by scrubbing, the necessary tanks for treatment and storage may trigger water permits, air permits, and RCRA permits, depending upon the nature of the material, the definition of source, and the water treatment train.

The moral of the above discussion can best be described as "no good deed goes unpunished."

Source reduction is not always technologically or economically feasible. The obvious second-best goal is to ensure that waste is not a potential hazard to health or the environment.

In developing a minimization program, it is advisable to set indices of performance, long-range goals, and specific yearly numerical goals. Perhaps the best index of performance is a ratio of waste generated to product produced. This gives you an easily measurable goal that recognizes rises and falls in production.

Long-range goals should include the following: maximum reduction of manufacturing, mining, and processing discharges to all media; no emission, discharge, or disposal of any hazardous waste without treatment that minimizes or removes the hazard(s) to the extent feasible; and regular review of all processes or operations to ensure minimization of potential employee or community exposure. Your company should develop prioritization criteria, review a certain number of processes each year, and review all processes by a specific date.

Annual quantitative goals should implement the maximum-reduction and no-emission objectives and should also specify reductions in wastes generated; wastes treated, destroyed, or disposed of on site; and wastes treated, destroyed, or disposed of off site. As discussed in Chapter 4, it is usually preferable for divisions to set these goals so that they will have a proprietary interest in meeting them.

As noted above, 3M's successful program is entitled "3P" (Pollution Prevention Pays). Dow calls its program "WRAP" (Waste Reduction Always Pays). The concept of "pays" gets management attention, but it is equally important that regulatory pressures will eventually require such reductions. Whether minimization programs are voluntary or mandatory, however, they can "improve productivity, increase product yields, decrease treatment costs and conserve energy while reducing potential liability costs."[25]

Notes to Chapter 7

1. McDonald's Corporation/Environmental Defense Fund, Waste Reduction Task Force, Final Report, Apr. 1991, at 9.

2. *Id.* at 9-10.

3. *Id.* at iii.

4. *Id.*

5. 42 U.S.C. §§11001-11050, ELR STAT. EPCRA §§301-330. (enacted as Title III of the Superfund Amendments and Reauthorization Act of 1986 and often referred to as "SARA Title III").

6. See generally Friedman & Rosenberg, *Opportunities Under Community Right-to-Know Reporting*, TOXIC TORTS & HAZARDOUS WASTE NEWSL. (Aug. 1989). The assistance of Ernie Rosenberg, Director, External Affairs and Compliance, Health, Environment and Safety, Occidental Petroleum Corporation, on the section relating to EPCRA is gratefully acknowledged.

7. EPCRA §313, 42 U.S.C. §11023, ELR STAT. EPCRA §313. This section only applies to facilities in SIC Codes 20-39 with 10 or more employees.

8. EPCRA §312, 42 U.S.C. §11022, ELR STAT. EPCRA §312. This requirement applies to facilities covered by the Occupational Safety and Health Administration's Hazard Communication Standard, 29 C.F.R. §1910 (1991), which now includes virtually all commercial and industrial facilities. *See also* Arnett, *Risky Business: OSHA's Hazard Communication Standard, EPA's Toxics Release Inventory, and Environmental Safety*, 22 ELR 10440 (July 1992).

9. Environmental Protection Agency, Estimating Releases and Waste Treatment Efficiencies for the Toxic Chemical Release Inventory Form (EPA 560/4-88-002, Dec. 1987).

10. Inflated initial reports will also make it easier to show "decreases" in future years.

11. In contrast, other provisions of EPCRA, such as those addressing emergency plans and material safety data sheets, deal with lower probability events that facilities and companies have direct stakes in avoiding entirely.

12. Fugitive emissions are emissions from equipment leaks rather than from point sources such as stacks and vents.

13. This release was timed for maximum effect on members of Congress, who were home for the Easter recess.

14. On April 12, 1989, EPA issued corrected figures. It estimated releases of 2.7 billion pounds of toxic chemicals to air and 9.7 billion pounds to water. However, 95 percent of these releases were of sodium sulfate, a relatively innocuous by-product of water pollution control. EPA delisted sodium sulfate because it is not particularly toxic.

15. 42 U.S.C. §7408, ELR STAT. CAA §108. These ozone precursor controls will

be required in over 100 urban areas that do not meet the ozone and PM_{10} standards. In an effort to address pollutant transport, forthcoming legislation is likely to extend the controls to some areas that do meet the standards.

16. It may be advisable, if your existing auditing program is not sufficient, to consider a specific review of air quality issues. It has been suggested that "(t)he resulting snapshot often indicates important safety, engineering practice, and compliance issues and highlights areas where the company could improve its regulatory, legal or economic status and avoid or reduce liability." Van Wormer, *Air Quality Auditing: A Strategy for the 90s,* ENSR NEWSL., Nov. 2, 1990, at 1.

17. B. SMART, BEYOND COMPLIANCE, A NEW INDUSTRY VIEW OF THE ENVIRONMENT 14 (1992). See pages 11-36 for description of a variety of company waste and source reduction programs.

18. *3M's Aim: Slash Emissions 90% by 2000,* ENVTL. MANAGER, June 1990, at 1.

19. *Id.*

20. *Id.*

21. For a description of the Dow program, see Dombrowski, *Product Stewardship Offers a Safe and Profitable Future,* 139 SAFETY & HEALTH 62 (National Safety Council, May 1989).

22. *See Waste Minimization,* UCLA HAZARDOUS SUBSTANCES CONTROL BULL. (Spring 1989).

23. Pollution Prevention Act §6603(5)(B), 42 U.S.C.A. §13102(5)(B) (1992 Supp.).

24. I am indebted to Ernie Rosenberg, Director, External Affairs and Compliance, and Catherine DeLacy, now Vice President, Health, Environment and Safety, Occidental Petroleum Corporation for the following analysis.

25. Dombrowski, *supra* note 21, at 63.

Chapter 8:
Dealing With Lawyers, Engineers, Business Managers, and Consultants

As an environmental manager, you will deal with three primary types of specialists: lawyers, engineers, and consultants. Your primary clients will be business managers. Members of these groups can be very helpful or can be counterproductive. In some instances you will have authority to hire in-house people or specialists to handle specific situations. [1] At other times you may be stuck with people you didn't hire and wouldn't hire if given a choice. This chapter gives some suggestions for dealing with each group.

Dealing With Lawyers

The environmental manager must learn to work closely with lawyers if he or she is to have a successful program. Some managers may view this as analogous to learning to work closely with porcupines. If an environmental manager is lucky or knows how to work with lawyers, or both, in-house or outside counsel can be valuable allies in developing a program. If the environmental manager is unlucky or is unable to work with lawyers because of either an inability to understand the importance of legal issues or a simple clash of cultures, counsel can be a major pain in the neck.

The first step in establishing a productive relationship with your environmental counsel is picking the right counsel. To the extent you control the selection decision, you should consider several factors. First, environmental law is a recognized professional specialty. Modern federal environmental laws and regulations have been in place now for more than 20 years and have generated a complex body of administrative and judicial authority. Thus, one criterion for selecting an environmental lawyer should be the lawyer's experience in handling environmental matters, including specific areas such as air, water, hazardous waste, and Superfund. This is not to say that one of the legal department's "general practitioners" would not be a suitable choice, but, as in environmental management, experience helps considerably. In addition, effective environmental counsel recognize that environmental law is not limited to protection of health and the environment, but extends to implementation of broad-ranging social policies in areas of major public concern. Finally, to the extent possible, you should avoid counsel who respond to every potential risk by "just saying no."

Whether you choose your environmental counsel with great care or have the choice made for you, it helps to be lucky. The skill and personality of the lawyer can make a major difference in the success of your program. Despite your best efforts, you are likely to face problems in dealing with counsel at some point in your career. The following discussion provides tips on handling two common types of "problem" lawyers.

The first type is the lawyer who says no to everything. For the conservative or perhaps lazy lawyer, it is always easier to say no than to develop a creative solution to a complex problem. Saying no eliminates all obvious risk. Some lawyers use this rationale to advise against doing environmental assessments, for example. As discussed under "Legal Exposure" in Chapter 5, there is no question that these assessments do present legal risks. However, the creative lawyer, like the creative manager, recognizes that the risks of not finding problems can be much greater. The difference is that failure to discover a problem until too late cannot be pinned directly on the overly cautious lawyer.

Fortunately, we are now seeing fewer "Dr. No's" in environmental legal practice. However, they are still too often found, particularly in companies that have not faced environmental crises. Companies that have faced such crises recognize that they are better off dealing with problems before they become major.

Before you conclude that your lawyer is overcautious about environmental assessments, remember that the decision to conduct such assessments must include the decision to deal with any issues discovered. Both the lawyer and the manager must be certain that senior management recognizes this. Otherwise, the cautious lawyer is not being overly cautious but *properly* cautious.

The second type of problem lawyer, who fortunately is fast approaching or has passed retirement age, is the lawyer with a strong traditional litigation background who attempts to read environmental laws and regulations narrowly. This lawyer thinks Superfund cases call for extensive motion practice, not realizing that the only realistic approach is negotiation. He or she also sees a potential constitutional challenge in every statute or regulation. Many of these more traditional lawyers have had limited experience with administrative law, particularly the broad interpretations characteristic of environmental law. Environmental law differs from some older fields in that the narrow approach will usually get you nowhere. As one commentator has noted, "[Y]ou would be better advised to accept EPA's legal interpretations and to base your arguments for change on factual and policy grounds."[2]

A lawyer in either of these categories can be a major impediment to your program. If you encounter a "Dr. No," your natural response may be simply to insist that he or she recognize that you are the client and that it is his or her job to tell you "no, but" rather than merely "no." This forces your lawyer to justify his or her position, including the lack of alternatives. Similarly, if your lawyer is a "strict constructionist," you may be tempted simply to demand that he or she accept the very different realities of environmental practice. As discussed below, this emotional, combative approach may work in extreme cases. Under ordinary circumstances, however, it can be counterproductive, just as it would be in dealing with any other problem staffer. There are usually better ways to deal with these attorneys and the views they represent.

Contradictory as it may sound, one major way to deal with the problem lawyer is to increase his or her participation in your program. For example, if the lawyer is concerned about environmental assessments, have him write the guidelines governing those assessments, participate in the assessments themselves, and/or review assessment team reports. (See also discussion of the Assessment Team in Chapter 5) To gain the support of a conservative legal department, you may also find it helpful or necessary to place your assessment program under the attorney-client relationship, even though this approach usually does not help protect documents, and often delays and obfuscates action on identified issues.

Another way to increase attorney participation, and hopefully cooperation, in your program is to ask for—and listen to—legal advice when appropriate. The environmental manager needs legal advice in many areas, and needs to know when to request it. Lawyers usually welcome these requests. They recognize that preventive law is the best means of avoiding exposure, and they like to know that their clients recognize this as well. Asking for advice can therefore help cement a relationship with a lawyer. By regularly requesting advice, you can assure the lawyer that you want your program to comply with the law. More importantly, you can subtly convey the message that you want to use the lawyer on a regular basis, but not if the lawyer will only take the easy way out by saying no rather than trying to be creative.

Sometimes a perceived problem with a lawyer is simply a failure of communication. The answer here is engaging in more dialogue. For example, a lawyer's apparent conservatism may rankle a manager who is anxious to proceed with a program. Simply asking the lawyer for the basis of his or her opinion (and I do not mean in a long formal memo) can make a major difference in communication. If "Dr. No" has to justify his or her opinion, he or she may be more willing to develop a solution. Conversely, if the manager understands the lawyer's rationale, he or she may come to agree that caution is appropriate. In either case, the lawyer and the manager may find a creative solution by working together.

When I was a lawyer at ARCO giving advice to clients (before I moved to my position at Occidental of implementing my own advice, which I expect many managers view as the ultimate revenge on a lawyer), one of my best clients had the reputation of being impossible for lawyers. However, what I found was that this client had never been given common sense reasons for legal opinions. When I gave him those reasons, the client, who was very bright, frequently raised additional factors that either I or he had not considered. Together, in informal dialogue, we could usually find ways to obtain the desired results. In the few instances when the legal answer simply had to be "no," the client understood the reasoning and accepted the decision.

This anecdote illustrates two important points. First, the key is maintaining dialogue that enables the lawyer to understand the business, and the businessman to understand the law. Neither side can hold back its respective facts and rationales. It is particularly important for the manager to make sure the lawyer knows and understands all the facts. Many managers (and, unfortunately, some lawyers) do not recognize that most law is not a matter of principle but of facts applied to principle. If both the lawyer and the manager fully understand the facts, both can adequately perform their jobs. However, there is nothing more frustrating for a lawyer than preparing an extensive legal opinion and then finding out that he or she was given the wrong set of facts. Second, the manager must recognize that he or she is dealing with laws and regulations and that understanding the application and interpretation of legal requirements is the specific expertise of lawyers. Sometimes even the best lawyer cannot enable the manager to implement a particular program element.

Education is another technique for curing "Dr. No's" and "strict constructionists." Many of these lawyers improve after attending a few seminars or appropriate trade association committee meetings. A wide variety of trade associations and private groups have been giving seminars on the importance of, and the means of structuring, environmental assessments. There are also numerous programs on environmental law and practice. Suggest to the lawyer that he or she attend an appropriate program. If he or she is reluctant, it might be appropriate to suggest to his or her boss that you feel such a program would benefit the lawyer and assist in advising you. Similarly, the lawyer may also benefit from trade association work with peers who are experienced in environmental law. There is nothing better than practical experience and peer review to change outmoded behavior patterns.

If, after trying the suggestions above, you are still stuck with an ineffective counsel, more drastic measures may be necessary. One option is to make sure that the record shows that decisions not to take action, or to take actions with which you disagree, were made on counsel's advice. You should make clear to the lawyer that you plan to do this. A lawyer trying to take the easy way out will then recognize that he or she must take responsibility for that advice as well. Similarly, if the lawyer's advice is simply not timely, it is helpful to document the request for the advice and the timing of the reply. In either case, documentation will help if it is necessary to go to the lawyer's superiors for relief. Care must be taken, however, that this documentation does not itself create legal problems.

Although, as I cautioned earlier, you should not overuse the tactic of simply demanding good legal advice, this alternative may be appropriate in extreme situations. General counsel recognize the importance of happy clients and are willing to act if there is a personality clash, or if it is clear that inadequate advice is being given. Your general counsel is more likely to take your complaint seriously if you have a history of recognizing the need for legal advice and appropriately requesting that advice, and if you have the backing of your boss.

An attempt to replace a lawyer demands much the same approach as an attempt to replace any other staffer whose performance is inadequate. As mentioned above, before you take this serious step, it is important to document the problems, although it is equally important to ensure that the documentation attempts do not themselves create major legal problems. Unless you have a good track record with the legal department, the effective burden of proof will probably be on you, because most general counsels have heard too many managers complain that a lawyer refused to support a scheme that seemed illogical or was clearly illegal. As discussed previously, facts make the law, and your argument to the general counsel must be bolstered by facts, not generalities.

To return to the positive side: If you have good, creative environmental counsel who are sensitive to environmental program needs, you are indeed fortunate. Competent counsel can be extremely helpful in the health, environment, and safety area, which is becoming intensely legal. Indeed, there is a growing trend toward placing lawyers in senior management positions in this area. In an ideal world this would not be the case. Solutions should focus on technical responses, not legal constraints. However, a whole generation of environmental law is not going to be repealed; the legal constraints are simply facts of life, and legal training helps managers deal with them.

While obeying these legal constraints, most lawyers in management positions nevertheless attempt to focus on technical solutions rather than legal solutions—and if they don't, they should. The lawyer-manager's development of technical solutions benefits from his or her recognition of legal constraints. For example, it is a lot easier to eliminate a waste stream, if possible, than to obtain a permit for it or to worry about the long-term impacts of its disposal. However, a lawyer who does not understand technology may tend to focus on the legal responses he or she does understand. The legally trained manager thus needs strong technical support.

Conversely, the technically trained manager needs strong legal support. Legal exposure is simply too great a risk to ignore. Your title may be manager, director, or vice president, but if you ignore the law, you risk acquiring the additional title of "designated inmate." Whatever the senior manager's training, the technical and legal sides must function as a team if the operation is to be successful. One purpose of this book is to give both the manager and the lawyer an understanding of the basic tools of environmental management so that they can complete an aggressive environmental program and remain within present and future legal constraints.

A word is in order regarding ways to use counsel in dealing with other departments or divisions. You will run into situations in which you suggest a program—for example, as a corporate staffer, you suggest a program to a division—and the response is, "We suggested that earlier, but Legal said we couldn't do it." This kind of comment should not be taken at face value. It is usually helpful for you and your counsel to meet with the division manager who claims he or she can't do something because of legal advice, along with the person giving that advice. I have seen many occasions, both as a lawyer and as a manager, where the advice was not understood in context.

Conversely, managers can often use legal advice to justify potentially unpopular programs. All managers are concerned about potential liability, and it is easy to "blame Legal" for a program. The smart lawyer will often encourage that approach, just as the corporate group may encourage a divisional manager who doesn't want to take heat for a program to "blame Corporate" for it.

Dealing With Engineers and Business Managers

In the previous section we had a few kind (and a few not so kind) words for the lawyers. This section deals with the best means of using the expertise of—and, when necessary, educating—engineers, as well as those business managers or senior managers who share the prejudices common among engineers. Unfortunately, many of us have had the pleasure of working for business managers who, out of frustration at their inability to understand the environmental management process, demanded long memoranda from us to justify everything we were doing or planning that did not fit into traditional business management. This section also includes some hints for dealing with this breed.

The unreconstructed lawyer, discussed in the previous section, who attempts to practice environmental law from a strict constructionist viewpoint and who, like the proverbial Bourbon kings, forgets nothing and learns nothing, has his or her counterpart in the engineering and business area. This engineer is usually technically competent, but environmentally insensitive. He or she might be an older engineer who remembers the days when environmental engineering consisted of a pipe to the nearest body of water. Today, he or she recognizes that this is not good environmental engineering, but he or she is very dubious about the need for certain environmental controls. He or she firmly believes that many environmental laws and regulations are unnecessary and without sound scientific foundation. He or she will therefore resist any changes unless he or she is convinced that the law absolutely requires them, and then he or she will try to do the bare minimum that the law requires. This individual may very well be right that many of the laws and regulations have serious technical flaws or are motivated strictly by politics, but this is irrelevant. As a manager, you must educate your staff to accept "regulatory truth" rather than "scientific truth," and to make whatever technical changes are necessary to either comply with or legally avoid a regulation, rather than quibbling over whether compliance is necessary from a technical standpoint. Lawyers may find this approach more congenial than engineers. [3]

Another individual who can make your life difficult is the business manager or senior manager who resists changes both because, like the engineer discussed above, he or she believes they are scientifically unnecessary, and because he or she wants to hold down short-term costs. Such a manager or engineer is even harder to deal with if he or she demands "engineering certainty" to back up any suggestion for change. He or she is particularly skeptical about the importance of emission and effluent inventories and the economics of solving problems cost-effectively now rather than waiting for additional and more costly regulation. The concept of "pay me now or pay me later" is not sufficiently concrete for this individual.

A third problem category includes engineers and business managers who assume that all government employees are idiots or ideologues attempting to ruin industry, or are just plain arrogant. Although these views are extreme and counterproductive, there are unfortunately enough examples of technical idiocy, ideology, and arrogance to keep these prejudices alive.

There is a story, perhaps apocryphal, about an early regional administrator of EPA who became involved in a negotiation over the effluent quality requirements to be included in an NPDES permit. The negotiations turned to Ph and the industrial applicants indicated that they would be willing to attain a Ph of 7. The regional administrator, a lawyer without technical training, responded angrily, "What do you mean, 7? We want the Ph at 1!" Fortunately, there are fewer of these technical idiots around today.

Environmental issues can get very ideologically polarized. This polarization is particularly common regarding risk assessment or scope of cleanup at RCRA or Superfund sites. Moreover, even seemingly minor events not directly related to particular sites can fuel suspicions about the ideological agendas of government employees. For example, in a speech to EPA employees, Dr. Barry Commoner delivered what the *New York Times* called "a fairly savage critique of their efforts to protect the nation's health from pollution. . . . He even dared use, in proposing a solution for the nation's pollution problems, what he called 'the S-word: socialism.'" Dr. Commoner further stated that we must end " 'the taboo against social intervention in the production system' " and that "[r]emedying the nation's 'environmental failure' would 'require the courage to challenge the taboo against even questioning the present dominance of private interest over the public interest.'" At the end of his speech, "he received thunderous applause from the audience he had so unsparingly criticized." The *Times* further quoted an EPA staffer, identified by name and as "a frequent critic of the agency's policies," as saying that the Agency staff "agreed with 80 to 90 percent of what he said."[4] Needless to say, while this is an extreme case and not, in my view, representative of the views of most EPA staff, such reports seem to support the belief of some engineers and managers that agency staffs are irrevocably biased against industry, and perhaps even against capitalism.

Most government employees are competent and try to be objective, especially if you give them a basis for doing so. But whatever the government employee's competence level or ideological preferences, it may do your cause irreversible damage to have a combative engineer as your technical expert. The government employee may not like the specific technical standard either, but he or she has to enforce it or be kept on a very tight leash in negotiating. An arrogant technical expert will hurt your cause, especially if the government employee is equally arrogant or is making up for lack of experience with bravado. As mentioned above regarding lawyers, you win agency proceedings on facts, not on law. It is therefore important to produce technical experts who can persuade the agency of the facts supporting your positions. Even the majority of government employees who try to be objective will in many instances be deeply suspicious of your motivations and your credibility. An arrogant, insensitive technical person in your organization not only will fail to persuade the government employee in the particular case, but will reinforce the employee's prejudices against industry, thus making it more difficult for you to deal with that agency in the future. Although staff turnover can be heavy, agencies have long institutional memories. A few bad experiences can give your company a damaging reputation for intransigence. In short, no matter how strong technically, an arrogant, insensitive person should take no part in an agency negotiation.

Another reason to keep such people out of negotiations is that they may be more susceptible to a common tactic analogous to the "country lawyer" ploy. Many of the more intelligent young government technical and legal staff will take advantage of their youth and act more inexperienced and naive than they are. The industry representative who sees his or her stereotype confirmed and rushes in soon finds himself or herself bested in the negotiation. Many of us who are former regulators recall the success of this ploy fondly and are conscious of it when we represent industrial clients.

Note that I am not suggesting that the only technical person who can handle an agency negotiation is some outside expert with a long resume. The most effective "expert" is usually the operational engineer with a local accent who can explain the situation in practical terms, stick to his or her area of expertise, and ignore the regulatory "dance." I am also not suggesting that only the younger engineer can represent industry effectively. The older engineer who has strong operational experience but is not condescending can be very impressive and may often be looked at as a "father figure," particularly if it is clear that he or she understands the agency point of view and can offer practical solutions benefiting both sides.

Assuming technical competence, how do we make the engineer or manager who falls into one of the three problem categories environmentally conscious and politically aware? If the person is basically intelligent, a dose of reality should be helpful. Activity in a trade association committee with his or her peers, as well as specific courses in environmental law, can help the engineer just as they can help the lawyer. Trade association or other educational activities in Washington are particularly useful in acquainting the individual with the legislative process.

Engineers with government experience can also be very helpful in educating other engineers and business managers. Such engineers are hopefully on your staff; they are also found in most trade association groups and courses.

Dialogue within your organization is another method of educating engineers and managers. It is at times very frustrating, particularly when seeking technical specialists' advice on legislation, to hear requests for basic amendments to laws or regulations that have been in effect for years and are politically sacrosanct. In-house discussion on legislation and regulation can help acquaint technical staffs with the parameters of legislative and regulatory change. Communication among the technical, legal, and government relations staffs is critical here. This does not mean a variety of memoranda back and forth but frank, one-on-one discussions ensuring that everyone understands various points of view and political realities, and feels that he or she has all the facts and that his or her point of view has been considered.

Another helpful technique, particularly if you have good government contacts and credibility, is to arrange nonconfrontational opportunities for your engineers and managers to talk to government staff. You might arrange an informal social meeting with your friends from government, letting them know ahead of time that you are trying to educate a member of your staff or a business manager. If the problem is that someone higher up in management does not understand the process, it may be useful to arrange meetings between management and government and environmental group staff so that management can see that government employees and environmentalists not only are human beings, but may also understand your operations better than management realizes. These meetings should always be out of the context of specific issues of concern to the company, or there is the danger of further polarization and unnecessary role playing. I have found this technique very helpful with senior managers who, in a nonadversarial setting, have come away with a new appreciation of government and environmentalist concerns. Following these dialogues, these internal "bottlenecks" can become your best supporters.

Incidentally, you should use the reverse of this approach if a negotiation reaches an impasse because of an unfortunate run-in with a stereotypically arrogant, ideological, or uninformed agency employee. Allowing a more senior manager to tag along may help bolster your position within the corporation by showing that manager your difficulties and the agency's refusal to understand "logic" as perceived within your company or industry.

Some engineers, like some lawyers, simply will never have the proper approach to environmental engineering or dealing with their agency counterparts. The only solution in those instances is simply to move heaven and earth to keep them out of your department, and to get them out if they are already in it. Chapter 3 discussed some hiring techniques designed to avoid the unfortunate necessity of firing or transferring someone for inability to do the job.

Dealing With Consultants

Many of us have heard the consultant defined as an individual who borrows your watch and then charges you for telling you the time. This definition has received wide circulation because in far too many cases it is correct. To avoid getting into this situation, you must know when to use, how to choose, and how to manage consultants.

Use of consultants is most productive when they provide specific expertise that is not available in house and that is necessary for a specific, limited purpose. For example, consultants may be useful in preparing or evaluating training programs. Use of consultants with specific technical expertise in preparing an EIS can also be cost-effective.

Some companies have outside consultants perform environmental audits. I do not generally recommend this because of consultants' lack of inside credibility and understanding of operations, as well as the importance of having the operations themselves feel responsible for environmental awareness and compliance. If used at all, consultants should generally be part of a team, filling in specific expertise that is lacking in house. However, an outside consulting firm may be useful in performing an initial assessment if you feel that is the only way to bring the need for assessments to management's attention. There are also times when a third party, such as a consultant, can provide an objective, unbiased review of an existing audit program. A good consultant with expertise in diverse areas may bring constructive and different approaches to the table. This may be particularly helpful if you are attempting to upgrade your audit program and need to verify to yourself or to senior management that the upgrade is necessary.

Finally, consultants, like outside lawyers, are frequently used simply because in-house people are unwilling to take the heat for an unpopular decision or because management is not satisfied unless a recommendation has the imprimatur of an outside expert. Reliance on consultants may be part of the corporate culture. Even if you resent this and know that you could do the job just as well, you will be stuck with using consultants.

The decision to use consultants does not terminate your management responsibilities, however. Your next task is to select the right consultant.

Few consulting firms—and few law firms—won't claim expertise on a specific subject if you ask them about it. It is your job as a manager to ascertain that this expertise really exists.

Referrals from other companies can be helpful. Bar associations may also be good sources for determining the value of environmental consultants. For example, the Los Angeles County Bar Association Environmental Law Section has "a program for identifying environmental consultants and associating names of lawyers with the consultants if there has been a working relationship between them."[5] As in hiring any contractor, an in-person interview is imperative. You need to ask tough questions such as, "How much will the work cost? Will the price include preparation of written materials and a presentation, if necessary, to public agencies?" In addition, "[a]sk the consultant about prior experience with public agencies and individuals in public agencies with whom he or she has had contact."[6]

There has been enormous growth in the use of consultants regarding Superfund and other hazardous waste management issues, as well as acquisitions and sales. Even the best consulting firms are straining their available expertise. Managers may have had either excellent or poor experiences with consulting firms depending on the specific personnel utilized. An individual with a degree in environmental science and not much else will not be able to give cost-effective suggestions for dealing with issues, and/or may make recommendations that do not fit operational reality. Thus, in hiring consultants, just as in hiring outside counsel, it is important to insist not only that the firm have a good reputation for expertise in the area you are addressing, but that it use specific individuals who justify that reputation and that the use of those individuals be specified in the agreement with the consulting firm. If outside consultants are required for environmental assessments, acquisitions, or sales, it is imperative that some of the individuals on the job have operational experience. If nothing else, this will establish credibility with in-house operational personnel.

Once the consulting firm is hired, it should not receive carte blanche. *Your job is to manage that consultant.* If you define the scope of work explicitly and manage the consultant properly, a good consultant can provide what you want at the appropriate cost. However, a consultant will study everything in depth or prepare fancy reports that you do not need unless you remain in close coordination and set adequate guidelines. In addition, unless you keep a close watch, use of consultants tends to create problems characteristic of the particular type of job the consultant is doing.

For example, consultants specializing in EISs are usually scientists rather than engineers and are usually very concerned about their scientific credibility. Of course, this credibility is key to a successful project, and it is important to have on your staff people who understand its importance. However, in seeking to prove that he or she has not "sold out" to industry, a consultant may overcompensate and reach conclusions unfavorable to you. These conclusions may not be fully thought out. Questioning the consultant closely on the conclusions may reveal any inherent weaknesses, but the individual's ego or suspicion that industry is trying to limit his or her objectivity may get in the way of reasoning. The best way to avoid unsatisfactory conclusions is to avoid having the consultant draw conclusions at all. The scientist should stick to science; he or she is not the decisionmaker. Similarly, environmental assessments should stick to facts, rather than reaching conclusions such as, "This is a violation of RCRA." Once the consultants have given them the information they need, other members of your organization are responsible for drawing the proper conclusions.

Two other problems commonly arise when consultants conduct environmental assessments. First, some consultants "low ball" future environmental costs for fear of being "deal killers." Conversely, consultants may make overly broad recommendations, particularly if their firm is looking for long-term business or provides additional engineering or design services. Many consultants are "technology-happy" and will propose effective, but gold-plated, solutions to your problems. This tendency also appears in areas such as fire protection. Operating personnel frequently harbor the deep suspicion that a consultant will not feel fire protection is adequate unless it involves a steel beam cast in concrete and buried in a lake. In-house staffs often can find ways to provide equivalent protection at lesser cost.

A final consideration in dealing with consultants is confidentiality. If you hire a consultant to do a specific audit where you suspect legal problems, or to evaluate the environmental impacts of an acquisition, you may wish to protect the material the consultant obtains or generates. You can do this by structuring the agreement properly through your counsel and ensuring that the consultant follows the provisions designed to protect confidentiality. A nondisclosure agreement to prevent unauthorized disclosure of client information or consultant work product is advisable. Another means of protection is to have attorneys retain the consultant and to have the consultant bill the attorneys. The agreement may also need to state expressly that the consultant is being retained to provide advice in anticipation of litigation. The data gathered and any other written material should be the property of the attorneys, and its dissemination should be restricted. Like other material with legal implications, any written or oral reports from the consultant should be transmitted to the attorney, data should be segregated and marked as confidential communications, and sensitive material should be distributed only to those with a need to know. [7] Be aware, however, that there is no sure way of protecting environmental studies from disclosure.

This discussion illustrates the fact that all consultants are not merely out to tell you the time from your own watch. Like other resources, consultants are valuable if you know how to choose and manage them. Indeed, by leveraging consultants' expertise, you can greatly increase the effectiveness of your program.

Notes to Chapter 8

1. *See* "Recruiting Environmental Professionals" in Chapter 3 for a discussion of techniques for hiring competent staff.

2. Eckert, *Representing Private Clients in EPA Rule Making*, NAT. RESOURCES & ENV'T, Winter 1985, at 27, 30.

3. The U.S. Supreme Court's recent decision in Daubert v. Merrell Dow Pharmaceuticals, Inc., __ U.S. __, No. 92-102 (June 28, 1993), did not significantly change this situation.

4. Shabecoff, *E.P.A. Critic Enters the Lion's Den And Is Showered by Wild Applause*, N.Y. TIMES, Jan. 15, 1988.

5. Dennis, *How to Select and Use an Environmental Consultant*, 4 PRAC. REAL EST. LAW. 83, 88 (1988).

6. *Id.*

7. *See id.* at 88-89.

Chapter 9:
Dealing With Federal and State Agencies, Citizen Groups, the Press, and the Public

The purpose of this chapter is not to guide the corporate manager or legal practitioner through the maze of environmental laws and regulations, but to give helpful hints on dealing with the issues and people involved. However, the chapter does discuss some legal issues, including those regarding the scope of review of agency decisions. [1]

The Regulators

Federal Regulators

Although federal and state decisions are often intertwined, it is important to distinguish between federal and state regulators. The federal regulators, specifically EPA employees, are divided among the Washington, D.C., headquarters and 10 regions. On its face, EPA is a decentralized organization, but major policy issues require decisions from Washington.

The centralized-decentralized dichotomy breaks down on an issue-specific basis. For example, in the hazardous waste area, each region seems to have its own view of policy, and headquarters has found it almost impossible to ensure uniformity. [2] Each region is jealous of its "turf," and often views headquarters as out-of-step with the real world and difficult to work with in terms of obtaining decisions. Headquarters returns the compliment, generally viewing the regions as not being totally aware of the Agency's mission and not always cognizant of the implications of its decisions. If these characterizations sound familiar to those of you attempting to deal with business organizational stresses, you probably now realize that one key to dealing with the Agency is recognition that in many respects its internal stresses are no different from those of any large organization. Of course, as a government agency, it is more vulnerable to congressional pressure. It is also slower to make decisions because it lacks incentives (other than statutory deadlines) for timely decisionmaking.

To deal successfully with EPA, or any other large government agency, it is critical to analyze the organizational structure and find out what moves the agency along. To obtain a favorable decision, it is also critical to determine what EPA will gain from such a decision, as well as what political and legal "heat" the decision will generate. [3] Your role as an advocate will be to craft a solution for the Agency that will fulfill its purposes and minimize the "heat." The solution probably will not include everything your management desires, but this is also true of the outcome of litigation. [4]

If you are involved in an Agency rulemaking, you must bear in mind that EPA holds almost all the cards.

> [A] private party should recognize the character of the proceeding into which he is entering. The major federal environmental statutes (e.g., the Clean Air Act, Clean Water Act, Resource Conservation and Recovery Act) are goal-oriented. EPA has been given broad authority under each to deal with risk to public health or welfare from pollution of the air, water, or lands of the United States; however, specific guidance from Congress on how EPA is to interpret and implement these broad statutory mandates is generally sparse.
>
> Also, the rule-making procedures that implement these statutes do not follow the rules of "fair play" of a judicial proceeding. These are legislative rule makings where none of the judicial rules apply. In effect, EPA itself is witness, prosecutor, judge, and jury. Even the elemental features of reasonably accurate transcripts of proceedings and access to the record upon which the rule making is based are sometimes (as a practical matter) not available. [5]

You should also know that most EPA staffers, particularly the lawyers, are competent, committed to environmental protection, and inherently skeptical about industry. There has been a strong Agency bias against hiring personnel with industry experience, so very few EPA staffers have ever worked in industry. Many very capable lawyers come to the Agency because they strongly believe in environmental protection and because they feel that they will have excellent job opportunities upon leaving the Agency. The legal staff at EPA (and at the U.S. Department of Justice's Environment and Natural Resources Division, which often represents EPA in litigation [6]) is of a very high quality, although many staffers are young and inexperienced. In contrast, although many EPA technical personnel are competent, their qualifications are generally lower than those of the lawyers. They have not necessarily had the same sense of mission and/or future career opportunity. This is now changing, particularly with the dramatic growth in opportunities for technical personnel experienced in hazardous waste. These opportunities have attracted more qualified technical personnel to EPA. Unfortunately, they have also led to rapid turnover.

In short, if you represent an applicant for a permit or an alleged violator of a regulation, you will usually face skilled but inexperienced staffers who are inherently skeptical about the merits of your position. You must overcome their skepticism. In most cases, this means you must engage in intelligent, good-faith negotiating. Patience in explaining your position and waiting for a decision must be the rule. It is usually not advantageous to come on strong with the regulator. Threats of political pressure, going over his or her head, or other attempts to throw your weight around normally will not help your client. Even the most inexperienced regulator has heard it all before, and all you will do is reinforce his or her derogatory image of industry.

There are times, however, when it is advisable to suggest to the staffer that you discuss the issue together with his or her boss so that you can both have the benefit of his or her wisdom. Again, this advice may sound familiar in terms of working within a business system. It illustrates the importance of working with an agency's decisionmaking process much as you would work with the decisionmaking process of any other organization. Similarly, attempts to go "right to the top" to obtain a decision—without doing the necessary spadework beforehand—are not advisable. Your ability to achieve this kind of access may impress your management, but it usually will not obtain the desired decision. Going over a staffer's head without his or her knowledge, except in the most extreme cases, will only antagonize the staffer and make it harder to achieve the appropriate decision for your client. Agency managers are accustomed to this kind of maneuvering and will normally back their staff, unless there is a significant error in policy or judgment. Moreover, unless there are policy issues involved that must be decided immediately, the higher level official will want a briefing from his or her staff before making a decision. The usual time to "go to the top" is when lower level staff agree with you and you need a quick decision on the issue. With the staffer on your side, the decision will be quicker, and usually the right one.

If a region is not handling an issue satisfactorily, the temptation is to try to bypass it and go directly to Washington. This is analogous to appealing to headquarters because of unsatisfactory dealings with a district in the business sector. Obviously, the region will not look favorably on this approach, and you must use it cautiously. EPA headquarters personnel are well aware of regional sensitivities, including the importance of protecting "turf." Trying to get Washington involved in a strictly local controversy is usually a waste of time and will antagonize the decisionmakers in the region.

Merely trying to determine whether there is a central policy that deals with your issue, or to obtain a general counsel's opinion, [7] is safer.

Even if there is an official policy, however, the region will not necessarily follow it. Many of us who practice in this area have experienced the frustration of referring to a memo from Washington on a subject, only to be told that the region will make its own decision. A memo that has been published in the *Federal Register* is more likely to be followed. Even published memos are sometimes disregarded, however. For example, the former Superfund settlement policy established a general rule that the federal government would not settle for less than 80 percent of cleanup costs, but also provided for exceptions to this rule. [8] Regional Agency personnel interpreted the exceptions very narrowly, and high-level personnel knew this. Nevertheless, Washington would rarely overrule the regions. Moreover, with the intense political pressure for hazardous waste site cleanup, regions simply had no incentive to negotiate. One commentator has noted that in the hazardous waste cleanup context, "inaction [by EPA] provokes fewer penalties than action and it is safe to spend or sue but dangerous to negotiate." [9] This comment applies equally well to other politically charged issues (including most environmental problems). Therefore, you cannot assume that official guidance from Washington will force the regions to work constructively with you.

You may find it useful to hire a former regulator to assist you in dealing with EPA. You should not assume, however, that such a person will automatically be able to obtain the right decision within a reasonable time. The ability to understand how the Agency thinks and who pushes what buttons is quite helpful, but, as discussed in Chapter 4, this advocate has his or her limits. His or her strength with his or her former colleagues is his or her competence and credibility. In short, successful advocates in the environmental area will not and should not jeopardize their credibility for the sake of victory on a specific issue. This means that if your position is unsound, simply hiring a former "insider" will not solve your problem. [10]

In working with EPA, remember that the Agency is not monolithic. In some cases, EPA's technical staff or program managers may be more sympathetic to your position than its lawyers are. While it is dangerous to try to "play off" one group against another, and while you cannot rely on "deals" that have not been approved by the lawyers, it can be helpful to focus on working with technical personnel to develop a reasonable position that they can support. You should not try to deal with program managers in the absence of counsel, however; EPA counsel are very sensitive about this, especially if you are a lawyer or if you are involved in actual litigation. [11] While direct communication with "EPA program managers below the level where final decisions are made" is not unethical, since they are not "parties," [12] EPA attorneys feel that this is going behind their back. "[F]ew actions will earn the distrust of government litigation counsel more surely than attempts to negotiate with program managers while excluding their counsel." [13]

There are also times when EPA program managers themselves mistrust their lawyers (or lawyers in general), and it can be helpful for you to meet with the program manager, accompanied by counsel on both sides. At that point, if you can encourage a dialogue between the two managers, while keeping both counsel as quiet as possible, settlement becomes more likely. Agency counsel, like private counsel, get caught up in the "chase" of litigation and tend to forget the objective. Getting the principals together under these circumstances can be extremely helpful, unless you have had little experience with Agency personnel and have little patience with the necessary (or unnecessary) bureaucratic constraints. The frustration level can be quite high, especially for those trained in technical disciplines.

Finally, you should be aware that negotiations can be particularly difficult when EPA contractors are involved. EPA often picks contractors based primarily on the lowest bid. Many of us have found that issues in complex litigation are resolved when the Agency finally spends the money to hire the most qualified contractor, rather than the cheapest. The competence and credibility of EPA's outside technical personnel are therefore critical.

Notwithstanding the desire of lawyers to be lawyers, the most important point to remember in dealing with EPA is that *most issues with the Agency are won, not on the law, but on technical arguments within the Agency.* "[Y]ou would be better advised to accept EPA's legal interpretations and to base your arguments for change on factual and policy grounds." [14] Your counsel's primary job should be to ensure that the best arguments are presented in as noncombative a manner as possible.

The role of good technical and policy experts cannot be overemphasized. Small businesses do not have these people in house, and few large companies have technical people with the patience and "people ability" to deal with their federal counterparts, who are usually young and inexperienced. Arrogant or patronizing industry representatives will jeopardize your case. If your in-house staffers do not have the necessary expertise and the proper attitudes, you may have to use outside specialists in EPA negotiations. Sometimes, however, small businessmen or in-house people can be more successful than outside experts. If these people are sincere and credible, they can make their points even if they are not familiar with Agency jargon. The Agency's technical people will respond to sincerity and openness. Counsel's job will be to ensure that the proper record is made and to step back as far as possible. If the issue becomes a "spitting match" between lawyers, you are being done a disservice.

When considering litigation, it is important to recognize that the Agency's burden of proof in upholding its decision is usually easy to meet. [15] Conversely, if your internal advocacy with the Agency has been successful, a challenge to an Agency decision in your favor is also unlikely to prevail.

> Where an Agency policy eases compliance with pollution control legislation, the challengers to that policy have the burden of proving that the policy is clearly precluded. The Court will not conduct a searching review in order to determine whether the Agency considered all of the environmental consequences of its actions and whether the purposes of the legislation have all been met. Thus, the Court will uphold an Agency action that eases strict mandates, except where the particular action is precluded by unambiguous statutory language or where the Agency failed to compile any record. [16]

Because courts are likely to uphold statutory interpretations, your best strategy for overturning an Agency determination in court is trying to distinguish your case on factual or policy grounds rather than making a head-on attack on the law. [17]

I am not suggesting that you should never threaten litigation. But if the Agency perceives that threats to its authority or position are not being made in good faith, both sides will find their positions cast in concrete. Conversely, if EPA perceives that a company will settle anything rather than litigate, the company's ability to negotiate reasonable settlements will quickly evaporate. If EPA perceives that the company will settle when there is a reasonable opportunity to settle, but will take a strong position when it firmly believes it is right, the company's credibility and, in turn, its settlement posture will improve. When EPA realizes that threats to litigate are real and that the company has a good track record in winning, there are more opportunities to resolve matters reasonably. [18]

State and Local Regulators

Many of the difficulties discussed above in working with EPA to develop optimum solutions are compounded when you must also work with state and local agencies. Almost every one of the major federal environmental statutes "establishes a framework for a federal-state 'partnership.'" [19] However, the partnerships are troubled.

> The utopia envisioned by Congress in which the state and federal governments work together combining broad technical

and scientific knowledge with intimate acquaintance with local conditions rarely works out in practice. Instead, the highly complex environmental statutes with their overlapping responsibilities, particularly in enforcement, give rise to a constant tension between federal and state agencies that runs all the way from differing interpretations of the same regulatory language to differing views on the seriousness of a particular regulatory violation. [20]

State and local agencies are important players on the environmental scene. As a representative of the regulated community, you need to be familiar with the characteristics of those agencies and with the consequences of the flaws in the federal-state "partnership" model. Most state and local agencies have limited resources. Federal statutes have increased the burden on states by requiring them to implement federal regulations, but federal funding has not been significantly increased and state funds have also been limited. Most state salary levels are substantially below federal levels, which makes it difficult for states to recruit and keep competent and experienced attorneys and technical staff. Despite their lower salaries, however, senior management officials in many states seem to be more career-oriented than EPA officials. Because of long tenure, they also have more practical experience.

State and local agencies are in some ways easier to deal with than EPA. First, perhaps because they don't have time for bureaucratic niceties, these agencies are generally much less formal than EPA in dealing with applicants or alleged violators, and higher level personnel who can make decisions are readily accessible. Lower level officials are also much more likely to be willing to bring matters to higher level personnel, who are more accustomed than their federal counterparts to making decisions. Furthermore, having a manager or technical specialist explain your company's situation, as suggested above regarding EPA, may be even more helpful here, where a local accent or shared acquaintances may increase credibility.

However, state and local officials are also much more susceptible to political pressures than is EPA. If a political situation gets too hot, the federal government can simply walk away from a local powder keg, as long as it doesn't have broader implications. State and local officials cannot do this. Moreover, ambitious local and state officials have been known to exaggerate the political pressures on agencies to further their own political careers. If a state attorney general or a local city attorney wants to make an issue of your project or problem, finding a practical solution can be extremely difficult. It becomes even more complicated when "the head of the environmental agency and the attorney general come from different political parties and follow different agendas."[21]

Political pressure against your project can become intense if a citizen group claims significant local health problems. "If the agency perceives itself as being accountable for a public emergency, appeals to its rules and policies may have some effect in restraining and directing it, but all too frequently in those circumstances the political powers in the government will sow the wind and the private defendant will reap the whirlwind."[22]

Political pressure can ensure that no matter what you do, either technically or legally, the matter will be decided by litigation in order to avoid political heat. Like EPA, state and local agencies frequently find that when an issue is politically hot, "inaction provokes fewer penalties than action and it is safe to spend or sue but dangerous to negotiate."[23]

The political sensitivities of state and local agencies can sometimes work to your advantage. State and local officials may respond to political pressures exerted on your own or your client's behalf. Great care must be used in exercising such pressure, however. Some state and local governments will be very receptive to the arguments of industrial clients in order to keep jobs in the community. However, some of these agencies may not fully understand the law. You thereby risk the "Lord, protect me from my friends" syndrome of obtaining a favorable decision that is not legally supportable. Your counsel can be very helpful in keeping you from being misled by such assurances.

On the federal level, political pressure will rarely help your client obtain the right decision, and indeed is usually counterproductive. Because the federal authorities are generally more mission-oriented and less susceptible to political pressures, their broad authority over programs delegated to states also makes a political strategy at the state or local level very risky. You should use such a strategy only if the settlement or solution you propose is clearly within the law and within "policy." As a general rule, government agencies have an "inherent instinct for rules and policies."[24] In the field of environmental problem-solving and litigation,

> it is important to set the arguments within the terms of the policies, since those are the terms in which the government attorneys are thinking. It is generally more advantageous to justify a desired result in terms of congruence with a policy than to suggest that the policy does not fit the facts and that disinterested analysis of the facts should prevail.[25]

If there are no direct policies on a particular point, the obvious answer is to find an analogous policy.[26] It is also important to recognize that if a settlement is significant, or if a rulemaking is involved, it will in one way or another be subject to public comment. [27] Inconsistencies with policy or federal law will be brought out, and a loosely crafted resolution will not stand up.

Dealings with state and local agencies are further complicated by frequent "turf" fights between these agencies and federal officials. It is important to check whether the federal government disagrees with state and local officials over policy or regulatory interpretation. Such disagreements frequently arise, for example, regarding implementation of the Clean Air Act through approved state implementation plans. States and localities are required to write regulations meeting federal standards. A regulation that does not meet those standards will not obtain federal approval, but may remain on the books of the state or locality. Thus, a state or local regulation may allow a proposed operation, but the regulation may not have federal approval. If this situation occurs in an area that has not attained the air quality required under the Clean Air Act, the federal government may prohibit the project even if state and local officials approve it. Your "friends" may have helped you win the battle, but you will have lost the war.

For example, there is continuing controversy between the federal government and the South Coast Air Quality Management District (SCAQMD) over the banking of emissions as a result of shut-downs and other means of reducing emissions. The federal government will approve banking of some emission reductions but not others. The SCAQMD will accept some banking that the federal government would not, and will not accept some banking that the federal government would. A permit applicant must therefore take care to comply with both sets of regulations, regardless of any assurances by the SCAQMD that compliance with its regulations is all that is necessary.

Overlapping agency jurisdiction can be particularly critical in litigation.

> [I]t is especially important to establish and understand the authority of the attorneys on the other side of the table in an environmental suit. The private litigant should anticipate that, if settlement is reached with only part of the governmental structure, another office will look for the opportunity to add some icing to the settlement cake in order to justify and maintain its position within the government. [28]

However, this does not mean that settlements can be negotiated with all agencies together. "The nature of the state-federal relationship often breeds rivalries and antagonisms that make common negotiation or settlement difficult and perhaps impossible. The different governments run on different timetables and have different frameworks for the review of settlements that often make coordination difficult." [29]

If you face this situation, "there will be times when settlement with one government and litigation against the other may be the most advisable course; for instance, if a reasonable settlement is available with the party with the strongest legal claim and no compromise is possible with the other."[30] Most compromises (especially in the hazardous waste area) must be approved by a court through some form of consent decree. Ideally, an experienced judge will be in a good position to place pressure on the nonsettling agency. As a practical matter, that agency has the burden of showing why it has not acted "reasonably" in trying to resolve a difficult matter. But if there is a perception of a "sweetheart deal" with the settling agency, this strategy can backfire, increasing the political pressure on the non-settling agency to "hang tough."

In summary, it is much more difficult to generalize about state and local agencies, or even about agencies with the same mission in different states, than about EPA and the Department of Justice, which have certain generic characteristics. State and local agencies' "turf" fights with federal agencies complicate the situation further. However, some of the common sense suggestions above may make interaction with these agencies a little easier.

Citizen Groups

As with federal, state, and local regulatory agencies, it is important to recognize what motivates citizen groups. Different groups may have different motivations, and their levels of competence and sophistication also vary substantially.

National organizations such as the Natural Resources Defense Council, the Sierra Club Legal Defense Fund, and the Environmental Defense Fund are well funded and employ extremely capable and generally experienced counsel. Their technical staffs are also usually quite competent, but have their own ideological biases. These groups engage in litigation on broad national issues.[31] They will often back up local organizations if the issues have broader range significance. The national organizations are also quite expert at mobilizing grassroots support for their positions. Since agency staff are concerned about public criticism, this ability to influence public opinion is a valuable asset for these citizen groups.

The national organizations' litigation track record is also quite good, perhaps partly because they pick and choose their cases. Thus, if a national group has joined a local organization against your project, you know there is a problem. While these groups still need to make the necessary record, that may not be an insurmountable difficulty.[32]

Local citizen groups vary much more than the national groups. Existing or proposed industrial projects frequently spur local involvement. If an EIS is required under NEPA because the federal government is involved at some decision point, public involvement is specifically required. [33] (See Chapter 10 for specific issues and concerns with respect to the EIS.) The state versions of NEPA also require public involvement.

There are a variety of strategies for handling public involvement in both NEPA and non-NEPA matters. [34] In general,

> [l]ocal opposition (as well as that of national groups if the project appears to be precedent-setting or of specific interest) should be defused as quickly and as early as possible. Usually, the initial concern stems not from an ideological commitment to stop a project, but rather from economic or personal (subjective) values, such as a fear that the project will lower real estate or home values. There is a rule of reason, of course, for determining when this discussion should begin. If it begins too early, the local population understandably gets agitated because adequate data is not yet available. Conversely, if the process starts too late, the local population may feel the project is a *fait accompli*; they might then conclude that the only answer is to "pass the hat" and start litigation, and/or increase the involvement of state and local politicians seeking easy political mileage by being "pro-green." Rather, the time to make sure the populace and local groups are aware of the project is when [you have] a solid data base so that the various questions and legitimate concerns of the groups can be answered. [35]

In either a NEPA or a non-NEPA context, it is critical that the applicant have a strong database with which to address local concerns.

Don't conclude from this that early involvement of local and national groups will necessarily prevent later litigation, particularly if the project appears to be precedent setting or of specific local interest. However, it has an excellent chance of at least narrowing the issues and reducing the time required for a final decision on the permit. A final decision is made not when the permitting agency issues a permit, but when the final opportunity for appeal in the court system is exhausted.

Opportunities for settlement of these issues vary. The attorneys for citizen groups, particularly national groups, may often be willing to compromise. However, they must also answer to clients. A businessman may feel strongly about an issue on ideological grounds, but may be persuaded to give in because of the ultimate economic impact. However, the statutes, regulations, and agency staff all have inherent biases against broad consideration of economic values. Citizen group clients who have brought or are preparing to bring litigation on the basis of strong ideological positions also are not motivated by economics. Therefore, potential settlements must often be formulated in terms of providing the greatest benefit to the environment.

Some argue that mediation, conciliation, or settlement can expedite a project.[36] These processes work best, however, within a very narrow structure, and then only if there is no major ideological dispute involving fundamental principles of concern to various environmental groups.[37]

It is imperative for managers and counsel representing development interests to be aware of the potential for ideological warfare over certain projects. If a major issue of principle is involved, the potential for delay must be considered in evaluating the economics of the project.

Public Relations

Dealings with the public are absolutely critical to environmental management. The previous section mentioned the importance of meeting with the public early in the project context. Chapter 4 noted that Occidental considers public relations issues "significant matters" that must be reported in its environmental management system. Chapter 5 discussed the public relations benefits of environmental assessments. Many companies use the term community relations to describe dealing with the public rather than public relations, which connotes press relations. I will use the terms interchangeably in this section.

Most companies have public relations departments, but the environmental manager must also understand the importance of this area of expertise. Most of us do not consider ourselves experts in dealing with the press and the public, in developing campaigns that will persuade the public, or in managing disasters. However, public relations is a constant in our jobs and we therefore need sufficient expertise to be able to give advice in all of these areas in coordination with our public relations departments. A detailed analysis of public relations techniques and detailed case studies on public relations triumphs or disasters are beyond the scope of this book, but the following sections explain some key public relations rules for environmental managers.

Dealing With the Press

Company positions must be clearly enunciated and presented uniformly to all media at all times. There is nothing worse than different people in an organization saying slightly different things on the same issue. On an evolving issue, the company position might change, and continuity must be maintained.

It is also particularly important that the company develop its position with input from the various staff disciplines involved, including environmental, legal, and public relations. Should any one of these groups become over-bearing, there can be serious repercussions. For example, if the legal department is not flexible and creative, the company may give the press too few facts and lose credibility.

Some company public relations departments are very careful to limit press contacts to specific public relations spokespeople. This position is not usually a move to protect turf, but is based on a legitimate concern that unless you know the press mentality and the rules under which the press operates, it is very easy to have a public relations disaster.

Perhaps the greatest danger in dealing with the press is a false assumption that you are speaking off the record. The number of people burned by this false assumption is legion. If you have developed a long-term relationship with a reporter who has a reputation for integrity, your background briefing or "off the record" comment may indeed be off the record. You can develop such a relationship by being a technical source for the reporter, not necessarily regarding specific matters involving your company. Most reporters who cover environmental issues do not have environmental experience or technical expertise. Their natural inclination is to be cynical about industry and assume the worst. Unless, by serving as a resource for technical data, you have educated a reporter, reduced his or her cynicism, and developed a long-term relationship, you must not assume you are off the record. The safest position is to assume that anything you say to a reporter is on the record.

Despite the risks of dealing directly with the press, limiting press contacts strictly to your public relations department is not necessarily the most effective means of getting your story across. In many companies, a call from the press brings the standard answer of "I'll get back to you." Corporate bureaucracy prevents the call from being returned immediately, and then the reporter is past his or her deadline. The reporter will not only be unable to include your comments, he or she may also conclude that you have something to hide, particularly if the eventual contact is a public relations person who cannot answer his or her specific questions.

Indeed, the public relations department would prefer that your spokesman be an operating or staff person who has specific expertise and understands relations with the press. If the public relations spokesman is an expert in your field, which is usually not the case, he or she can be effective. In addition, many public relations departments run programs training management to deal with the press. Those programs probably should be expanded. Technical and legal specialists should become more involved in public relations, just as they have become more involved in Washington advocacy. Ideally, a reporter will talk to the technical expert and the public relations expert together; this gives him the best opportunity to understand your position clearly.

A company should have a policy on dealing with the press. Even in the absence of a policy, it is vital to check with a public relations expert about the credentials of the reporter requesting information. I learned the importance of such a check the hard way almost 20 years ago.

I was interviewed for a future radio program. What I didn't know was that the reporter would edit the interview and insert questions that he hadn't asked me in order to make his points. The "fixed" questions were asked to someone else whom the reporter favored. When the program aired, it sounded like a face-to-face debate. What I also didn't know was that this reporter had a reputation for playing this kind of game. I have done other radio debates since, but always live. The danger of having your statements taken out of context by editing is greater than you may think. Indeed, I have seen the raw and edited tapes of a well-known television investigative reporting program that pulled similar stunts.

It is also important to be certain that what you say cannot be taken out of context even without reportorial "dirty tricks." Reporters are looking for catch statements and sometimes lose qualifiers. When I first began to work for industry in 1970, I made a statement that could have been taken out of context with disastrous results. As a member of an unusual breed at that time, an environmental lawyer working for a corporation, I was on a New York City Bar Association panel entitled "Young Lawyers and the Legal Revolution," and I made a comment that received extensive coverage in the *New York Times*. I first stated: "There are too many Neanderthals in corporations that have nearly wrecked the corporate system." If that comment had been reported without my qualifier, "but a surprising number of corporate executives have consciences," my career in the industrial sector might have been very short-lived. Instead, my company was delighted with the publicity. This publicity also bolstered the general counsel's arguments to management that in the new fields with broad social policy considerations, particularly environmental law and civil rights law, it was important to hire lawyers who normally would not have considered corporate legal departments as a place of employment. However, I realized that I had been lucky to escape trouble, and learned a valuable lesson on being very careful about statements with qualifiers.

Dealing With the Public

Credibility is critical to good public relations. You may have a public relations disaster, such as the Ashland tank disaster in Pennsylvania, but there are opportunities for salvage. You can often maintain credibility by promptly acknowledging your responsibilities and taking corrective action. Ashland, for example, moved very rapidly, recognizing that its legal defenses were minimal. It faced up to its responsibilities immediately and the chief executive made a variety of public statements that were well received. Another example, in a different context, of a good effort to turn around a disaster was Johnson & Johnson's response in the Tylenol™ poisoning case. Here was a situation totally beyond the company's control, but recognizing the imperative of consumer confidence, the company spent a huge amount in recalling and redesigning its product.

Conversely, Exxon's response to the *Valdez* tanker spill can be perceived as a classic miscalculation. [38] In the event of a perceived environmental or safety incident, the public expects the company's senior executives to be actively and openly involved in mitigation. The public also expects an apology. The company does not have to admit liability, but it must indicate that it cares. Nothing could undo the Bhopal tragedy, but the chairman of Union Carbide went immediately to India at some considerable personal risk. Exxon's failure to send its chairman immediately to Valdez, and the resulting public perception that it did not care, has been viewed as making a bad situation worse. One crisis management expert stated, "As phony as it sounds, sending the chairman to the scene would have shown genuine concern for what happened there." [39] Apparently the Chairman of Exxon agrees with that statement since "[h]e stated that although his instinct had been to head to Alaska, he was persuaded not to by a consensus of his fellow Exxon executives." [40]

In the hazardous waste context, credibility can be extremely difficult to achieve. This was particularly true in the early days, just before Superfund, when there was strong political pressure to develop a groundswell for a Superfund law. As mentioned earlier, the public and most politicians and reporters don't recognize the distinction between trace amounts and harmful quantities of hazardous pollutants, or between situations in which exposure is unlikely and those in which there is an immediate pathway of exposure. If you attempt to take these issues head-on, you will be accused of being callous.

A citizen group can make outrageous statements without any technical backup, and can release so-called health studies that may be full of holes. [41] If you attempt to refute these statements and studies with technical arguments, normally your audience's eyes will glaze over. Even if they listen, they probably won't believe you. After all, you are the polluter as opposed to the victimized citizen. Even if the health studies are eventually discredited, the "exposed" citizens will not believe that the studies are invalid and will sue. Of course, any population includes cases of cancer and birth defects. The public (and some juries) immediately assume that your activities caused these conditions. Your only response to this kind of situation, commonly known as chemophobia, is longer term, low-key, nonthreatening programs that attempt gradual education.

The previous discussion should not be considered a statement that company activities can never cause health problems. Far too often, however, public fear greatly exceeds the actual risks.

The environmental manager is often in the unenviable position of being the local spokesman. As in working with the government, patience is critical. If you do your homework and retain your cool, particularly through the first few meetings, the furor will gradually diminish. There will be individuals who for political reasons want to maintain public frenzy, and will not be turned around. The public may also look on you as a "good guy," while continuing to be suspicious about your company. This is still a good start.

To prevent chemophobia from developing in the first place, you must maintain your image in the local community through grassroots efforts. Employees should be encouraged to participate in local organizations so that they become known as individuals and not industry ogres. Arranging an "open house" at your local facility can also be helpful. The public normally assumes that a factory or plant is a horrendous place. If you have a well-run and well-kept facility, these visits may improve your local image. It is particularly useful to have the actual operators explain the processes. Usually, their pride in their work and in the facility will come through to the visitors.

Where the issue is siting, concern for real estate values will awaken formerly latent environmental instincts. If it feels, rightly or wrongly, that your siting decision will reduce the value of its housing, even the most conservative and pro-business community will turn out in droves, pass a large hat, and give you major difficulties. You may have all the facts in the world indicating that your project will not harm the environment, but you still have to dispel the concern about real estate values.

It is also important from a business standpoint for senior managers in industries viewed by the public as polluters to recognize that, whether or not they are right, they and their companies will not be loved. This is particularly troublesome to senior managers who have devoted their lives to a company and in turn want the company to be liked. This is an unrealistic expectation. At best, the public may look upon you as a responsible company within a polluting industry. Even achieving this level of acceptance will be particularly difficult if your industry is considered a polluter and doesn't generate many jobs. Unfortunately, some senior managers have become virtually obsessed with attacks on their companies and spend an inordinate amount of time trying to change positions taken by public groups that simply are beyond the persuasive power of the senior managers or anyone else, to the detriment of their primary job of managing a company or a specific operation. Of course, in a major disaster, the chief executive must step in and, if nothing else, make it clear that he or she is on top of the situation. For example, senior executives of Union Carbide (Bhopal), Ashland, and Johnson & Johnson have acted as spokesmen following their respective crises. But senior executives have to recognize that some forces are beyond their control.

Managers should also remember that, over time, many disasters, unless they bear the name of a company (such as the AMOCO *Cadiz* tanker disaster), become generic, and the involvement of the company becomes obscure. This is little comfort at the time of the disaster, but the longer view must be borne in mind in developing a good public relations campaign.

Notes to Chapter 9

1. For a general discussion of environmental law, see LAW OF ENVIRONMENTAL PROTECTION (S. Novick ed. 1987, 1992), and D. SIVE & F. FRIEDMAN, A PRACTICAL GUIDE TO ENVIRONMENTAL LAW (1987). The first two sections of this chapter are derived from Friedman, *Dealing With Federal and State Agencies and Citizen Groups,* in A PRACTICAL GUIDE TO ENVIRONMENTAL LAW. Adapted by permission of the publisher, the American Law Institute-American Bar Association Committee on Continuing Professional Education.

2. *See generally* F. ANDERSON, NEGOTIATION AND INFORMAL AGENCY ACTION: THE CASE OF SUPERFUND (report to Administrative Conference of the United States, May 25, 1984).

3. *See generally* Eckert, *Representing Private Clients in EPA Rule Making,* NAT. RESOURCES & ENV'T, Winter 1985, at 27.

4. Macbeth, *Settling With the Government,* NAT. RESOURCES & ENV'T, Winter 1985, at 9, 12: "Like private litigation, successful resolution of disputes with the government depends on understanding what the other side wants and why it wants it, so that creative lawyers can find the common ground that will make settlement possible." *Id.* at 12.

5. Stein, *EPA Administrative Rule Making: A View From the Outside,* NAT. RESOURCES & ENV'T, Winter 1985, at 33.

6. Habicht, *Settling a Case With the Land and Natural Resources Division,* NAT. RESOURCES & ENV'T, Winter 1985, at 5:

> The [Land and Natural Resources] Division represents the United States, its agencies, and its officials in matters relating to environmental protection and management of public land resources, including the acquisition of land for public use. In addition to the Environmental Protection Agency and the Department of the Interior, the Division's most frequent clients include the departments of Agriculture, Commerce, Defense, Energy, and Transportation, as well as the General Services Administration. In its affirmative litigation as plaintiff, the Division represents agencies that are suing either to enforce a statute involving environmental protection or resource management or to acquire property through the power of eminent domain.

Id.

7. These opinions are published by EPA and are also available from the Environmental Law Institute in Washington, D.C.

8. This policy was published by EPA and is available from the Environmental Law Institute in Washington, D.C.

9. F. ANDERSON, *supra* note 2, at 46.

10. Friedman, *60s Activism and 80s Realities—We've Come a Long Way,* ENVTL. F., July 1983, at 8, 11. *See also* Eckert, *supra* note 3, at 32:

> You or your client will never live down a reputation for supplying false or unreliable information. There is a small but elite "bar" well known to EPA. These lawyers represent their clients vigorously, but treat agency staff, counsel, and managers with courtesy and respect. They are scrupulously fair in their dealings with EPA counsel; they can be counted on to keep their word. Their comments and pleadings are reliably accurate and well written. They are cooperative in administrative arrangements such as extensions of time, printing of the record, and scheduling of oral argument. They present their arguments forcefully, but without threats or insults. They persuade their clients to adopt reasonable positions likely to be acceptable to EPA before negotiations commence. It is plain that these lawyers are far more likely to help their clients get the relief they seek than those who approach the task of representation with less balance and finesse.

Id.

11. Eckert, *supra* note 3, at 32.

12. *Id.,* citing D.C. Bar Legal Ethics Comm., Op. 80 (Dec. 18, 1979).

13. *Id.*

14. *Id.* at 30.

15. Stukane, *EPA's Bubble Policy After* Chevron v. NRDC: *Who Is to Guard the Guards Themselves?,* 17 NAT. RESOURCES LAW. 647 (1985). See also Eckert, *supra* note 3, at 30: "The case reports are strewn with the wreckage of attempts to reverse EPA interpretations on fundamental questions of interpretation of Agency-administered statutes."

16. Stukane, *supra* note 15, at 675 (footnotes omitted).

17. Eckert, *supra* note 3, at 30.

18. *See generally* Macbeth, *supra* note 4. *See also* Friedman, *Corporate Environmental Programs and Litigation: The Role of Lawyer-Managers in Environmental Management,* 45 PUB. ADMIN. REV. 766 (1985).

19. Macbeth, *supra* note 4, at 9.

20. *Id.*

21. *Id.* at 10.

22. *Id.* at 12.

23. F. ANDERSON, *supra* note 2, at 46.

24. Macbeth, *supra* note 4, at 11.

25. *Id.*

26. *Id.*

27. *Id.* at 11: "Justice Department regulations provide for public comment on all proposed settlements in pollution abatement cases."

28. *Id.* at 10.

29. *Id.*

30. *Id.*

31. Citizen groups have been involved in most major litigation in the air, water, and hazardous waste areas. *See* J. MILLER, CITIZEN SUITS: PRIVATE ENFORCE-MENT OF FEDERAL POLLUTION CONTROL LAWS (1986); Reisel, *Citizen Suits in Environmental Litigation,* in D. SIVE & F. FRIEDMAN, *supra* note 1, at 301.

32. Stukane, *supra* note 15, at 675 n.139 (citing Motor Vehicle Mfrs. Ass'n v. State Farm Mut. Auto Ins. Co., 463 U.S. 29 (1983)) (agency's decision to repeal rule designed to promote safety must be supported by the record).

33. 40 C.F.R. §1501.7 (1991).

34. *See generally* Friedman, *NEPA—An Industry Perspective,* ENVTL. F., Jan. 1985, at 39, 43.

35. *Id.*

36. The Conservation Foundation, among others, is acting as a mediator in several disputes. EPA is utilizing negotiated rulemaking.

37. Friedman, *supra* note 34.

38. Sherman, *Smart Ways to Handle the Press,* FORTUNE, June 19, 1989, at 69. *See also* Sandler, *Courting Public Opinion,* ENVTL. F., May/June 1992, at 10.

39. Sandler, *supra* note 38, at 14.

40. *Id.* at 14-15.

41. The report prepared for Congress by a study group under §301 of CERCLA notes:

> The popular concern over the consequences of exposure to hazard-ous wastes has also resulted in overreaction. The "ghost dump" of Frayser, Tennessee, is one example where a highly charged atmos-phere resulted in emotional meetings, Congressional hearings and talk of evacuating the area, even though no actual dump site existed. See *The Dump That Wasn't There,* 215 SCIENCE 645 (Feb. 5, 1982). There is an ongoing dispute, too, over the Love Canal scare, frequently referred to during the passage of CERCLA, and the quality of the May 1980 study of alleged chromosome defects among the residents of houses near the site. See Havender, *Assessing and Controlling Risk,* in Bardach and Kagen, SOCIAL REGULATION: STRATEGIES FOR REFORM 21, 47 (1982); Levine, LOVE CANAL: SCIENCE, POLITICS AND PEOPLE (1982); *Psycho-Social Impact of Toxic Waste Dumps,* 127 CONG. REC. E5894 (Dec. 16, 1981) (Cong. LaFalce); Kolata, *Love Canal: False Alarm Caused By Botched Study,* 208 SCIENCE 1239 (June 13, 1980); Holden, *Love Canal Residents Under Stress,* 208 SCIENCE 1242 (June 13, 1980).

INJURIES AND DAMAGES FROM HAZARDOUS WASTES—ANALYSIS AND IMPROVEMENT OF LEGAL REMEDIES, 97th Cong., 2d Sess., at §I, n.5 (Comm. Print 97-12, Sept. 1982).

Chapter 10:
The Environmental Impact
Statement Process

It is beyond the scope of this book to describe specific permitting processes in detail, although the previous chapter outlines general considerations in dealing with the permitting constituency (federal and state agencies and citizen groups). It is also beyond the scope of this book to discuss NEPA[1] or state NEPAs[2] in detail. However, this chapter gives some basic suggestions on handling the EIS process.

For those of you who are new to this area, NEPA was the first statute of the environmental "revolution" and was designed to ensure that projects' environmental impacts would be fully considered. The key section of NEPA is §102(2)(c), which requires an EIS for "major Federal actions significantly affecting the quality of the human environment." The EIS must address the following subjects:

- the environmental impact of the proposed action,
- any adverse environmental effects that cannot be avoided if the proposal is implemented,
- alternatives to the proposed action,
- the relationship between local short-term uses of man's environment and the maintenance and enhancement of long-term productivity, and
- any irreversible and irretrievable commitments of resources that would be involved if the proposed action were implemented.

States have promulgated similar laws, usually using the term "environmental impact report" instead of "environmental impact statement."

The law itself is simple, but the politics of completing an adequate EIS are complicated and need to be addressed in detail. EIS preparation involves all the issues and skills discussed in the previous chapters. It is particularly important to assure that a project will not be stopped by an injunction because of "irreparable harm that would result absent such an injunction."[3] Environmental groups have to show more than just the fact that an impact

261

statement is inadequate to obtain an injunction, and the courts have become increasingly reluctant to "second-guess the scientists, experts, economists, and planners who make the environmental [impact] statement."[4] However, this does not mean that inadequate EISs will not be successfully challenged. It is important to meet the criteria of an adequate EIS. As one court has stated,

> [I]n our opinion an EIS is in compliance with NEPA when its form, content, and preparation substantially (1) provide decision-makers with an environmental disclosure sufficiently detailed to aid in the substantive decision whether to proceed with the project in the light of its environmental consequences, and (2) make available to the public, information of the proposed project's environmental impact and encourage public participation in the development of that information.[5]

It is clear that trying to fight or undermine the EIS process generally will not work. Industry representatives have therefore recognized that their most important function in the EIS process is to ensure that adequate studies are completed for use in the statement. This approach reduces the risks of delay and additional expense in the litigation process.

It is particularly important to ensure that agency shortcuts in the name of "policy" do not actually delay projects substantially. Both government and industry attorneys have learned to advise their clients of the danger of encouraging projects that will not withstand environmental scrutiny. Consequently, this chapter will discuss how you and your counsel can ensure the adequacy of environmental impact statements.

The Lead Agency

Many projects are subject to the jurisdiction of more than one federal or state agency. Any of the agencies could prepare the EIS, but one agency will act as the "lead agency" to assume supervisory responsibility for preparation of the statement.[6] The competence of this agency and the expedition with which it will undertake to prepare the EIS are important to the applicant. In addition, jealousies often develop among the agencies, and it is important to determine the attitudes of the agencies toward each other as early as possible.

It is also essential to establish what personnel will be available and whether the federal lead agency can work together with the state lead agency. Selection of the federal and state lead agencies must be coordinated, particularly in a state such as California where the state EIR will be prepared at the same time as the federal EIS. It may be possible to use part or all of the federal EIS as part of the state EIR, so the two statements will be consistent.

In a controversial project involving several agencies, selection of the lead agency may take from three to six months. "Any Federal agency, or any State or local agency or private person substantially affected by the absence of lead agency designation, may make a written request to the potential lead agencies that a lead agency be designated."[7] The Council on Environmental Quality (CEQ) has federal responsibility for supervising the EIS process and can be helpful in mediating conflicts. An agency should not be selected because it is known for its speed, as opposed to its competence, in developing EISs. An agency notorious for shortcuts that will help an applicant expedite the EIS process is not necessarily the best lead agency, since shortcuts can lead to delays in the review process and probable litigation.

In conjunction with selection of the lead agency, the applicant should prepare a full outline of what it believes the EIS should include. Its own legal analysis will be extremely helpful in avoiding agency shortcuts. A suggested outline of the areas that need to be covered can also help expedite the process, since it gives an agency at least a working draft at an early time. This is particularly useful if the staff is inexperienced or unfamiliar with the project.

Assembling a Task Force

Neither federal nor state agencies normally have the personnel readily available to devote substantial time to a complicated project. Considerable effort may be necessary in Washington, D.C., or in the state to ensure the assignment of competent personnel. Agencies are reluctant to remove staff from their normal duties for long periods even if a project has some form of national priority. Consequently, it may take three months just to assemble the necessary task force to work on the EIS.

An applicant may feel greatly frustrated when, after doing a substantial amount of environmental work, it finds that the task force assigned to the project has had no or limited previous experience in the EIS process. Months may be necessary merely to understand what is involved in the project and to develop the necessary writing techniques. Thus, the applicant's early assembly of data in a usable form is quite important.

Preparation of an Environmental Impact Analysis

Unless extensive data are readily available and the agency is very experienced in the area, the applicant should prepare a complete environmental impact analysis for use by the agency or agencies involved. This can be very expensive, but cutting the time required for preparing the EIS can save money, particularly if you and/or your financing institution is anxious to begin the project.

Accurate Data

First-rate data may dispel some of the opposition, or at least cause the opposition to consider the possible outcome seriously before it decides to litigate. Many times I have teased my friends in the environmental community that they will have a hard time finding competent experts to challenge a project because we have already hired the best. It is important to use credible consultants in developing the environmental analysis. If the consultants have solid reputations in the scientific community, the agency may determine that only limited cross-checks are necessary to ensure a perception that the agency, rather than the applicant, has completed the EIS. Thus, complete duplication of the applicant's work and analysis will be avoided.

It is particularly helpful to get the advice of local environmental groups who may be opposed to a project as to the scope of the available studies and additional studies that they feel are necessary. An early meeting with them can correct many misconceptions before their positions harden and they raise funds to attempt to stop the project. Their input can also be extremely helpful in planning the project. While early contact may not eliminate litigation, it does narrow the issues that will be litigated. As indicated in Chapter 9, patience and control of temper are critical to avoid early and irrevocable polarization.

Time Factors

It is also important to recognize that one or more years of baseline data may be necessary in order to determine the environmental impacts of a complicated project. The agency needs to know the air quality, water quality, and biological bases for that period. Alternative sites for the project and the impacts on these sites must also be considered. Agencies may have extensive information and, on rare occasions, additional studies may not be necessary, but usually the schedule for the project must include time for obtaining data.

Moreover, some agencies, such as the Federal Power Commission and the Nuclear Regulatory Commission, require an applicant to prepare an EIR before the agency begins drafting the EIS. It can take a full year to prepare such an impact report. Agencies that do not require an EIR before beginning the EIS can have some of the baseline analysis and data prepared concurrently with the drafting of the EIS.

Preparation of a Draft EIS

If no additional studies are necessary and the project has some priority within the agency, nine months to a year should be enough time to complete an adequate draft EIS. During the preparation period, discussions should be held with the agencies that would normally review the statement to determine what areas they consider critical. All agencies concerned with the project should be involved at the earliest possible time. Prior contact can expedite the formal review of the draft EIS and limit potential negative comments. Courts will consider negative comments by environmental agencies such as EPA significant.

Agencies should be encouraged to seek the advice of the applicant, environmental groups, and other interested agencies in preparing the EIS. The agency that ignores them may complete a very poor draft statement. If all groups are essentially satisfied with the scope of the EIS and its consideration of the issues, litigation and costly additional delays may be eliminated.

Too often the agencies simply will not have the expertise of the applicant, who may have devoted years to analysis and study before making a major financial decision to build the project. Both the agency and the applicant should designate liaison personnel to ensure that materials are received and continuous contact is maintained.

The CEQ regulations do not provide specific timetables for comment because of the feeling that they would be too "inflexible." [8] However, the regulations do provide for a minimum of 45 days for interested agencies to review a draft EIS. [9] This period, as well as a two- to three-week period for printing the EIS, should be considered in arranging a time schedule.

Public Hearings

Although most federal agencies do not require public hearings on a draft EIS, public hearings are usually held if the project is of any size or is controversial. Early guidelines adopted by the CEQ prior to the promulgation of regulations require at least 15 days' notice, but if the project is controversial, an additional 15 to 30 days are usually provided prior to the hearing. [10] The applicant should review the draft EIS thoroughly and be prepared at the public hearing to criticize it.

The hearing is a good time to indicate where the agency has overstated the environmental impacts of the project. The applicant may also see understated impacts, and it is good practice in ensuring the adequacy of the EIS and improving the applicant's credibility to indicate potentially understated impacts at the public hearing. Because it is virtually impossible to hide the negative environmental impacts of a project, it is to the applicant's advantage to reveal them and reap the benefits of credibility and EIS soundness. NEPA is essentially a full disclosure law. [11]

Written Comments

Written comments are also extremely important in ensuring EIS adequacy. Written comments are considered part of the EIS. [12] Agencies must respond to them. [13] Thus, if areas in the EIS are weak or need expansion or revision, the applicant should prepare extensive written comments and thus force the agency to do the necessary work to complete an adequate EIS. Note that EISs have never been rejected for being too voluminous and that sometimes the "weight of the evidence" in reviewing an EIS is measured in pounds.

If there are extensive written comments and hearings, the agency should not be encouraged to expedite completion of the final statement until the applicant is certain that the agency can adequately respond to the comments. Usually, it takes about three months to respond properly to both oral and written comments.

Outside Consultants

The EIS process is time-consuming and expensive. Use of outside consultants by applicants and, to a certain degree, by the agencies themselves, usually at the applicant's expense, is rapidly coming into favor. As long as the agency and not the applicant prepares the EIS, these consultants appear to be legally acceptable. [14]

An outside consultant experienced in preparation of impact statements can shorten the process by three to six months. Even if the time is not shortened, at least the final product will have a better chance of being satisfactory. However, some agencies will continually second-guess consultants and nullify their value.

Both the agency and the applicant should be certain that the consultant has a good idea of the scope of the project and the areas that an adequate EIS must include. Thus, the proposal should indicate the scope of the consultant's work. He or she must be given room to make independent decisions, but time schedules should be set and the scope of the necessary studies should be predetermined, allowing flexibility to revise provisions or studies as various problems are discovered.

Public Involvement

As discussed generally in Chapter 9, the EIS scoping process specifically requires public involvement. [15] Usually it is preferable to arrange meetings with potential opposition before the formal scoping process in order to defuse opposition before it coalesces. As follows from the discussion in the section "Citizen Groups" in Chapter 9: "[I]t is critical, when the scoping process is approached, that the applicant have a strong data base with which to answer local concerns." [16]

Conclusion

In EIS preparation, as in almost all areas of environmental interface with regulators, the most significant job of the manager and the attorney is handling the administrative process prior to litigation. It is critical to use environmental counsel early on to ensure that there is no litigation. Far too often, attorneys are not included in the earliest stages of EIS planning and preparation. Counsel is brought in only when litigation has become imminent and it is too late to make the necessary record. NEPA cases are won or lost on records and the most important record is the intangible one of working early on with *all* parties, including potential opposition, to ensure that the matter does not proceed to litigation, or at least that the issues are narrowed and that your position is backed up by a sound and voluminous EIS that will be difficult to challenge.

The best example I know of the importance of this advice occurred in the early 1970s. I was engaged in some frustrating attempts to convince an agency to broaden both the scope and the depth of a proposed EIS. My concern was primarily based on what appeared to be substantial vulnerability to a citizen suit. At the same time, a colleague of mine with a national environmental organization was equally frustrated by the agency's recalcitrance. I suggested and he agreed that we both meet together with senior agency officials to express our concerns. This unusual request provoked the action we were both seeking, and the EIS was greatly improved. No litigation was filed, although another citizen group unsuccessfully challenged that EIS in another context several years later.

Notes to Chapter 10

1. *See* Sive & Cohen, *NEPA Practice*, in D. SIVE & F. FRIEDMAN, A PRACTICAL GUIDE TO ENVIRONMENTAL LAW 169 (1987). Much of this chapter in an earlier form originally appeared in Friedman, *The Environmental Impact Statement Process*, 22 PRAC. LAW. 47 (1976). Adapted by permission of the publisher, the American Law Institute-American Bar Association Committee on Continuing Professional Education. The original version was reprinted in G. COGGINS & C. WILKINSON, FEDERAL PUBLIC LAND AND RESOURCES LAW (2d ed. 1987).

2. Practice varies from state to state. As an example of the complexity of state NEPAs, see S. DUGGAN, J. MOOSE & T. THOMAS, GUIDE TO THE CALIFORNIA ENVIRONMENTAL QUALITY ACT (CEQA) (1987).

3. Kleppe v. Sierra Club, 427 U.S. 390, 6 ELR 20532 (1976).

4. National Helium Corp. v. Morton, 486 F.2d 995, 1001, 4 ELR 20041 (10th Cir. 1973) (Breitenstein, J., concurring), *cert. denied*, 416 U.S. 993 (1974).

5. Trout Unlimited v. Morton, 509 F.2d 1276, 1283, 5 ELR 20151 (9th Cir. 1974).

6. 40 C.F.R. §1501.5 (1991).

7. 40 C.F.R. §1501.5(d) (1991).

8. 40 C.F.R. §1501.8 (1991).

9. 40 C.F.R. §1506.10(c) (1991).

10. CEQ Guidelines, 38 Fed. Reg. 20550 (Aug. 1, 1973).

11. Committee for Nuclear Responsibility v. Seaborg, 463 F.2d 783, 1 ELR 20469 (D.C. Cir. 1971). "The only role for a court is to insure that the agency has taken a 'hard look' at environmental consequences; it cannot 'interject itself within the area of discretion of the executive as to the choice of the action to be taken.' Natural Resources Defense Council v. Morton, 458 F.2d 827, 838, 418 U.S. App. D.C. 5, 16 (1972)." Kleppe v. Sierra Club, 427 U.S. 390, 410 n.21, 6 ELR 20532 (1976).

12. National Helium Corp. v. Morton, 486 F.2d at 1001, 4 ELR at 20043.

13. 40 C.F.R. §1503.4 (1991).

14. *See* CEQ Guidelines, *supra* note 10. The rationale for allowing consultants to prepare EISs is discussed in Natural Resources Defense Council v. Callaway, 524 F.2d 79, 87, 5 ELR 20640, 20644 (2d Cir. 1975):

> The evil sought to be avoided by the holdings in Conservation Society and Greene County is the preparation of the EIS by a party, usually a state agency, with an individual "axe to grind," i.e., an interest in seeing the project accepted and completed in a specific manner as proposed. Authorship by such a biased party might prevent the fair and impartial evaluation of a project envisioned by NEPA. Here no problem of self-interest on the part of the author exists. As the Navy's hiree, the independent consultant has no interest but the Navy's to serve and is fully responsible to the Navy for any shortcomings in the EIS.

Therefore, we see no difference for NEPA purposes between this procedure and preparation of the EIS by Navy personnel. In both cases the preparers are guided exclusively by the interests of the Navy and the dictates of the NEPA process.

15. 40 C.F.R. §1501.7 (1991).

16. Friedman, *NEPA—An Industry Perspective*, Envtl. F., Jan. 1985, at 39, 43.

To infer, we use the Gaussian ID MERA processes, and the procedure and preparation of the life by library personnel, in both of the appearance to profile results of by an alteration of the life and to alteration of the MERA process.

Chapter 11:
Conclusion

This book summarizes many of the environmental management lessons that I and others have learned over the years. Some of its suggestions, such as those on dealing with regulators, are unique to the environmental area. Many others, such as those on interactions between staff and line management, simply apply good general management techniques in the environmental context. Basic good management is vital in the environmental area, if only because environmental costs are so high. Occidental's 1991 environmental costs related to ongoing operations were $257 million and reserves for remediation expenses provided for past operating and disposal sites totaled $149 million. These costs are typical for large companies; for many smaller companies, costs are disproportionately larger.

Many environmental management techniques come down to getting the most out of the people in your organization. An environmental management system, like any other management system, must ensure that each individual's performance is recognized, so that good work receives credit and bad work cannot be blamed on committees. Effective environmental management also requires an interdisciplinary approach. No one discipline has all the solutions, and turf problems must be resolved so that the organization can make full use of engineers, lawyers, consultants, and other professionals. The ability to work with people is thus a critical ingredient of successful environmental management.

This book makes many recommendations that do not cost much, and that can save significant amounts. Effective use of personal and lap-top computers, for example, is fairly inexpensive. So is minimization of turf problems, which creates major opportunities for cost savings. Even the recommendations that require significant up-front investments can pay for themselves in the long run by making management more cost-effective. For example, computerized management systems cost money, but by enabling you to detect problems early and handle information efficiently, they can save far more.

An effective environmental management department can be a profit center. Occidental's operating management paid its environmental department the ultimate compliment by recognizing this several years ago. A consulting firm had inquired whether Oxy would be interested in using some of the department's time to work as outside consultants. A senior operations executive responded that, hour for hour, the amount the department saved the company by working in house substantially exceeded the amount it would bring in by working out of house.

Reduction of costs—especially transaction costs—is one main theme of this book. As discussed in Chapter 4, pollution control is frequently cheaper outside the United States because less must be spent on studies, consultants, lawyers, paperwork, and resulting delays. Reducing these transaction costs in the United States would clearly be in the public interest. This interest is often ignored, which is frustrating for the environmental manager. High transaction costs result partly from the history of environmental regulation and partly from widespread paralysis in decisionmaking. Regulatory agencies are frequently paralyzed by the intense and conflicting demands they face, and companies may be paralyzed if decisionmaking moves slowly upward through numerous organizational levels. It is indeed unfortunate that so much time and money are devoted to transactional issues rather than to the environmental protection we all desire. A detailed analysis of the impediments to potential ways to reduce environmental transaction costs such as market based techniques instead of "command and control" (e.g. emission trading to limit sulfur dioxide and reduce acid rain under the Clean Air Act Amendments of 1990) is beyond the scope of this book, but such analysis is sorely needed. Indeed, additional work is needed on environmental management in general. The existing literature is surprisingly sparse. This book hopefully will help inspire further work in this important field.

Appendix A:
Organization Chart

REPRESENTATIVE CORPORATE ORGANIZATION CHART

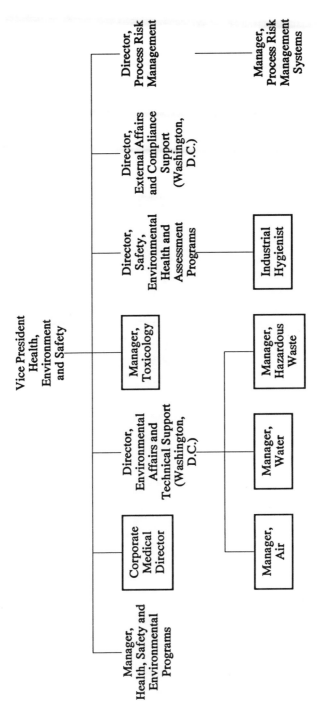

* Occidental model boxes in ☐ are suggested for larger organizations where expertise is not readily available in divisions.

Appendix B:
Sample Internal
Monthly Report

Figures have been omitted from this sample Occidental Petroleum Corporation report. When circulated internally, these reports include figures generated by the Oxy-EAS^{TM} system.

To: **Distribution**   Date: **February 19, 1988**
From: **F. B. Friedman**
Subject: **Health, Environment and Safety**
           Monthly Report, January 1988

Environmental Compliance:

There were __ environmental citations and __ excursions or reportable incidents recorded for January. In January 1987, on a pro forma basis, there were __ environmental citations and __ excursions or reportable incidents. __ of the citations were at OxyChem plants, the other __ were at ICC locations. Cities/OOG and MidCon did not report any citations, excursions, or reportable incidents this month.

Environmental Legislative and Regulatory Matters:

N.J. Environmental Audit Review Act—This bill, N.J. A. 1822, would establish a program for the certification of environmental auditors and would require owners or operators of industrial establishments as defined by the New Jersey Environmental Cleanup Responsibility Act to have such sites audited annually by a certified auditor until the site is closed, terminated, or transferred.

Mexican Environmental Law—On March 1st, a new, comprehensive environmental law will go into effect. The current law emphasizes correction of problems, primarily through sanctions. The new law aims at decentralizing enforcement and will focus on prevention, requiring environmental impact analysis prior to permitting of new facilities. The new law also has expanded penalty provisions, including possible prison terms as well as fines. This is a further indication of the direction environmental protection legislation is going in other countries and supports the prompt implementation of the OPC policy of maintaining functional equivalents to U.S. levels of environment, health and safety protection in our international operations.

Environmental Matters:

Toxic Chemicals Emission Reports—EPA has completed work on a general guidance document to help facilities estimate their annual toxic chemical emissions as required by Section 313 of the Emergency Planning and Community Right to Know Act. The emission reports on the 329 chemicals listed are due by July 1st for emissions in calendar year 1987 from the facilities covered by the law. Copies will be available from EPA in mid-February.

Potential Superfund Waste Sites—The General Accounting Office has estimated that the United States may have as many as 427,000 potential

Superfund hazardous waste sites. The bulk of these are municipal or industrial landfills. This is well above the 27,000 that EPA has identified and currently has under investigation. This would imply that there could be a continuing stream of EPA PRP notices received in the foreseeable future.

Safety:

The Injury Incidence Rate (IIR) was __ for the month of January compared to __ for January 1987.

ENVIRONMENTAL FACT SHEET
January 1988

	Current Month		Year to Date	
	1988	1987	1988	1987

I. CITATIONS

    Number received
    Number closed
    Number open
    Payments
    Citations requiring payment

II. PERMIT EXCURSIONS AND
    REPORTABLE INCIDENTS

    Number reported

III. ASSESSMENTS OF FACILITIES

    Reports received
    Reviewed by Board Committee

IV. IBP
    CITATIONS RECEIVED
    EXC. & REPORTABLE INCIDENTS

NOTE: Statistics on citations and excursions are subject to further
verification and are as of: 05/09/88

OCCIDENTAL PETROLEUM CORPORATION
MONTHLY ACCUMULATED WORK ACCIDENT SUMMARY
COMPARISON December 1987 vs. December 1986

A. SAFETY STATISTICS

	Fatalities/Total Recordable Cases			Total Incidence Rates		
	MONTH 87	YTD 87	YTD 86	MONTH 87	YTD 87	YTD 86
OCC						
ICC						
OOG						
CITIES*						
IBP						
CORPORATE						
MIDCON						
Total						

Note: Due to a revised interpretation, by OSHA, of what constitutes a recordable incident, the 1987 figures cannot be compared with past years' statistics.

*Cities Service now included in Occidental Oil and Gas.

Data are correct as of: 01/15/88

Appendix C:
Auditing Policy of the United States Environmental Protection Agency

Environmental Protection Agency
Environmental Auditing Policy Statement
51 Fed. Reg. 25004 (July 9, 1986)

SUMMARY: It is EPA policy to encourage the use of environmental auditing by regulated entities to help achieve and maintain compliance with environmental laws and regulations, as well as to help identify and correct unregulated environmental hazards. EPA first published this policy as interim guidance on November 8, 1985 (50 FR 46504). Based on comments received regarding the interim guidance, the Agency is issuing today's final policy statement with only minor changes.

This final policy statement specifically:

• Encourages regulated entities to develop, implement and upgrade environmental auditing programs;

• Discusses when the Agency may or may not request audit reports;

• Explains how EPA's inspection and enforcement activities may respond to regulated entities' efforts to assure compliance through auditing;

• Endorses environmental auditing at federal facilities;

• Encourages state and local environmental auditing initiatives; and

• Outlines elements of effective audit programs.

Environmental auditing includes a variety of compliance assessment techniques which go beyond those legally required and are used to identify actual and potential environmental problems. Effective environmental auditing can lead to higher levels of overall compliance and reduced risk to human health and the environment. EPA endorses the practice of environmental auditing and supports its accelerated use by regulated entities to help meet the goals of federal, state and local environmental requirements. However, the existence of an auditing program does not create any defense to, or otherwise limit, the responsibility of any regulated entity to comply with applicable regulatory requirements.

States are encouraged to adopt these or similar and equally effective policies in order to advance the use of environmental auditing on a consistent, nationwide basis.

DATES: This final policy statement is effective July 9, 1986.

FOR FURTHER INFORMATION CONTACT:

Leonard Fleckenstein, Office of Policy, Planning and Evaluation, (202) 382–2726;

or

Cheryl Wasserman, Office of Enforcement and Compliance Monitoring, (202) 382–7550.

SUPPLEMENTARY INFORMATION:

ENVIRONMENTAL AUDITING POLICY STATEMENT

I. Preamble

On November 8, 1985 EPA published an Environmental Auditing Policy Statement, effective as interim guidance, and solicited written comments until January 7, 1986.

Thirteen commenters submitted written comments. Eight were from private industry. Two commenters represented industry trade associations. One federal agency, one consulting firm and one law firm also submitted comments.

Twelve commenters addressed EPA requests for audit reports. Three comments per subject were received regarding inspections, enforcement response and elements of effective environmental auditing. One commenter addressed audit provisions as remedies in enforcement actions, one addressed environmental auditing at federal facilities, and one addressed the relationship of the policy statement to state or local regulatory agencies. Comments generally supported both the concept of a policy statement and the interim guidance, but raised specific concerns with respect to particular language and policy issues in sections of the guidance.

General Comments

Three commenters found the interim guidance to be constructive, balanced and effective at encouraging more and better environmental auditing.

Another commenter, while considering the policy on the whole to be constructive, felt that new and identifiable auditing "incentives" should be offered by EPA. Based on earlier comments received from industry, EPA believes most companies would not support or participate in an "incentives-based" environmental auditing program with EPA. Moreover, general promises to forgo inspections or reduce enforcement responses in exchange for companies' adoption of environmental auditing programs—the "incentives" most frequently mentioned in this context—are fraught with legal and policy obstacles.

Several commenters expressed concern that states or localities might use the interim guidance to *require* auditing. The Agency disagrees that the policy statement opens the way for states and localities to require auditing. No EPA policy can grant states or localities any more (or less) authority than they already possess. EPA believes that the interim guidance effectively encourages *voluntary* auditing. In fact, Section II.B. of the policy states: "because audit quality depends to a large degree on genuine management commitment to the program and its objectives, auditing should remain a voluntary program."

Another commenter suggested that EPA should not expect an audit to identify all potential problem areas or conclude that a problem identified in an audit reflects normal operations and procedures. EPA agrees that an audit report should clearly reflect these realities and should be written to point out the audit's limitations. However, since EPA will not routinely request audit reports, the Agency does not believe these concerns raise issues which need to be addressed in the policy statement.

A second concern expressed by the same commenter was that EPA should acknowledge that environmental audits are only part of a successful environmental management program and thus should not be expected to cover every environmental issue or solve all problems. EPA agrees and accordingly has amended the statement of purpose which appears at the end of this preamble.

Yet another commenter thought EPA should focus on environmental performance results (compliance or non-compliance), not on the processes or vehicles used to achieve those results. In general, EPA agrees with this statement and will continue to focus on environmental results. However, EPA also believes that such results can be improved through Agency efforts to identify and encourage effective environmental management practices, and will continue to encourage such practices in non-regulatory ways.

A final general comment recommended that EPA should sponsor seminars for small businesses on how to start auditing programs. EPA agrees that such seminars would be useful. However, since audit seminars already are available from several private sector organizations, EPA does not believe it should intervene in that market, with the possible exception of seminars for government agencies, especially federal agencies, for which EPA has a broad mandate under Executive Order 12088 to provide technical assistance for environmental compliance.

Requests for Reports

EPA received 12 comments regarding Agency requests for environmental audit reports, far more than on any other topic in the policy statement. One commenter felt that EPA struck an appropriate balance between respecting the need for self-evaluation with some measure of privacy, and allowing the Agency enough flexibility of inquiry to accomplish future statutory missions. However, most commenters expressed concern that the interim guidance did not go far enough to assuage corporate fears that EPA will use audit reports for environmental compliance "witch hunts." Several commenters suggested additional specific assurances regarding the circumstances under which EPA will request such reports.

One commenter recommended that EPA request audit reports only "when the Agency can show the information it needs to perform its statutory mission cannot be obtained from the monitoring, compliance or other data that is otherwise reportable and/or accessible to EPA, or where the Government deems an audit report material to a criminal investigation." EPA accepts this recommendation in part. The Agency believes it would not be in the best interest of human health and the environment to commit to making a "showing" of a compelling information need before ever requesting an audit report. While EPA may normally be willing to do so, the Agency cannot rule out in advance all circumstances in which such a showing may not be possible. However, it would be helpful to further clarify that a request for an audit report or a portion of a report normally will be made when needed information is not available by alternative means. Therefore, EPA has revised Section III.A., paragraph two and added the phrase: "and usually made where the information needed cannot be obtained from monitoring, reporting or other data otherwise available to the Agency."

Another commenter suggested that (except in the case of criminal investigations) EPA should limit requests for audit documents to specific questions. By including the phrase "or relevant portions of a report" in Section III.A., EPA meant to emphasize it would not request an entire audit document when only a relevant portion would suffice. Likewise, EPA fully intends not to request even a portion of a report if needed information or data can be otherwise obtained. To further clarify this point EPA has added the phrase, "most likely focused on particular information needs rather than the entire report," to the second sentence of paragraph two, Section III.A. Incorporating the two comments above, the first two sentences in paragraph two of final Section III.A. now read: "EPA's

authority to request an audit report, or relevant portions thereof, will be exercised on a case-by-case basis where the Agency determines it is needed to accomplish a statutory mission or the Government deems it to be material to a criminal investigation. EPA expects such requests to be limited, most likely focused on particular information needs rather than the entire report, and usually made where the information needed cannot be obtained from monitoring, reporting or other data otherwise available to the Agency."

Other commenters recommended that EPA not request audit reports under any circumstances, that requests be "restricted to only those legally required," that requests be limited to criminal investigations, or that requests be made only when EPA has reason to believe "that the audit programs or reports are being used to conceal evidence of environmental non-compliance or otherwise being used in bad faith." EPA appreciates concerns underlying all of these comments and has considered each carefully. However, the Agency believes that these recommendations do not strike the appropriate balance between retaining the flexibility to accomplish EPA's statutory missions in future, unforeseen circumstances, and acknowledging regulated entities' need to self-evaluate environmental performance with some measure of privacy. Indeed, based on prime informal comments, the small number of formal comments received, and the even smaller number of adverse comments, EPA believes the final policy statement should remain largely unchanged from the interim version.

Elements of Effective Environmental Auditing

Three commenters expressed concerns regarding the seven general elements EPA outlined in the Appendix to the interim guidance.

One commenter noted that were EPA to further expand or more fully detail such elements, programs not specifically fulfilling each element would then be judged inadequate. EPA agrees that presenting highly specific and

prescriptive auditing elements could be counter-productive by not taking into account numerous factors which vary extensively from one organization to another, but which may still result in effective auditing programs.
Accordingly, EPA does not plan to expand or more fully detail these auditing elements.

Another commenter asserted that states and localities should be cautioned not to consider EPA's auditing elements as mandatory steps. The Agency is fully aware of this concern and in the interim guidance noted its strong opinion that "regulatory agencies should not attempt to prescribe the precise form and structure of regulated entities' environmental management or auditing programs." While EPA cannot require state or local regulators to adopt this or similar policies, the Agency does strongly encourage them to do so, both in the interim and final policies.

A final commenter thought the Appendix too specifically prescribed what should and what should not be included in an auditing program. Other commenters, on the other hand, viewed the elements described as very general in nature. EPA agrees with these other commenters. The elements are in no way binding. Moreover, EPA believes that most mature, effective environmental auditing programs do incorporate each of these general elements in some form, and considers them useful yardsticks for those considering adopting or upgrading audit programs. For these reasons EPA has not revised the Appendix in today's final policy statement.

Other Comments

Other significant comments addressed EPA inspection priorities for, and enforcement responses to, organizations with environmental auditing programs.

One commenter, stressing that audit programs are *internal* management tools, took exception to the phrase in the second paragraph of section III.B.1. of the interim guidance which states that environmental audits can 'complement' regulatory oversight. By using the word 'complement' in this context, EPA does

not intend to imply that audit reports must be obtained by the Agency in order to supplement regulatory inspections. 'Complement' is used in a broad sense of being in addition to inspections and providing something (i.e., self-assessment) which otherwise would be lacking. To clarify this point EPA has added the phrase "by providing self-assessment to assure compliance" after "environmental audits may complement inspections" in this paragraph.

The same commenter also expressed concern that, as EPA sets inspection priorities, a company having an audit program could appear to be a 'poor performer' due to complete and accurate reporting when measured against a company which reports something less than required by law. EPA agrees that it is important to communicate this fact to Agency and state personnel, and will do so. However, the Agency does not believe a change in the policy statement is necessary.

A further comment suggested EPA should commit to take auditing programs into account when assessing all enforcement actions. However, in order to maintain enforcement flexibility under varied circumstances, the Agency cannot promise reduced enforcement responses to violations at all audited facilities when other factors may be overriding. Therefore the policy statement continues to state that EPA may exercise its decretion to consider auditing programs as evidence of honest and genuine efforts to assure compliance, which would then be taken into account in fashioning enforcement responses to violations.

A final commenter suggested the phrase "expeditiously correct environmental problems" not be used in the enforcement context since it implied EPA would use an entity's record of correcting nonregulated matters when evaluating regulatory violations. EPA did not intend for such an inference to be made. EPA intended the term "environmental problems" to refer to the underlying circumstances which eventually lead up to the violations. To clarify this point, EPA is revising the first two sentences of the paragraph to which this comment refers by changing "environmental problems" to "violations and underlying environmental problems" in the first sentence and to "underlying environmental problems" in the second sentence.

In a separate development EPA is preparing an update of its January 1984 *Federal Facilities Compliance Strategy,* which is referenced in section III. C. of the auditing policy. The Strategy should be completed and available on request from EPA's Office of Federal Activities later this year.

EPA thanks all commenters for responding to the November 8, 1985 publication. Today's notice is being issued to inform regulated entities and the public of EPA's final policy toward environmental auditing. This policy was developed to help (a) encourage regulated entities to institutionalize effective audit practices as one means of improving compliance and sound environmental management, and (b) guide internal EPA actions directly related to regulated entities' environmental auditing programs.

EPA will evaluate implementation of this final policy to ensure it meets the above goals and continues to encourage better environmental management, while strengthening the Agency's own efforts to monitor and enforce compliance with environmental requirements.

II. General EPA Policy on Environmental Auditing

A. Introduction

Environmental auditing is a systematic, documented, periodic and objective review by regulated entities [1] of facility operations and practices related to meeting environmental requirements. Audits can be designed to accomplish any or all of the following: verify compliance with environmental requirements; evaluate the effectiveness

of environmental management systems already in place; or assess risks from regulated and unregulated materials and practices.

Auditing serves as a quality assurance check to help improve the effectiveness of basic environmental management by verifying that management practices are in place, functioning and adequate. Environmental audits evaluate, and are not a substitute for, direct compliance activities such as obtaining permits, installing controls, monitoring compliance, reporting violations, and keeping records. Environmental auditing may verify but does not include activities required by law, regulation or permit (e.g., continuous emissions monitoring, composite correction plans at wastewater treatment plants, etc.). Audits do not in any way replace regulatory agency inspections. However, environmental audits can improve compliance by complementing conventional federal, state and local oversight.

The appendix to this policy statement outlines some basic elements of environmental auditing (e.g., auditor independence and top management support) for use by those considering implementation of effective auditing programs to help achieve and maintain compliance. Additional information on environmental auditing practices can be found in various published materials. [2]

Environmental auditing has developed for sound business reasons, particularly as a means of helping regulated entities manage pollution control affirmatively over time instead of reacting to crises. Auditing can result in improved facility environmental performance, help communicate effective solutions to common environmental problems, focus facility managers' attention on current and upcoming regulatory requirements, and generate protocols and checklists

---

[1] "Regulated entities" include private firms and public agencies with facilities subject to environmental regulation. Public agencies can include federal, state or local agencies as well as special-purpose organizations such as regional sewage commissions.

[2] See, e.g., "Current Practices in Environmental Auditing," EPA Report No. EPA–230–09–83–006, February 1984; "Annotated Bibliography on Environmental Auditing," Fifth Edition, September 1985, both available from: Regulatory Reform Staff, PM–223, EPA, 401 M Street SW, Washington, DC 20460.

which help facilities better manage themselves. Auditing also can result in better-integrated management of environmental hazards, since auditors frequently identify environmental liabilities which go beyond regulatory compliance. Companies, public entities and federal facilities have employed a variety of environmental auditing practices in recent years. Several hundred major firms in diverse industries now have environmental auditing programs, although they often are known by other names such as assessment, survey, surveillance, review or appraisal.

While auditing has demonstrated its usefulness to those with audit programs, many others still do not audit. Clarification of EPA's position regarding auditing may help encourage regulated entities to establish audit programs or upgrade systems already in place.

B. EPA Encourages the Use of Environmental Auditing

EPA encourages regulated entities to adopt sound environmental management practices to improve environmental performance. In particular, EPA encourages regulated entities subject to environmental regulations to institute environmental auditing programs to help ensure the adequacy of internal systems to achieve, maintain and monitor compliance. Implementation of environmental auditing programs can result in better identification, resolution and avoidance of environmental problems, as well as improvements to management practices. Audits can be conducted effectively by independent internal or third party auditors. Larger organizations generally have greater resources to devote to an internal audit team, while smaller entities might be more likely to use outside auditors.

Regulated entities are responsible for taking all necessary steps to ensure compliance with environmental requirements, whether or not they adopt audit programs. Although environmental laws do not require a regulated facility to have an auditing program, ultimate responsibility for the environmental

performance of the facility lies with top management, which therefore has a strong incentive to use reasonable means, such as environmental auditing, to secure reliable information of facility compliance status.

EPA does not intend to dictate or interfere with the environmental management practices of private or public organizations. Nor does EPA intend to mandate auditing (though in certain instances EPA may seek to include provisions for environmental auditing as part of settlement agreements, as noted below). Because environmental auditing systems have been widely adopted on a voluntary basis in the past, and because audit quality depends to a large degree upon genuine management commitment to the program and its objectives, auditing should remain a voluntary activity.

III. EPA Policy on Specific Environmental Auditing Issues

A. Agency Requests for Audit Reports

EPA has broad statutory authority to request relevant information on the environmental compliance status of regulated entities. However, EPA believes routine Agency requests for audit reports [3] could inhibit auditing in the long run, decreasing both the quantity and quality of audits conducted. Therefore, as a matter of policy, EPA will *not* routinely request environmental audit reports.

EPA's authority to request an audit report, or relevant portions thereof, will be exercised on a case-by-case basis where the Agency determines it is needed to accomplish a statutory mission, or where the Government deems it to be material to a criminal investigation. EPA expects such requests to be limited, most likely focused on particular information needs rather than the entire report, and usually

---

[3] An "environmental audit report" is a written report which candidly and thoroughly presents findings from a review, conducted as part of an environmental audit as described in section II.A., of facility environmental performance and practices. An audit report is not a substitute for compliance monitoring reports or other reports or records which may be required by EPA or other regulatory agencies.

made where the information needed cannot be obtained from monitoring, reporting or other data otherwise available to the Agency. Examples would likely include situations where: audits are conducted under consent decrees or other settlement agreements; a company has placed its management practices at issue by raising them as a defense; or state of mind or intent are a relevant element of inquiry, such as during a criminal investigation. This list is illustrative rather than exhaustive, since there doubtless will be other situations, not subject to prediction, in which audit reports rather than information may be required.

EPA acknowledges regulated entities' need to self-evaluate environmental performance with some measure of privacy and encourages such activity. However, audit reports may not shield monitoring, compliance, or other information that would otherwise be reportable and/or accessible to EPA, even if there is no explicit 'requirement' to generate that data.[4] Thus, this policy does not alter regulated entities' existing or future obligations to monitor, record or report information required under environmental statutes, regulations or permits, or to allow EPA access to that information. Nor does this policy alter EPA's authority to request and receive any relevant information—including that contained in audit reports—under various environmental statutes (e.g., Clean Water Act section 308, Clean Air Act sections 114 and 208) or in other administrative or judicial proceedings.

Regulated entities also should be aware that certain audit findings may by law have to be reported to government agencies. However, in addition to any such requirements, EPA encourages regulated entities to notify appropriate State or Federal officials of findings which suggest significant environmental or public health risks, even when not specifically required to do so.

---

[4] See, for example, "Duties to Report or Disclose Information on the Environmental Aspects of Business Activities," Environmental Law Institute report to EPA, final report, September 1985.

B. EPA Response to Environmental Auditing

1. General Policy

EPA will not promise to forgo inspections, reduce enforcement responses, or offer other such incentives in exchange for implementation of environmental auditing or other sound environmental management practices. Indeed, a credible enforcement program provides a strong incentive for regulated entities to audit.

Regulatory agencies have an obligation to assess source compliance status independently and cannot eliminate inspections for particular firms or classes of firms. Although environmental audits may complement inspections by providing self-assessment to assure compliance, they are in no way a substitute for regulatory oversight. Moreover, certain statutes (e.g. RCRA) and Agency policies establish minimum facility inspection frequencies to which EPA will adhere.

However, EPA will continue to address environmental problems on a priority basis and will consequently inspect facilities with poor environmental records and practices more frequently. Since effective environmental auditing helps management identify and promptly correct actual or potential problems, audited facilities' environmental performance should improve. Thus, while EPA inspections of self-audited facilities will continue, to the extent that compliance performance is considered in setting inspection priorities, facilities with a good compliance history may be subject to fewer inspections.

In fashioning enforcement responses to violations, EPA policy is to take into account, on a case-by-case basis, the honest and genuine efforts of regulated entities to avoid and promptly correct violations and underlying environmental problems. When regulated entities take reasonable precautions to avoid noncompliance, expeditiously correct underlying environmental problems discovered through audits or other means, and implement measures to prevent their recurrence, EPA may exercise its discretion to consider such actions as honest and genuine efforts to assure compliance. Such consideration applies particularly when a regulated entity promptly reports violations or compliance data which otherwise were not required to be recorded or reported to EPA.

2. Audit Provisions as Remedies in Enforcement Actions

EPA may propose environmental auditing provisions in consent decrees and in other settlement negotiations where auditing could provide a remedy for identified problems and reduce the likelihood of similar problems recurring in the future.[5] Environmental auditing provisions are most likely to be proposed in settlement negotiations where:

• A pattern of violations can be attributed, at least in part, to the absence or poor functioning of an environmental management system; or

• The type or nature of violations indicates a likelihood that similar noncompliance problems may exist or occur elsewhere in the facility or at other facilities operated by the regulated entity.

Through this consent decree approach and other means, EPA may consider how to encourage effective auditing by publicly owned sewage treatment works (POTWs). POTWs often have compliance problems related to operation and maintenance procedures which can be addressed effectively through the use of environmental auditing. Under its National Municipal Policy EPA already is requiring many POTWs to develop composite correction plans to identify and correct compliance problems.

C. Environmental Auditing at Federal Facilities

EPA encourages all federal agencies subject to environmental laws and regulations to institute environmental

auditing systems to help ensure the adequacy of internal systems to achieve, maintain and monitor compliance. Environmental auditing at federal facilities can be an effective supplement to EPA and state inspections. Such federal facility environmental audit programs should be structured to promptly identify environmental problems and expeditiously develop schedules for remedial action.

To the extent feasible, EPA will provide technical assistance to help federal agencies design and initiate audit programs. Where appropriate, EPA will enter into agreements with other agencies to clarify the respective roles, responsibilities and commitments of each agency in conducting and responding to federal facility environmental audits.

With respect to inspections of self-audited facilities (see section III.B.1 above) and requests for audit reports (see section III.A above), EPA generally will respond to environmental audits by federal facilities in the same manner as it does for other regulated entities, in keeping with the spirit and intent of Executive Order 12088 and the EPA *Federal Facilities Compliance Strategy* (January 1984, update forthcoming in late 1986). Federal agencies should, however, be aware that the Freedom of Information Act will govern any disclosure of audit reports or audit-generated information requested from federal agencies by the public.

When federal agencies discover significant violations through an environmental audit, EPA encourages them to submit the related audit findings and remedial action plans expeditiously to the applicable EPA regional office (and responsible state agencies, where appropriate) even when not specifically required to do so. EPA will review the audit findings and action plans and either provide written approval or negotiate a Federal Facilities Compliance Agreement. EPA will utilize the escalation procedures provided in Executive Order 12088 and the EPA *Federal Facilities Compliance Strategy* only when agreement between agencies cannot be reached. In any event, federal agencies are expected to report pollution

---

[5] EPA is developing guidance for use by Agency negotiators in structuring appropriate environmental audit provisions for consent decrees and other settlement negotiations.

abatement projects involving costs (necessary to correct problems discovered through the audit) to EPA in accordance with OMB Circular A–106. Upon request, and in appropriate circumstances, EPA will assist affected federal agencies through coordination of any public release of audit findings with approved action plans once agreement has been reached.

IV. Relationship to State or Local Regulatory Agencies

State and local regulatory agencies have independent jurisdiction over regulated entities. EPA encourages them to adopt these or similar policies, in order to advance the use of effective environmental auditing in a consistent manner.

EPA recognizes that some states have already undertaken environmental auditing initiatives which differ somewhat from this policy. Other states also may want to develop auditing policies which accommodate their particular needs or circumstances. Nothing in this policy statement is intended to preempt or preclude states from developing other approaches to environmental auditing. EPA encourages state and local authorities to consider the basic principles which guided the Agency in developing this policy:

• Regulated entities must continue to report or record compliance information required under existing statutes or regulations, regardless of whether such information is generated by an environmental audit or contained in an audit report. Required information cannot be withheld merely because it is generated by an audit rather than by some other means.

• Regulatory agencies cannot make promises to forgo or limit enforcement action against a particular facility or class of facilities in exchange for the use of environmental auditing systems. However, such agencies may use their discretion to adjust enforcement actions on a case-by-case basis in response to honest and genuine efforts by regulated entities to assure environmental compliance.

• When setting inspection priorities regulatory agencies should focus to the extent possible on compliance performance and environmental results.

• Regulatory agencies must continue to meet minimum program requirements (e.g., minimum inspection requirements, etc.).

• Regulatory agencies should not attempt to prescribe the precise form and structure of regulated entities' environmental management or auditing programs.

An effective state/federal partnership is needed to accomplish the mutual goal of achieving and maintaining high levels of compliance with environmental laws and regulations. The greater the consistency between state or local policies and this federal response to environmental auditing, the greater the degree to which sound auditing practices might be adopted and compliance levels improve.

Dated: June 28, 1986.

Lee M. Thomas,
Administrator.

Appendix—Elements of Effective Environmental Auditing Programs

Introduction: Environmental auditing is a systematic, documented, periodic and objective review by a regulated entity of facility operations and practices related to meeting environmental requirements.

Private sector environmental audits of facilities have been conducted for several years and have taken a variety of forms, in part to accommodate unique organizational structures and circumstances. Nevertheless, effective environmental audits appear to have certain discernible elements in common with other kinds of audits. Standards for internal audits have been documented extensively. The elements outlined below draw heavily on two of these documents: "Compendium of Audit Standards" (©1983, Walter Willborn, American Society for Quality Control) and "Standards for the Professional Practice of Internal Auditing" (©1981, The Institute of Internal Auditors, Inc.). They also reflect Agency analyses conducted over the last several years.

Performance-oriented auditing elements are outlined here to help accomplish several objectives. A general description of features of effective, mature audit programs can help those starting audit programs, especially federal agencies and smaller businesses. These elements also indicate the attributes of auditing EPA generally considers important to ensure program effectiveness. Regulatory agencies may use these elements in negotiating environmental auditing provisions for consent decrees. Finally, these elements can help guide states and localities considering auditing initiatives.

An effective environmental auditing system will likely include the following general elements:

I. *Explicit top management support for environmental auditing and commitment to follow-up on audit findings.* Management support may be demonstrated by a written policy articulating upper management support for the auditing program, and for compliance with all pertinent requirements, including corporate policies and permit requirements as well as federal, state and local statutes and regulations.

Management support for the auditing program also should be demonstrated by an explicit written commitment to follow-up on audit findings to correct identified problems and prevent their recurrence.

II. *An environmental auditing function independent of audited activities.* The status or organizational locus of environmental auditors should be sufficient to ensure objective and unobstructed inquiry, observation and testing. Auditor objectivity should not be impaired by personal relationships, financial or other conflicts of interest, interference with free inquiry or judgment, or fear of potential retribution.

III. *Adequate team staffing and auditor training.* Environmental auditors should possess or have ready access to the knowledge, skills, and disciplines needed to accomplish audit objectives. Each individual auditor should comply

with the company's professional standards of conduct. Auditors, whether full-time or part-time, should maintain their technical and analytical competence through continuing education and training.

IV. *Explicit audit program objectives, scope, resources and frequency.* At a minimum, audit objectives should include assessing compliance with applicable environmental laws and evaluating the adequacy of internal compliance policies, procedures and personnel training programs to ensure continued compliance.

Audits should be based on a process which provides auditors: all corporate policies, permits, and federal, state, and local regulations pertinent to the facility; and checklists or protocols addressing specific features that should be evaluated by auditors.

Explicit written audit procedures generally should be used for planning audits, establishing audit scope, examining and evaluating audit findings, communicating audit results, and following-up.

V. *A process which collects, analyzes, interprets and documents information sufficient to achieve audit objectives.* Information should be collected before and during an onsite visit regarding environmental compliance(1), environmental management effectiveness(2), and other matters (3) related to audit objectives and scope. This information should be sufficient, reliable, relevant and useful to provide a sound basis for audit findings and recommendations.

a. *Sufficient* information is factual, adequate and convincing so that a prudent, informed person would be likely to reach the same conclusions as the auditor.

b. *Reliable* information is the best attainable through use of appropriate audit techniques.

c. *Relevant* information supports audit findings and recommendations and is consistent with the objectives for the audit.

d. *Useful* information helps the organization meet its goals.

The audit process should include a

periodic review of the reliability and integrity of this information and the means used to identify, measure, classify and report it. Audit procedures, including the testing and sampling techniques employed, should be selected in advance, to the extent practical, and expanded or altered if circumstances warrant. The process of collecting, analyzing, interpreting, and documenting information should provide reasonable assurance that audit objectivity is maintained and audit goals are met.

VI. *A process which includes specific procedures to promptly prepare candid, clear and appropriate written reports on audit findings, corrective actions, and schedules for implementation.* Procedures should be in place to ensure that such information is communicated to managers, including facility and corporate management, who can evaluate the information and ensure correction of identified problems. Procedures also should be in place for determining what internal findings are reportable to state or federal agencies.

VII. *A process which includes quality assurance procedures to assure the accuracy and thoroughness of environmental audits.* Quality assurance may be accomplished through supervision, independent internal reviews, external reviews, or a combination of these approaches.

Footnotes to Appendix

(1) A comprehensive assessment of compliance with federal environmental regulations requires an analysis of facility performance against numerous environmental statutes and implementing regulations. These statutes include:
Resource Conservation and Recovery Act
Federal Water Pollution Control Act
Clean Air Act
Hazardous Materials Transportation Act
Toxic Substances Control Act
Comprehensive Environmental Response, Compensation and Liability Act
Safe Drinking Water Act
Federal Insecticide, Fungicide and Rodenticide Act
Marine Protection, Research and Sanctuaries Act
Uranium Mill Tailings Radiation Control Act

In addition, state and local government are likely to have their own environmental laws.

Many states have been delegated authority to administer federal programs. Many local governments' building, fire, safety and health codes also have environmental requirements relevant to an audit evaluation.

(2) An environmental audit could go well beyond the type of compliance assessment normally conducted during regulatory inspections, for example, by evaluating policies and practices, regardless of whether they are part of the environmental system or the operating and maintenance procedures. Specifically, audits can evaluate the extent to which systems or procedures:

1. Develop organizational environmental policies which: a. implement regulatory requirements; b. provide management guidance for environmental hazards not specifically addressed in regulations;

2. Train and motivate facility personnel to work in an environmentally-acceptable manner and to understand and comply with government regulations and the entity's environmental policy;

3. Communicate relevant environmental developments expeditiously to facility and other personnel;

4. Communicate effectively with government and the public regarding serious environmental incidents;

5. Require third parties working for, with or on behalf of the organization to follow its environmental procedures;

6. Make proficient personnel available at all times to carry out environmental (especially emergency) procedures;

7. Incorporate environmental protection into written operating procedures;

8. Apply best management practices and operating procedures, including "good housekeeping" techniques;

9. Institute preventive and corrective maintenance systems to minimize actual and potential environmental harm;

10. Utilize best available process and control technologies;

11. Use most-effective sampling and monitoring techniques, test methods, recordkeeping systems or reporting protocols (beyond minimum legal requirements);

12. Evaluate causes behind any serious environmental incidents and establish procedures to avoid recurrence;

13. Exploit source reduction, recycle and reuse potential wherever practical; and

14. Substitute materials or processes to allow use of the least-hazardous substances feasible.

(3) Auditors could also assess environmental risks and uncertainties.

Appendix D:
Checklist for
Acquisition Review

GUIDELINES FOR ACQUISITIONS

CONTENTS

GUIDELINES FOR ACQUISITIONS

o OPERATIONS

   For all present and past facilities, including jointly-owned
   facilities operated by others, review

   - Name of the facility.

   - Address.

   - General description of products and functions.

   - Contact names, positions and phone numbers.

   - Facility's environmental, health and safety organization and
     manpower.

   - Whether the facility is still in operation.

   - The facility's operating history including all prior uses by
     all prior owners and operators with respect to the a) raw
     materials used, and intermediates, products and wastes produced
     in the past, b) raw materials presently used, and
     intermediates, products and wastes presently produced. For
     materials in category b) above, Material Safety Data Sheets
     (MSDSs) should be obtained or reviewed for all raw materials
     used at the plant, and for all intermediate streams and
     products. Obtain all MSDSs or similar documents, or chemical
     analyses, that describe current wastes and waste streams.
     Cross references: Onsite Corrective Action, page 8; plans and
     drawings, page 20.

- 2 -

o TOXIC SUBSTANCES CONTROL ACT (TSCA) COMPLIANCE

- Review available records concerning whether all components of
  current and planned commercial products, and current and
  planned isolated intermediates, are listed on the TSCA
  Inventory of commercial chemical substances. Review status of
  all Premanufacture Notifications (PMNs) that have been
  submitted. If any PMNs have been withdrawn prior to agency
  action, determine why. Determine whether any substance for
  which a PMN has been submitted is subject to a section 5(e)
  (Regulation Pending Development of Information) or 5(f)
  (Protection Against Unreasonable Risks) order.

- Determine whether any chemical substance that is a component of
  a commercial product is subject to a Significant New Use Rule
  (SNUR).

- Obtain a list of all chemicals manufactured, processed, used or
  distributed for which the company or another party has filed
  either a TSCA §8(e) substantial risk notice or a §8(d) health
  and safety data reporting notice, and obtain a summary of the
  information whicn has been submitted to the U. S. Environmental
  Protection Agency (EPA) pursuant to those reporting
  requirements.

- Obtain the number(s) assigned to the §8(e) notice(s) by the
  EPA, and copies of that agency's analyses of the submitted
  information.

- Review records of allegations of significant adverse health or
  environmental effects maintained pursuant to TSCA §8(c) to
  ascertain alleged effects and public concern with operations or
  with products and product lines.

- Review products and product components that are subject to testing under a Section 4 test rule, and products/product components that are likely candidates for future agency action under Section 4.

- Review all EPA TSCA inspection reports, and internal records of follow-up by the company and/or the Agency.

- List by location any known or suspected carcinogens, teratogens, other reproductive toxins, and mutagens manufactured, processed, used or distributed. List all carcinogens by the classifications used by the International Agency for Research on Cancer (IARC). This list is to be inclusive of chemical substances handled by formulation contractors. Cross reference: Industrial Hygiene, page 15.

- Review use and handling of PCBs, and procedures for helping ensure compliance with PCB requirements.

o EXCURSION LOGS AND ENVIRONMENTAL AUDITS/ASSESSMENTS

- List the types of events that excursion logs, call-in systems or similar systems that are designed to serve as a record of permit excursions, spills, etc. are intended to capture.

- Review and assess the latest annual or other summary of such events, and review and assess actions taken.

- Review all environmental audit or assessment reports pertaining to each currently operating facility including but not limited to owned, leased, and tolling facilities, and formulation contractors, and reports pertaining to follow-up activity.

- 4 -

- Determine if there is a system in place for identifying
excursions from governmental, generally accepted, or internal
workplace exposure limits. If such a system exists, determine
the events that it is intended to capture, review and assess
the latest annual or other summary of such events, and review
and assess actions taken. Cross reference: Industrial
Hygiene, Page 15.

- Review probable regulations that may impact excursion logs and
environmental audits/assessments.

- Review internal estimates of costs to remedy any existing
deficiencies in compliance, etc. as noted in excursion logs and
in audits/assessments.

- Based on all of the above, estimate future capital costs and
operating expenses to remedy existing deficiencies.

o PRODUCT SAFETY AND TESTING EXPENSES

- Review product safety and toxicology organization, staffing and
support, including laboratory facilities that are owned, leased
or otherwise dedicated to the company.

- List all current products, product components and intermediate
streams and review the results of past product safety (i.e.
toxicology) testing programs pertaining to those materials.
Cross reference: Operations, page 1.

- List all ongoing toxicity testing whether on products, product
components, or intermediate streams, including testing for
chronic effects (carcinogenicity and reproductive effects), and
the operations or products that may be impacted by the results

- 5 -

of such testing. Obtain status reports and preliminary results when available. Include ongoing testing by trade associations, the Chemical Industry Institute of Toxicology (CIIT), etc. that may impact the company's operations or products.

- List all probable testing requirements by federal agencies during the next 5 years that may impact the company's operations or products.

- List all internal product safety testing recommendations and relevant recommendations within trade association, CIIT, etc. which have not yet been acted on by commencing such testing.

- Review internal estimates of and actual costs to the company of all toxicity testing currently in progress, and cost estimates for all testing which has been recommended but not yet commenced.

- Review toxicity testing budgets and actual costs for the past 5 years for products, product components and intermediate streams, including testing that is carried on by trade associations, CIIT, etc. for which the company has financial responsibility.

- Based on the above information, make a forecast of toxicity testing expenses for the company for each of the next 5 years.

o SUPERFUND SITES AND NOTIFICATIONS

- Review §103(c) notifications under the Comprehensive Environmental Response, Compensation and Liability Act (CERCLA or "Superfund").

- Review Eckhardt list submissions regarding waste disposal.

- 6 -

- Review status of each site where company has been named a PRP with respect to Remedial Investigation (RI), Feasibility Study (FS), Record of Decision (ROD), steering committee organization and chairman/contact.

- Review status of each Superfund site where company has not been named a PRP, but where involvement is known or suspected, with respect to RI, FS, groundwater surveys, ROD, etc.).

- Review compliance with Superfund Amendment and Reauthorization Act (SARA) Title III requirements.

- Review consultants' reports and internal company reports on significant Superfund sites and significant problem areas to ascertain nature and magnitude of potential liability.

- Review volumes and types of wastes sent to each site by the company. Cross references: Eckhardt list submissions, page 5; §103(c) notifications, page 5.

- List sites for which toxicity (in addition to volumetric share) is being considered by the steering committee or other appropriate group in apportioning liability. Review status of negotiations on liability apportionment, and ascertain the volume and nature of wastes generated by the company and sent to those sites.

- Review internal estimates of percentile volumetric share and total cost share (including all future costs) to remediate each site.

- Review sources of wastes (i.e. identity of plants or other operations) that led to involvement at each site.

- 7 -

- Review all consultants' reports and internal company records concerning any alleged or potential groundwater contamination at present or past sites or facilities. Cross references: Onsite Corrective Action, page 8; plans and drawings page 20.
- Review all of the above with respect to the company's joint ventures, partnerships, etc.
- Review identity of disposal sites currently used by the company's facilities together with any audits or assessments of those sites. Cross reference: Eckhardt list submissions, page 5; §103(c) notifications, page 5; company's "list of approved disposal sites," page 20.
- Considering all of the above, estimate future costs to remediate each site for which the company has or will probably have financial responsibility under CERCLA, and company's share of those costs.

o INSURANCE CLAIMS
   - Review all insurance claims, including the nature and amount of each claim, made by the company and pertaining to any environmental matter.

o NEW JERSEY ECRA STATUS AND EXPENSES (AND COMPLIANCE WITH SIMILAR REQUIREMENTS OF OTHER STATES)
   - Review status of New Jersey facilities under ECRA.
   - Review Site Evaluation Submissions and current status of sampling plans and remediation efforts.

- 8 -

- Review company's projected costs for ECRA compliance for each facility.

- Based on all available information, estimate future capital costs and operating expenses for ECRA compliance.

- Review all of the above for other applicable states that have requirements similar to New Jersey ECRA.

o LAND-BAN AND RETROFIT IMPACTS

- Review all facilities that require permitting under RCRA.

- Review required annual RCRA reports for offsite locations and amounts sent offsite each year. Cross reference: company's "list of approved disposal sites," page 20.

- Review records concerning financial responsibility requirements.

- List types and volumes of wastes (including wastewaters) generated at each site.

- List and characterize all onsite treatment, storage and disposal facilities, including but not limited to surface impoundments, waste piles, incinerators, waste treatment tanks, and deepwells. Cross reference: Deepwells, page 10; plans and drawings, page 20.

- Review the expected impact of RCRA retrofit rules on surface impoundments and landfills, including RCRA-exempt surface impoundments.

- Review the expected impacts of the land-ban decisions under RCRA for both onsite and offsite disposal.

- Review any variance requests made related to land ban or retrofit.

- 9 -

- Review internal projected costs for alternate disposal, treatment or retrofit.
- Based on all of the above information, estimate future capital costs and operating expenses associated with land ban and retrofit.

o ONSITE CORRECTIVE ACTION

- Review descriptions of present and past solid waste management units and treatment, storage or disposal facilities at each site. Cross reference: plans and drawings, page 20.
- Review Eckhardt list submissions regarding onsite disposal.
- Review plant history and lists of materials handled, and locations at which materials were or are handled, as they may relate to soil or groundwater contamination potential. Cross references: plant operating history, page 1; plans and drawings, page 20.
- Review hydrogeology characterization of present and past sites when available. Cross reference: plans and drawings, page 20; potential groundwater contamination, page 6.
- Review RCRA and non-RCRA groundwater monitoring and assessment data for each present and past site. Cross reference: potential groundwater contamination, page 6.
- Review data on soil contamination at each present and past site.
- Review internal estimates of costs for remediation of known and suspected soil or groundwater contamination problems.
- Based on the above information, estimate future capital costs and operating expenses associated with onsite corrective action.

- 10 -

o <u>STORAGE TANKS AND INCINERATORS</u>

- Other than the situations covered under land-ban and retrofit requirements and onsite corrective actions (above), review any upgrading expected in order to meet the RCRA standards for incinerators and storage tanks, including ancillary equipment and piping.

- Review present and past use and current inventory of storage tanks for petroleum and related materials and hazardous substances, and compare with probable upgrade rules. Include locations, types, and conditions of tanks and their present and past contents. Note whether tanks are aboveground, or partially or wholly underground. Cross reference: plans and drawings, page 20.

- Review whether storage tanks are associated with known or suspected soil or groundwater contamination. Cross reference: Onsite Corrective Action, page 8; plans and drawings, page 20.

- Review permits for upgrading of incinerators and storage tanks. Cross reference: Current Permits and Recent Compliance, page 12.

- Review internal cost estimates associated with required or advisable upgrading of storage tanks and incinerators.

- Based on the above information, estimate future capital costs and operating expenses associated with storage tanks and incinerators.

o <u>INVENTORIED WASTES FOR DISPOSAL</u>

- Determine whether there are any hazardous or other wastes (drums, lab wastes etc.) in inventory for disposal, and the

- 11 -

chemical nature of such wastes. Prepare a listing of such wastes and estimate cost of disposal.

o **DEEPWELLS**

- List all facilities which use deepwells for waste disposal.
- Review the nature of each deepwell, and results of any tests for mechanical integrity.
- Review the State and Regional regulatory environment, bans, actions and probable actions related to deepwells.
- Review selected technologies, available cost estimates, established cost reserves and any existing capital forecasts associated with current deepwell disposal.
- Determine past and present deepwell waste characteristics (flow, toxicity, etc.).
- Estimate costs to withdraw from each well including any remediations, including capital costs and operating expenses necessary for alternate disposal.

o **WASTEWATER TREATMENT AND COMPLIANCE**

- Characterize types and volumes of wastewater (direct and indirect discharges) for all pollutants including conventional pollutants, priority pollutants and pesticide pollutants.
- Review wastewater toxicity and biomonitoring results for all discharges and assess the impact of any probable in-stream limits.
- Review expected adverse impacts of direct discharges on water quality of receiving streams including any water quality

- 12 -

limited streams, and review waste load allocations either
presently imposed or projected.

- Review internal assessments of expected technologies and costs
to comply with any guidelines, toxicity limits, pretreatment
standards, water-quality forced limits, etc.

- Estimate future capital costs and operating expenses associated
with meeting present and probable future requirements.

o AIR COMPLIANCE AND ISSUES

- Review data base on air emissions of pollutants that are
subject to National Emissions Standards for Hazardous Air
Pollutants (NESHAPs) regulations.

- Separately review any studies and/or submissions relating to
any radionuclides.

- Review air quality attainment status at domestic manufacturing
facilities, and review facility emissions expected to be
impacted under the State Implementation Plans (SIPs).

- Determine whether there are any Class I areas that could be
impacted by any facility, and the facility's regulatory status.

- Review Waxman list submissions.

- Review all studies and/or submissions conducted or made because
of or in connection with Prevention of Significant
Deterioration (PSD) requirements.

- Review monitoring systems and control equipment at each
facility.

- Review current production rate information for consistency with
permit applications and for emission inventory data.

- 13 -

- Review internal forecasts of costs to achieve probable abatement requirements, and the nature of the technology needed to achieve abatement.
- Estimate future capital costs and operating expenses associated with meetings present and probable future requirements.

o CURRENT PERMITS AND RECENT COMPLIANCE

- List all current environmental permits and their expiration dates. Include names of compliance officers and contacts.
- Assess the frequency and nature of reportable and non-reportable water discharge permit and Publicly Owned Treatment Works (POTW) ordinance violations and exceedances for the last 5 years. Cross reference: Excursion Logs and Environmental Audits/Assessments, page 3.
- Assess the frequency and nature of reportable and non-reportable air permit violations and exceedances for the last 5 years. Cross reference: Excursion Logs and Environmental Audits/Assessments, page 3.
- Assess the frequency and nature of Superfund (CERCLA)-reported releases for the last 5 years. Cross reference: Excursion Logs and Environmental Audits/Assessments, page 3.
- Review community complaint issues (whether or not included in the TSCA §8(c) file) and litigation with respect to emissions, odor, noise or other releases for the last 5 years. Cross reference: TSCA §8(c) file, page 2; past and present environmental and toxic tort litigation; page 20.

- 14 -

- Review RCRA, water, and air regulatory inspection findings, federal, state and local, and list any deficiencies and company or agency follow-up, during the last 5 years. Cross reference: Excursion Logs and Environmental Audits/Assessments, page 3.

- Determine if there is a system in place for assuring RCRA manifest closeout.

- Review internal estimates of costs to remedy significant compliance problems.

- Based on all of the above, estimate future capital costs and operating expenses to remedy significant compliance problems.

o COMPLIANCE ORDERS

- Review all Compliance Orders, Administrative Orders, Notices of Violation or any similar documents received during the last 5 years, and list separately those currently active. Review and assess internal cost estimates to bring the facility or facilities into compliance. Cross reference: Current Permits and Recent Compliance, page 12.

o 10-K AND 10-Q SUBMISSIONS

- Review the most recent submissions for environmental matters, as well as 10K and 10Q submissions for the past 5 years.

o OCCUPATIONAL HEALTH

- Review medical health organization, staffing, budget and responsibilities at the general office and at other locations.

- 15 -

- Review and assess existing medical surveillance programs for employees.
- Separately identify any special examinations or biological monitoring conducted on employees.
- Obtain a summary of all anecdotal medical information and case studies that may indicate a relationship between products, processes, or workplace conditions and human health.
- List all completed, ongoing and planned epidemiology studies of any type, e.g. cross-sectional studies, prospective or retrospective morbidity or mortality studies, etc., whether carried out internally, by consultants, or by government authorities such as the National Institute for Occupational Safety and Health (NIOSH). Note any follow-up action recommended or taken by any party.
- Based on the above, and on available toxicology information, assess potential future liabilities. Estimate future capital costs and operating expenses associated with minimizing relevant risks.

o INDUSTRIAL HYGIENE

- Review industrial hygiene organization, staffing and responsibilities at the general office and at each facility including analytical support.
- Identify chemical and physical agents to which employees are potentially exposed at each site. Cross reference: Operations, page 1.

- 16 -

- Using the above list of chemicals, identify chemical substances that are within the following categories: Known or suspect human carcinogens and other categories of carcinogens by IARC classification; teratogens or other reproductive toxins; mutagens; systemic toxins; OSHA or American Conference of Industrial Hygienists (ACGIH) listed chemicals; chemicals regulated under comprehensive OSHA health standards (29 CFR 1910.1001ff); chemicals with internal company exposure limits. Cross reference: TSCA Compliance, page 2.

- Review the personnel and area exposure monitoring data collected at each facility over the past 3 years on the chemical and physical agents noted above.

- Review the asbestos management program for each facility and assess the status of asbestos identification and of any abatement or removal projects either planned or underway.

- Review internal projected costs to complete any asbestos removal or abatement projects. Estimate future costs to achieve "asbestos-free" status at facilities.

- Identify any major ongoing or planned engineering projects to achieve reduction of workplace exposures to chemical or physical agents along with respective estimated costs.

- Review internal hearing conservation program for employees.

- Based on the above, estimate future capital costs and operating expenses to achieve goals.

o OSHA COMPLIANCE

- Review results of OSHA inspections that have occurred during the past 5 years. Determine the types and severities of

- 17 -

citations received and status of their resolution, including any outstanding items under contest. Note the circumstances and resolution with OSHA of all employee deaths that were or that were alleged to be work-related.

- Review the company's hazard communication program designed to comply with the federal OSHA Hazard Communication Regulation (OSHA HCR).

- Review the results of OSHA inspections specifically with respect to OSHA HCR compliance, and whether any violations involve failure to warn employees of chronic health risks, and the chemical substances involved in such failure to warn.

- Ascertain compliance with the OSHA comprehensive health standards (29 CFR 1910.1001ff). Cross reference: Industrial Hygiene, Page 15.

- Review any internal "written compliance programs" specific to chemical agents covered by the above comprehensive health standards, and describe efforts to reduce workplace exposures below the respective PELs. Cross reference: Industrial Hygiene, page 15.

o EMPLOYEE SAFETY

- Review the company's policies and guidelines pertaining to the safety of its employees.

- Using the OSHA 200 logs, and cross-referencing the TSCA §8(c) file, review the company's occupational injury and illness experiences at each facility for the last 5 years. Cross reference: Company's workers' compensation experience, page 20.

- 18 -

o PROCESS SAFETY

- Review available process descriptions for major processes at each facility.

- Review layout drawings for each site and assess spacing of process structures, control centers, auxiliary process equipment, tank farms, truck/rail docking stations, and office complexes. Cross reference: plans and drawings, page 20.

- Review any studies conducted on potential process failures that could lead to major releases of hazardous materials.

- Review the Emergency and Hazardous Chemical Inventory Form submitted pursuant to §312(a) of Title III of the Superfund Amendments and Reauthorization Act of 1986 (SARA) for each facility. Ascertain maximum quantities handled/stored at each site, manners of use, and general locations of such chemicals.

- Review internal safety design standards pertaining to process interlock/trip systems, instrumentation, containment and emergency relief systems, emergency release control, and piping systems.

- Review internal guidelines or standards pertaining to inspection and/or testing of critical safety devices (e.g. special alarms, process shut-downs, interlocks, and rupture relief).

- Review the most recent safety audit reports covering processes in both domestic and foreign locations and assess status of major recommendations.

- Determine occurrences of any major process-related adverse events (major fires, explosions, etc.) within the last 10 years

- 19 -

and review incident investigation reports produced internally or by external consultants or others such as insurance carriers.

- Review internal estimates of costs for both ongoing and planned projects to reduce the risks of potentially dangerous process events.

- Based on the above, estimate future capital expenditures and operating costs in the process safety area for both ongoing and planned projects.

o FIRE PROTECTION AND CONTROL

- Obtain a list of combustible and flammable liquids and solids handled in bulk at each manufacturing and formulation site. Ascertain maximum quantities handled or stored at each site and manner of storage.

- Review internal fire protection standards or codes pertaining to inerting and to explosion protection for atmospheric storage tanks, gas and oil-fired furnaces, and tank car and tank truck unloading.

- Assess the application of internal fire protection standards in locations handling combustible and flammable materials.

- Review site drawings showing installed fire protection systems, including water supply and distribution, and sprinkler and deluge control. Ascertain likely fire demand and adequacy of existing water supply at each facility. Cross reference: plans and drawings, page 20.

- Review the adequacy and technology of sprinkler systems and deluge protection.

- 20 -

- Review fire occurrences during the past 10 years, and the investigation reports covering major events resulting in significant property damage and/or process outage.

- Review fire protection surveys that have been conducted during the past 10 years either internally or by outside consultants, e.g., by insurance carriers. Ascertain status of major recommendations and company's projected cost to remedy deficient items.

- Based on the above, estimate future capital costs and operating expenses associated with fire protection and control.

o OTHER

- Obtain plans and drawings for all current and former plant sites showing locations of production and storage facilities, potential waste "problem areas," and waste discharges.

- Note plant locations in relation to Superfund sites.

- Review the company's list of approved disposal sites for wastes, and its list of approved recycling facilities.

- Review reserves for mine or other reclamation.

- Review copies of all consultants' reports pertaining to mining or other facilities.

- Note the states in which the company's facilities are located, and the nature of state environmental, safety or health laws and regulations that are more stringent than federal laws.

- Review how those more stringent requirements may affect the assessments made pursuant to these Guidelines for Acquisitions.

- 21 -

- Review permitting files for the sites for which permits are being sought to incinerate or to dispose of hazardous wastes. Cross reference: Storage Tanks and Incinerators, page 9, Onsite Corrective Action, page 8.

- Review status of past and present product liability litigation, and of past and present environmental and toxic tort litigation and relate such litigation to past and current plants, processes and waste disposal sites. Review nature of claims, amounts of damages and/or nature of other relief which is sought, and current status of litigation. Note whether litigation tends to focus on particular products, product lines, plants, processes or waste disposal sites.

- Review the company's workers' compensation experience for the last 5 years. Ascertain the status of outstanding employee claims and review the projected costs to close existing costs. Note whether claims tend to focus on particular plants or processes.

- Determine the nature of all occupational disease workers' compensation claims, and note their relationship to specific plants, processes, etc. Estimate future costs to close the existing cases, and estimate the extent of potential future liability from employees who have not yet filed claims. Note the potential for third party liability from spouses, etc.

- Review any Environmental Impact Statements (EISs) and Environmental Assessments (EAs), and any Clean Water Act §404 studies. For EISs and EAs that are required pursuant to the National Environmental Policy Act (NEPA), assess status, and note existence and status of any litigation.

- 22 -

- Review contract provisions regarding environment safety and health liabilities associated with jointly-owned facilities, whether those facilities are operated by the company being reviewed or operated by others.
- Review sales of facilities, subsidiaries, etc. for environmental indemnification responsibilities.

JRW/tls-1749H

Appendix E:
Sample Internal Environmental and Safety Audit Questionnaire

Objectives

- To determine that corporate, industry group, and/or plant procedures adequately address environmental and safety concerns.

- To determine that a recent environmental assessment has been performed and items identified have been addressed.

- To determine that all applicable regulations, training and required reporting is properly documented.

- To determine compliance with all permit and regulatory requirements is properly documented.

- To determine that all work related injuries and illnesses are recorded.

Questions	Yes	No	N/A

ENVIRONMENTAL

Organization and Facility Description

1. Does the entity or function being audited maintain copies of all applicable company environmental policies and procedures?

2. Do internal reporting requirements exist delineating a clear reporting structure within the local environmental organization?

3. Do these requirements clearly note which organizations are obligated to provide data and information to the environmental group?

4. Does a mechanism exist for reporting excursions, incidents, significant matters, etc. to the appropriate individuals and organizations in the company and to the applicable government agencies?

5. Do recordkeeping requirements exist to ensure adherence to permits, rules and regulations?

6. Do these recordkeeping requirements clearly define responsibility for safekeeping of these records? (These procedures should include provisions for maintaining permits, monitoring reports and other records.)

7. Are records kept in a central file or by a designated individual at each facility providing for good control and accessibility? If a central control is not in place, at a minimum, is a reference folder maintained that includes file and location references?

8. Is access to records adequately controlled, and are the records maintained in an orderly fashion?

9. Is the record filing system consistent for all environmental activities?

10. Has a recent environmental assessment been performed? What is the date of the last report prepared? _____ Obtain a copy.

11. Has the facility documented a summary of all environmental compliance requirements which apply to their plant or location? (This information may be found in the environmental assessment reports, applicable environmental reference manuals or operating permits.) Has documentation been updated within the last 12 months?

Revised: 1-1-91

Questions	Yes	No	N/A

12. Does the facility have copies or access to applicable federal, state and local regulations?

13. Does the facility have or have access to a system (such as the environmental action system (EAS)) or a service that provides it with the following information:

 A. A listing of matters such as significant incidents or reportable excursions?
 B. Legal actions taken or pending?
 C. A listing of all environmental issues by a control or folio number?
 D. An action plan for resolution of each environmental issue with timetables and milestones?
 E. Compliance requirements applicable to items listed in (A) through (D)?
 F. Community Right-to-know program (required for all facilities)?

Water Quality

14. Does a list of waste water discharge permits that are presently in force exist? (This information may be summarized in the environmental assessment reports or applicable environmental reference manuals.) If so, obtain a copy.

15. If the plant has waste or waste water ponds, are the required permits maintained? If so, obtain a copy.

16. Is the facility in compliance with water quality requirements during storm periods?

17. If the facility is not in compliance with water problems during storm periods, do they have a program for correction?

18. If the facility has any monitoring wells, are the required permits maintained? If so, obtain a copy.

19. If the facility has any injection wells, are current permits maintained for each of these wells?

Air Quality

20. Does a list of air emission permits presently in force exist? (This information may be found in the environmental assessment reports or applicable environmental reference manuals.) If so, obtain a copy.

21. Has a recent regulatory air inspection been performed? If so, when was the last inspection? _____ Obtain a copy.

22. Has there been any change in the operation since the last assessment, either a new process or significant change to an existing process that would have required new permits or changes in existing permits? Have these permits been secured? If not, have they been applied for?

23. Is an emission inventory maintained to help monitor emission levels?

Revised: 1-1-91

Questions	Yes	No	N/A

24. Are these inventories periodically updated?

25. Are periodic emissions tests performed by company and/or air pollution control agency personnel?

Solid and Hazardous Waste Management

26. Does the facility maintain a list of solid and hazardous generated wastes? Is the amount generated shown? Obtain a copy.

27. Do manifests exist for each off-site shipment of hazardous waste?

28. Does the facility have a system to verify and maintain receipt of a copy of each manifest required to be returned by the off-site disposal operator?

29. Is an annual hazardous waste summary provided to the state.

30. Is a statement regarding the plants "waste reduction efforts" issued annually to the state? Obtain a copy.

31. Is an inventory of drummed waste maintained?

32. Is a listing of this drummed waste inventory maintained? Obtain a copy.

33. Are drums dated as to when hazardous waste is first placed in the drum?

34. Is there an industry group or division list or other form of record denoting authorized disposal sites?

35. If not, has the disposal site used by the plant been reviewed and approved, and has this information been adequately documented?

36. Does a list of hazardous wastes disposed of on-site exist? If so, obtain a copy.

Vinyl Chloride Monomer (VCM)

36. If the plant has any VCM related activities, is this information documented?

37. Is there a fugitive emission identification and control program? (This information may be found in applicable environmental reference manuals.)

38. Are the results of the fugitive emission identification and control program adequately documented?

Polychlorinated Biphenyls (PCBs)

39. Does this facility contain polychlorinated biphenyls (PCBs), PCB equipment. (e.g., transformers, capacitors, electromagnets, electric motors, hydraulic systems, heat transfer systems, compressors), or containers of PCBs or PCB mixtures? (This information may be found in the environmental assessment reports, or applicable environmental reference manuals.)

40. Are periodic inspections made of any PCB equipment that is in service? Are these inspections adequately documented?

Revised: 1-1-91

<u>Questions</u>

	Yes	No	N/A

<u>Asbestos</u>

41.　Has the facility conducted and documented a survey of asbestos located within the facility? If friable asbestos is present, is there a plan for encasement, removal, disposal or other appropriate action under applicable regulations? Obtain a copy of each document.

<u>Spill Control and Emergency Plans</u>

A Spill Prevention, Control, and Countermeasure (SPCC) Plan is a specific requirement of 40 Code of Federal Regulations (CFR), and pertains to the storage and use of oil, (including gasoline diesel, crude oil, fuel oil, and vegetable oil). The requirement is in addition to any other requirement (regulatory or company) for a spill contingency plan.

<u>Questions</u>

	Yes	No	N/A

42.　Does the facility have an SPCC plan updated within the last 3 years?

43.　Has the facility been without any reported spills within the last six months?

44.　Does the facility have any emergency response or other disaster control contingency plan?

45.　Does this emergency response plan include a community hazard communication program, and does it cover fire, storm, bomb threat, gas releases, etc.?

<u>General</u>

46.　If the facility transfers product via pipeline, is there an in-house pipeline inspection, surveillance and maintenance program?

47.　Are environmental regulations and requirements communicated to on-site contractors in documented form?

48.　Are all AFEs reviewed by environmental personnel at the appropriate levels to determine if the project may have an environmental effect and that the effect is provided for?

<u>Safety</u>

<u>Organization and Facility Description</u>

1.　Does the facility have corporate and/or local safety policies and procedures (i.e., training, hazard communication, etc.)? Obtain a copy.

2.　Has there been a recent safety assessment report issued? Obtain a copy.

<u>General</u>

3.　Does the facility maintain a list and/or inventory of all chemicals (raw materials, intermediates, finished products)?

Revised: 1-1-91

Questions	Yes	No	N/A

4. Are material safety data sheets (MSDSs) available for all chemicals for which an MSDS is required?

    Note: The MSDSs are required under two different sets of regulations. The occupational Safety & Health Administration (OSHA) requires the MSDSs for compliance with its Hazard Communication Standard and the Environmental Protection Agency (EPA) requires the MSDSs as part of its Community Right-to-Know regulations.

5. Is the purchasing department aware of the requirement to obtain the MSDSs for purchased raw materials?

6. Are safety regulations and requirements communicated to on-site contractors in documented form?

7. Is there an industry group or facility drug and alcohol abuse policy meeting the OPC policy requirements?

8. Are outside consultants used in a cost-effective manner?

Chemical Exposure

For all chemicals in your facility for which there are OSHA Permissible Exposure Limits (PELs) or Threshold Limit Values (TLVs), employee exposure should be determined or estimated. A listing of these limits and values may be obtained from Corporate Industrial Hygiene. Sometimes, a careful review of the exposure potential will result in the conclusion that exposure is minimal or non-existent. In other cases, it will be necessary to actually sample to determine the extent of exposure. If exposure (without regard to the use of personal protective equipment) is above the action level (1/2 of the limit), then a program of routine sampling must be established, and an engineering solution investigated. Chemicals for which there are substance-specific standards (asbestos, formaldehyde, vinyl chloride, etc.) should be sampled routinely to generate sufficient data to allow exposure to be estimated with more confidence. (See Substance Specific Standards Section).

Questions	Yes	No	N/A

9. If as a result of sampling an overexposure is believed to exist, have the individual employees who were monitored been provided with proper personal protective equipment?

    A. Is its use enforced?

10. Is there an action plan to engineer out the source of overexposure?

11. Is ventilation checked regularly and results documented?

12. Have representative exposure samples been taken for all chemicals with OSHA-PELs or American Conference of Governmental Hygienists-Threshold Limit Values (ACGIH-TLVs) at your facility?

13. Are samples taken on a scheduled basis?

14. Are they representative of an 8-hour TWA?

15. Are area Standard Threshold Exposure Level (STEL) and Ceiling samples taken?

16. Are employees notified of monitoring results?

17. Is there prompt follow-up on high exposures?

Questions	Yes	No	N/A
18. Is there proper documentation of:			
A. Monitoring data?			
B. Sampling/Analytical procedures?			
C. Results?			

Substance Specific Standards

If your facility handles chemicals which have been specifically regulated by OSHA as listed below, the requirements of that standard(s) must be met.

Substance Specific Standards have been promulgated by OSHA for the following: Refer to Specific Reg: 29 CFR 1910

Asbestos	Dimethylaminoazobenzene
Coal tar pitch volatiles	N-Nitrosodimethylamine
4-Nitrobiphenyl	Vinyl chloride
a-Naphthylamine	Inorganic arsenic
Methyl chloromethyl ether	Lead
3,3'-Dichlorobenzidine and salts	Coke oven emissions
bis-Chloromethylether	Cotton dust
b-Naphthylamine	1,2-Dibromo-3-chloropropane
Benzidine	Acrylonitrile
4-Aminodiphenyl	Benzene
Ethyleneimine	Formaldehyde
b-Propiolactone	Ethylene oxide
2-Acetylaminofluorene	

19. Have the specific requirements of these standards been addressed as to:

    A. Sampling to measure action level?
    B. PEL, ceiling and STEL concentration?
    C. Change rooms and shower facilities?
    D. Medical monitoring?
    E. Medical removal from workplace exposure?
    F. Recordkeeping and training?
    G. Is there a written program where required?
    H. Have regulated areas been established and demarcated as required?

Access to Exposure and Medical Records

OSHA regulations require that employees be informed <u>annually</u> that they have a right to see and/or obtain a copy of their exposure and medical records. Should an employee ask to see his/her data, we have fifteen days to comply. Requests for exposure data will likely be minimized if you discuss the results of any sampling with employees as they are obtained. The notification of right of access can be done by posting an appropriate announcement on the bulletin board, or by discussion during a safety or communications meeting. If you use the latter method, you must document that fact. Records are required by the standard to be preserved and maintained for the duration of employment, plus thirty years.

Questions	Yes	No	N/A
20. Are employees informed annually of their right to exposure data and medical records, both past and present?			
21. Are employees notified of their personal exposure data as collected?			
22. Can the facility meet the 15-day time frame to supply requested records?			

Revised: 1-1-91

Questions	Yes	No	N/A
23. Do the employees know of the existence, the location and availability of records?			
24. Do employees know the designated person who maintains these records?			
25. Do employees know of their right of access?			
26. Is a copy of the standards (OSHA 1910.20) readily available for employee examination?			

Noise - Hearing Conservation

There is no OSHA requirement for a written noise program. The regulation does require that it be determined whether employees are exposed at or above the "action level" of 85 dBA as an eight-hour time-weighted average (TWA). If they are, the affected employees must be given training, access to hearing protection and audiometric testing.
There should be an up-to-date noise survey on file to show the compliance officer. Noise surveys should be updated whenever new noise sources are added, or at least every two years. If indicated by the survey, dosimetry should be performed on employees in high noise environments.

Mine Safety & Health Act (MSHA) does have requirements concerning noise levels, depending on the operation. Questions 39 an 40 refer only to MSHA Regulations.

Questions	Yes	No	N/A
27. Has a sound level survey of the facility been performed to identify areas above 85 dBA within the past two years?			
28. Are areas above 90 dBA posted with signs?			
29. Are workers offered an annual audiometric exam?			
30. Has representative 8-hour dosimetry been conducted on those individuals identified by the sound level survey?			
31. Are employees given annual training?			
32. Does this training include effects of noise on the ear, and the principles of noise generation?			
33. Is a copy of the OSHA Noise Standard 1910.95 readily available for employees to examine?			
34. Is proper hearing protection provided for identified employees? Are employees trained in care and use?			
35. In areas over 90 dBA, is hearing protection usage enforced?			
36. Does the program include documentation of:			
A. Area and personal sampling?			
B. Audiometric testing?			
C. Annual training?			
37. Is the documentation readily available?			
38. Is special training given to employees who have experienced a standard threshold shift?			

Questions	Yes	No	N/A
39. Has a program been implemented to provide hearing protection under MSHA regulations?			
40. If a program has not been implemented, have noise surveys been performed in areas above 85 dBA in accordance with MSHA regulations?			

Interview with: _____ _____ _____
                        (Name)   (Title)   (Date)

Revised: 1-1-91

<u>Objectives</u>

The general objective of this review is to provide assurance that all environmental and safety related activities are adequately documented where practical. Specific objectives of these reviews are listed below.

- To ensure that all OPC/Industry Group policies and procedures regarding environmental and safety issues are being adhered to.

- To ensure proper documentation exists for areas of concern noted in the most recent assessments and any other identified issues have been addressed and corrective action has been properly taken.

- To ensure that documentation of all applicable regulations, training, and required reporting is maintained.

- To ensure that compliance with all permit and regulatory requirements are properly and adequately documented in the environmental and safety records, and to ensure these files are maintained in an organized fashion.

- To ensure that all work related injuries and illness are recorded.

In satisfying the audit objectives, the auditor is encouraged to use the information included in the environmental and safety assessment reports, and applicable environmental and safety reference and standard operating procedure manuals located at the audit site. Information from these sources may help accomplish many of the following audit procedures.

	WORKPAPER REFERENCE	COMPLETED BY/DATE
<u>Procedures</u>		
<u>ENVIRONMENTAL</u>		
<u>ORGANIZATION AND FACILITY DESCRIPTION</u>		
1. Review all applicable company environmental policies and procedures.		
2. Review the most recent environmental assessment report issued, recognizing any confidentiality requirements, and determine that it contains a brief summary of all environmental activities, facilities, processes, and new construction. This information should include all facilities or processes that are related to, or could result in, air emissions, water effluents and outfalls, hazardous or solid waste etc. In short, this should include all activities which do or might have an environmental effect on land, air, or water. Review the environmental assessment to identify issues or activities not included on the related action plan and review action plan to determine if adequate follow-up had been performed and documented. Determine if the action plans were entered into the EAS system.		

Revised: 4-1-91

	WORKPAPER REFERENCE	COMPLETED BY/DATE

Use the following points as a guide to determine the following:

A.   Physical location in the plant?
B.   Operating status of the units or processes?
C.   Age and general condition?
D.   Pollution excursion incident and citation histories?
E.   Type and quantity of material processed?
F.   Proximity to environmentally sensitive/high exposure areas?
G.   Sensitive local or community factors?
H.   Presence and structure of environmental staff?
I.   Identification of hazardous processing locations?

3.   Using the information obtained in Step 2, determine the scope of this review. Select a sample (which should include some of the high risk facilities) to review in greater detail.

4.   Review the recordkeeping activity and determine the adequacy of controls, including entry of all excursions and other identified issues into the Environmental Action System (EAS). Recordkeeping procedures will vary by location, however, where applicable the following points can be used to determine the adequacy and reasonableness of controls:

A.   For the sample selected in Step 3, determine if the records are reasonably complete. Although all of the following will not always apply, they offer some types of data which might be included in environmental records. (This data may be included in the environmental assessment reports or applicable environmental reference manuals.)

1)   Applicable laws and regulations (ref. Step 4).
2)   Permits in effect and pending applications for new permits (ref. Steps 4,8,9 and 11 thru 13).
3)   Timeliness of application(s) for permit renewal(s).
4)   Names and telephone numbers of individuals to contact at the regulatory agencies.
5)   Facility layout and process descriptions (ref. step 3).
6)   Monitoring data and/or estimation methods on air emissions (ref. Step 13).
7)   Monitoring data on water effluents, and outfalls and overall water quality (ref. Steps 8 thru 12).
8)   Required data on solid and/or hazardous waste, waste descriptions, storage and treatment, disposal methods, disposal locations, manifests (ref. Steps 15 thru 21).
9)   Listing of disposal sites used in the past.
10)   Emergency response, disaster control, contingency, and other local community awareness and incident control plans (ref. Steps 27 thru 29).
11)   Company/division policies and procedures (ref. Step 1).
12)   Applicable reports to government agencies; routine and nonroutine (ref. Step 4). (Routine such as National Pollution Discharge Elimination System (NPDES) reports and nonroutine such as spill reports.)

Revised: 4-1-91

5. Determine the following information has been recorded and documented in accordance with the OPC Health, Environment and Safety Procedure No. 2.11, "Reporting Environmental Matters":

    A. A listing of matters such as significant incidents or reportable excursions?
    B. Legal actions taken or pending?
    C. A listing of all environmental issues by a control or folio number?
    D   An action plan for resolution of each environmental issue, with timetables and milestones?
    E. Compliance requirements applicable to items listed in (a) through (d)?
    F. Community Right-to-know program (required for all facilities)?

WATER QUALITY

6. Determine if any excursions occurred in the last 12 months. Determine if resolution of these incidents were properly documented and recorded. Determine analytical quality control and assurance tests have been properly documented? Select a sample period and perform a comparison of the agency reports to the laboratory results.

    A. From a review of the environmental records, is it evident that all incidents falling outside of permit requirements were properly reported and documented? In these cases was corrective action taken and adequately documented?

7. Review the permits required for waste or waste water ponds. (This information may be included in the environmental assessment reports or applicable environmental reference manuals.)

    A. If so, determine if they require groundwater checks and periodic reporting of these results.
    B. Are ground water checks documented?
    C. Have any exceptions to permit requirements (if applicable) been properly documented and reported?

8. Review the last assessment action plan, and determine if any temporary noncompliance water problems during storm periods have been addressed.

9. Review the permits that are required for monitoring wells.

    A. What reporting requirements are placed on the plant? (This information may be included in the environmental assessment reports or applicable environmental reference manuals.)
    B. Is there documentation to indicate that the well design and operation is within the permit and regulatory agency requirements?
    C. Select a sample period and perform a comparison of the agency reports to the laboratory results.
    D. Have reported monitoring results (last 12 months) been documented and transmitted to the Industry Group HQ?
    E. Have all exceptions to agency requirements been properly reported and entered into the EAS?

Revised: 4-1-91

	WORKPAPER REFERENCE	COMPLETED BY/DATE

10. Review the current permit for each injection well. (This information may be documented in the environmental assessment report or applicable environmental reference manuals.)

   A.   Do the permits or regulations require periodic testing and reporting?
   B.   If so, select a sample of test results and compare the lab results to the agency reports.
   C.   By review of the records, can we determine that all exceptions to permit requirements were properly reported and documented?

AIR QUALITY

11. Of the air emission permits presently in force, select a sample period and perform a comparison of the reports to the agency to the emission test results.

   A.   Have all exceptions to the permit requirements been reported as required?
   B.   Have steps been taken and documented to avoid these issues in the future?

12. Highlight any exceptions noted in the last regulatory air inspection performed. Determine if corrective action has been taken and if these efforts have been adequately documented and entered into EAS.

13. For facilities operating within a geographic area not meeting federal air quality standards (these issues are not restricted to nonattainment areas), perform the following:

   A.   Review applicable air pollution control agency emission standards. Obtain an understanding of the permitting process (i.e., preparation of the construction application by company personnel and the granting of an authority to construct by the agency and document procedures followed. Determine if the facility has had a change in operation (i.e., new process or significant change to an existing process) since the last environmental assessment was performed. If so, how does this change affect the permits? Are new permits or changes to the existing permits required? Have these permits been secured or applied for? Review the permits and their applicable requirements.
   B.   Select a sample of emission sources and test for proper authorization to construct from the agency.
   C.   Review company procedures followed and controls in place to ensure that emission standards are not exceeded.
   D.   For any fines or citations issued within the last year, determine that these have been adequately resolved and action taken to ensure the violation does not reoccur. Determine that information was entered into EAS.

Revised: 4-1-91

	WORKPAPER REFERENCE	COMPLETED BY/DATE

SOLID AND HAZARDOUS WASTE MANAGEMENT

14. Review the list of solid and hazardous wastes and the amount being generated. (This information may be included in the environmental assessment reports, or applicable environmental reference manuals.)

   A.   Is this information properly documented?
   B.   Does the document action indicate whether this waste is disposed of on or off-site and by what means?

15. Document the procedures for off-site disposals of hazardous waste.

   A.   How are these manifests controlled?
   B.   How are "manifest exceptions" handled?
   C.   Is the manifest record system properly maintained, and does it provide for adequate documentation of this activity?
   D.   Does the plant perform a periodic review of vendor performance, and is this review properly documented?
   E.   Determine if transporters not contracted by the waste disposal company are reviewed for EPA license prior to being used as a transporter of hazardous waste.

16. Review the inventory of drummed waste.

   A.   Is it in accordance with applicable state and federal requirements?
   B.   Determine how the drums are documented as to when hazardous waste is first placed in the drum?
   C.   From review of this documentation, determine if any hazardous drummed waste has been held over 90 days.
   D.   What controls are in place to ensure drummed waste is not held for over 90 days?
   E.   Is all of this information adequately documented?

17. Review the last assessment and determine that the disposal sites are within the provisions of the Resource Conservation and Recovery Act (RCRA), and other federal, state, or local regulations.

18. Select a sample of hazardous waste manifests, and determine if shipping destinations are included in the list of authorized disposal sites.

19. Determine if facility disposes of hazardous waste (either generated on-site or received from off-site). Obtain information regarding the disposal methods, and review documentation that disposal methods meet regulatory requirements including necessary permits.

20. Determine if there are any documented locations that were used as waste disposal sites in the past.

   A.   Determine if any groundwater tests have been performed.

   B.   Determine if there is any evidence of ground water contamination.
   C.   Determine if this information has been documented.

Revised: 4-1-91

	WORKPAPER REFERENCE	COMPLETED BY/DATE

<u>VINYL CHLORIDE MONOMER (VCM)</u>

21. Determine if the plant has any VCM related activities?

    A. Obtain a list of all equipment in place that is used to alert personnel as to the levels of emissions in the workplace. Has this information been documented?

    B. Determine if there is any documentation that shows what levels of emissions (fugitive or emergency venting/release) are acceptable. (This VCM related information may be found in the environmental assessment reports or applicable environmental reference and operating procedure manuals).

22. Determine if there has been any emergency venting/release incidents in the last three months?

    A. What is the status of the incidents?

    B. Was a notice of violation or penalty received?

    C. Was the cause of the problem identified and rectified?

    D. Was this activity properly documented?

23. Select a sample period and determine if there were any fugitive emission incidents.

    A. Is there adequate documentation for each emission?

    B. Were these incidents and their related effects properly documented and reported in accordance with applicable requirements?

    C. If periodic agency reports are required, perform a comparison of the emission levels in the agency reports and the on-site recorder levels.

    D. Is there consistency in the information reported and the data actually recorded?

<u>POLYCHLORINATED BIPHENYLS (PCBs)</u>

24. For any electrical equipment containing dielectric fluid, has a positive determination been made that the equipment does or does not contain PCBs? Is the equipment labeled properly?

25. Determine if the facility performs and documents an annual inventory of equipment containing PCBs. Determine the retention period for annual PCB inventory records. Do the annual reports contain information such as the following:

    A. Date and source of PCB articles, chemicals, and mixtures received?

    B. Date and type of article, chemicals, and mixtures removed from service?

    C. Accounting of amount received, amount removed, and amount remaining at facility?

    D. For amounts removed is there a complete record of disposition?

Revised: 4-1-91

26. For periodic inspections made of any PCB equipment that is in service, determine the following:

    A. Are the inspections documented?
    B. If any leaks or spills were found, was the appropriate corrective action taken and documented?
    C. Is there documentation of any contaminated soil disposal?
    D. Is adequate spill containment provided for in service PCB equipment?

27. Determine if the storage area appears to meet the regulatory requirements listed below and if appropriate documentation is maintained. The following are examples of items which should be considered in reviewing the storage areas:

    A. Roof to prevent rain water from reaching PCB items.
    B. Storage area properly labeled.
    C. Spill containment to contain twice the internal volume of the largest PCB containing article.
    D. Containment area should not have any drains, valves, expansion joints, sewer lines or other openings. Does the storage facility meet these requirements?
    E. All articles marked with the date they are placed in storage.
    F. All articles in storage checked for leaks at least every 30 days and records of checks maintained.
    G. Impervious (concrete) flooring with curbs.

28. Determine if a Food or Feed Risk Analysis has been conducted of PCB equipment and if all PCB transformers have been removed from Food or Feed conditions.

ASBESTOS

29. Has the plant conducted a survey to determine the presence and condition of any asbestos? (This information may be included in the environmental assessment reports or applicable environmental reference manuals.)

    A. Is there documentation to evidence that all insulation has been checked for asbestos content?
    B. Are all areas containing asbestos properly marked?
    C. Have all of these areas been adequately contained?
    D. Have all of these efforts been properly documented?

30. Determine if there is a procedure for notifying agencies prior to removal and disposal of asbestos containing materials and if proper handling and monitoring procedures are followed.

SPILL CONTROL AND EMERGENCY PLANS

A Spill Prevention, Control, and Countermeasure (SPCC) Plan is a specific requirement of 40 Code of Federal Regulations (CFR), and pertains to the storage and use of oil, (including gasoline, diesel, crude oil, fuel oil, and vegetable oil). The requirement is in addition to any other requirement (regulatory or company) for a spill contingency plan.

Revised: 4-1-91

	WORKPAPER REFERENCE	COMPLETED BY/DATE

31. Determine if an SPCC Plan is required for the facility based upon the amount of oil stored on site.

 A. Has the SPCC Plan been approved by a registered professional engineer?
 B. Has the SPCC Plan been updated at least every three years?
 C. Has the inspections required by the SPCC Plan been documented?

32. Determine if there have been any reported spills in the last six months. Determine if corrective actions have been taken and properly documented.

33. Determine if the facility operates a ship or barge dock.

 A. Does the spill control plan include the dock facilities?
 B. Do the environmental reference manual or the dock operating procedures address environmental concerns at the dock?
 C. Has this information been distributed to all affected personnel?
 D. Is the facility in compliance with U.S. Coast Guard regulations? (For example hydrostatic testing and recordkeeping of product transfer hoses).

34. For the emergency response or other disaster control contingency plan, determine the following:

 A. Has the emergency contingency plan been updated in the last 12 months?
 B. Has this plan been adequately communicated to the agencies required under SARA Section 3?
 C. What plans are there to update this program in accordance with the new right-to-know laws where applicable?

GENERAL

35. Determine if the in-house pipeline operations program addresses inspection, surveillance maintenance, and postings of line markers in accordance with Department of Transportation (DOT) regulations. Physically review portions of the pipeline (and related rights-of-way controlled by the facility), and ensure adequate markings have been placed and that the area is well maintained.

36. Determine that environmental or safety related areas have been marked with signs and markings in compliance with regulations, and if there is a plot plan or blueprint that identifies these areas. (Markings may include: boundaries, permit number, owner, and product name information. This information may be maintained by the safety department since in many cases this area is safety related.)

37. Determine if there is a central file where complaints from neighbors or other interested parties are maintained.

   A. Have there been any recent complaints?
   B. Did any of these complaints relate to a discharge or exception to a permit allowance, and were these incidents properly documented and reported to the appropriate agencies where required?
   C. Is this information properly documented?
   D. When corrective action was taken was the correction documented?

38. Determine if the facility sponsors training programs for all personnel involved in environmental activities to ensure the personnel are aware of the most current regulation and compliance requirements.

   A. Do these programs include information regarding the most current right-to-know regulations?
   B. Is this training activity properly documented? (This training may be included in the routine new employee orientation, or periodic operations safety meetings, and may also be included in the applicable environmental reference manuals.)

39. Determine that contractors perform in compliance with applicable environmental regulations and how the facility ascertains they are in compliance.

40. Determine if there is any threatened or pending legal action against the company. Determine if this information has been communicated to the appropriate industry group and corporate personnel and entered into the EAS.

41. Select a sample of AFEs and ensure all AFEs are reviewed by environmental personnel at the appropriate levels to determine if the project may have an environmental effect and that the effect is provided for.

SAFETY

ORGANIZATION AND FACILITY DESCRIPTION

1. Review all applicable safety policies and procedures and obtain a summary of local safety programs (i.e. ‑training, hazard communication, etc.).

2. Determine if local safety procedures address the following areas: (This information may be included in applicable safety manuals and/or standard operating procedure.)

   A. Internal reporting requirements delineating a clear reporting structure within the local safety organization. Do they clearly note what organizations are obligated to provide data and information to the safety group?
   B. A mechanism for reporting accidents, injuries and significant matters to appropriate individuals and organizations in the Industry Group and Corporation, and to the applicable government agency.

	WORKPAPER REFERENCE	COMPLETED BY/DATE

C.   Recordkeeping requirements to assure adherence to OSHA/MSHA recording and reporting requirements.

    1)   Do they clearly define responsibility for categorization of injuries/illnesses to determine which are recordable? Is there a review procedure on categorization?

    2)   Is there a review procedure to assure that appropriate worker compensation claims are recorded in the OSHA/MSHA logs?

    3)   Is there clearly defined responsibility for safekeeping of the records?

    4)   Is there a defined procedure and file documenting required safety and hazard communication training?

    5)   Are five years of OSHA logs maintained on file?

D.   Review OSHA guidelines for mercury level testing for workers exposed to mercury in the work environment, if applicable.

3.   Review the most recent safety assessment report issued including the action plan and any other areas of concern noted in the assessment report.

    A.   Determine if the facility or industry group has documented their follow-up on these items.

    B.   What is the follow-up system?

    C.   Are there adequate controls over documentation of these efforts?

4.   Review the facility's hazard communications activities. This information should include identification of hazardous materials purchased, produced or shipped; an inventory of hazardous material stored, used or produced on site; existence of material safety data sheets on these materials, their inclusion in training programs for both employees and on-site contractors. Determine if proper records are being maintained.

    A.   Select a sample of Material Safety Data Sheets (MSDSs) and ensure a MSDS is available for all chemicals for which a MSDS is required.

    Note: The MSDSs are required under two different sets of regulations. OSHA requires the MSDSs for compliance with its Hazard Communication Standard, and the EPA requires the MSDSs as a part of its Community Right-to-Know regulations.

    B.   Review shipping documents to determine compliance with DOT hazardous materials shipping regulations.

        1)   Are proper DOT product descriptions, quantity or weight identified?

        2)   Are approved containers being utilized?

        3)   Is the facility in compliance with cargo tank and railcar requirements?

        4)   Has the nature of the cargo and its hazards been communicated to the driver?

    C.   Is there a program for minimizing inventories of hazardous materials?

Revised: 4-1-91

	WORKPAPER REFERENCE	COMPLETED BY/DATE

5. Determine if the facility has documented the applicable OSHA or MSHA regulations and any local and/or company safety requirements. (This information may be found in the safety assessment reports or applicable safety reference manuals.) Does the facility have copies of, or access to, applicable federal, state, and local regulations?

6. Recordkeeping procedures will vary by location, however, the following points can be used to determine compliance with applicable government regulation. This includes such items as:

   A. Are the records kept in a central file or by a desig-nated individual at each facility providing for good control and accessibility to these records. If a central control is not in place, at a minimum is a reference folder maintained which includes file and location references?

   B. Is access to the records adequately controlled, and are the records maintained in an orderly fashion?

   C. Is the record filing system consistent for all safety activities?

   D. From the records identified in step b, select a sam-ple and determine if the records are reasonably com-plete and that the OSHA logs include all reportable items as defined in the U.S. Department of Labor - Bureau of Labor Statistics <u>Definitions of Recordable Injuries</u>, and for the MSHA logs, the Directorate of Technical Support--Denver Technical and Health Cen-ter--Division of Mining. Information Systems <u>Infor-mational Report for Notifying MSHA of Accidents, Injuries, Illnesses and Employment</u>.

   E. In order to assure conservative interpretation of the above guidelines, review the first aid logs to deter-mine if there have been any cases of multiple visits by the same individual in a short period of time for treatment of the same or similar injuries or illness that may have not been reported on every occasion. Determine if this review has been documented.

   F. Review recordkeeping concerning chemical exposure and determine compliance with OSHA requirements.

   G. Test for compliance with 29 CFR Part 1904.5 to deter-mine that:

      1) The annual summary of occupational injuries and illnesses was certified by the preparer as being true and correct.

      2) The annual summary was posted by February 1.

7. Review OSHA/MSHA noise conservation requirements and deter-mine adherence to applicable regulations.

<u>GENERAL</u>

8. Select a sample of on-site contractors and determine if there is documentation of contractor's compliance with the OPC and/or industry group contractor safety policy. Deter-mine if the contractor's safety program was reviewed prior to contract execution.

9. Select a sample of AFEs and ensure all AFEs are reviewed by safety personnel at the appropriate levels to determine if the project may have a safety effect and that the effect is provided for.

Revised: 4-1-91

	WORKPAPER REFERENCE	COMPLETED BY/DATE

10. Review the documentation of actions taken in response to Risk Engineering Report recommendations.

11. Determine if the facility or industry group has formal safety policies and procedures, and if they are documented and made available to all employees. To check implementation of the policies and procedures, perform a facility inspection, and make spot observations on the following points:

   A. Is jewelry (rings, necklaces, ear rings etc.) being worn where it is forbidden?
   B. Are workers using required eye protection, safety shoes and/or hard hats?
   C. Are workers wearing loose clothing around machinery?
   D. Where indicated, is breathing apparatus available and stored in easy access, in working condition and properly inspected? Determine if employees who use respirators have received a physician's certification in compliance with 29 CFR 1910.134.
   E. Are workers given respiratory training where breathing apparatus is required? Is the training documented? Are respirators in proper working condition?
   F. Are workers who use respirators required to be free of interfering facial hair?
   G. Are "NO SMOKING" and other required safety signs clearly posted in designated areas?
   H. Are fire alarm boxes, fire hose cabinets, and extinguisher areas clearly marked? Are these areas unobstructed? Is there a plot plan indicating the location of all fire fighting equipment in the plant? Has this plan been posted and adequately distributed to all employees? Determine if hydrostatic testing is performed and documented on fire extinguishers in compliance with 29 CFR 1910.157.
   I. Are fire extinguishers inspected regularly? Select a sample of extinguishers and determine inspections are being properly documented.
   J. Are safe containers available for the movement of small quantities of flammables?
   K. Are there safe disposal facilities for hazardous or flammable residues?
   L. Are antistatic electricity devices fitted where necessary?
   M. Determine if employees are receiving annual audiograms in compliance with 29 CFR 1910.95.

12. Document and test required annual medical examinations:

   A. Audiometric required by 29 CFR 1900.95, noise conservation program.
   B. Lung capacity test required by 29 CFR 1900.134, respiratory surveillance.
   C. Physicians clearance for operators to use respirators required by 29 CFR 1900.120.

ENVIRONMENTAL STATUTORY AND COMMON LAW

IN THE COMMERCIAL SETTING

I. INTRODUCTION

Hazardous materials are a fact of life. Their presence may profoundly affect the value of land and expose all parties involved in real estate transactions to significant liabilities. The transfer of real property which contains, or which may contain, hazardous substances, or operations which utilize such substances, can pose difficult problems for the buyer and the seller as well as for those in the financial community. In order to make informed business decisions, it is imperative that all parties are aware of the nature and the scope of the problem.

Environmental risks in a transaction can arise in two ways: responsibility for cleaning up contaminated property and responsibility for compliers with environmental protection laws. In this portion of the seminar we will outline basic environmental responsibilities. These will, in turn, highlight the need to identify, and where possible remedy, preexisting contamination in an effort to minimize the liability regardless of whether it arises under common law tort theories, statutory cleanup provisions, or general environmental compliance statutes.

II. SPECIFIC FEDERAL STATUTES

Prior to the 1970's, environmental law basically consisted of common law tort principles (see Section V, _infra_) and a few limited federal or state statutes. However, in response to increasing public awareness Congress quickly produced a series of major statutes which established a federally enforceable regulatory scheme covering most environmental media - the National Environmental Policy Act (1969), the Clean Air Act (1970), the Clean Water Act (1972), the Resource Conservation and Recovery Act (1976), and the Toxic Substance Control Act (1978). This meteoric growth in environmental legislation is graphically illustrated by Figure 1 which identifies some eighty or so enactments affecting the environment. See, also, Table 1.

With prospective controls well established, Congress in the 1980's began to look back at past practices and closed the loop with the enactment of the Comprehensive Environmental Response, Compensation and Liability Act of 1980 which quickly became known as "Superfund" (the Act is also known, as many environmental statutes are, by its acronym, CERCLA). The Emergency Planning and Community Right-to-Know Act (1986) added a new emphasis on public disclosure.

In this memorandum, only those major environmental laws most frequently encountered in real estate transactions are summarized. Where a single Congressional enactment contains several independent programs, each program is separately addressed. Like any other legal issue, the applicability and interpretation of each statute will depend to some extent on the location and use of the property as well as a number of other factors. Always seek the advise of qualified environmental legal counsel <u>before</u> determining your response.

TABLE 1. Federal Laws on Environmental Protection

RHAA	-	Rivers & Harbors Appropriations Act (Refuse Act) (1899)
OPA	-	Oil Pollution Act (1990)
OCSLA	-	Outer Continental Shelf Lands Act (1953)
NHPA	-	National Historic Preservation Act (1966)
WSRA	-	Wild & Scenic Rivers Act (1968)
NEPA	-	National Environmental Policy Act (1969)
CAA	-	Clean Air Act (1990)
OSHA	-	Occupational Safety & Health Act (1970)
FWPCA	-	Federal Water Pollution Control Act (1972)
MPRSA	-	Marine Protection Research & Sanctuaries Act (1972)
CZMA	-	Coastal Zone Management Act (1972)
NCA	-	Noise Control Act (1972)
FIFRA	-	Federal Insecticide, Fungicide & Rodenticide Act (1972)
MMPA	-	Marine Mammal Protection Act (1972)
MLAA	-	Mineral Leasing Act Amendments (1973)
ESA	-	Endangered Species Act (1973)
SDWA	-	Safe Drinking Water Act (1974)
HMTA	-	Hazardous Materials Transportation Act (1975)
TSCA	-	Toxic Substances Control Act (1976)
RCRA	-	Resource Conservation and Recovery Act (1976)
CWA	-	Clean Water Act (1977)
SMCRA	-	Surface Mining Control and Reclamation Act (1977)
UMTRCA	-	Uranium Mill Tailings Radiation Control Act (1978)
CERCLA	-	Comprehensive Environmental Response, Compensation, & Liability Act (1980)
SARA	-	Superfund Amendments and Reauthorization Act (1986)
EPCRA	-	Emergency Planning and Community Right-to-Known Act (1986)
AHERA	-	Asbestos Hazard Emergency Response Act (1986)
SPA	-	Shore Protection Act (1988)

Revised: 1-1-91

ATTACHMENT A

A.   Principal Federal Statutes

    1.   Comprehensive Environmental Response,
          Compensation and Liability Act - "Superfund"

Perhaps the most significant federal statute imposing liability for clean-up of contaminated soils and groundwater is the Comprehensive Environmental Response, Compensation and Liability Act of 1980 ("CERCLA") as amended in 1986 by the Superfund Amendments and Reauthorization Act ("SARA"). 42 U.S.C. Section 9601 et seq. Under CERCLA, where the United States Environmental Protection Agency ("EPA") determines there may be an imminent and substantial endangerment to the public health or the environment because of an actual release (or even the threat of a release) of a hazardous substance from a facility, it can either undertake response actions on its own or direct any one or more potentially responsible parties ("PRPs") to undertake certain response actions. Response actions can run the gamut from mere monitoring of the situation to simple removal and proper (re)disposal of the source materials to complete remediation and cleanup of all contaminated soils and groundwater.

Under CERCLA, both current and past owners or operators of a facility are among those that may be liable for the cost of response actions. The liability is strict (i.e., fault is not required) and can be joint and several (i.e., any one party can be required to bear 100 percent of the cost, where the resulting contamination is not easily divisible). The affirmative defenses are limited to the following: 1) an act of God, 2) an act of war, or 3) the act (or omission) of a third party having no direct or indirect contractual relationship with the PRP. Arguably only the latter, often called the third party defense, can be utilized.

CERCLA provides that a deed or other instrument transferring property is a "contract." Thus, environmental contamination of property by any predecessor in title can make the "third party defense" unavailable. However, CERCLA does provide somewhat of a "safe harbor" for the current owner who can show that at the time he acquired the property he had no knowledge or reason to know that the property was in fact contaminated. In order to be entitled to use the "innocent landowner defense," an owner must show that, <u>at the time of purchase</u>, he had undertaken the "appropriate inquiry" and "appropriate investigation" with respect to possible contamination. We will address the "innocent landowner" defense in greater detail in a forthcoming session.

Even where these initial studies do not reveal a problem, subsequent discovery of site contamination imposes a duty to notify any potential purchaser of the discovery. Failure to provide such information will result in the loss of the right to the "safe harbor," even though the seller was not responsible for the contamination and no longer holds title to the property. 43 U.S.C. 9601(f)(35).

Under CERCLA, EPA is authorized to recover costs from "responsible persons." The courts have recognized that personal liability may extend to directors, shareholders, officers, and employees of a corporation where they control or are actively involved in the conduct of corporate affairs. A secured lender may, as long as the lender does not participate in the management of the facility, escape liability. However, by foreclosing a security interest in property which becomes a "Superfund" site, the lender <u>may</u> be deemed an owner or operator liable for cleanup costs. The fact that the lender was not factually responsible for the contamination is legally irrelevant.

From a compliance audit standpoint, the most important requirements of CERCLA are those in Sections 102 requiring industrial and transportation facilities to report immediately to EPA's National Response Center releases of hazardous substances listed, as directed by CERCLA Section 102, if a release to the environment exceeds the "reportable quantity" for the substance specified in EPA's regulations. Release is broadly defined to include spills and discharges to soil, air, and water but excludes permitted and certain routine discharges and those confined to occupational exposures. Contemporaneous reporting to state and local environmental and emergency response agencies is often required.

2.   Resource Conservation and Recovery Act-Subtitle C

The Resource and Conservation and Recovery Act ("RCRA"), as amended by the Hazardous and Solid Waste Amendments of 1984 ("HSWA"). 42 U.S.C.

Section 6901 et seq., was the first federal legislation aimed solely at regulation of "hazardous wastes." RCRA created a "cradle-to-grave" regulatory system for controlling and tracking hazardous wastes from the time they are generated through their storage, treatment and disposal. Whenever a proposed acquisition involves an industrial operation along with real estate, the facility's compliance with environmental regulations will be at issue. For facilities producing hazardous wastes which the prospective purchaser plans to operate, it is imperative that any environmental property evaluation include the operation's current compliance status with RCRA's permit and manifesting systems. Thus, it has become critical to determine if you are looking at a facility which is, or has been, in some way connected with the generation, handling, storage or disposal of a RCRA hazardous waste.

The importance of waste characterization can not be over emphasized. RCRA (and EPA's implementing regulations) separates waste materials into two categories: "solid wastes" and "hazardous wastes." A solid waste includes practically any "discarded" (i.e., abandoned) material regardless of its physical form. A waste does not have to be a solid to qualify as a solid waste; it may be a solid, a liquid, a semi-solid (i.e., sludge), or even a containerized gas. See, 42 U.S.C. Section 6903(27), 40 C.F.R. Section 261.2.

Only a material determined to be a RCRA solid waste may also be a RCRA "hazardous waste." Any person producing a RCRA solid waste is legally obligated to determine if that waste is a RCRA hazardous waste. See, 40 C.F.R. Sections 261.3, 261.20. With certain exceptions, solid waste is also hazardous waste if it is "listed" on one of several regulatory lists or if it exhibits any of four identifying characteristics. EPA has established three lists: wastes from certain specific sources, 40 C.F.R. Section 261.32; certain enumerated wastes from nonspecific sources, 40 C.F.R. Section 261.31; and certain discarded commercial chemical products together with their containers and spill cleanup residue, 40 C.F.R. Section 261.33. A solid waste becomes classified as a "characteristic" hazardous waste, even if it is not included on one of these lists, if laboratory analysis indicates any one of four hazardous characteristics: ignitability, corrosivity, reactivity or extraction process toxicity ("EP Toxicity"). See, 40 C.F.R. Sections 261.3, 261.20. Almost any facility that produces a listed or characteristic hazardous waste is brought under one or more of EPA's rules for generation, storage, treatment or disposal of hazardous wastes.

Only where less than 100 kilograms (220 pounds) of hazardous waste is produced per month is the waste "generator" substantially exempt from full RCRA regulation; production of amounts between 100 kilograms and 1000 kilograms (2200 pounds) per month results in classification as a "small quantity generator" with the imposition of on-site storage restrictions together with substantial reporting and recordkeeping requirements.   Included in this is the preparation and use of Uniform Hazardous Waste Manifests to document custody transfer of the waste to transporter(s) and ultimately the disposal site operator.   Generators subject to full regulation are allowed to accumulate hazardous wastes on-site for no longer than 90 days without obtaining a permit for operation of a RCRA storage facility.   Treatment or disposal of hazardous waste also requires a permit. See, generally, 40 C.F.R. Section 264.

Under RCRA, companies engaged in treatment, storage and disposal of hazardous wastes are required to have operating permits which impose strict requirements for closure and post-closure care, including the maintenance of financial responsibility assurances. For most industrial facilities, historical "releases" of hazardous wastes or hazardous constituents from on-site waste management have resulted in some degree of soil and/or groundwater contamination. Permits for these facilities are also subject to "corrective action" requirements dictating cleanups analogous to CERCLA remediation projects. 42 U.S.C. Section 6924(u).

A RCRA permit can be transferred to a new purchaser but only after it has first been modified, or revoked and reissued to name the new owner and "incorporate such other requirements as may be necessary." 40 C.F.R. Section 270.40. Although permit transfer can sometimes be accomplished with only a "minor modification" to the permit, if material alterations

Revised: 1-1-91

ATTACHMENT A

are to be made to the facility after purchase, the permit and its limiting conditions may be modified by the agency. 40 C.F.R. Section 270.41-42. The impact of increasingly stringent standards on planned facility alterations must be factored into any proposed acquisition plans.

One of the more significant changes to the original RCRA hazardous waste program came through implementation of the "land ban" under HSWA which generally prohibits the disposal of specified untreated wastes in any landfill. The first type of waste to come under the land disposal ban was bulk or noncontainerized liquid hazardous waste. Rules addressing additional types of listed hazardous wastes have now been issued. The land ban program required EPA to set waste treatment standards that must be met by the waste generator prior to any landfilling. Only if, after testing and certification, the waste meets the applicable treatment standard can the material be land disposed. See 40 C.F.R. Section 268, et seq.

While primarily providing the framework for controlling the treatment and disposal of hazardous wastes, RCRA Section 7003 also authorizes actions against persons contributing to an "imminent and substantial endangerment" to human health or the environment caused by the handling, storage, treatment, transportation or disposal of any hazardous or solid waste, to compel the cleanup of the site.

If the transaction involves property which proves to be contaminated by hazardous wastes, the parties potentially liable for cleanup will include a new owner. Once EPA has determined that an "imminent and substantial endangerment" exists, it may seek an injunction that restrains activities contributing to the contamination and require remedial activities to be undertaken. 42 U.S.C. Section 6973. An "innocent" purchaser can be called upon to remediate problems created by former owners.

3.   RCRA Subtitle D - Solid Wastes

Pursuant to Subtitle D of RCRA, 42 U.S.C. Section 6941-6949(a), regulation of nonhazardous solid wastes is primarily to be the responsibility of the states. Subtitle D does, however, establish a federal prohibition against the disposal of either solid or hazardous wastes in "open dumps." 42 U.S.C. Section 6944(b), 6945(a) and (c)(2). Thus, if the purchased property includes an on-site dump operating without a permit or in violation of permit standards, the new owner may be subjected to federal enforcement action, even if no hazardous wastes have been discarded at the site. This possibility simply highlights the need for careful assessment of the historical and current use of the entire tract prior to acquisition.

4.   RCRA Subtitle I - Underground Storage Tanks

Transactions involving real estate with underground storage tanks are obvious situations in which a company may face unexpected environmental liability. If the new owner is found to have caused a leak or to now own or lease a UST system which has leaked, the company may face unexpected environmental liability.

The HSWA amendments to RCRA added Subtitle I, 42 U.S.C. Section 6991, et seq., which called for a comprehensive federal regulatory program for underground storage tanks ("USTs"). This legislation filled a gap which existed between CERCLA and RCRA Subtitle C. Neither CERCLA nor RCRA Subtitle C were amenable to clean up of releases from USTs. Due to the express exclusion of petroleum, EPA lacked the necessary authority under CERCLA to effect cleanup from leaking USTs containing petroleum products. See 42 U.S.C. Section 9601(14) (the "petroleum exclusion"). Since the primary thrust of RCRA is the regulation of waste disposal practices, EPA would have had to classify the use of leaking underground product storage tanks as a waste disposal practice to have utilized RCRA.

Under the amendments to RCRA, compliance can now be enforced through administrative orders or through the courts. Section 9003(h) empowers EPA to require the owner or operator of a leaking UST to cleanup petroleum releases while Section 9006 authorized EPA to issue administrative orders or initiate civil actions in federal district court to enforce compliance with Subtitle I regulations.

In addition to emphasis on corrective actions and cleanup of releases, Subtitle I establishes the framework for an extensive set of regulations addressing registration, design, construction, installation, and operational controls as well as proof of financial responsibility. See, 40 C.F.R. Subpart 280. RCRA required owners to register all tanks either in use after 1984 or abandoned since 1974 if they remained in the ground unused. 42 U.S.C. Section 6991(a), 50 Fed.Reg. 46602. Existing UST systems (i.e., those installed before December 1988) are required to be upgraded to provide for corrosion protection and leak detection over the next ten years. This retrofitting is scheduled on the basis of the tank's age; older tanks are to be addressed by December, 1989. Devices to prevent spills and overfills must also be retrofitted to existing systems.

Even existing UST systems on the property which are to be taken out of service (either temporarily or permanently) are subject to regulation. The permanent closure requirements include a requirement to conduct an evaluation of the subsurface around the tank. The discovery of any contamination within the excavation may trigger certain response and remediation obligations.

Any developer expecting to install a new UST system should consider that the system will be required to meet all new registration, design, installation and operational requirements at the time of installation.

    5.   The Clean Air Act

The Clean Air Act ("CAA"), 42 U.S.C. Section 7401 et seq., establishes an air quality management system centered on air quality goals (National Ambient Air Quality Standards or "NAAQS") for ubiquitous air pollutants and imposes a number of requirements for the attainment and maintenance of the NAAQS. States then develop their own control programs to attain and maintain the various NAAQS. These programs are combined into State Implementation Plans ("SIPs") which are reviewed and formally approved by EPA and are enforceable by that agency as well as the state. The SIP must demonstrate attainment of the NAAQS, describe state emission control strategies, contain legally enforceable regulations including procedures for new source review, and outline the state program for air quality monitoring.

Any new "major" source of air pollution (or any major modification to an existing source) is required to employ stringent emission controls to meet "new source performance standards" ("NSPS") set by EPA, but generally enforced by the states. These standards reflect the emission limitation and emission reduction achievable by applying the best demonstrated technology of continuous emission reduction. Thus, any anticipated expansion or modification of facilities on the property must consider not only the adequacy of current air pollution control systems but the impact of imposition of NSPS requirements as a result of modifying the existing facilities.

The proposed installation of any new major source of air pollution, or major modifications to an existing source, must also demonstrate that their emissions will not adversely impact ambient air quality. In "attainment areas," i.e., those meeting the NAAQS, the Act's prevention of significant deterioration ("PSD") program, may require on-site ambient air quality studies that can entail collection and analysis of monitoring data for up to a year prior to obtaining the permit necessary to begin construction. PSD permit applicants may also be required to conduct computerized modeling to predict their proposed emission impacts on air quality.

Areas in which the existing ambient air quality is not within NAAQS, i.e., "nonattainment areas," are required to apply even more stringent new and modified new source review regulations. Any proposed major source must agree to emission controls that will meet the "lowest achievable emission rate," it may then be required to obtain sufficient "offsets" before a permit to construct can be issued; the total allowable emissions from other existing sources together with those anticipated from the new source must be less than the total emissions from currently

Revised: 1-1-91

existing sources. A developer of property must consider whether he will be able to obtain the necessary offsets to allow the contemplated development in view of the ambient air quality in the area. In nonattainment areas, the ability to transfer air permits may prove to be an important economic aspect of real estate transactions.

In addition to standards for common air pollutants, i.e., particulate matter, sulfur dioxide, nitrogen oxides, carbon monoxide, and ozone, the act requires EPA to establish National Emission Standards for Hazardous Air Pollutants ("NESHAPs"). In 1971, EPA designated asbestos as such a hazardous air pollutant. 36 Fed.Reg. 5931; 40 C.F.R. Section 61.01(a). Property owners and developers must pay particular attention to the asbestos NESHAP since it regulates the renovation or demolition of any building or facility containing asbestos as well as the disposal of waste asbestos. 40 C.F.R. Section 61.140 et seq.

6. The Clean Water Act

The Clean Water Act ("CWA"), 33 U.S.C. Section 1251, et seq., (a/k/a the Federal Water Pollution Control Act, "FWPCA") imposes a number of requirements that can affect owners of real property. Under the National Pollutant Discharge Elimination System ("NPDES") a permit is required for the discharge of any "pollutant" from a "point source" (e.g., any pipe, ditch, conduit, etc.) into any of the various types of "waters of the United States." NPDES permits specify both the nature and the quantity of discharge that is allowable and can be technology-based requiring the use of the "best available technology" ("BAT") or be based on the water quality of the receiving stream. With the imposition of water-quality based standards, the uses of property may be limited if located along a water quality limited (i.e, a polluted) stream or a stream with a highly protective designated use. See, 40 C.F.R. Sections 122-124 (NPDES implementing regulations).

Section 404 of the CWA is overseen by the United States Army Corps of Engineers and requires a property owner to obtain a permit prior to any construction activity in "waters of the United States" as well as any "wetland," (a quite broadly defined term). As part of the process of obtaining a permit for activity in a wetland, a person may be required to obtain other wetlands which will be preserved in "mitigation" of those which are to be developed.

CWA Section 311, 33 U.S.C. Section 1321, prohibits the discharge of oil in "harmful quantities" (i.e., any amount which causes a film or sheen on water). 40 C.F.R. Section 110.3. Spill response and cleanup duties belong to the product custodian without regard to the fault. The "person in charge" of the facility also has an affirmative duty to immediately report any discharge of "harmful quantities" of oil to the National Response Center ("NRC") or the EPA regional office. 40 C.F.R. Section 110.10. Section 311(j) requires land based facilities to comply with EPA implementing regulations which now include the preparation of Spill Prevention, Control and Countermeasure ("SPCC") Plans for all locations with above-ground oil storage capacity greater than 1,320 gallons (42,000 gallons for underground storage). 40 C.F.R. Section 112.1(d)(2).

Purchasers should determine the adequacy of the facility's SPCC Plan and its associated spill history. See C.F.R. Section 112.7 (guidelines for preparation and implementation of SPCC plans).

7.   The Toxic Substances Control Act

The Toxic Substances Act ("TSCA"), 15 U.S.C. Section 2601 et seq., requires the testing, premanufacturing notice and recordkeeping for chemical substances or mixtures that will be produced in substantial qualities if they could be anticipated to enter the environment in substantial quantities or if there may be substantial human exposure.

TSCA Section 6(e) is devoted to the control of and ultimate elimination of polychlorinated biphenyls ("PCBs"). EPA's implementing regulations impose strict requirements on the use, storage and disposal of PCBs. Although PCBs are no longer manufactured, they are still found in the insulating fluids of many existing pieces of electrical equipment such as transformers and capacitors. Most PCB-containing transformers and certain large capacitors located in restricted-access areas may be used for the remainder of their useful lives, subject to routine inspection and recordkeeping under EPA rules. However, their use in locations creating a risk to food or feed has been prohibited since 1985. Thus, the existence of PCB-containing equipment may restrict the use of property.

PCBs can also be a serious concern where its use in equipment has resulted in contamination of building or grounds from leaking fluids. Additional care must be exercised when this equipment is serviced, retired, sold, disposed of or even when dismantled for salvage.

8. The Emergency Planning and Community Right-To-Know Act - SARA Title III

When Congress reauthorized the Superfund statute in 1986, it included what has become known as Title III or the "Right-to Know" provisions. Included in Title III of SARA is the Emergency Planning and Community Right-To-Know Act ("EPCRA") enacted as free-standing law within SARA. 42 U.S.C. Section 11001, et seq. The Act represents Congress' response to public concern raised by the disaster in Bhopol, India where in late 1984, thousands were killed as a result of the release of a toxic gas from a chemical facility. Title III mandated the establishment of state and local emergency response organizations charged with developing emergency release response plans and imposes a series of notification and reporting requirements on a wide range of facilities regarding the presence and release of specific chemicals.

Title III imposes rigorous notification requirements for releases (spilling, leaking, escaping, discharging, etc.) of over 600 EPCRA "hazardous substances" in amounts greater than or equal to certain specified reportable quantities ("RQs"). See, 40 C.F.R. 302.1 et seq. Although the requirements are closely related to CERCLA's reporting requirements, they are not identical.

The "Community Right-to-Know" provisions of Title III are intended to increase public access to information in order to facilitate the development of local emergency response planning. Any facility which has more than the designated "threshold planning quantity" of any listed "extremely hazardous substance" on-site is required to periodically report that information to the appropriate emergency response commission. Any release that may result in off-site exposures requires immediate notification of state and federal authorities.

    B.   Secondary Federal Statutes

        1.   Safe Drinking Water Act

The Safe Drinking Water Act ("SDWA"), 42 U.S.C. Section 300(f), et seq., in addition to specifying a scheme for primary and secondary standards for acceptable levels of contaminants in public water supplies, provides for the protection of underground drinking water supplies through a federal-state program regulating the disposal of hazardous wastes via underground injection wells. Both new and existing wells are required to obtain permits to operate.

It is important to note, however, that public water systems include "non-community" systems such as hotels, motels, factories and other businesses that produce their own drinking water. 40 C.F.R. Section 141.2. A third class of public water systems, the "non-transient non-community" system serving at least twenty-five of the same persons over six months per year, may be faced with the imposition of federal primary drinking water regulations. See, 52 Fed.Reg. 25695 (1987). The national primary drinking water standards specify maximum contaminant levels ("MCLs") and treatment techniques as well as stringent monitoring requirements. Any purchaser seeking to acquire commercial property which includes its own system for supplying drinking water should be familiar with the pertinent regulatory requirements imposed on these systems.

The 1986 SDWA amendments prohibited the use of lead pipe, solder or flux when installing or repairing any public water system and required that under certain conditions notice be given the persons that might be affected by lead contamination of their drinking water. 42 U.S.C. Section 300g-6. Other amendments in late 1988 provide for the recall of water fountains (coolers) with certain leaded pipes or solder. Pub. L. No. 100-572 (1988). While this may not be a "deal breaker," it does deserve the attention of any prospective purchaser.

2.   National Environmental Policy Act

The National Environmental Policy Act ("NEPA"), 42 U.S.C. Section 4321, et seq., as one of the first major pieces of federal environmental legislation forms the basic national charter for protection of the environment. NEPA requires federal agencies to: prepare a detailed statement on the environmental impact ("EIS") for every proposed "major federal action significantly affecting the quality of the human environment;" and, describe appropriate alternatives to any recommended course of action concerning alternative uses of available resources.

The statute indicates that actions which are subject to federal control and responsibility, i.e., federal permits, licenses, loans, grants, leases and so forth, may require preparation of an FIS even though actual federal involvement in the activity is minimal. Thus, in certain cases, permits required by any of the number of previously discussed statutes can fall within the definition of a major federal action under NEPA. NRDC v. USEPA, 859 F.2d 156, 167 (DC Cir. 1988) (Issuance of a new source discharge permit constituted a major federal action for NFPA purposes): Where this is the case, the proposal will result in the agency preparing an EIS addressing not only the proposed action but any alternatives which might mitigate the adverse impacts as well. Most agencies require the permit applicant to prepare an environmental assessment which the agency will use to determine whether the agency issues a finding of no significant impact or proceeds to prepare an EIS.

3.   National Historic Preservation Act

The National Historical Preservation Act ("NHPA"), 16 U.S.C. Section 470 et seq., requires that federal agencies consider the impact of their decisions on historical and cultural resources. 40 C.F.R. Section 6.301. If the activity may cause irreparable loss or destruction of significant scientific, prehistoric, historic or archaeological data, the owner may be required to undertake data recovery or preservation activities. See, 48 Fed.Reg. 44716 (September 29, 1983) (National Park Service Technical standards and guidelines regarding archaeological preservation). Where an undertaking may affect a property with historical, architectural, or cultural values and is on, or eligible for listing on, the National Register of Historic Places, a determination of eligibility from the Department of the Interior must be requested under the procedures in 36 C.F.R. Part 63. 40 C.F.R. Section 6.301(b). A company may be required to undertake an investigation of property to satisfy these requirements where it seeks a federal permit, etc.

4.   Rivers and Harbors Act

The Rivers and Harbors Appropriations Act of 1899 ("RHAA"), 33 U.S.C. Section 401, et seq., requires that any structure which may impede or impact a navigable waterway must be authorized by permit. Because of the definition of "navigable waterway", almost any development of property along any surface water must be evaluated in order to determine whether a permit will be necessary under RHAA.

5.   Occupational Safety And Health Act

The Occupational Safety and Health Act ("OSHA"), 29 U.S.C. Section 651, et seq., regulates the exposure of persons to contaminants in the workplace. The Occupational Safety and Health Administration, a division of the United States Department of Labor, has a number of areas in which it exercises what may appear to be overlapping statutory duties with EPA. For instance, both agencies are concerned with a number of issues surrounding the use and handling of hazardous materials such as asbestos and pesticides.

With its adoption of hazard communication regulations, sometimes known as the "workers right-to-know" rules, every employer must assess the toxicity of chemicals it uses and provide appropriate training as well as material safety data sheets ("MSDS") to inform their workers of potential chemical risks. 29 C.F.R. Section 1200.

The adequacy of the facility's compliance program should be identified prior to closing so that the purchaser can evaluate the impact of these rules on continued operation or planned expansion (or redirection) of activities at the facility.

6.   Federal Insecticide, Fungicide, and Rodenticide Act

The Federal Insecticide, Fungicide, and Rodenticide Act ("FIFRA"), 7 U.S.C. Section 136 et seq., first enacted in 1947 is a federal program for pesticides. The statute also imposes civil and criminal penalties for the sale or distribution of unregistered pesticides, for mislabeling of pesticides, and for the use of these products inconsistent with their labeling.

III. PRINCIPAL STATE LAWS

    A.   Oklahoma Statutes

    Although Oklahoma does not have a state counterpart to the federal CERCLA program, it does operate a number of the programs which parallel or in some cases administer many of the other federal programs. Therefore, State rules must not be overlooked when assessing the potential impact of environmental constraints on property transfers.

        1.   Oklahoma Controlled Industrial Waste Disposal Act

    The Oklahoma Controlled Industrial Waste Disposal Act ("CIWDA"), 63 O.S. Section 1-2001, et seq., is the state's counterpart to RCRA regulating hazardous wastes under the name of "controlled industrial waste." The State has been granted federal authority to operate its program in lieu of the federal hazardous waste program. 49 Fed.Reg. 50362 (December 27, 1984). Thus, Oklahoma, through the Oklahoma State Department of Health ("OSDH"), is responsible for carrying out most aspects of the RCRA program. OSDH has primary enforcement responsibility, although EPA Region VI retains some responsibility to conduct its own inspections and institute enforcement actions.

WHERE TO FIND SELECTED FEDERAL ENVIRONMENTAL REGULATIONS

ARMY CORPS OF ENGINEERS

Dam Permits	33 CFR Part 321
Definition of Navigable Waters of the United States	33 CFR Part 329
Enforcement, Supervision and Inspection	33 CFR Part 326
General Policies	33 CFR Part 320
Nationwide Permits	33 CFR Part 330
Permit Processing	33 CFR Part 325
Permits for Discharges of Dredged or Fill Material	33 CFR Part 323
Permits for Ocean Dumping of Dredged Material	33 CFR Part 324
Permits for Work Affecting Navigable Waters	33 CFR Part 322
Public Hearings	33 CFR Part 327

CLEAN AIR ACT

Air Quality Planning Areas	40 CFR Part 81
Ambient Air Monitoring Reference and Equivalent Methods	40 CFR Part 53
Ambient Air Quality Surveillance	40 CFR Part 58
Citizen Suit Notification	40 CFR Part 54
Clean Air Act Exemptions	40 CFR Part 69
Delayed Compliance Orders	40 CFR Part 65
Motor Vehicle and Aircraft Controls	40 CFR Parts 85-87
National Ambient Air Quality Standards (NAAQS)	40 CFR Part 50
National Emission Standards for Hazardous Air Pollutants	40 CFR Part 61
Noncompliance Penalties	40 CFR Parts 66-67
Performance Standards for New Stationary Sources	40 CFR Part 60
Regional Consistency	40 CFR Part 56
State Implementation Plan Requirements (SIP; PSD)	40 CFR Parts 51-52
Stratospheric Ozone Protection	40 CFR Part 82

CLEAN WATER ACT

Citizen Suit Notification	40 CFR Part 135
Discharge of Oil and SPCC Plans	40 CFR Parts 109-112
Effluent Limitation Guidelines and Performance Standards; Pretreatment Standards	40 CFR Parts 405-471
List of Conventional and Toxic Pollutants; pH Limits	40 CFR Part 401
NPDES Criteria and Standards	40 CFR Part 125
NPDES Permit Program	40 CFR Part 122
Permit Decisionmaking Procedures	40 CFR Part 124
Pretreatment Regulations	40 CFR Part 403
Procedures for Improving State Water Quality Standards	40 CFR Part 131
Secondary Treatment Regulations	40 CFR Part 133
State Certification of Activities Requiring a Federal License or Permit	40 CFR Part 121
State SPDES Permit Program Requirements	40 CFR Part 123
Test Procedure Guidelines for Pollutant Analysis	40 CFR Part 136
Water Quality Planning and Management	40 CFR Part 130

EMERGENCY PLANNING AND COMMUNITY RIGHT-TO-KNOW ACT

Emergency Planning Notification Procedures-Spill Reporting	40 CFR Parts 302 & 355
Hazardous Chemical Reporting (MSDS)	40 CFR Part 370
Toxic Chemical Release Reporting (Form R)	40 CFR Part 372
Trade Secrecy Claims and Disclosure to Health Professionals	40 CFR Part 350

ENVIROMENTAL IMPACT STATEMENTS, COASTAL ZONE MANAGEMENT ACT, AND ENDANGERED SPECIES ACT

Coastal Zone Management Act NOAA Regulations	15 CFR Parts 921-933
Environmental Impact Statements Council on Environmental Quality Regulations	40 CFR Parts 1500-1508
Joint Agency Endangered Species Regulations	50 CFR Parts 17:401-453

FREEDOM OF INFORMATION ACT

EPA Procedures	40 CFR Part 2

OCEAN DUMPING

Ocean Dumping	40 CFR Parts 220-229

OCCUPATIONAL SAFETY AND HEALTH ADMINISTRATION

General	29 CFR Parts 1900-1928
Hazard Communication	29 CFR Part 1910.1200
Occupational Health and Safety Standards	29 CFR Part 1910

PESTICIDES

Agricultural Commodity Tolerances and Exemptions	40 CFR Part 180
Agricultural Worker Protection Standards	40 CFR Part 170
Animal Feed Tolerances	40 CFR Part 186
Certification of Pesticide Applicators	40 CFR Part 171
Certification of Usefulness	40 CFR Part 163
Emergency Use Exemptions	40 CFR Part 166
Enforcement	40 CFR Part 162
Experimental Use Permits	40 CFR Part 172
Food Tolerances	40 CFR Part 185
Good Laboratory Practice Standards	40 CFR Part 160
Hearings	40 CFR Part 164
Labeling Requirements	40 CFR Part 156
Packaging Requirements	40 CFR Part 157
Pesticide Acceptance; Disposal and Storage Procedures	40 CFR Part 165
Pesticide Registration and Classification Procedures	40 CFR Part 152
Policies and Interpretations	40 CFR Part 153
Procedures Governing the Rescission of State Primary Enforcement Responsibility for Pesticide Use Violations	40 CFR Part 173
Production and Distribution Books and Records	40 CFR Part 169
Registration Data Requirements	40 CFR Part 158
Registration of Pesticide-Producing Establishments; Reports and Labeling	40 CFR Part 167

Registration Standards	40 CFR Part 155
Special Review Procedures	40 CFR Part 154

RCRA HAZARDOUS WASTE MANAGEMENT REGULATIONS

Final Permit Standards for Treatment, Storage, and Disposal Facilities	40 CFR Part 264
General-Definitions and Delisting Procedures	40 CFR Part 260
Generator Standards	40 CFR Part 262
Identification and Listing of Hazardous Waste-Definition of Solid/Hazardous Waste; Recycling; Small Quantity Generators	40 CFR Part 261
Interim Status Standards for Treatment, Storage, and Disposal Facilities	40 CFR Part 265
Land Disposal Restrictions	40 CFR Part 268
Permit Issuance Procedures	40 CFR Part 270
Recyclable Material Standards; Used Oil/Waste Combustion; Batteries	40 CFR Part 266
State Programs	40 CFR Parts 271-272
Transporter Standards	40 CFR Part 263
Underground Storage Tanks	40 CFR Part 280

SAFE DRINKING WATER ACT

Drinking Water Standards (MCL and MCLG)	40 CFR Parts 141-143
National Secondary Drinking Water Regulations	40 CFR Part 143
Underground Injection Control Programs	40 CFR Parts 144-148

SUPERFUND

Citizen Rewards for Information on Superfund Criminal Violations	40 CFR Part 303
National Contingency Plan	40 CFR Part 300
National Priorities List	40 CFR Part 300, Appendix B
Natural Resource Damage Assessments (Department of Interior)	43 CFR Part 11
Reimbursement to Local Governments for Emergency Response to Hazardous Substance Releases	40 CFR Part 310
Spill Reporting-Reportable Quantities	40 CFR Parts 302 & 355

TOXIC SUBTANCES CONTROL ACT

Allegations that Chemical Substances Cause Significant Adverse Reactions to Health or the Environment (TSCA & 8(c))	40 CFR Part 717
Asbestos	40 CFR Part 763
Chemical Imports and Exports	40 CFR Part 707
Chemical Information-Preliminary Assessment Information Report-Production, Use, Exposure (TSCA &8(a))	40 CFR Part 712
Data Reimbursement	40 CFR Part 791
Dibenzo-Para-Dioxins/Dibenzofurans	40 CFR Part 766
Fully Halogenated Chlorofluoroalkanes	40 CFR Part 762
General	40 CFR Parts 700-702
Good Laboratory Standards	40 CFR Part 792
Health and Safety Data Reporting (TSCA & 8(d))	40 CFR Part 716
Identification of Specific Substance and Mixture Testing Requirements	40 CFR Part 799
Inventory Reporting (TSCA & 8(b))	40 CFR Part 710
Metal Working Fluids	40 CFR Part 747
PCB Use	40 CFR Part 761
Premanufacture Notification Exemptions	40 CFR Part 723
Premanufacture Notification (TSCA &5)	40 CFR Part 720
Reporting and Recordkeeping	40 CFR Part 704
Section 6 Rulemaking Procedures	40 CFR Part 750
Significant New uses of Chemical Substances	40 CFR Part 721
Testing Consent Agreements and Test Rules	40 CFR Part 790
Testing Guidelines; Health, Chemical Fate, Environmental Effects	40 CFR Parts 795-798

WETLAND REGULATIONS

EPA

Section 401(b) Guidelines	40 CFR Part 230
Section 404 Program Definitions; Exempt Activities	40 CFR Part 232
Section 404(c) Veto Procedures	40 CFR Part 231
State 404 Programs	40 CFR Part 233

Revised: 1-1-91

Appendix F:
DOJ Policy on
Criminal Prosecutions for
Environmental Violations

Factors in Decisions on Criminal Prosecutions for Environmental Violations in the Context of Significant Voluntary Compliance or Disclosure Efforts by the Violator (Department of Justice July 1, 1991)

I. Introduction

It is the policy of the Department of Justice to encourage self-auditing, self-policing and voluntary disclosure of environmental violations by the regulated community by indicating that these activities are viewed as mitigating factors in the Department's exercise of criminal environmental enforcement discretion. This document is intended to describe the factors that the Department of Justice considers in deciding whether to bring a criminal prosecution for a violation of an environmental statute, so that such prosecutions do not create a disincentive to or undermine the goal of encouraging critical self-auditing, self-policing, and voluntary disclosure. It is designed to give federal prosecutors direction concerning the exercise of prosecutorial discretion in environmental criminal cases and to ensure that such discretion is exercised consistently nationwide. It is also intended to give the regulated community a sense of how the federal government exercises its criminal prosecutorial discretion with respect to such factors as the defendant's voluntary disclosure of violations, cooperation with the government in investigating the violations, use of environmental audits and other procedures to ensure compliance with all applicable environmental laws and regulations, and use of measures to remedy expeditiously and completely any violations and the harms caused thereby.

This guidance and the examples contained herein provide a framework for the determination of whether a particular case presents the type of circumstances in which lenience would be appropriate.

II. Factors to be Considered

Where the law and evidence would otherwise be sufficient for prosecution, the attorney for the Department should consider the factors contained herein, to the extent they are applicable, along with any other relevant factors, in determining whether and how to prosecute. It must be emphasized that these are examples of the types of factors which could be relevant. They do not constitute a definitive recipe or checklist of requirements. They merely illustrate some of the types of information which is relevant to our exercise of prosecutorial discretion.

It is unlikely that any one factor will be dispositive in any given case. All relevant factors are considered and given the weight deemed appropriate in the particular case. See *Federal Principles of Prosecution* (U.S. Dept. of Justice, 1980), Comment to Part A.2; Part B.3.

A. *Voluntary Disclosure*

The attorney for the Department should consider whether the person[1] made a voluntary, timely and complete disclosure of the matter under investigation. Consideration should be given to whether the person came forward promptly after discovering the noncompliance, and to the quantity and quality of information provided. Particular consideration should be given to whether the disclosure substantially aided the government's investigatory process, and whether it occurred before a law enforcement or regulatory authority (federal, state or local authority) had already obtained knowledge regarding noncompliance. A disclosure is not considered to be "voluntary" if that disclosure is already specifically required by law, regulation, or permit.[2]

---

1. As used in this document, the terms "person" and "violator" are intended to refer to business and nonprofit entities as well as individuals.

B. Cooperation

The attorney for the Department should consider the degree and timeliness of cooperation by the person. Full and prompt cooperation is essential, whether in the context of a voluntary disclosure or after the government has independently learned of a violation. Consideration should be given to the violator's willingness to make all relevant information (including the complete results of any internal or external investigation and the names of all potential witnesses) available to government investigators and prosecutors. Consideration should also be a given to the extent and quality of the violator's assistance to the government's investigation.

C. Preventive Measures and Compliance Programs

The attorney for the Department should consider the existence and scope of any regularized, intensive, and comprehensive environmental compliance program; such a program may include an environmental compliance or management audit. Particular consideration should be given to whether the compliance or audit program includes sufficient measures to identify and prevent future noncompliance, and whether the program was adopted in good faith in a timely manner.

Compliance programs may vary but the following questions should be asked in evaluating any program: Was there a strong institutional policy to comply with all environmental requirements? Had safeguards beyond those required by existing law been developed and implemented to prevent noncompliance from occurring? Were there regular procedures, including internal or external compliance and management audits, to evaluate, detect, prevent and remedy circumstances like those that led to the noncompliance? Were there procedures and safeguards to ensure the integrity of any audit conducted? Did the audit evaluate all sources of pollution (i.e., all media), including the possibility of cross-media transfers of pollutants? Were the auditor's recommendations implemented in a timely fashion? Were adequate resources committed to the auditing program and to implementing its recommendations? Was environmental compliance a standard by which employee and corporate departmental performance was judged?

D. Additional Factors Which May [Be] Relevant

1. Pervasiveness of Noncompliance
Pervasive noncompliance may indicate systemic or repeated participation in or condonation of criminal behavior. It may also indicate the lack of a meaningful compliance program. In evaluating this factor, the attorney for the Department should consider, among other things, the number and level of employees participating in the unlawful activities and the obviousness, seriousness, duration, history, and frequency of noncompliance.

2. Internal Disciplinary Action
Effective internal disciplinary action is crucial to any compliance program. The attorney for the Department should consider whether there was an effective system of discipline for employees who violated company environmental compliance policies. Did the disciplinary system establish an awareness in other employees that unlawful conduct would not be condoned?

3. Subsequent Compliance Efforts
The attorney for the Department should consider the extent of any efforts to remedy any

---

2. For example, any person in charge of a vessel or of an on shore facility or an offshore facility is required to notify the appropriate agency of the United States Government of any discharge of oil or a hazardous substance into or upon *inter alia* the navigable waters of the United States. Section 311(b)(5) of the Clean Water Act, 33 U.S.C. 1321(b)(5), as amended by the Oil Pollution Act of 1990, Pub. L. 101-380, §4301(a), 104 Stat. 485, 533 (1990).

ongoing noncompliance. The promptness and completeness of any action taken to remove the source of the noncompliance and to lessen the environmental harm resulting from the noncompliance should be considered. Considerable weight should be given to prompt, good-faith efforts to reach environmental compliance agreements with federal or state authorities, or both. Full compliance with such agreements should be a factor in any decision whether to prosecute.

III. Application of These Factors to Hypothetical Examples[3]

These examples are intended to assist federal prosecutors in their exercise of discretion in evaluating environmental cases. The situations facing prosecutors, of course, present a wide variety of fact patterns. Therefore, in a given case, some of the criteria may be satisfied while others may not. Moreover, satisfaction of various criteria may be a matter of degree. Consequently, the effect of a given mix of factors also is a matter of degree. In the ideal situation, if a company fully meets all of the criteria, the result may be a decision not to prosecute that company criminally. Even if satisfaction of the criteria is not complete, still the company may benefit in terms of degree of enforcement response by the government. The following hypothetical examples are intended to illustrate the operation of these guidelines.

Example 1:
This is the ideal case in terms of criteria satisfaction and consequent prosecution leniency.

1. Company A regularly conducts a comprehensive audit of its compliance with environmental requirements.

2. The audit uncovers information about employees' disposing of hazardous wastes by dumping them in an unpermitted location.

3. An internal company investigation confirms the audit information. (Depending upon the nature of the audit, this follow-up investigation may be unnecessary.)

4. Prior to the violations the company had a sound compliance program, which included clear policies, employees training, and a hotline for suspected violations.

5. As soon as the company confirms the violations, it discloses all pertinent information to the appropriate government agency; it undertakes compliance planning with that agency; and it carries out satisfactory remediation measures.

6. The company also undertakes to correct any false information previously submitted to the government in relation to the violations.

7. Internally the company disciplines the employees actually involved in the violations, including any supervisor who was lax in preventing or detecting the activity. Also, the company reviews its compliance program to determine how the violations slipped by and corrects the weaknesses found by that review.

8. The company discloses to the government the names of the employees actually responsible for the violations, and it cooperates with the government by providing documentation necessary to the investigation of those persons.

Under these circumstances Company A would stand a good chance of being favorably considered for prosecutorial leniency, to the extent of not being criminally prosecuted at all. The degree of any leniency, however, may turn upon other relevant factors not specifically dealt with in these guidelines.[4]

Example 2:
At the opposite end of the scale is Company Z, which meets few of the criteria. The likelihood

---

3. While this policy applies to both individuals and organizational violators, these examples focus particularly upon situations involving organizations.

of prosecutorial leniency, therefore, is remote. Company Z's circumstances may include any of the following:

1. Because an employee has threatened to report a violation to federal authorities, the company is afraid that investigators may begin looking at it. An audit is undertaken, but it focuses only upon the particular violation, ignoring the possibility that the violation may be indicative of widespread activities in the organization.

2. After completing the audit, Company Z reports the violations discovered to the government.

3. The company had a compliance program, but it was effectively no more than a collection of paper. No effort is made to disseminate its content, impress upon employees its significance, train employees in its application, or oversee its implementation.

4. Even after "discovery" of the violation the company makes no effort to strengthen its compliance procedures.

5. The company makes no effort to come to terms with regulators regarding its violations. It resists any remedial work and refuses to pay any monetary sanctions.

6. Because of the non-compliance, information submitted to regulators over the years has been materially inaccurate, painting a substantially false picture of the company's true compliance situation. The company fails to take any steps to correct that inaccuracy.

7. The company does not cooperate with prosecutors in identifying those employees (including managers) who actually were involved in the violation, and it resists disclosure of any documents relating either to the violations or to the responsible employees.

In these circumstances leniency is unlikely. The only positive action is the so-called audit, but that was so narrowly focused as to be of questionable value, and it was undertaken only to head off a possible criminal investigation. Otherwise, the company demonstrated no good faith either in terms of compliance efforts or in assisting the government in obtaining a full understanding of the violation and discovering its sources.

Nonetheless, these factors do not assure a criminal prosecution of Company Z. As with Company A, above, other circumstances may be present which affect the balance struck by prosecutors. For example, the effect of the violation (because of substance, duration, or amount) may be such that prosecutors would not consider it to be an appropriate criminal case. Administrative or civil proceedings may be considered a more appropriate response.

Other examples:

Between these extremes there is a range of possibilities. The presence, absence, or degree of any criterion may affect the prosecution's exercise of discretion. Below are some examples of such effects:

1. In a situation otherwise similar to that of Company A, above, Company B performs an audit that is very limited in scope and probably reflects no more than an effort to avoid prosecution. Despite that background, Company B is cooperative in terms of both bringing itself into compliance and providing information regarding the crime and its perpetrators. The result could be any of a number of outcomes, including prosecution of a lesser charge or a decision to prosecute the individuals rather than the company.

2. Again the situation is similar to Company A's, but Company C refuses to reveal any information regarding the individual violators. The likelihood of the government's prosecuting the company are [sic] substantially increased.

3. In another situation similar to Company A's, Company D chooses to "sit on" the audit

---

4. For example, if the company had a long history of noncompliance, the compliance audit was done only under pressure from regulators, and a timely audit would have ended the violations much sooner, those circumstances would be considered.

and take corrective action without telling the government. The government learns of the situation months or years after the fact.

A complicating fact here is that environmental regulatory programs are self policing: they include a substantial number of reporting requirements. If reports which in fact presented false information are allowed to stand uncorrected, the reliability of this system is undermined. They also may lead to adverse and unfair impacts upon other members of the regulated community. For example, Company D failed to report discharges of X contaminant into a municipal sewer system, discharges that were terminated as a result of an audit. The sewer authority, though, knowing only that there have been excessive loadings of X, but not knowing that Company D was a source, tightens limitations upon all known sources of X. Thus, all of those sources incur additional treatment expenses, but Company D is unaffected. Had Company D revealed its audit results, the other companies would not have suffered unnecessary expenses.

In some situations, moreover, failure to report is a crime. *See, e.g.,* 33 U.S.C. §1321(b)(5) and 42 U.S.C. §9603(b). To illustrate the effect of this factor, consider Company E, which conducts a thorough audit and finds that hazardous wastes have been disposed of by dumping them on the ground. The company cleans up the area and tightens up its compliance program, but does not reveal the situation to regulators. Assuming that a reportable quantity of a hazardous substance was released, the company was under a legal obligation under 42 U.S.C. §9603(b) to report that release as soon as it had knowledge of it, thereby allowing regulators the opportunity to assure proper clean up. Company E's knowing failure to report the release upon learning of it is itself a felony.

In the cases of both Company D and Company E, consideration would be given by prosecutors for remedial efforts; hence prosecution of fewer or lesser charges might result. However, because Company D's silence adversely affected others who are entitled to fair regulatory treatment and because Company E deprived those legally responsible for evaluation cleanup needs of the ability to carry out their functions, the likelihood of their totally escaping criminal prosecution is significantly reduced.

4. Company F's situation is similar to that of Company B. However, with regard to the various violations shown by the audit, it concentrates upon correcting only the easier, less expensive, less significant among them. Its lackadaisical approach to correction does not make it a strong candidate for leniency.

5. Company G is similar to Company D in that it performs an audit and finds violations, but does not bring them to the government's attention. Those violations do not involve failures to comply with reporting requirements. The company undertakes a program of gradually correcting its violations. When the government learns of the situation, Company G still has not remedied its most significant violations, but claims that it certainly planned to get to them. Company G could receive some consideration for its efforts, but its failure to disclose and the slowness of its remedial work probably mean that it cannot expect a substantial degree of leniency.

6. Comprehensive audits are considered positive efforts toward good faith compliance. However, such audits are not indispensable to enforcement leniency. Company H's situation is essentially identical to that of Company A, except for the fact that it does not undertake a comprehensive audit. It does not have a formal audit program, but, as a part of its efforts to ensure compliance, does realize that it is committing an environmental violation. It thereafter takes steps otherwise identical to those of Company A in terms of compliance efforts and cooperation. Company H is also a likely candidate for leniency, including possibly no criminal prosecution.

In sum, mitigating efforts made by the regulated community will be recognized and evaluated. The greater the showing of good faith, the more likely it will be met with leniency.

Conversely, the less good faith shown, the less likely that prosecutorial discretion will tend toward leniency.

IV. Nature of this Guidance

This guidance explains the current general practice of the Department in making criminal prosecutive and other decisions after giving consideration to the criteria described above, as well as any other criteria that are relevant to the exercise of criminal prosecutorial discretion in a particular case. This discussion is an expression of, and in no way departs from, the long tradition of exercising prosecutorial discretion. The decision to prosecute "generally rests entirely in [the prosecutor's] discretion." *Bordenkircher v. Hayes*, 434 U.S. 357, 364 (1978).[5] This discretion is especially firmly held by the criminal prosecutor.[6] The criteria set forth above are intended only as internal guidance to Department of Justice attorneys. They are not intended to, do not, and may not be relied upon to create a right or benefit, substantive or procedural, enforceable at law by a party to litigation with the United States, nor do they in any way limit the lawful litigative prerogatives, including civil enforcement actions, of the Department of Justice or the Environmental Protection Agency. They are provided to guide the effective use of limited enforcement resources, and do not derive from, find their basis in, nor constitute any legal requirement, whether constitutional, statutory, or otherwise, to forego or modify any enforcement action or the use of any evidentiary material. See *Principles of Federal Prosecution* (U.S. Dept. of Justice, 1980) p.4; *United States Attorneys' Manual* (U.S. Dept. of Justice, 1986) 1-1.000.

---

5. Although some statutes have occasionally been held to require civil enforcement actions, *see, e.g., Dunlop v. Bachowski*, 421 U.S. 560 (1975), those are unusual cases, and the general rule is that both civil and criminal enforcement is at the enforcement agency's discretion where not prescribed by law. *Heckler v. Chaney*, 470 U.S. 821, 830-35 (1985); *Cutler v. Hayes*, 818 F.2d 879, 893 (D.C. Cir. 1987) (decisions not to enforce are not reviewable unless the statute provides an "inflexible mandate").

6. *Newman v. United States*, 382 F.2d 479, 480 (D.C. Cir. 1967).

Appendix G:
Standards for Performance of Environmental, Health, and Safety Audits

Standards for Performance of Environmental, Health,
and Safety Audits
Environmental Auditing Roundtable
January 22, 1993
©1993

Introduction

These standards have been prepared by the Environmental Auditing Round-table (EAR), a professional organization, to provide minimum criteria for the conduct of environmental, health, and safety audits (EHS audits). These are the generally accepted auditing standards that EAR members believe are necessary for the professional conduct of EHS audits.

Some important points about these standards are:

1. An EHS *audit* is defined as an activity directed at verifying a site or organization's environmental, health, or safety status with respect to specific, predetermined criteria. An audit is distinct from other evaluation methods that may involve conclusions based on professional opinion or limited evaluation, or unique instances not associated with specific criteria.

2. These standards apply to activities that take place within the scope of an audit engagement. Standards of audit program design and implementation are a natural extension of these standards; however, to emphasize only core issues, these standards focus solely on the audit engagement.

3. These standards are deliberately concise. They intend to define *what* is required to conduct a competent audit, not *how* to implement each aspect of the standard.

4. In these standards, the word "must" denotes a mandatory practice, while "should" denotes a desired "best practice" recommendation.

5. Throughout this document, "audit" and "auditor" mean "environmental, health, and safety" audit or auditor.

The scope of EHS auditing is broad, and the term EHS *audit* is used in a variety of ways. Activities that could be covered by these standards range from internally motivated audits (such as those for property transfer or regulatory compliance) to audits conducted with the intent of disclosing findings to the public (such as reporting on the goals and performance of the environmental program of an organization). A "client" authorizes the performance of an audit, and must assure the consent and cooperation of the "auditee" (the organizational unit or facility) to be audited. The scope of an audit must be defined in advance, and the verification criteria selected and agreed on prior to beginning the audit. Agreement on required audit resources is part of the scope. The organization being audited must provide the auditors with access to documentation, information, location, and other resources needed to make judgments and form opinions required to achieve the objectives of the audit. Audit "findings" are the conclusions reached by auditors regarding elements of the audit scope and verification criteria. Audits must be conducted in an ethical manner. The EAR Code of Ethics governs the activities of its members in performing audits. The Code is attached to these standards.

Standards are developed in the complex legal and regulatory environment of auditing. Standards must be sufficiently flexible to be adaptable to the unique needs and circumstances of any individual audit. Although these standards define good commercial and customary practices for performing audits, there are specific circumstances that might mandate a departure from the standards established here. This document reflects a consensus of environmental professionals on key components of the performance of audits. It is not indicated to serve as a legal analysis of liability issues or as legal advice. This document will be updated periodically, as judged appropriate to changing audit practices and legal requirements. The EAR Standards Committee will review this standard at least annually for possible revision.

I. General Standards

A. Auditor Proficiency

Auditors must have adequate qualifications, technical knowledge, training, and proficiency in the discipline of auditing to perform their assigned audit tasks. Proficiency is the responsibility of the organization managing auditing activities and of each individual auditor. Qualifications of the audit team assigned must be commensurate with the objectives, scope, and complexities of the audit assignment.

　　1. Auditors must be qualified to perform audits. Organizations and individuals responsible for planning the audit engagement must establish suitable educational and professional experience criteria for auditors. Auditor proficiency and professional experience in the following areas must be adequate to achieve audit objectives.

　　　　a. Auditing processes, procedures, and techniques.
　　　　b. Characteristics and analysis of management systems.
　　　　c. Regulatory requirements and environmental policies.
　　　　d. Environmental, health, and safety protection systems

and technologies.

 e. Facility operations.

 f. Potential environmental, health, and safety impacts and hazards/risks associated with the types of facilities and operations to be audited.

2. Auditors should have training and demonstrated abilities in areas needed to perform audits, including, but not limited to:

 a. Interpersonal and communication skills.

 b. Work scheduling and planning.

 c. Analytical abilities to evaluate potential deficiencies noted during the audit.

3. Auditors should understand the operations of the facility/organization to be audited as they relate to the audit scope.

B. Due Professional Care

Due professional care is the application of diligence and skill in performing audits. Exercising due professional care means assuring accuracy, consistency, and objectivity in the performance of audits; using good judgment in choosing tests and procedures; developing conclusions and, if necessary, recommendations; and preparing reports.

1. Auditors must conscientiously complete audits in compliance with these auditing standards.

2. Auditors must apply the diligence and skills expected of a competent, reasonably prudent and knowledgeable auditor in the same or similar circumstances.

3. Auditors must apply established auditing standards consistently, and should seek authoritative interpretations when such standards are conflicting or vague.

4. Auditors must conclude that sufficient and reasonable evidence exists to allow formation of opinions.

C. Independence

Auditors must be objective and independent of the audit site and/or activity to be audited, free of conflict of interest in any specific situation, and not subject to internal or external pressure to influence their findings.

1. Factors that can impair independence include personal or organizational bias, and external or internal influence on the auditor's judgment or authority, whether implied or direct.

2. Where a conflict of interest exists, it must be communicated to the client. In some cases, the client may waive the conflict of

interest. A statement of this waiver should be provided in the audit report.

3. An objective auditor must base findings on observed, measurable, and verifiable evidence, and not allow personal opinions or beliefs to influence the conduct of audits or conclusions that might be reached.

II. Conduct of Audits

A. Clear and Explicit Objectives

The objectives of an audit must be clearly established and fully communicated beforehand to the client and to the auditee. The objectives of specific audits should be consistent with the needs of intended recipients of audit results and the provisions of these standards.

B. Systematic Plans and Procedures for Conducting Audits

Audits must be based on use of systematic plans and procedures that provide uniform guidance in audit preparation, field work, and reporting. Explicit written plans and procedures promote consistency and uniformity of approach.

1. The audit planning process and procedures must include the use of protocols, checklists, and/or guidelines consistent with the audit scope to provide a clear methodology for conducting the audit.

2. Audit documentation must be consistent with the defined scope of the audit.

C. Planned and Supervised Fieldwork

Fieldwork must be properly planned, implemented, and supervised, to foster efficiency and consistency and to achieve audit objectives. Effective supervision and leadership are necessary parts of environmental auditing.

1. A team leader must supervise fieldwork performed by members of the audit team.

2. Audit fieldwork should be conducted in accordance with a prepared protocol and an established audit plan.

3. While on site, auditors must gather information necessary to fulfill the audit objectives. The information collected must be relevant, accurate, and sufficient to support findings, conclusions, and recommendations. Appropriate sampling schemes should be utilized in selecting samples.

D. Audit Quality Control and Assurance

Audits must undergo quality checks to assure accuracy and encourage continuous improvement of audit management systems, procedures, and implementation. Quality control measures the extent to which an audit is conducted according to the objectives and scope of the audit, and to these standards.

1. Quality checks should be conducted to ensure that audit findings are consistent with evidence recorded by the auditors.

2. Quality checks should be conducted to ensure that audit findings are reliably communicated in reports.

E. Audit Documentation

The auditor prepares documentation of ongoing activities during an audit in "working papers."

1. Each subject reviewed in an audit should be documented sufficiently so that another auditor of similar skill could confirm the conclusions of the auditor without consulting further resources.

2. Disposition of working papers should be consistent with established policies of the auditing organization or as agreed upon when defining the scope of the audit with the client.

III. Audit Reporting

A. Clear and Appropriate Reporting

A formal report must be prepared for each audit to communicate information, consistent with the audit scope and objectives. Reports should clearly communicate information and findings in a timely manner to the intended recipients, and in sufficient detail and clarity to facilitate corrective action.

1. The audit report should describe the audit scope and conduct, and report the audit results and conclusions, consistent with audit objectives.

2. Audit findings must be documented and based on relevant, accurate, and sufficient evidence. Audit reports may contain recommendations to correct the deficiencies identified in the audit report. An auditor's opinion as to the overall status of the facility may also be included, if the opinion is consistent with the defined scope and objectives.

Environmental Auditing Roundtable
CODE OF ETHICS

Introduction

The reliance of the public and business community on the information reported by environment, health and safety auditors imposes an obligation that auditors maintain high standards of technical competence and integrity.

Professional Conduct

Article I.	Members as professionals shall exercise honesty, objectivity, and diligence in the performance of their professional duties and responsibilities.
Article II.	Members shall not engage in any act or omission of a dishonest, deceitful, or fraudulent nature.
Article III.	Members shall continually seek to maintain and improve their professional knowledge, skills, and competence.
Article IV.	Members shall not knowingly misrepresent facts and when expressing an audit opinion shall use reasonable care to obtain sufficient facts to support statements. In their reporting, members shall reveal facts which if not revealed could distort the report.
Article V.	Members shall avoid any activity which would prejudice their ability to carry out their professional duties and responsibilities objectively.
Article VI.	Members shall not use confidential information gained in the course of an audit for personal gain. Members shall not disclose confidential information acquired in the course of an audit unless disclosure of such informatio is required by law.

Conduct of Members

Article I.	Members shall abide by this Code of Ethics and support the objectives of the Environmental Auditing Roundtable.
Article II.	Members shall not represent their acts or statements in such a way as to lead others to believe that they officially represent the Environmental Auditing Roundtable unless they are duly authorized to do so.
Article III.	Members shall not directly market their professional services at Roundtable meetings.

Article IV.	Applicants for membership and candidates for elective office in the Roundtable shall not misrepresent any credentials submitted in support of their application or candidacy.
Article V.	Members in good standing may communicate their membership and their acceptance of this Code of Ethics. However, they may not in any way imply that they are endorsed by the Roundtable or its Board of Directors.

Glossary

AFE:	Authorization for Expenditure
APA:	Administrative Procedure Act
CAA:	Clean Air Act
CEQ:	Council on Environmental Quality
CERCLA:	Comprehensive Environmental Response, Compensation, and Liability Act
D.C. Circuit:	U.S. Court of Appeals for the District of Columbia Circuit
EIR:	environmental impact report
EIS:	environmental impact statement
EPA:	Environmental Protection Agency
EPCRA:	Emergency Planning and Community Right-to-Know Act
FWPCA:	Federal Water Pollution Control Act
MACT:	maximum available control technology
MIS:	management information system
NEPA:	National Environmental Policy Act
NPDES:	national pollutant discharge elimination system
OSH Act:	Occupational Safety and Health Act
OTA:	Office of Technology Assessment
PC:	personal computer
PRP:	potentially responsible party
PSD:	prevention of significant deterioration
RCRA:	Resource Conservation and Recovery Act
SCAQMD:	South Coast Air Quality Management District
SEC:	Securities and Exchange Commission
TSCA:	Toxic Substances Control Act

The Environmental Law Institute
Transforming Law Into Action

Improving Professional Expertise ELI publications are critical working tools for attorneys and other environmental professionals. The Institute's flagship publication, the *Environmental Law Reporter*, and its series of treatises, deskbooks, and monographs form a core environmental reference library for law firms, corporations, government agencies, public interest groups, and universities.

Improving Dialogue Through the ELI Associates Program, the Institute has become the nation's premier society for professionals in environmental law, policy, and management. Program participants receive *The Environmental Forum*, ELI's award-winning policy journal, a membership directory, invitations to ELI seminars, and discounts on ELI publications.

ELI Publications

Environmental Law Reporter $995/year	*Oil Pollution Deskbook* $85
ELR's News, Analysis and Update $795/year	*RCRA Deskbook*...$85
The Environmental Forum (subscription fee	*Superfund Deskbook*...$85
included in Associates Program dues.)	*Wetlands Deskbook* $85
Full rate...$75/year	*Practical Guide to Environmental*
Nonprofit/govt./academic rate $50/year	*Management* $35
National Wetlands Newsletter $48/year	*A Guide to Environmental Law in*
Law of Environmental Protection..................$297	*Washington, DC* $28
(available through Clark Boardman	*Environmental Regulation of Coal Mining:*
Callaghan Co. 800-221-9428)	*SMCRA's Second Decade* $28
Sustainable Environmental Law $130	*Fundamentals of Negotiation: A Guide*
(available through West Publishing Co.	*for Environmental Professionals* $28
800-328-9352)	*Wetlands Protection: The Role*
Clean Air Deskbook...$85	*of Economics*...$28
Clean Water Deskbook $85	*ELI Research Briefs* $10
European Community Deskbook......................$85	

Use this postage-paid card to request more information or call ELI at (800) 433-5120.

YES! I'd like to learn more about the Environmental Law Institute. Please send me the following information:

❏ ELI Annual Report ❏ ELI Publications brochure

❏ ELI Associates Program information

NAME

ORGANIZATION

ADDRESS

CITY/STATE/ZIP